The front cover photograph, taken at the Jesse Lee Home in Unalaska c. 1920,
and the winter panorama on the back cover are from the girlhood album
of the late Annie Swanson Hatch, courtesy of the Hatch family.
The frontispiece photo of Unalaska c. 1925, by the late Charles H. Hope,
is used with the permission of his daughter, Gertrude Svarny.

Printed in the United States of America.

First printed August 2007.

Hardscratch Press, 2358 Banbury Place,
Walnut Creek, California 94598-2347.

Library of Congress Control Number: 2007929081

ISBN: 978-0-9789979-0-8

2 4 6 8 9 7 5 3 1

Cataloging-in-Publication Data

Hudson, Raymond L.
    Family after all : Alaska's Jesse Lee Home. Vol. 1, Unalaska, 1889–1925 / by Raymond L. Hudson.

        p.   cm.
    Includes bibliographical references and index.

    ISBN 978-0-9789979-0-8
        1...Jesse Lee Home (Unalaska, Alaska) 2. Indian children -- Institutional care -- Alaska --
Unalaska. 3. Eskimo children -- Institutional care -- Alaska -- Unalaska. 4. Unalaska (Alaska) --
History. 5. Unalaska (Alaska) -- Social life and customs. 6. Methodist Episcopal Church --
Missions -- Alaska -- Unalaska. I. Title.

F914.U63H93 2007

                                                                        2007-929081

FAMILY AFTER ALL

Alaska's Jesse Lee Home

VOLUME I
UNALASKA, 1889–1925

by

Raymond L. Hudson

A HARDSCRATCH PRESS BOOK

Publisher's Note

BY THE TIME IT CLOSED IN SEWARD after the cataclysmic Good Friday earthquake of 1964, the Methodist Jesse Lee Home had housed hundreds of children, mostly Alaska Native children, over a period of 75 years. That is a considerable portion of Alaska's history under the U.S. flag.

Even so, this project was first envisioned not as the story of the Home per se but as a collection of interviews with former "Jesse Lee kids" that would incidentally tell something of the workings of the institution. For me, born at Seward while the Home was in operation there, Jesse Lee had always meant Jesse Lee at Seward. But of course there would have to be mention of its Unalaska beginnings.

That was the sketchy notion when I wrote to a number of librarians and other knowledgeable Alaskans asking whether the Jesse Lee story hadn't already been told. No, they all said. Except for mention in one or two individual accounts, it had not. And it should be.

One person went further. Poet-artist-historian Ray Hudson, whose book *Moments Rightly Placed* is a memoir of his own introduction to Unalaska, offered access to his files and sent a lengthy inventory of documents on the Home's early years in the Aleutians—whereupon the original notion underwent a sea change and a new question was asked and answered: Yes, he would be willing to write the Unalaska portion of the story.

Now the finished work is more nearly what it should have been all along, a full history of the Jesse Lee Home. From his already existing scholarship on Unalaska, from further research and his own lyrical bent, Ray Hudson has written in Volume I about the sometimes tumultuous opening years, about the faith and foibles of the people who established the Home and persevered there, about the neighbors who saw that perseverance as a threat. And about the children, whose well-being—however defined—was everyone's announced aim. The Seward story will follow in its own book.

The shared title of these two volumes was not chosen out of second-hand sentiment. Clearly Jesse Lee was not "home" or "family" in the traditional sense, at Unalaska or at Seward. But despite sadness and storms and occasional dysfunction—not so unusual in any clan—it was as close to home as most of the children and even some of the adults could hope to be.

This story is dedicated to all of the Jesse Lee family.

Jacquelin B. Pels
Hardscratch Press
April 2007

Jackie Pels
12·28·07

CONTENTS

Author's Note

As with anything I write about the history of the Aleutians, this account of the Jesse Lee Home began with conversations with Anfesia Shapsnikoff (1900–1973) and Henry Swanson (1895–1990). I am indebted to several members of the Newhall family. In the 1970s Edith Newhall Drugg was exceptionally generous and enthusiastic about the work of her parents. I wish I had had more than one brief conversation with her brother, Chester Newhall, to whom I was introduced by Philemon and Flora Tutiakff. The material Flora shared was surpassed only by her insights into the work of the Home. Indispensable material was supplied early on by Dr. David S. Newhall. I benefited from conversations with other Newhall grandchildren, Virginia Drugg and Donna Larrow. Dr. Newhall's nephew, Frank Newhall, also shared material he had assembled. I want to thank Margaret Boaz for a copy of the diary kept by her grandparents, Noah and Clara Davenport; Darrell Langley for information on Mary Tuck; Elizabeth Caroline Haralson and Kenneth Hatch for material on their relatives.

I am very grateful to Robert Collins for allowing the use of his collection of Clara Cook letters and to Martha Murray for genealogical information. The staff members at several institutions were invaluable: L. Dale Patterson, at the United Methodist Church Archives at Drew University; Hayden Lawrence, at the Alaska Missionary Conference Commission on Archives and History, Anchorage; Gladi Kulp at the Alaska State Historical Library; Stephanie Miller at Alaska Children's Services in Anchorage; and the staff at the Presbyterian Historical Society in Philadelphia. The Unalaska City School District kindly allowed photographs from their collections to be scanned. Jeffery Dickrell did the scanning. All who visit Unalaska owe Coe and Phyllis Whittern a debt of gratitude for the care and thoughtfulness with which they have restored and preserved the Boys' Home. As it has for over a century, this building continues to grace the eastern end of Unalaska Village.

Jacquelin Pels suggested the project. Her careful editing, perceptive questions, and deep respect for the residents and staff at the Jesse Lee Home have made this book what it is.

Raymond L. Hudson
Middlebury, Vermont
January 2007

Unalaska Bay, Alaska.

SHIPS AT DOCK *in Unalaska Bay, early 1900s. Tinted photograph published by the Portland Post Card Co.,*
F.H. Nowell, photographer. Courtesy of the Anchorage Museum at Rasmuson Center
(John Urban Collection, B64.1.182).

1

Arrival at Unalaska

In mid-September the thousand-mile arc of the Aleutian Islands is beautiful beyond imagining. Green treeless hills, like velour cascading to the sea, are bordered with swaths of lupine, monkshood and fireweed. Waist-high blueberry bushes and towering salmonberry thickets droop with ripe fruit. Shallow streams rustle with returning salmon. The Bering Sea and the North Pacific Ocean break against beaches and cliffs and channel through passes with currents so strong that, even today, ships seek shelter in deep protected bays.

Unalaska Island, in the eastern or Fox Islands group, is 175 miles from the tip of the Alaska Peninsula and 810 miles from Anchorage. It is the second largest island in the Chain, and its numerous fjords, inlets and bays give it the longest coastline. The broad north end opens into vast Unalaska Bay, which encompasses smaller bays, islands and harbors. Today the city of Unalaska incorporates much of Unalaska Bay, but in the 19th century the village was confined to a long narrow peninsula, curved like a smile and formed by the pebbled beach of the inner harbor and a shallow stream that flows from a freshwater lake at the head of a wide valley. The beach, sandy at low tide but rocky most days of each month, is edged with high wild rye grass. Northwest from the village, across the protected waters of the inner harbor, the low bluffs on nearby Amaknak Island roll upward to the graceful slope of Ballyhoo rising above Dutch Harbor, a sheltered deep-water port. At the eastern end of the peninsula is the community cemetery, two small mounds of white crosses. Rising wave on wave above the graveyard stands Mount Newhall, the first summit of a ridge that extends northeast toward Summer Bay and southeast to form the backdrop of the wide valley. When this story began, the mountain was unnamed.

In 1889 the village was still known by its Aleut name *Iliuliuk*, a word describing the curved shoreline. The population was about 300, almost entirely Unangan, as the eastern Aleuts call themselves. The western end of the village peninsula was dominated by buildings of the Alaska Commercial Company. The founders of this firm, headquartered in San Francisco, had purchased the holdings of the Russian-American Company in 1867 and 1868. The A.C. Co. soon built a new store and in 1873 constructed a wharf at the tip of the peninsula. By 1889 it had peppered the land between the wharf and the store with warehouses for drygoods and furs, a fenced-in coal yard, and the largest building in the village. The impressive three-story company house held offices, living quarters for the general agent, a kitchen for the Chinese cook, a library, and guest rooms. A tall flagpole surrounded by Russian cannons stood in front. Next to the company house was the store itself, looking somewhat diminutive sandwiched between the company house and a second three-story building. This laundry and storage building had a community meeting room upstairs.

Since 1880 Rudolph Neumann had been the A.C. Co.'s general agent overseeing stations from the Kuskokwim River region in Alaska's interior to the tip of the Aleutian Islands at Attu. Bavarian by birth, Neumann was a lifelong bachelor known for his high spirits and sophisticated nature. The library he maintained included the latest literature and his apartments were furnished with fine paintings. He spoke Russian and English and was an astute administrator.

When the A.C. Co. steamer *St. Paul* tied up at the wharf on Sept. 18, 1889, John and Mary Tuck of Middletown, Connecticut, were aboard. He was the newly assigned government schoolteacher. She was to be the matron of a Methodist mission, unbuilt but already named the Jesse Lee Memorial Home and Industrial School. The *St. Paul* was floating proof of the wealth of the A.C. Co. When it was built, by William Cramp & Sons of Philadelphia, no expense had been spared, from steam engines to double topsails and royals. Two hundred feet in length with a registered tonnage of 1,000 tons, at its launching in January 1876 the ship presented "the appearance of a yacht rather than of a vessel designed for business purposes."[1] Beautiful cabin work graced the interior in burl walnut, black walnut, mahogany and Spanish cedar. Traveling on the *St. Paul* with company men, the Tucks were surrounded by evidences of the power of a firm that challenged all competitors. It was a power they would unsuccessfully confront.

John Tuck had been hired for $1,000 a year by the Rev. Dr. Sheldon Jackson, special agent for education for Alaska. Jackson, a Presbyterian minister, was a man of vision, persuasion, and not a little controversy. He viewed education and Christianity as parallel enterprises, both necessary if the Indians, Eskimos and Aleuts of the newly purchased territory were to survive. After working in the western United States, he had established the first Protestant mission at Wrangell in 1877. In January 1880, in New York City, he met with representatives of several Protestant denominations to divide Alaska like Joseph's coat of Biblical times. The Presbyterians had kept the Southeast to themselves and agreed to begin work at Barrow. Baptists, Episcopalians, Moravians and Congregationalists each had taken different regions. The Mission Board of the Methodist Episcopal Church had selected the Aleutian chain, including the farthest east Shumagin Islands. In 1885 the Woman's Home Missionary Society established an Alaska Bureau. Its first secretary, Lydia Hill Daggett, commenced three and a half years of recruitment that ended only when John and Mary Tuck stepped forward. After they reached Unalaska, Daggett exulted: "No other missionaries of the Methodist Church are so isolated as these."[2]

John and Mary Tuck arrived with no place to live and nowhere to teach. They had left San Francisco with the understanding that the Home would be constructed within the year and that the public school would occupy one room in it.[3] They introduced themselves to Rudolph Neumann, who saw a tall, thin, severe-looking man in his early 30s and a woman a few years younger whose delicate, youthful beauty was now tempered by anxiety. Mary had wavered between staying in Connecticut and accepting the "call" to the mission field. After welcoming them, Neumann offered to provide a six-room house for $25 a month.[4] The rent would remain at $200 a year through 1897. The house was just past a row of small red cottages the company had built for its best sea otter hunters. As the Tucks made their way from the company complex to their new dwelling, they passed two large structures, reminiscent of San Francisco and for good reason. These were the Bishop's House, residence of the Orthodox bishop when he was in town, and the Russian school building; both had been designed by Mooser & Pissis of San Francisco and built 10 years earlier by the A.C. Co. Just beyond the Bishop's House was the most prominent reminder of the century that Russia had been in Alaska: the Church of the Holy Ascension, erected in 1858 under the leadership of the Aleut priest Innokentii Shaishnikoff, who had died in 1883. The church was now showing signs of the rough unforgiving Aleutian weather and would soon be replaced with a larger building, the fourth on the site since the first chapel was constructed around 1808.

Just outside the fenced churchyard stood the late priest's impressive house, also constructed by the company. When the naturalist John Muir visited Father Shaishnikoff in 1881 he had been "ushered into a room which for fineness of taste in furniture and fixtures might well challenge the very best in San Francisco or New York."[5] Muir attributed the excellence of the home to the refinement of the priest or his wife, Maria Alekseev Shaishnikoff, who was living there when the Tucks arrived. Her son Vasilii had been elected chief of Unalaska in September 1887. She welcomed the establishment of a government school.

The Tucks would have noticed other frame houses and several of the semi-underground dwellings called *barabaras*. With sheltered front doorways and two or three small windows, barabaras were ideally suited to a treeless environment buffeted by strong winds and yielding little heating material. By 1889, however, only a half-dozen such homes were in use at Unalaska. Most residents lived in small frame cottages.[6]

With its mixture of Aleuts, Russians, eastern and northern Europeans, and Americans who hailed from Vermont to California, Unalaska was a diverse community. There was extensive literacy in Aleut and Russian—a school had been operated by the church with some regularity since the 1820s. Both the Russian-American Company and the Alaska Commercial Company had supported education. The Russian school had a small dormitory for promising boys from outlying villages. The English language was gaining strength with the arrival of more Americans and as instructors were available. The A.C. Co. was required to operate schools in the Pribilof Islands under its contract with the government to harvest fur seals; it also sponsored limited schooling at Unalaska, at times in conjunction with the Orthodox clergy and on other occasions when the wives of various company

THE CHURCH OF THE HOLY ASCENSION *as seen by the Tucks on their arrival in 1889. It was rebuilt in the mid-1890s. This photograph was in a junior fiction book: Kirk Munroe,* The Fur-Seal's Tooth, A story of an Alaska Adventure. *Harper & Bros., New York, 1894.*

agents conducted classes in English. In 1880 the company hired Nicholas Gray as a teacher. He had immigrated to the United States from Russia as a teenager and was fluent in Russian and English. In 1883 he was transferred to St. Paul in the Pribilof Islands, where he taught for several years.

Sheldon Jackson was determined to build on the foundation that had been laid by several generations of educated Aleuts. "You are well aware," he wrote in May 1885 to the U.S. commissioner of education, "that that most advanced and civilized portion of the native population of Alaska live from Kadiak westward along the Aleutian Islands."[7] Lydia Daggett, of the mission society, also acknowledged that the Aleutians were, as far as education and religion went, "one of the brightest parts on the bright side." She credited the Orthodox Church for this and also praised "the influence of the A.C. Co." She put her own twist onto this assessment, however, and remarked that this was an illustration "of what the Gospel, even when adulterated by ignorant priests, can do for these *home heathen*."[8]

. .

HOW HAD THE TUCKS ARRIVED at this isolated community in the heart of the eastern Aleutians? In 1885, after 11 years of possession, the federal government had finally acknowledged responsibility for education in the territory. Jackson had been the obvious choice as special agent for education. However, the deputy U.S. commissioner at Unalaska, Chester Seeber, was alarmed when he learned a Presbyterian minister had been appointed. Jackson would be useless, he wrote the secretary of the interior, for people living from Belkofski to Attu where there were Russian church schools in most villages. Seeber questioned the very premise of educating Aleuts. After all, he argued, they were sea otter hunters and fishermen. "I believe that education will never better their condition," he said. And for God's sake, he concluded, whatever happens don't send a missionary: "The natives here have no earthly or heavenly need of learning to sing 'Nearer My God to Thee' or 'There is a fountain filled with blood.'"[9]

In his 1886 general instructions to Alaskan teachers Jackson called attention to the prominent positions held in Aleut villages by priests and other Orthodox officials. He encouraged the teachers to take "special pains" to "secure the hearty cooperation of the Priest and leaders of the Greek Church."[10] He urged teachers to encourage parents and priests to visit the government schools. He suggested that teachers sponsor entertainments of singing and recitations "during the long winter evenings."[11] After a visit to the region in 1886 Jackson wrote that half of the population at Unalaska was literate in the Aleut language.[12] Nevertheless, when it came to formulating the "Rules and Regulations for the Conduct of Public Schools and Education in the Territory of Alaska" in 1887, Jackson moved to eradicate one of the great achievements of Orthodoxy among the Aleuts: literacy in their own language. "The children shall be taught in the English language," he wrote, "and the use of school books printed in any foreign languages will not be allowed.

The purpose of the Government is to make citizens of these people by educating them in our customs, methods and language. The children are primarily to speak, read and write the English language. . . ." The last sentence was amended by the secretary of the interior to read, "The children are primarily *to be taught* to speak, read and write the English language. . . ."[13] That altered little the effect of the order.

During his first year as agent, Jackson sent Solomon Ripinsky to Unalaska. He was a Polish immigrant who had been recommended by a former superintendent of schools in Oregon. Ripinsky, whom Jackson described as "a Russian Hebrew," was initially hired for Kodiak. He set sail from Sitka in September 1885, but within days the vessel had sprung a leak and a storm had driven it onto a beach. He returned to Sitka by canoe just as the A.C. Co.'s steamship *Bonita* was preparing to depart for Unalaska. Jackson immediately arranged for Ripinsky to go aboard and after a voyage of 1,278 miles he arrived with a few desks, books, slates and other supplies from the school in Sitka. The A.C. Co. provided a building for the school and rented him a room.

School opened with 45 pupils, 20 boys and 25 girls. Ripinsky could speak Russian, a second language for most of the Aleut population. To facilitate learning, he allowed Russian in the school. In fact, he arranged for the priest to teach Russian on Tuesdays, Thursdays and Saturdays. Ripinsky taught English on Mondays, Wednesdays and Fridays. Commissioner Seeber was horrified. ". . . What the cross [of languages] will produce it is difficult to imagine," he wrote, and wondered "whether it will revive in the children some dead language or create a new one."[14]

There would be little opportunity to find out. Within four months of Ripinsky's arrival Jackson wrote to Lydia Daggett, "If you will find a Methodist man (married) who will go to Unalashka, I will have him appointed by the Government as a teacher."[15] Faced with the monumental task of providing education across Alaska's vast territory on an appropriation of only $25,000, Jackson had turned to missionary societies. By offering subsidies through contracts, he encouraged these groups to open schools in the more isolated regions of the territory.[16] No Methodist man, however, was forthcoming. Ripinsky stayed only a little over a year. Neumann was impressed with him and offered him a position with the A.C. Co. at one of its stations along the Kuskokwim River. Ripinsky settled instead in Haines (Fort Chilkoot), where he taught school, drew maps for the government, worked for canneries, and eventually owned a store. A resident of Haines recalled him as a short elderly man who wore a black yarmulke and doted on the children who came into his store on errands.[17] After his death in March 1927 a prominent peak in the area was named in his honor.[18]

The school at Unalaska remained vacant for three years, during which the Woman's Home Missionary Society (WHMS) continued its recruiting campaign for what was now defined as an industrial and training school. In addition to teaching day students from the village, the school would provide room and board for children, primarily girls, from Unalaska

THE ALASKA COMMERCIAL COMPANY STORE, *probably dating from the 1860s, was east of the large company house built in 1874. Beyond the company house can be seen roofs of some of the cottages the company built for its best sea otter hunters. Courtesy of the Alaska and Polar Regions Collections, Elmer E. Rasmuson Library, University of Alaska Fairbanks (William Gerstle Collection, 76-132-8).*

LYDIA HILL DAGGETT, *first secretary of the Alaska Bureau established by the Woman's Home Missionary Society in 1885. From* Woman's Home Missions, *August 1901.*

THE REV. SHELDON JACKSON *(identified in the original caption as vice president of the Alaska Geographical Society, in a photo by La Roche, Seattle, May 15, 1899). Courtesy of the Alaska State Library, Historical Collections (ASL-Jackson-Sheldon-1).*

and other communities. The Home would concentrate on girls because the Orthodox church had a boarding school for boys. Any students living at the Home would be "indentured." That is, a formal contract would tie the students to the institution. No copies of this early agreement have been found, but it is clear that the contract guaranteed children access to Orthodox church services and to ministrations of the priest. Daggett made clear that the teacher would have ample time outside of school for the real work of proselytizing. She insisted in her 1886 report, "These people can be civilized and Christianized."

> No claim is made upon the time of the wife, and very little upon that of the teacher out of school hours, and none on the Sabbath, thus giving them the privilege of doing the same work that many missionaries in foreign lands have long done, and are doing today, at the expense of Missionary Societies. The Government salary is ample for the support of the teacher and his family.[19]

Still no one volunteered. By October 1887 the proposed school had been named after Jesse Lee (1758–1816), a Methodist clergyman who served as chaplain to both the U.S. House and the Senate. Considering his early pioneering work in New England, the easternmost part of the United States, it was felt appropriate that his name reside in the extreme west of the nation. Building funds were raised by selling "Autograph leaves" for 50 cents each. A person could purchase only one in his or her own name, but others could be subscribed in the "names of friends, living or dead." The leaves were to be bound in special volumes. More substantial donations allowed donors to name a room in the Home. Contributions arrived earmarked for specific needs. A boys' band somewhere came up with funds to pay for a front door. An organ was donated.

In 1888 Daggett summarized the society's expectations. The Home would be established among "the brightest and best class of natives" in the Territory. It would provide a safe place for "friendless girls" who within a few years could be trained "for missionary work among the heathen tribes." She was referring to people of interior Alaska. That summer Daggett began corresponding with 33-year-old John A. Tuck, of Farmington, Maine. His career as a teacher had begun in Glidden, Iowa, where he lived with his aunt and uncle in 1880. There he had met the daughter of a clergyman from Iowa City, and in 1883 he and Mary Penelope were married. (Mary's family name is unknown.) She supported her husband's pursuit of a job in Alaska as she felt called to mission service. She agreed to act as matron of the proposed Home and to teach "industrial work," provided John could be employed as government teacher. However, that year there was no funding for a school at Unalaska and Tuck agreed to go to Unga, a mining and fishing community on the largest of the Shumagin Islands, off the Alaska Peninsula at the head of the Aleutians. Daggett pleaded with Jackson that he use all his power—"which I do hope will be greatly increased this year—shackles all stricken off"—to send a teacher to Unalaska even if some other location had to be short-changed.[20] She was concerned that Catholic priests, specifically the

Jesuits, would get to the Aleutians first. "It is to my mind *fearful* that our Govt should have ordered its officials to extend all courtesies possible to the great Mogul churchmen from Russia," she wrote to Jackson. "Then [Alaska Governor] Swineford's report frightens me out of my senses."[21] (When Swineford was replaced in 1889 by Lyman Knapp, she was greatly relieved "in as much as he [Knapp] is a Vermonter!") She worried that Orthodox Church officials would forbid the children from attending "our" government school. "I do not so much fear at Unga," she wrote, "on account of the white men there but if the Greeks are as loyal to their ch[urch] as Jesuits the wives of these will cling to Priest instead of husband." At the same time she expressed unease about the "miners & their 'hangers on'" who were arriving at Unga "at a fearful rate" with no one to curb their appetites.

Daggett also, however, had misgivings about Tuck and his wife. A Mr. and Mrs. Baker had expressed interest in Alaska, and Daggett favored them over the Tucks for Unga. Baker was a physician, and his wife was "a downright missionary" who had worked for the Woman's Christian Temperance Union. Daggett felt that Tuck "has not consecration enough to do outright mission work" outside of his duties as a hired teacher in the public school. However, because Unalaska had less promise as a missionary site than Unga, Tuck might do all right there. During this long delay, Mary Tuck began to have second thoughts. Her friends' alarms had become contagious. Tuck must have communicated his wife's feelings because he offered to sail to Alaska without her. Daggett was firm, however, and told Mary the work would be ruined if she did not go, and go cheerfully.[22] Then in April another candidate, G.F. Arms, appeared, and Daggett preferred him and his wife to all others.

In the meantime, Tuck had accepted Jackson's offer of the position at Unga on the condition that he be transferred to Unalaska as soon as a school was allocated there. In April 1889 and before he could get to Unga, he heard from Jackson that a school at Unalaska had been authorized.[23] Tuck wrote to N.H.R. Dawson, commissioner of education in Washington, D.C., requesting transfer from Unga to Unalaska. If he could not work at Unalaska, he explained to Dawson, his wife could not initiate the home for orphan girls that the Woman's Home Missionary Society had been trying for years to establish. "I am quite sure that a failure on my part to go to Ounalaska," he wrote, "would so discourage the projectors of this Home for girls that it would not be built for a long time, if ever."[24] The commissioner agreed and on July 27 Tuck accepted an appointment to Unalaska.

The Unga job went to John Carr, who sailed with the Tucks from San Francisco. This was not his first time in the Aleutian region, and he would have been able to supply information about the territory on the voyage north. He and his wife, Ethelda, had gone to Unga in April 1886. A year later she had fallen ill. Confined to her bed, she had been attended by women from the village who Carr acknowledged "did all they could." He could not understand their language, however, and he felt that their nursing techniques were not those "Americans are accustomed to."[25] Ethelda died on June 15, 1887. For the women of the Methodist church, she became a martyr, referred to as John Carr's "now

Sainted wife." Daggett used Ethelda Carr's death to rally support for the Unalaska home. Evidencing exasperation at the slowness with which the faithful responded to her repeated calls for funds and personnel, she scolded, "The Methodists have—well they have a spot on the Island of Unga . . . made sacred by the grave of the first Methodist woman sent out—not by them."[26]

And so, after many false starts and uncertainties, John and Mary Tuck sailed to the Aleutians accompanied by Carr and the new wife he "had married on purpose." Although Mary Tuck's own health was stable at the moment, she had a history of heart trouble. The tragic story of Ethelda Carr may have struck a chord in her. Would she also lay down her life among the heathen?

NOTES

1. *Daily Alta California*. March 14, 1876. See also a description of the vessel published on March 19, 1876. Kitchener incorrectly gives the construction date as 1865 (*Flag Over the North*, 94).

2. *Woman's Home Missions* [hereafter *WHM*]. October 1889:151.

3. Tuck to N.H.R. Dawson, commissioner of education. July 17, 1889. NARA. RG 75. Letters Received, 1883–1907.

4. Rudolph Neumann to Alaska Commercial Company, June 17, 1895. Stanford University, Special Collections JL006.

5. Muir, *The Cruise of the Corwin*, 16.

6. Applegate, Samuel. "The Third or Unalaska District," 89.

7. Sheldon Jackson to John Eaton. May 20, 1885. NARA. RG 75. Letters Received, 1883–1907.

8. Quoted in Daggett, "Report from the Bureau of Alaska." Woman's Home Missionary Society. 1886. Sheldon Jackson Scrapbook, Vol. 63. PHS. RG 239.

9. Chester Seeber to secretary of the interior. July 15, 1889. NARA. RG 75. Letters Received, 1883-1907.

10. All Eastern Orthodox churches—whether Greek, Russian, Slavic or American—were frequently lumped together by Protestant writers of the 19th century and referred to as "Greek." This misleading practice arose because of the historical links of Eastern Orthodoxy with the Eastern Roman Empire and Byzantium (Constantinople).

11. Sheldon Jackson. Sept. 1, 1886. NARA. RG 75. Letters Received, 1883–1907.

12. *Proceedings of the Department of Superintendence . . .*, 197.

13. Rules and Regulations for the Conduct of Public Schools and Education in the Territory of Alaska. June 14, 1887. NARA. RG 75. Letters Received, 1883-1907. Emphasis added.

14. Seeber to the secretary of the interior. Oct. 15, 1885. NARA. RG 75. Letters Received, 1883–1907.

15. Sheldon Jackson Scrapbook, Vol. 63. Presbyterian Historical Society [hereafter PHS]. RG 239.

16. Haycox, Stephen W. "Sheldon Jackson in Historical Perspective: Alaska Native Schools and Mission Contracts, 1885–1894."

17. Mary Meacock, personal conversation with Ray Hudson, August 1980.

18. See also Hakkinen, "Col. Sol Ripinsky."

19. Quoted in Daggett, "Report from the Bureau of Alaska." Woman's Home Missionary Society. 1886. Sheldon Jackson Scrapbook, Vol. 63. PHS. RG 239.

20. Daggett to Jackson, Feb. 14, 1889. Sheldon Jackson Papers, PHS. RG 239. Box 4, folder 33.

21. Daggett to Jackson, April 19, 1889. Sheldon Jackson Papers, PHS. RG 239. Box 4, folder 33.

22. Daggett to Jackson, April 19, 1889. Sheldon Jackson Papers, PHS. RG 239. Box 4, folder 33.

23. As of June 21, the Territorial Board of Education had not heard about the Unalaska opening. When they met for their semi-annual meeting, they appointed Tuck to the Unga position at a salary of $1,000 for nine months.

24. Tuck to N.H.R. Dawson, commissioner of education. July 17, 1889. NARA. RG 75. Letters Received, 1883-1907.

25. *WHM*. Sept. 1887.

26. *WHM*. May 1888:69.

2

First Students, First Misgivings

AFTER JOHN AND MARY TUCK MOVED INTO THEIR rented quarters, they converted the living room into a schoolroom. At 11 by 20 feet, it comfortably held a dozen desks. With a kitchen, an upstairs bedroom for themselves, and a few other rooms, the building was adequate for a beginning. They expected to move out of these temporary quarters the next summer as the society had appropriated $7,000 for a building.

John opened school to an enthusiastic reception. Thirty students were enrolled, although there were never more than 19 present for any one month. The average attendance for the first eight months was 12, a perfect number considering they had only the 12 desks. The schoolroom "was filled to overflowing with the daughters of all the upper ten of the town." Separately it was noted that among the girls attending were "the grown-up daughters of the Russian priest,"[1] and another report noted that "the grandchildren of a former priest were among the first to ask admission to our school." The girls would "stay until dark" and even attended classes on some of the church holidays.[2] Maria Alekseev Shaishnikoff, the grandmother of these girls, had lived with Protestants herself in Sitka and had been educated there. She knew the value of education and had taught in the school overseen by her late husband. Three of her daughters had married men who were associated with the A.C. Co., and it was children from these marriages who were noted in Tuck's reports. Children of Maria's sons also attended, but with Russian names and darker complexions they were not acknowledged by whites as being in the town's "upper class." Among books in Russian that have survived from the Shaishnikoff family are three that belonged to the wife of Maria's oldest son, Alexander: two volumes of plays and Tolstoy's *War and Peace*.[3]

That winter an epidemic swept through the eastern Aleutians. At Unalaska 15 people died. An even more severe epidemic had struck two years earlier, during which the Aleut priest at Belkovski, Father Moisei Salamatoff, had died, leaving an 18-year-old daughter, Matrona. She took a position teaching in the Belkovski school, and in 1889 Sheldon Jackson arranged with Rudolph Neumann to send her to the California Normal School for teachers at San Jose. When she returned to Alaska, she would join the Tucks at Unalaska.

In May 1890 Taissa and Ludmelia Prokopeuff, ages 15 and 14, arrived from Attu, the village at the western tip of the Aleutian Chain. The father of a third girl approached the Tucks because he was concerned about his daughter's welfare. Sheldon Jackson happened to be in town for three days, and the Tucks consulted him. They agreed with his suggestion to open their cottage as a home "and fill it with girls as fast as possible."[4] Jackson said he would even go from church to church soliciting money for them if needed. "I had the satisfaction of seeing the 'Home' commenced," he wrote, "by Professor and Mrs. Tuck taking into their family two orphan girls from the island of Attu."[5] With the Home established as an industrial boarding school, the WHMS received a $713.99 subsidy from Jackson for operations during the 1890–1891 year. This was paid in January 1892, and the following year the subsidy was increased to $1,000.[6]

Daggett received word of girls arriving at the Home and increased her appeals for funds. "How long shall these devoted missionaries be allowed to suffer thus," she wrote, "and the orphan girls left to be devoured by the human wolves that prowl about these localities?"[7] When the chosen contractor in San Francisco, Captain Charles Goodall, received building plans along with the initial payment, he discovered that they specified a building that could not be shipped. He returned the money. Daggett had a new facility designed and worked with a different contractor to get material ready before September first, the last date for shipments leaving San Francisco. She described the anticipated building:

> Our new home will have upon the first floor the Eliza Jane Baker Chapel and school room (24 x 30 feet), a recitation room, industrial school room, a small room for kindergarten work, kitchen and store rooms, dining room, parlor and reading room, sleeping rooms upon second floor, and an attic that can be finished for additional rooms if needed. There are several rooms not yet named, and several others not furnished.[8]

A gift of $100 allowed donors the privilege of naming a room after someone "here or among the angels." Daggett noted that "Little Lee's" room had been completely paid for by his parents and included "a beautiful picture, in wide gilt frame, of their angel boy." A large life-like picture of another dead child had been received for mounting on a different door. Referring to these necrological mementos, she wrote, "Of course these are not requisite, but they are *very* acceptable."

Tuck was counting on a new building when he petitioned the U.S. commissioner at Unalaska, Louis H. Tarpley, for legal custody of a total of 17 girls on Sept. 16, 1890. Tuck and his successors would become their guardians until they were 18 years old. The Jesse Lee Home would provide room and board, clothing, instruction in English "and in all the industries that pertain to good house-keeping and in the principles of morality and religion that will fit them for good and virtuous citizenship." In addition to the two girls from Attu, eight others were described as "full orphans." They were Anna Ignatieff (age 12), Eudokia Krukoff (12), Hortina [?] Krukoff (12), Priscilla Krukoff (15), Maria Lochnikoff (14), Maria Popoff (5), and sisters Antonina (13) and Glykeria (unrecorded age) Sherebernikoff. Seven girls at the school who were being raised by widowed mothers were classified as "half orphans." They were the three sisters Alexandra (16), Sossipatra (12), and Irene (6) Sovoroff; sisters Zoya (14) and Palaktia (no age recorded) Tutiakoff; and sisters Katarina (15) and Olga (no age given) Repin.

"BUILDING USED BY METHODIST MISSION, *Unalaska. Mr. and Mrs. John A. Tuck and pupils."*
This was the structure rented from the Alaska Commercial Company. From Sheldon Jackson,
Education in Alaska, 1891–1892. *Washington, Government Printing Office, 1894.*

Commissioner Tarpley, whose office and living space was donated by Rudolph Neumann, let Tuck know that he would not grant the request and allowed him to withdraw it so as to "avoid the precedent of an adverse decision." Tarpley felt the law did not allow for the "binding out of minor children except on the ground of pauperism." Tuck's reasons went beyond poverty to encompass what he considered unsuitable living conditions. This was seen in his description of Katarina Repin: "Illegitimate daughter of wealthy father living in San Francisco but not owning his daughters, mother dead, under no control, a smart, pretty girl going to ruin fast." Her sister Olga, he said, was in the same condition. The two girls were living with their maternal grandparents. The "wealthy father" was Alfred Greenbaum, who had served as general agent for the A.C. Co. at Unalaska from 1873 to 1880. He had a long-term relationship with Maria Repin and acknowledged the paternity of their first child, who had died in infancy, and of Katarina (Ekatrina). After Alfred left the Aleutians, Maria remained at Unalaska where she died in 1885. Perhaps as a result of Tuck's agitation, Greenbaum brought Katarina to San Francisco for schooling around 1891. She drowned at Unalaska in 1895. Greenbaum denied he was the father of Olga, the only one of the three girls to live to adulthood.[9]

Tuck was not surprised by Tarpley's decision; the commissioner and his wife were not great supporters of the school. However, the Tucks had another, more effective ally.

On Sept. 13, 1890, six girls were sent from St. Paul Island to the school at Unalaska aboard the U.S. Revenue Cutter *Bear*, commanded by Captain Michael A. Healy. His wife, Mary Healy, had promised to take care of the girls as they traveled the 180 miles south.[10] The girls were listed as Tatiana Shapsnikoff, Avdotia Sedick, Salorn Pahomoff, Nadesda Shaishnikoff, Lukeria Krukoff and Parascovia Shutyagan. Mary described the trip to Unalaska in a letter to Sheldon Jackson.

> . . .we directed our course again towards Ounalaska with our precious freight of six little virgins (as the Captain calls them) and oh what a time we had, the storm . . . was about the worst we could possibly have, we were obliged to lay to for a couple of days, and let the ship fight it out with the wind and sea as best she could, there was no sleep or comfort of any kind for anybody on board.[11]

Upon arrival, Captain Healy took the girls to the Home, where Mary Tuck received them with open arms while confiding to Mary Healy that she "felt discouraged at the sight of so many for so small a space as she had to put them." Healy had made a collection among the ship's officers to help clothe the girls. The captain and his wife, both members of the Catholic Church, were enthusiastic about the work of the Home. Mary Healy invited Mary Tuck aboard the cutter, gave her clothing for the girls, and provided fancy handkerchiefs as presents. Mary Tuck quickly got to work.

Mrs. Tuck received oh such quantity of things from the East and two very large boxes from Oakland filled with clothes for the children, a number of pieces of furniture and forty blankets. I cannot begin to tell all of her wealth in this line, she has been very busy making flannel underclothes to keep them warm . . . she now has fourteen living constantly with her. . . .[12]

On September 28 the agent at St. Paul noted in the government logbook, "Mr. Tuck wrote that the children sent from St. Paul to his school were all in good health and getting along very well." One girl, however, had abandoned the Tucks' house the day after arriving and fled to Maria Shaishnikoff's home. John Tuck went after her but with no success. He enlisted Captain Healy's assistance, but Maria explained that the girl (probably Nadesda Shaishnikoff) was her goddaughter and that she had promised the girl's dying mother to care for her. Maria Shaishnikoff had no objection to the girl attending school but was adamant about her not living with the Tucks. Healy suggested that Tuck retreat and concentrate on the girls he had. If they could become his "banner pupils," parents "would be more than anxious to have their children under his charge" when the new Jesse Lee Home was built.

Word was already out, however, that education wasn't the only goal of this school. *The Alaskan*, a newspaper published in Sitka, noted that Mary Tuck was "nobly assisting her husband in the good work of evangelization and education."[13] Misgivings about the newly established school were expressed in the 1890 U.S. census report.

The report of the school at Unalaska, the most important point in western Alaska, is somewhat confusing. The teacher reported the establishment as a public day school, supported by the United States government, with 1 male teacher and 40 pupils, of which 2 were males and 38 females, with an average daily attendance of 13 for 196 days. The fact is that the institution is a home for girls, established under the auspices of the Methodist church, and the average daily attendance of 13 represents the number of boarders (girls) who are confined to the house. The number of boarders has since been much increased.[14]

What with "full orphans" and "half orphans" and the daughters of the town's "upper ten" coming and going, attendance at the school was erratic. But then, the government school under John Tuck wasn't the only one in session. The Russian school continued to hold classes attended by both girls and boys, and there were boys living at the Orthodox boarding facility. In February 1891 Daggett renewed the society's contract with the government for schools at Unalaska and Unga. In April Jackson requested $2,500 for payment to the society.

"CAPT. M.A. HEALY, U.S.R.M., *Commanding U.S. Revenue Cutter 'Bear.'" Courtesy of the Alaska State Library, Historical Collections (ASL-Healy-MA-1). The late-19th century photograph of the* Bear *with a steam launch is courtesy of the Consortium Library, University of Alaska Anchorage, Archives & Special Collections (Thomas W. Benham Photographs, c. 1880–1890, hmc-0069-b4). Written on the photo, "Northward Ho. U.S. Rev. Stmr 'Bear' bound out."*

That spring the Tucks welcomed an assistant, Lydia F. Richardson, from Middletown, Connecticut. She had been the superintendent of a state industrial school, and Tuck had written several letters to Daggett asking for her appointment. Richardson appears to have been a woman of energy and flair who expected to do good work in Alaska. She signed an early report, "Yours for God and Alaska." Richardson arrived just in time to relieve an ailing Mary Tuck of some of her responsibilities. In May 1891 John Tuck wrote that the new assistant was providing valuable and much needed help. "I realize each day more and more," Richardson wrote shortly after arriving, "how overworked and run down [Mary Tuck] is. Sometimes I think she may never recover."[15] Soon after Richardson's arrival, Daggett published a letter from her appealing for assistance to the Home. Reminded of local predators prowling the dock, the secretary urged again that the Unalaska missionaries "not be left helpless to relieve the sufferings of these destitute children—girls which wolves in human shape are seeking to devour."[16]

All was not harmonious between the newcomer and the Tucks, however. Richardson made friends with Commissioner Tarpley's wife, who had little use for the Tucks. As the summer went on, Lydia Richardson and Mary Tuck had several disagreements. In fact, Mary Healy wondered whether Mary Tuck would survive the help of her new assistant. "My first visit was ashore to see if Mrs. Tuck still lived," she wrote on October 13 to Sheldon Jackson, "for I fancied she must have had a fierce struggle with Miss Richardson."[17]

Despite appeals made by and on behalf of Lydia Richardson, it became clear to John that Mary's health was being further undermined by her anxiety over the new assistant. He wrote numerous letters to Daggett detailing Richardson's behavior. Finally, he asked Richardson to vacate the house. Mary Healy reported that on hearing this, Richardson ran to the A.C. Co. store where she created a scene by asking for protection from the Tucks. She then ran along the front beach "declaring she would drown herself." The deputy marshal, Ney B. Anthony, was sent for, and he managed to quiet her down. After talking with her for several hours, he informed the Tucks that "she was really insane and remained so for twelve hours when she became calm." She reluctantly agreed to return to the States but before leaving made an attempt to take control of the Orthodox church school. In the end, she sailed away, a victim of that very 19th century diagnosis "nervous prostration."

Daggett was offended when Tuck, after having asked repeatedly that Richardson be sent to Alaska, suggested the bureau secretary use better judgment in selecting assistants. She was further offended when he cautioned her not to repeat what he had written about Richardson. Nothing could have induced her to speak of this to anyone, she stormed to Jackson while urging him "not to refer to it in the least to any one—officers nor others." If a reason for Richardson's departure was required, "failure of health is sufficient."[18] Somewhat ingenuously she wrote to the women of the missionary society that doctors had ordered Richardson home "if she wanted to save her life."

ABOARD THE *BEAR, left to right, back row: Mary and John Tuck of the Jesse Lee Home, Capt. Michael Healy, Mary Healy, and a man whose name is not known. In the 1890s a number of girls from St. Paul Island in the Pribilofs traveled to Unalaska on the* Bear, *but the identities of these five girls are not known. (NARA, RG 26, Records of the U.S. Coast Guard, 26-CB, "Cruise of the U.S.R.C. Bear, Alaska and Eastern Siberia, Summer, 1895, John M. Justice.")*

The one letter Richardson had written to Daggett was filled with human interest tidbits that were useful in raising funds. "I had it copied & sent it from Dan to _____ [Bathsheba]," Daggett wrote. She also had it printed in *Woman's Home Missions*. Tuck's own reports were minimal, with never any financial accounting. Daggett demanded and pleaded for more information. When Tuck did write, he tended to complain. Finally, he described six girls. "Is six girls all we have to show for [$]2000 & over we have expended?" Daggett asked Jackson incredulously. She desperately needed material to augment her annual report. She called for two women to take up the challenge at Unalaska. "Where are they," she asked, "and the money to send them?" At the Home conditions returned to normal although, as Mary Healy cryptically informed Sheldon Jackson, "they have much to undo that Miss Richardson taught the girls."

Ten days after Commissioner Tarpley and his wife left on vacation, the mothers of several of the girls living with the Tucks came and asked for their daughters to return home. Tuck refused. "I kept the mothers off by bluffing them," he wrote to Jackson. As soon as Captain Healy arrived on the *Bear*, Tuck presented the same petition to him that Tarpley had allowed to be withdrawn. Because no action had been taken on it, Healy—newly named a justice of the peace—was free to render a decision. The captain, his wife explained, didn't feel that a hearing was required because he knew "all these people on this Spit and the children are better off" with the Tucks "than with their mothers who are not proper custodians of their children." Healy had recently been on a campaign to eradicate alcohol from Alaskan villages. "Hell-Roaring Mike," as he had been dubbed, had destroyed barrels of homebrew from the Alaska Peninsula to Atka and threatened whole villages with punishment. He immediately granted Tuck's custodianship for a year. The captain wrote to Jackson, "I enclose [for] you my first recorded decision as J. P. [justice of the peace]. There may not be much law in it but there is a heap of Justice."[19] Tuck was gratified but a bit worried; there were rumors that as soon as the *Bear* left, the mothers would use force to pry their children from the Home.

During his visit to Unalaska in the spring of 1890, Jackson had recruited three men to form a school board committee. They were Rudolph Neumann, Nicholas S. Resoff—the Aleut Orthodox priest in the village since 1884—and Ney B. Anthony, the newest of the three to the community. Their appointment from the U.S. commissioner of education was dated January 1891. In mid-October Neumann and Resoff wrote acknowledging their appointments and simultaneously submitting their resignations in protest. Neumann's letter summarized the state of affairs and reflected the attitude of much of the local population.

> All the natives born citizens of the Western Aleutian Islands, which are of Russian or Aleutian descent, profess the Christian religion, and are members of the Greco-Russian Church.

The school which has been in operation here very nearly two years, is at present located in one of the buildings owned by the Alaska Commercial Co. and offers very limited accommodations. A new and commodious school-house, in connection with the Jesse Lee Home, is to be erected next spring.

The home contains at present, I think, about twenty-one girls and one boy, the public day-school consists of about eight girl pupils.

The children living at the home are permitted to attend divine service at the Russian Church only under the supervision of their teachers, and to quote Mr. J.A. Tuck, Superintendent of the Jesse Lee Home, "when I think it is conscientiously required."

The Revd. N.S. Reesoff, priest of the Russian Church here, naturally objects to any such arrangement and insists that the church regimen should not be infringed on. Admitting the necessity and usefulness of a public, non-sectarian school, he protests against the insidious attempts at proselytism, which must necessarily tend to a deplorable estrangement between parent and child.

All the inmates of the home being girls, with the exception of one, and various means are resorted to increase their numbers still, whose connection with that institution will presumably cease upon their attaining their legal majority; what is their fate to be then?

Raised by their education and training above their surroundings they will find themselves in an anomalous and most unfortunate condition. Estranged from relations and friends, excluded from the membership of their church, unfit and incapable to become the wives of those who were their equals by birth, surrounded by circumstances that will preclude the majority to become self-supporting, their future will be such as I do not care to participate in creating.

Therefore, I beg to tender my resignation of a position, which as far as I can see, does not present a field of useful and beneficent action, nor enables me to prevent a great deal of misery and unhappiness.[20]

Mary Healy had warned, a bit after the fact, that the Tucks should not expect a bed of harmless roses. "Many thorns will prick them severely," she had written to Jackson. Troubles at the Jesse Lee Home had only begun. The Methodists' General Conference was about to cut all funding to Alaska.

NOTES

1. Report of the General Agent for the Year 1889–90. Education in Alaska, 1245.

2. Daggett. Report, September 1890. Sheldon Jackson Scrapbook. Volume 63. PHS. RG 239.

3. Department of Anthropology and Museum, Central Washington University, Ellensburg, Washington.

4. Tuck. "History and needs of our mission in Alaska." *New York Christian Advocate*. Nov. 21, 1895.

5. Report of the General Agent for the Year 1889–90. Education in Alaska, 1264. During his visit to Unalaska, Jackson received several donations to the museum he was establishing in Sitka. Mary Tuck provided lava from Makushin Volcano and Bogoslov Island. Rudolph Neumann contributed three Russian carbines and an ivory depiction of a "potlatch dance" from the Kuskokwim region (*The North Star*. November 1890:2).

6. Education in Alaska. 55th Congress, 2d Session, Senate, Doc. No. 137. Serial 3599.

7. *WHM*. December 1890:181–182.

8. Daggett. Report September 1890. Sheldon-Jackson Scrapbook. Volume 63. PHS. RG 239.

9. Andrews, Sharon J. "Remembrance of Our Ancestors," typescript dated April 7, 1988. This was supplied by Diana Kierce.

10. *St. Paul Island Log Books*. NARA, RG 22.

11. Mary Healy to Jackson, Oct. 20, 1890. PHS. RG 239. Box 5, folder 4.

12. Ibid.

13. *The Alaskan*. Oct. 4, 1890.

14. *Report on population and resources of Alaska at the eleventh census, 1890*. No specific author is given for this section. Information on the Aleutians came from both Ivan Petroff, who was unacknowledged in the publication, and from Samuel Applegate, who wrote the regional description.

15. *WHM*. August 1891:120.

16. Ibid.

17. Mary Healy to Sheldon Jackson, Oct. 13, 1889. NARA. RG 75. Letters Received, 1883–1907.

18. Daggett to Jackson, Oct. 20, 1891. PHS. RG 239. Box 5, folder 33.

19. Healy to Jackson. Oct. 15, 1891. NARA. RG 75. Letters Received, 1883–1907.

20. Rudolph Neumann to William T. Harris, Commissioner of Education. Oct. 14, 1891. NARA. RG 75. Letters Received, 1883-1907.

3

Crisis

ANOTHER WINTER PASSED. ANOTHER SNOWY SPRING. There was still no sign of the promised building. In November 1891 Lydia Daggett renewed the government school contract until June 1892, after which it would be dependent on the construction of a suitable building. In the spring of 1892 she herself traveled to San Francisco to oversee the purchase and shipment of materials for which $10,000 had been appropriated and raised. The funds were deposited in a bank in Cincinnati. Then on May 9 the General Conference of the Methodist Church adopted a resolution prohibiting cooperation with the government in operating contract schools, an action taken in support of a proposed 16th Amendment to the U.S. Constitution. Twenty-one states had approved the amendment, intended to protect public schools by a strict separation of church and state. No money whatever could be used to pay "for services, expenses or otherwise, any church, religious denomination or religious society, or any institution or undertaking which is wholly or in part under sectarian or ecclesiastical control."[1] In other words, the church could not contract to operate schools for the government.

Dissatisfaction over contract schools had been growing within the government itself. By 1892 the commissioner of Indian affairs had determined the policy was "an unwise one, partly because it is using public funds for sectarian uses, which is certainly contrary to the spirit of the Constitution and directly opposed to the letter of many of the State constitutions." Of equal concern, it was impossible for his office to adequately inspect or supervise these schools, many of which had as their "chief aim" the teaching of particular religious beliefs.[2] Congress agreed and began gradually to cut appropriations. By 1894–1895 the subsidizing of contract schools was discontinued.

On learning of the action of the General Conference, the Executive Board of the WHMS immediately halted efforts to secure a building for the Jesse Lee Home. In a summary later in the year, the Executive Board concluded that money would be better spent elsewhere. "More than half the people in the older States reside in cities of 5,000 and upwards, and a much larger proportion of vice and wretchedness is found in them," the society reported. "The entire population of Wyoming, Colorado, Nevada, Oregon, Washington, Montana, and North and South Dakota . . . is less than that of New York City." Alaska was comparatively insignificant and its costs considerable. A school for 60 pupils at Unalaska would cost at least $8,000 a year.[3] In general, contract schools did not pay for themselves but became a drain on the church. There was also a bit of sectarian jealousy in this decision to support the amendment. All Protestant churches combined received $500,000 less than the Catholic Church alone for annual contract work throughout the U.S. and its territories.[4] The WHMS attempted to put the best face possible on the decision of the General Conference by insisting that withdrawing from this work would force the government to step in. This, they wrote, "will eventually promote the best interests of all concerned." "The character of Government schools" would be "elevated," and once land was distributed to Indians they would be endowed "with the rights and privileges of citizenship."

Faced with the refusal of the society to act, Lydia Daggett stepped in and contracted personally with the government for $6,480 to ensure the Alaska work continued.[5] She traveled to Washington state where she arranged to ship supplies to the Tucks and sought a possible contractor for the anticipated Home even without the government school. The North American Commercial Company had recently received the government contract to harvest fur seals in the Pribilof Islands, replacing the Alaska Commercial Company. The new firm had built a fine dock and several buildings at Dutch Harbor, on Amaknak Island within Unalaska Bay. Company officials offered Daggett free passage to Unalaska, and by mid-July 1892 she found herself "seated in our dilapidated Jesse Lee Home, surrounded by the bright faces of our fifteen girls, with a background of two such sad, discouraged ones [the Tucks], that my heart was nearly broken."[6] She had notified Mrs. S. Hamilton of the society of her impending trip. "If she goes," Hamilton wrote, "the cause will prosper, for she has a strange power to move people to help."[7]

She had arrived, Daggett wrote, without a building and with no one "to help Mrs. Tuck." Her visit must have been an intense several weeks. Tuck's only comment on record was made to Sheldon Jackson a year later. "Unfortunately," he wrote, "Mrs. Daggett gained for us the active enmity of the A.C. Co."[8] She had, after all, traveled to Unalaska through the generosity of their main competitor, and she soon began to purchase coal and coal oil for the Home from the N.A.C. Co. and to use them to ship goods to Unalaska. Relations between Tuck and Neumann cooled even further. Although the company continued to rent the government a school building for $200 a year, it now charged the Home what was called "Native prices," a higher cost than was charged to ships or traders who did business with the company.[9] Another employee of the company, Nicholas Gray, back from teaching school at St. Paul Island and working as an accountant and storekeeper, was forthright in his opposition to the Tucks. "Mr. Gray," wrote Tuck, "is an open enemy to us and will annoy us I have no doubt in every way he can." Without actually violating the contract the company had with the home, Gray sold them inferior coal. He sided with anyone opposed to them. Daggett found Ney B. Anthony, the only remaining member of the school board, friendly, but he was soon to leave the community. In Daggett's estimation, Louis H. Tarpley, the deputy U. S. commissioner, was useless. He was, she wrote, "no terror to evil doers." And he was, of course, a friend of the A.C. Co. The next commissioner, she said, "should be a man, not a tool in the hands of such as desire to keep law from the place; a

"Pupils at mission home, *Unalaska, 1892. Supported by Methodist Woman's Home Mission Society of the United States." From Sheldon Jackson's* Education in Alaska, 1891–1892. *Washington, Government Printing Office, 1894.*

lawyer and a judge, a righteous one, too."[10] She preferred someone other than Lycurgus Woodward, who had no love for her for "various and sundry reasons."[11] Woodward eventually received the appointment, however, and became a stout defender of the Home.

Some sense of equanimity had been restored between the Home and the Orthodox community by the time Daggett arrived. The bishop was in residence, and Daggett enjoyed the company of one of his aides who joined them at prayers at the Home, read from their Bible, played the Hamilton organ, and sang their hymns. He even informed them that the bishop hoped one of the girls would remain with them until she was 18. This mutual respect was due in part to the work of Home assistants Matrona Salamatoff and Anna Fulcomer, who had arrived in the summer of 1892. Matrona had completed her courses in California. Without permission of the WHMS, Daggett arranged for Fulcomer to transfer from the Stickney Home in Washington state to Alaska. Anna Fulcomer wrote, "I suppose you know that if we did not take the girls to the Russian (Greek) church on Sundays and holidays that we could not get any. This has always been done." She reviewed a few past difficulties and went on to acknowledge, "For a while it looked as if the home would stop for lack of children, through the influence of the priests." However, good relations were established with the two new teachers at the Russian school, Father Metrofan and a deacon, Mr. Alexine.[12]

When Daggett returned to the States she wrote a general letter trying to dispel any lingering rumor that the government was going to build a school at Unalaska. It was not. Nor was the money that had been raised for the Jesse Lee Home going to be used for any other purpose. She had gone to Alaska "empty handed and heavy hearted." But she remained resolute. "O Lord, give us patience," the letter ended.[13] From Lynden, Washington, she wrote Jackson that the funds raised for the Jesse Lee Home were being used "to meet other obligations of the Society." "Had the other Bureaus worked as hard as ours," she wrote, "they might not have been so far behindhand as they are."[14] She urged him to lobby to restore the church's commitment to the Jesse Lee Home.

She had done two important things to safeguard the work, however. First, she had sent Anna Fulcomer to assist the Tucks. Second, she had arranged for the A.C. Co. to build an annex onto the rented facility and had ensured that a year's worth of supplies would be sent to the Tucks. The addition, she was convinced, was necessary "to save Mr. Tuck's life and that of his wife as well." She wrote her report about the visit while on the steamer leaving Alaska. She did not send it or communicate with the society, however, until she was assured that materials for the addition had left the port and that there was no way for officials to revoke the order. The society in effect fired her as bureau secretary. "I should do it again," she wrote defiantly to Jackson, "only twice as much." She was replaced by "Mrs. Senator H.M. Teller" of Washington, D.C. "This gives them all power over the money unmolested—officially—& leaves me at liberty to take any other position in behalf of Alaska that may come to me."[15]

For several months Lydia Daggett continued to argue that the decision of the Methodist General Conference to withdraw from contract schools did not apply to Alaska. She argued that if the society had a suitable building, the government would not build a school. When challenged that the "spirit" of the conference resolution encompassed Alaska, she replied that "if men at the head of such a movement can't frame a paper to cover all they mean I disregard all 'spirits of it'"—especially when they had supported the project year after year.

The discussions continued into the annual meeting of the missionary society in the autumn. Again, Daggett argued that Alaska was exempt from the conference resolution. Jeannette Crippin Fisk, widow of General Clinton B. Fisk, was her primary opponent.[16] When Fisk found herself unable to refute Daggett's argument, she "*venomously* came to the front of the platform and asked in defiant tones"[17] if Daggett hadn't made a $6,000 contract with the government for Alaska despite the action of the general conference. Fisk referred to a letter from W.T. Harris, the commissioner of education, in which he promised funds. It took Daggett a couple of days during which she telegrammed Harris and studied the original letters before she uncovered what had happened. The $2,000 in Harris's letter had been changed by someone to $6,000. Whether the alteration had been done "from ignorance or malice" she didn't know, but the result was the same: By the time she had her proof, the vote had gone against her and Alaska was abandoned.

With the termination of society support for the Home, there was an attempt to rename the Unalaska project after a generous donor. This prompted another letter from Daggett to Jackson in which she appealed to him to safeguard the name "under which over $10,000 was raised." She continued to lobby for the restoration of funds to Alaska. "I expected to be beheaded for doing without orders what I did," she wrote to him. She attempted to find out where the money raised for Unalaska had been spent. Some of it, she suspected, had gone to one of the mission's offices already "carpeted throughout with Brussels carpets." At the end of her letter, she again urged Jackson, "You will not consent nor allow this name to be taken from that Home even tho only the old house remains? Will you?" Her trip to Alaska had been "a never to be forgotten one. To see with my own eyes was more than I can express." She was clearly leaving a project that had been dear to her heart. "Write me all you can," she said, "I have time for I shall ask for no information from any one else. What comes voluntarily is all right—but none sought. I remain as sincerely as ever for Alaska, Mrs. L. H. Daggett."[18]

. .

IN LETTERS WRITTEN BY Salamatoff and Fulcomer there is a sense of camaraderie and support among the Tucks and their young assistants. Matrona Salamatoff, or Mattie as she called herself, referred to the others as "lovely people." She found Mary Tuck sympathetic and helpful. "We banded together very closely," she wrote, "trying to lift up the native

MATRONA SALAMATOFF, *Unalaska, and* ANNA FULCOMER *(right), Circle City. From Sheldon Jackson's* Education in Alaska, 1895–1896. *Washington, Government Printing Office, 1897.*

children, who came to us from homes where sloth, immorality, and intemperance pre-vailed."[19] She experienced success in teaching and found "the pupils are quite ready to comprehend all branches except arithmetic. . . ." However, she left the following summer. Perhaps it was Mary Tuck's chronic illness or the general lack of medical care available in the community that led her to reassess her training. She enrolled at a hospital in Portland, Oregon, to become a trained nurse.

Anna Fulcomer found the Tucks to be wonder-workers, making do with so very lit-tle, as she put it, and paying for necessities out of their own pockets.[20] A glimpse of Fulcomer was given in a letter by Ellen Kittredge.

> I had a splendid time at Unalaska. One of the two white women living there, a Methodist mission teacher, met us and took us to her school. It is a boarding school for eighteen girls from other islands. She had us write our names in an authograph book she had. Then we wrote our names on a big piece of cotton cloth that had a great many names on it, and the children are to sew our names where we wrote. The cloth is going to the World's Fair 1893 [Columbian Exposition in Chicago]. You can look for it there.[21]

In late 1893 Fulcomer expressed a desire to return to school to study anthropology. She stayed at Unalaska through the summer of 1894, however, because of Mary's poor health and John's absence. His father had died and he made a trip east to visit his mother. Fulcomer eventually attended the University of Chicago and in 1896 applied to return to Unalaska, hoping to arrive before school started in order to do some anthropological work. There was no opening, so she accepted a position at Circle City in the interior of Alaska.[22] Fulcomer was the first to suggest that "an experienced medical missionary" be sent to Unalaska. This recommendation would not be implemented for several years, but it would prove of incalculable value.

The Tucks were ignorant of the decision of the General Conference of the WHMS to make no appropriation for the Jesse Lee Home in 1892, and they went on with their work fully expecting a new building in the summer of 1893. By September 1892 there were 26 pupils at the Home. In November Michael Healy wrote a letter of glowing support, urging "the ladies of the Methodist society" to "provide it with better facilities with which to continue and enlarge its work for the elevation of these poor, neglected members of their sex."[23] A sentence from his letter would circulate in mission reports for years to come: "In all my experience in the country I have seen nothing that has rendered so much good to the people." The addition to the Home was completed around the first of December. This almost doubled the living space, but the Home was still overcrowded. "Twenty-eight of us sit down to eat in a room where we can hardly turn around," wrote Anna Fulcomer. "We must pass through the kitchen and well-room to reach the school-room; the girls' dormitories are over the school-room; in the attic above we must keep flour, meal, dried fish, sugar, shoes, extra cooking utensils, all kinds of clothing, and, in fact everything. It is most inconvenient."[24] Mattie Salamatoff compared their sleeping arrangements to "the fashion of berths on board a ship."[25] Their new stove was inefficient. Wet clothes hung indoors took days to dry.

The Woman's Home Missionary Society was under a "constitutional obligation" to submit its plans and budget to the men, generally bishops, of the Board of Managers of the Missionary Society. Elizabeth Rust, corresponding secretary, summarized the result in a "statement" published on page four of *Woman's Home Missions* in January 1893. Two articles set the stage for this "statement." The first, titled "Alaska," extolled "the indomitable Secretary, Mrs. Daggett," "the revered name of Jesse Lee," and the society's hope "to help end the dreadful tale of the Alaskan woman's fate." It acknowledged "the expense, annoyance, and . . . distress of mind" Daggett experienced trying to balance the high cost of Alaskan work with missionary funds and government aid. Men like Sheldon Jackson and Michael Healy, accustomed to the deep pockets of the government, had no idea "how inadequate is a missionary treasury to such stupendous prices" as were found in Alaska. While a mission school was now impossible, the society hoped to station "an evangelist" at Unalaska and another at Unga. The Unalaska minister could work with "the school the government will build" to "bring forth a Divine harvest on those volcanic islands where men are few but gross wickedness abounds." However, this first article concluded, the bishops were hesitant to do even this much.

This article was immediately followed by one about a man who was not afraid to undertake unpopular causes. Prince Albert, husband of Queen Victoria, had pushed for the first World's Fair despite severe criticism, opposition and ridicule. In the end, he had succeeded. Now, in 1893, the United States was preparing for a great world's fair in Chicago on the occasion of the 400th anniversary of the arrival of Columbus. The juxtaposition of articles was anything but subtle.

The "statement" itself provided a detailed account of the presentation made before the Board of Managers. The women urged stationing a preacher at Unalaska if operating a school was impossible. He should be under the supervision of the Puget Sound Conference, as the nearest and most knowledgeable about Alaskan conditions. They informed the Board of Managers that support from the Missionary Society or the U.S. government was vital if missionaries were to surmount the control "a great commercial company" held over the territory. This was a reference to the Alaska Commercial Company, although the company was at this time reducing its stations in Alaska after losing its lease on the Pribilof Islands. "United States law has little authority in Alaska," the statement said, repeating information from L.H. Daggett. Naming each member of the Board of Managers, the statement quoted the decision to close the work in Alaska "in view of the smallness of the population accessible in said islands and the occupancy of the mainland of Alaska by other evangelical churches." The article concluded by assuring readers that the

Jesse Lee Home school would continue through July 1893. Sufficient supplies had already been shipped. After that, if the government did indeed build the promised school, John Tuck would continue as teacher. Although the women's society would "be obliged to be content with this arrangement," negotiations were ongoing with the "authorities at Washington, and of the church" in the hope of finding a way to resume missionary work in Alaska. In the meantime, the funds collected would remain with the WHMS as their board of managers "alone has the authority to appropriate moneys."

This statement was written by Elizabeth L. Rust and also signed by Eliza G. Davis. Significantly, both women used their given and surnames. This in itself was unusual, in light of the general subservience of women to men exemplified by references to the new secretary of the Alaska Bureau as "Mrs. Senator H.M. Teller." Clearly, the fight for the Home had not been surrendered. Elizabeth Rust continued her efforts, gaining support from men and women in authority.

Part of Rust's statement was quoted when Mrs. M.E. Griffith appeared before the annual conference of the U.S. Board of Indian Commissioners and representatives of missionary boards on Jan. 12, 1893. Sheldon Jackson had just concluded a summary of the introduction of reindeer to Alaska and the work of the 14 contract schools in the territory. He had referred to the decision of the Methodist Church to withdraw from the Aleutians. "It will be a positive injury," he told the representatives. Although the church, in his opinion, had "abundant wealth," the work in western Alaska "must be abandoned because the church has concluded not to take any Government money and the Woman's Home Missionary Society say they can not, without the help of the Government raise the funds."

> That church has built up a boarding school of 25 girls, some of them having come 1,000 miles. Two of them were picked up by captains, found without homes, almost without clothes, eating fish for food when they could, and eating carrion along the shore when they could not get anything better. Of these 25, I suppose not more than 5 have homes. That Christian church, through the warm hearts of its women, has taken these girls out of those conditions, has placed them in a Christian home, has kept them there three years, and when the steamer goes up next spring the word will go, "You must disband." Where can those girls go if the church that has brought them out of the old conditions simply drops them? If the denominations will go on with their work, I do not care whether they take Government funds or not, but I do not want the work stopped.[26]

Mrs. Griffith then took the floor. It was not that the WHMS did not have sufficient funds, she said: "We have raised $10,000 for the work in Alaska." The problem was that some members of the society "had been deceived in regard to the location of our mission." No church member had actually visited Alaska before agreeing to work in the Aleutians.

She then referred to the high cost of serving the sparse population in the islands. The society, she affirmed, stood behind the decision of the church to refuse any government aid. Although she offered no plan, she concluded, "I hope no one will believe that we propose to allow our twenty girls to go back to heathenism."

1893 marked the end of the contract school at Unalaska. The government theoretically assumed direct control. For residents in the village, however, nothing seemed changed. Tuck remained as teacher and his wife as matron of the Home. Everything—public education and the "industrial school"—took place in the Tucks' home. The WHMS continued as the dominant power behind both. "We now have the school under our care," reported Jeannette Fisk, president of the WHMS, at its October 1894 meeting. "Government supplies the school-house, and we support the children."

· ·

DURING THE SUMMER OF 1893 the Tucks said farewell to some of their first students, including several of the girls who had arrived from the Pribilof Islands with Captain Healy in 1890. Paraskovia Shutyagan, now a young woman of 22, left to live and work in Portland, Oregon, as a "nurse girl" with the family of the former customs agent. The Tucks did not like to see her go, but as a resident of the Pribilof Islands she was a ward of the government, and the treasury agent gave his approval.[27] In August the Tucks took 10 girls and traveled to St. Paul Island where Tatiana Shapsnikoff was married "to one of the best men on the island," John Kochutin, a first-class sealer.[28] Although Tuck "had some trouble to keep one of the younger girls from following her example" they returned with all of their students and one more to take Tatiana's place.[29]

There were weddings at Unalaska also. Annie Kudrin married Peter Shaishnikoff, and Sophia Reinken married Henry Swanson. He was a Swedish immigrant who had previously lived in the False Pass area. Swanson Lagoon on Unimak Island is named for him. Sophia was the daughter of Adolph Reinken, a long-time employee of the A.C. Co., and his late wife, Evdokiia, a daughter of Father Innokentii Shaishnikoff. Adolph Reinken had placed Sophia and his other children in the Home while he and his second wife, Alexandra Kudrin, lived at Chernofski on the southern end of the island. On the occasion of his daughter's wedding, Reinken hosted a dance on a Sunday evening. For Orthodox Christians, the Sabbath ends at sunset on Sunday (and begins at sunset on Saturday). He wanted his other children to attend this happy occasion, but John Tuck refused permission. "I felt that then was the time to make a stand," he wrote. "The present is no time for yielding an iota of principal [sic], especially concerning the Sunday question, about which so large a portion of the public is inclining the wrong way."[30] Reinken had been the only person paying tuition and board for his children. Now he was furious. Years later, Reinken's grandson, Henry Swanson the younger, recalled the old man frequently swearing, "Gott in Himmel!"

Whether he said that or not on this occasion, he removed all his children from the Home and after the wedding celebration took them to Chernofski for the winter.

More than 15 residents of the Home had left within a little over a year. By October 1893 enrollment stood at 19 girls. The new manager for the North American Commercial Company in the Pribilof Islands had ties to the Baptist orphanage at Kodiak, and the Jesse Lee Home could expect few students from St. Paul or St. George. The A.C. Co. would do nothing to add to the enrollment of the school. Tuck's friend Michael Healy told him it looked as if the Home "were doomed to die a natural death from starvation or suffocation, our pupils gradually growing up and leaving and no new ones coming to take their places." Sheldon Jackson himself remained upbeat. The Unalaska school "has had a very successful year," he wrote in June 1893, "the pupils connected with the boarding department having made marked progress." That summer he visited Unalaska and encouraged the Tucks to persevere. He wrote that they continued "bravely and heroically." He promised to continue efforts to secure funding until the Methodist authorities "understand the real condition and authorize the women to resume their work in the Home."[31]

The fall of 1893 saw another epidemic strike Unalaska. Within three days the entire population of the Home was bedridden except for Anna Fulcomer and three girls. Five people died in the village, and the A.C. Co. doctor had almost 150 patients to treat.[32] Mary Tuck's health continued to decline. She had a serious case of "capillary bronchitis" and was urged by the doctor to move to a warmer climate. John Tuck also had been ill and continued to find himself unable to concentrate for extended periods of time.

His report covering the school year 1893–1894 sought to explain the low attendance. First, Unalaska was the seat of the Orthodox Church for the region and its officials opposed anything that would "Americanize" or "derussianize" the people. Second, in comparison with Unga, at Unalaska there were far fewer white men who acknowledged their natural children and sought to have them educated. Tuck felt he and his wife had made appreciable progress in teaching English.

> Contrary to the prevalent opinion, Russian is not the vernacular of any large proportion of the people of the Aleutian District of Alaska. Beginning work in this place in Sept. '89, I soon discovered that most of the people had a very limited knowledge of any language except the Aleut and that by the use of English I could come quite as near to their ways of thought and feeling as by any other available means. Although nearly all had some knowledge of English, yet there existed an intense prejudice against its use which was very hard to overcome. Russian was the language of their church and the people seemed to regard its use as a religious duty. The Church schools gave only the merest smattering of knowledge, in most instances only the ability to count and to pronounce from the written or printed page. . . .[33]

Other sources make clear that a sizable proportion of the community understood Russian. Certainly all those who attended the Russian school, boys and girls, knew the fundamentals of the language and had a basic vocabulary. Russian continued to be used by educated Aleuts until World War II. Tuck subordinated everything to the teaching of English and now could report that "most of their talking and thinking at work and at play is done in English and not in Aleut; and the younger children talk as fluently if not as idiomatically in English as any American children would do. These have even lost the use to a large extent of their native Aleut."

If and when a building for the Jesse Lee Home arrived, there would have to be a piece of property on which it could be erected. On July 18, 1891, Tuck had sent a hand-drawn map to U.S. Commissioner of Education William Harris showing land that he requested be set aside as a reservation for the Jesse Lee Home.[34] The site covered fully half of all the inhabitable land on the peninsula. Its western border was the barn and cattle yard of the A.C. Co. It extended east to the base of a mountain and the shores of the large Unalaska Lake that separated the peninsula from Unalaska Valley. Tuck said that the property totaled between 15 and 20 acres, and he asked Harris to send the request to the appropriate official in the Department of the Interior. And then this entire claim seems to have slipped Tuck's mind.

When the Alaska Commercial Company purchased the holdings of the Russian-American Company at Unalaska it thought it had its property safely in hand. In 1884 and again in 1887 Neumann filed maps indicating the company's claims to land that lay, basically, between the church and the western end of the peninsula. It also claimed a pasture lying east of the main residential cluster of barabaras in the village. But in 1891 territorial Governor Lyman Knapp claimed the eastern tip of the peninsula for a thousand feet. This included land occupied by many of the A.C. Co. buildings. (The government would take no actions regarding the land until 1906.) In July of 1891 Neumann had the A.C. Co. property claims verified by Ivan Petroff, then a U.S. deputy surveyor.[35] In 1892 Neumann had about 3½ acres surveyed for the Home at the request of the visiting Mrs. Daggett. Later, about 5 acres were added, and the total 8½ acres were set aside as a school reserve. At the same time Neumann agreed to have his company erect the anticipated new building for the Home behind the rented facility, with the understanding that it would have to be moved to its own land once that had been received. Of course, the building did not arrive that year. In June 1895 Tuck again asked Neumann for land on which to erect the Home, now expected to arrive that summer. The 8½ acres had been taken by the government for the public school. Neumann said the mission would need to contact the A.C. Co.'s home office.

Neumann protested when he realized how much land was being claimed for the Jesse Lee Home, citing Tuck's apparent ignorance of any earlier claims for land.[36] If the Home received title to all the land at the eastern end of the peninsula, "an extension of the town would be an impossibility." It seemed ludicrous, Neumann said, that the government would allow 25 acres of a townsite no larger than 96 acres to be tied up "for school and mission purposes." The A.C. Co. itself claimed only 26 acres. His computation of 96 acres included his company's 26 acres, 8 acres for the school and 25 for the mission, 3 acres claimed by the Orthodox Church, 6 acres claimed by the government (including the custom house), and 26 acres of river, lake and mountains—leaving only 2 acres for the entire local population. Land issues at Unalaska have frequently been confusing. In the 1893–1894 report of the Woman's Home Missionary Society, Mrs. H.M. Teller incorrectly reported that the society had secured title to 160 acres of property at Unalaska. This was not an announcement calculated to win over the A.C. Co.

As the new deputy U.S. commissioner at Unalaska, Lycurgus R. Woodward wrote to Jackson that he was sorry there was a conflict over land. His solution was ingenious if a bit unrealistic. He suggested that the women of the missionary society transfer their facility to an abandoned island where in addition to the regular work of the Home they could raise foxes. Not only would the Home be self-supporting in a few years, he wrote, but the girls "would be away from bad influences . . . [and] out from under the laws of the Greek church."[37]

Eventually it was Lydia Daggett's nemesis, Jeannette Fisk, who brought about the resumption of the work. By the fall of 1893, Fisk was aware that the closing of the Unalaska mission had produced "a ban of censure" on the Methodist Church itself. She was assigned the job of ascertaining "the real condition of things." The WHMS met that October and elected Fisk president. The society also voted $3,560 for the construction of a building at Unalaska. It was to have two stories and an attic and was to measure 72 by 36 feet. Fisk immediately met with the board of bishops in Minneapolis. "I there learned that the cause of suspension," she wrote, "was because of the opinion that we had never had permission to enter upon this work."[38] Considering what had transpired for almost 10 years, this explanation seems incredible.

Once again Sheldon Jackson came to the rescue. He produced a letter written in 1884 authorizing the WHMS to begin its work in Alaska. General Fisk had been the chairman of the committee that wrote the letter. The bishop who had objected to reopening the Unalaska school made a resolution supporting continuation. It passed on a voice vote. Jackson also appeared by invitation at the annual meeting of the General Missionary Committee. When he finished speaking the committee stood up in a show of unanimous support for the Alaskan program. In April 1894 the society published a summary of the financial status of the Alaska project showing that the special fund for Alaska had received $14,621.21. After disbursements and withholding funds for outstanding bills, about $3,900 remained.

Further support for the Home appeared in an 1894 report from Dr. J.M. Buckley, who was requested to investigate conditions at Unalaska. Able to get no nearer than Sitka (some

Unalaska, June 20, 1894
Mrs. H.M. Teller:

Dear Madam, ——I have been in Unalaska for several days, and have spent my time at your school. I thought it might be interesting to you to hear the impressions of a stranger concerning it.

I am just on the way up the Yukon to begin just such a school under the Rev. John W. Chapman of the Episcopal Church, of whom you may have heard; and so I have been especially interested in it myself, and have taken pains to learn all the details of the work. And it gives me new courage to see what wonderful results may be accomplished by patient, faithful work in Christian faith. Mr. and Mrs. Tuck, under the great disadvantages of crowded quarters, and, I should judge, limited means, very great opposition, the influence of the Greek Church, and the terrible immorality of the natives, and so many incoming sailors,——how they have stood their ground and accomplished the results they have is wonderful.

I was there twelve hours yesterday, and a good part of the day before as well as of Sunday, and saw the girls at work, at play, at meals, in school, and at worship. A happier, more contented, more harmonious set I never saw. There was no quarrelling anywhere; and each did her own share of work, like a hive of busy bees. They laugh and play and sing and bustle about, bright and happy and natural, and yet as orderly as one would find anywhere.

The discipline is excellent without depressing them; and, if the babel of voices gets too high, a tap of the bell or a word is sufficient to bring quiet. They stand well in reading with girls in any public schools anywhere, and write well; and yet these girls were wild untaught Indians, or half-breeds, speaking only their own language, and dirty beyond conception, and unused to any civilized habits. I wish you could see the neat rooms, clean floors, wash hanging on the line, ironed aprons and dresses, nicely made beds, dresses they themselves had made,——all the work of these girls, even the tiny ones taking part as far as they are able; and the lunch and dinners, with excellent bread, was entirely their own doing, etc.

I am glad to tell you of Mrs. Tuck's work, and I wish she could have many interested in it as well. It is saving these girls from a most horrible degradation, such as one shudders even to know of; and every Christian woman who values her sacred womanhood ought to feel it a privilege to do any, even a small part, in helping to keep them out of it, and to save them not only to do their work in the world and make it so much the better, but for eternal life.

I remain
Yours sincerely,
Bertha W. Sabine [39]

1,200 miles away) he relied on information from a Captain Thomas, who had just arrived from the island. Thomas had high praise for the work of John and Mary Tuck. Buckley also received a favorable report from another missionary who had visited the Home over a six-week period. "The girls were carefully guarded in a bright, homelike atmosphere," the report stated, "and their progress in learning was astonishing."[40] This missionary was Bertha W. Sabine, who was on her way to the Episcopal mission at Anvik on the Yukon.

The members of the WHMS were relieved that their work could resume. Alaska had proved "to be not only a field of strange interest, but one of the most important and promising."[41] Anna F. Beiler was appointed secretary of the Alaska Bureau. Like Daggett, she was a skilled administrator able to focus her considerable energy and moral authority on the project. She would tolerate nothing that stood in the way of accomplishing her goals. Under her leadership the Jesse Lee Home would be built, the staff reorganized, and its mission clarified.

NOTES

1. *WHM*. December 1892:181–182.

2. Report of the Commissioner of Indian Affairs, Aug. 27, 1892. Serial 3088:56.

3. *WHM*. July 1892:98.

4. *WHM*. December 1892:181. The commissioner of Indian affairs had commented on the jealousy in his report of Aug. 27, 1892. Serial 3088.

5. Report of the Commissioner of Indian Affairs, Aug. 27, 1892. Serial 3088:56.

6. Woman's Home Missionary Society. Reports from Bureaus. 1891–1892:76.

7. Mrs. S. Hamilton to Jackson, Nov. 18, 1891. PHS. RG 239. Box 5, folder 14.

8. Tuck to Jackson. Oct. 21, 1893. NARA. RG 75. Letters Received, 1883–1907.

9. Mrs. H.M. Teller to Jackson, June 2, 1894. PHS. RG 239. Box 5, folder 32.

10. 54th Congress, 1st session. Senate Document No. 113. Feb. 11, 1896. Her letter was written Aug. 24, 1892.

11. Beiler to Jackson, Jan. 15, 1899. PHS. RG 239. Sheldon Jackson Papers Box 6, folder 18.

12. *WHM*. September 1894:138.

13. This letter was published on Aug. 22, 1892, in an unnamed newspaper in Port Townsend, Washington. Sheldon Jackson Scrapbook, Volume 63. PHS. RG 239.

14. Daggett to Jackson, March 17, 1893. PHS. RG 239. Box 5, folder 24.

15. Ibid.

16. Clinton B. Fisk died July 9, 1890. In church publications Jeannette Fisk was always referred to as Mrs. Clinton B. Fisk or, occasionally, as Mrs. General Clinton B. Fisk. Her given name was located at The African American Registry where Clinton Fisk is noted as an early prohibitionist and the founder of Fisk University. http://www.aaregistry.com/african_american_history/2398/Clinton_Fisk_freedman_bureau_pioneer.

17. Daggett to Jackson, Jan. 23, 1894. PHS. RG 239. Box 5, folder 29.

18. Ibid.

19. *Christian Advocate*. Oct. 25, 1893. PHS. RG 239. Vol. 63.

20. *WHM*. September 1894:138-139.

21. Lopp. *Ice Window*. 2001:24–25.

22. For her stay at Circle City, see Fulcomer, Anna, "The Three R's at Circle City." *Century Magazine*, Vol. 66, June 1898:223–229.

23. Jackson, "Education in Alaska 1895–96." *Annual Report of the Secretary of the Interior for the Fiscal Year Ended June 30, 1896.* Vol. V, Part 2. Washington. Government Printing Office. 1897:1444

24. Anna Fulcomer to H.M. Teller, May 12, 1894. *WHM.* September 1894:138.

25. Matrona Salamatoff. *Christian Advocate.* Oct. 25, 1893. *Sheldon Jackson Scrapbook*, Volume 63. PHS. RG 239.

26. Journal of the Twenty-Second Annual Confference [sic] of the United States Board of Indian Commissioners with Representatives of Missionary Board and Indian Rights Associations. Serial 3088: 1418–1419.

27. People living in the Pribilof Islands at the time the Alaska Commercial Company received its 20-year contract to manage and harvest the fur seals were considered "wards" of the government and were subject to strict regulatory control over their lives.

28. *St. Paul Island Log Books.* NARA, RG 22.

29. Tuck to Jackson. Oct. 21, 1893. NARA. RG 75. Letters Received, 1883–1907.

30. Ibid.

31. *WHM.* February 1896:26.

32. Tuck to Jackson. Oct. 21, 1893. NARA. RG 75. Letters Received, 1883–1907.

33. Tuck to Jackson. June 1, 1894. NARA. RG 75. Letters Received, 1883–1907.

34. Tuck to William T. Harris. July 18, 1891. NARA. RG 75. Letters Received, 1883–1907.

35. This ubiquitous person was gathering material for the 1890 census, a position he would soon be fired from because of fake translations he prepared for the government's fur seal hearings in Paris.

36. Rudolph Neumann to Alaska Commercial Company, June 17, 1895. Stanford University, Special Collections JL006.

37. Woodward to Jackson. July 15, 1895. NARA. RG 75. Letters Received, 1883–1907.

38. Fisk, Mrs. Clinton B. [Jeannette], *Methodist Church Work in Alaska.* Lake Mohonk Conference. 12th Annual Meeting. 1894: 135–136

39. Quoted in Fisk, *Methodist Church Work in Alaska.* Lake Mohonk Conference. 12th Annual Meeting. 1894:136.

40. *WHM.* January 1909:6.

41. *WHM.* December 1894.

4

The Home Arrives

"I AM HAPPY TO ASSURE YOU THAT I AM A SINCERE CHRISTIAN," wrote Mattie J. Short from Little Rock, Arkansas, on May 29, 1894, "trying to serve God as best I know." Although raised with a Methodist grandfather, she had never actually joined the church. She would, "at once," if the Woman's Home Missionary Society wished it. She had lived something of an unsettled life, she explained in her letter to Mrs. Teller. She pledged the interim secretary of the Alaska Bureau that she was "willing to endure all the privations and hardships of a missionary's life."

John and Mary Tuck had been pleased with the help given by Matrona Salamatoff and Anna Fulcomer, and they looked forward to Mattie Short's arrival. No sooner had she stepped through the door, however, than she announced that she would be of no practical use in the everyday operations of the Home.[1] She could neither cook nor sew and would prefer just to pay a small amount for room and board. The Tucks were shocked, of course, but they were horrified to learn that she approved of drinking wine, playing cards, and dancing—though all in moderation. She was, from all accounts, an attractive and vivacious woman who quickly made friends. Among them were the Tucks' allies Michael Healy, Commissioner Woodward, and the new deputy U.S. marshal Willard B. Hastings.

When Captain Healy invited Short to accompany him on a trip to St. Paul, she wanted to take along four of the older girls. However, Mary Tuck and three other girls were very ill at the time and John would have been left with everything. He said no. Mattie became angry and scolded him in front of the girls. Tuck ordered her out of the house and she moved in with Commissioner Woodward and his wife. Woodward found her "fiery and high spirited." Healy, according to Tuck, was "very seriously offended and called it taking an unfair advantage of a woman." Nevertheless, without her underfoot, the work at the home was easier to manage although several of the older girls, following Mattie's example, had become "dissatisfied and disobedient." Whether with or without guile, Mattie informed Mrs. Teller that she had "grave fears for Mrs. Tuck's health if she is not speedily relieved."[2] According to a November 1894 letter to Teller from Irene Sovoroff, one of the girls brought from the Pribilof Islands in 1889, Mary Tuck had not left her bed for the previous eight weeks.[3]

"I am at a loss as to how to take Mr. Woodward in various ways," wrote Tuck. Indeed, Woodward was a bundle of contradictions. He felt the girls at the Home would be in moral danger from whalers and other men and yet he thought the girls were too closely watched by the Tucks. He certainly understood the power of the Orthodox church at Unalaska and yet he wanted the missionaries to confront the priests directly. ". . . To do as he wishes," wrote Tuck, "would be a declaration of war with the Orthodox Russian Church and . . . we are not yet strong enough to assume such an attitude." Tuck was not completely opposed to the idea. "Let us wait until we at least have a good building," he added, "and ample support as well as a full corps of teachers."

Woodward for his part wrote to Jackson that "Mr. Tuck has the unhappy faculty of getting on the wrong side of almost everybody." He suggested that Tuck be replaced. Not, however, with such as Mattie Short. "It would be much better for the cause of Christian education," he wrote, "to have a person baptized with the Holy Ghost and fire appointed to this school."[4] Two days after he wrote to Jackson, his wife, Edith, applied for the assistant teacher position. When Tuck wrote that he and his wife felt the need to leave Unalaska during the summer of 1894, Jackson suggested to Mrs. Teller that Woodward and his wife might be willing to oversee the Home.[5]

Woodward's attitude toward the Orthodox Church was not exceptional among government officials. Allan H. Dougall, an examiner for the Department of Justice, had praised the Home in 1892. In contrast, he wrote, "The Greek church is not in any sense an American church, or a church for Americans." He went on to add, with flagrant ignorance, "American citizens who have never heard a prayer for the President of the U.S. or know not the meaning of the 4th of July . . . are taught to pray for the Emperor of Russia, to celebrate his birthday and commemorate the victories of ancient Greece."[6] He had obviously never been at Unalaska for the religious and community festivities on the national holiday.

The Tucks were looking forward to saying farewell to Mattie Short in the early summer of 1895. They were startled to hear rumors of her engagement to an employee of the A.C. Co. They were dumbfounded when this employee turned out to be Willard B. Hastings, recently appointed deputy U.S. marshal. After the June wedding she became an integral part of Unalaska's officialdom, a powerful, well-placed, energetic opponent. The wedding was made even more unpleasant for the Tucks because William Hamilton, assistant agent of education, was visiting from Washington, D.C. He boarded with the Woodwards for a month while awaiting the arrival of the *Bear*.[7] Hamilton described the arrival of a fleet of revenue cutters that coincided with the coming of spring.

> Officers and sailors gave life to the hitherto deserted street, dainty revenue cutters and a trimly built British gunboat rode at anchor in the harbor; saucy little steam launches and natty, white boats darted about; bugle calls floated out over the tranquil waters. . . . All was life and action, where there had been silence and stagnation. There were calls upon the officers of the various ships, photographic excursions, climbing of mountains whose ravines still held the winter snows, balls, and even a wedding at high noon in which the contract-

Nov. 23, 1894

MY DEAR MRS. TELLER: —I know that you will be glad to receive a letter from a little girl who you never saw before. I have heard Mr. and Mrs. Tuck talk about you so much that I felt like as if I wanted to write to you this Sunday morning. Mrs. Tuck has been sick nearly all this summer but she is sick in bed yet but she gets up and stays in her room once in a while. She goes down in the front room when there is a fire built there. We began to have school in September. We have a few scholars come in from outside to go to school with us. We have so many girls that Mr. Tuck made a new store house to keep our clothing in it.

When it was a nice day we saw some whales standing in a line by the Priest Rock. We thought it was some sailors that had escaped from the whaler. There is going to be a wedding. Parsha's cousin is going to be the bride. We have snow on the ground and over the mountains. We have classes in the school room and in the dining room. Miss Short teaches the smaller children and Mr. Tuck teaches the larger ones. I am in the class with the larger girls.

This summer we had a lot of berries. Saturday evening we always bake for Sunday. Mr. Tuck makes candys out of sugar and molasses or sometimes out of maple sirup. Mrs. Tuck has not been out of her bed for eight weeks. Bertha (the steamer) went away November 1st and it is not here yet. I think that something has happened to her.

We have no room so we cook and eat in the dining room both. Mr. Tuck made a longer table so as to give room and we could not be quite crowded as we were before, and he made several benches. They have put up a new paper in the front room. One day it stormed so hard that our fence broke down and some of the natives' boats were blown away. There was a woman by her house watching to see if her barrels would blow away. At once one of her barrels blew away and she ran and caught it.

In the afternoon Mr. Woodward comes and gives us papers to read to ourself. I have a mental arithmetic and also one of the little girls. Few of the big girls have mental arithmetics.

I thank you for that coat that you sent me. I think it is very nice. It is a little bit too big for me. I am going to fit it when I get time to do it. I am in Mrs. Tuck's room writing this letter and also some of the girls are staying up here sewing. Mr. Tuck killed all the chickens that we had and we have none at all. The first one they killed jumped into the well room. They killed them all for Thanksgiving. Mrs. Tuck is going to teach me how to make biscuits and also bread. I could make bread just a little bit.

This summer we did not have so much sickness as we did last summer, only a few of the girls were sick. I help Mrs. Tuck a great deal. I make my own dresses and sometimes I sew my own dresses on the machine. Some of the natives are poor and don't hardly get anything to eat. Some of them have no money to buy their food with. They pay all their money for sugar to make quass out of.

On Monday we always wash and when it is a bad day we always leave them in the tub until the next day. We have school every day in the mornings and afternoons, except Saturday afternoon we don't have school, we have to get things ready for Sunday. I am studying in elementary geography, also a few of the big girls. I have a sister here in school with me. We have about twenty-eight girls and only two boys, which make altogether about thirty. We have about five tables. Two of them we don't use. We sometimes knead bread or biscuits on them. In the morning's recess Mr. Tuck always read from Physiology, and in the afternoons we always have spelling, then after school we mend our underclothes. We have a few foxes here in winter. We saw some on the hill. I am learning lot of verses from the Bible.

To-day is Thanksgiving and Mrs. Tuck went down stairs and eat breakfast with Mr. Tuck and Mr. Anthony in the front room. I have been here with Mrs. Tuck four years. I know how to read notes and sing them, but sometimes I don't like to read them. This is my first letter I ever wrote to you. I know that you will be very glad to get it. I have written this letter by myself without anything to help only Mr. Tuck corrected a few words for me I did not know how to spell. I hope that you will get this letter on the Bertha. May God bless you and keep watch over you through the night. Mrs. Tuck makes table cloths and napkins out of white muslin.

From Irene Sovoroff,
Unalaska, Alaska, Jesse Lee Home

ing parties were Miss Short, who had been the public-school teacher at Unalaska during the past year, and Mr. Hastings, one of the agents of the Alaska Commercial Company.[8]

In April 1895 the WHMS learned the government had appropriated $19,500 for the support of people in the Pribilof Islands. For three years the Home had been caring for 16 girls from the islands at a cost of about $50 a year per girl. The society thought it only fair that the share of money that would have gone to those girls come to the Home. A letter was sent to Assistant Secretary of the Treasury Hamlin explaining, "We are anxious to 'enlarge our borders' and take in more of this same class who knock continually for admission, but [whom] we have had to turn away for want of room and support." [9] Ten days later Hamlin replied that he was unable to comply with the society's request as the appropriations bill restricted the money "to native inhabitants on the Islands of St. Paul and St. George, Alaska."[10]

. .

AT LONG LAST, ON Aug. 14, 1895, a vessel carrying lumber for the Jesse Lee Home—and for a public school—arrived. The A.C. Co. had bid $5,540 for the school construction, but both jobs were awarded to the firm of David William Starrett of Port Townsend. That company had bid $4,745 for the school construction. Twelve of Starrett's workmen arrived along with the lumber. They expected to have the Home and the school completed within 45 days. The school was a frame building, 1½ stories, 55 feet long and 31 feet wide. Tuck oversaw the work on the Home while Commissioner Woodward was hired as superintendent of construction for the school. Woodward later admitted he knew nothing about carpentry or construction. He made the strange confession that he had shown the building specifications to "leading members of the Alaska Commercial Company" who had declared "the building would not stand." Yet he raised no concerns to Jackson or the Commissioner of Education.

Halfway through the school project, Starrett received $2,135.25.[11] On October first, Woodward accepted the school on behalf of the government. Twenty-four days later a severe gale from the southeast blew the school off its foundation. Two weeks later a northwest wind righted the building and returned it almost to its original position. It was badly damaged, however, and required new timbers within and without. Jackson received word of this disaster in the same mail that brought Starrett's bill for the remaining $2,609.75. Also in the mail was a letter from Tuck stating that the school building had not been constructed in accordance with plans and specifications. Tuck had made what repairs he could despite the fact that Gray at the A.C. Co. wanted to charge him the same price charged for rescuing a vessel, which in Tuck's view amounted to extortion. Tuck bought timbers from the A.C. Co. and did the work himself.

"U.S. public school, *Unalaska, Alaska,*" by photographer P.S. Hunt (1866–1917). Courtesy of the Alaska and Polar Regions Collections, Elmer E. Rasmuson Library, University of Alaska Fairbanks (Mary Whalen Photograph Collection, 75-84-554).

When Jackson arrived to inspect the school in June 1896, he found that the contractor had shorted the specifications in numerous ways. For example, the foundation posts were to be 5 feet long and buried 3 feet 10 inches into the ground. They were in fact between 2 feet 10 inches and 3 feet 9 inches long and placed only 10 to 15 inches into the soil. The building had been left open around the ground, and the wind simply swept under and lifted it. Smaller timbers and second-class lumber were used throughout construction. The rafters were not secured, and the shingling was sloppy. Jackson concluded, "The schoolhouse can neither be repaired to advantage or used in its present condition. It will have to be taken down and rebuilt." He urged that the contractor be sued for fraud or for damages if he were unwilling to reconstruct the building. Jackson was able to resolve the question of land ownership during this visit. He was given authority by the Secretary of the Interior to select and post land for both the mission and the school "in the proposed town site of Unalaska."[12] Captain Francis Tuttle of the *Bear* detailed a party of sailors to assist him.

The Jesse Lee Home stayed on its foundations but was damaged and could not be occupied. Built according to Tuck's basic floor plan, the home was 72 feet long by 36 feet wide. It had two stories plus an attic. Tuck saw to it that "additional lumber . . . [was] put in to strengthen it above what the specifications called for,"[13] and this may have mitigated the effect of the gale. Despite his best efforts, however, Tuck was blamed for the damage.

A little over two weeks before the great wind, the number of workers at the mission had doubled with the arrival of two women, Agnes Sowle and Elizabeth Mellor. Hired as an assistant teacher, Mellor would remain only a few years. Sowle, on the other hand, would devote her entire life to the Jesse Lee Home. Eventually her name would become synonymous with the good work people associated with the Home. This was a position she grew into gradually, however. She stepped off the boat bearing the worst of tidings for the Tucks and about to make several errors of judgment that would compromise the mission's work.

1. Tuck to Jackson. Nov. 27, 1894. NARA. RG 75. Letters Received, 1883–1907.

2. Woman's Home Missionary Society. Report from Bureaus, 1893–1894:88.

3. *WHM*. February 1895:27.

4. Woodward to Jackson. Feb. 21, 1895. NARA. RG 75. Letters Received, 1883–1907.

5. June 2, 1894. Mrs. H.M. Teller to Sheldon Jackson. PHS. RG 239. Reel 13, 1894–1897.

6. Report from Allan H. Dougall, Examiner, Department of Justice. Oct. 12, 1892. NARA. U.S. Department of the Interior. Territorial papers, Alaska, 1869–1911. MF 720, Roll 7.

7. The Woodwards charged $2 a day. *Education in Alaska*. 55th Congress. Senate Doc. No. 137. Serial 3599:155.

8. Hamilton, "The Itinerary for 1895," 586.

9. *WHM*. February 1895:35.

10. April 6, 1895; April 16, 1895. NARA. RG-26. MF 720, Roll 10.

11. This was actually paid on Oct. 28, 1895, and was one-half the contract price less 10 percent.

12. Jackson, *Education in Alaska 1895–96*, 1457.

13. Maria Freeman Gray to William Harris. Feb. 18, 1897. NARA. RG 75. Letters Received, 1883–1907.

"MISS AGNES I. SOWLE *(next page)*, *Missionary at Unalaska, Alaska,*" *from* Woman's Home Missions, *February 1896.*

5

Agnes Sowle

THERE ARE NO METHODIST SAINTS EXCEPT in the most general and meaningless way. If there were a rite of canonization, a process for nominating and vetting candidates, Agnes Sowle Newhall would certainly be in the running. Her life reflected an energetic spirit devoted to good works. She possessed a pure and disciplined will. She had an experience of transcendent enlightenment. She was steadfast. She displayed a spontaneous generosity of heart. She died in the field of action. All saints are saints within sectarian limits. The perimeters allowed to late 19th century Methodist female missionaries were not expansive. She lived within those boundaries and yet the kindness for which she was remembered flowed beyond them.

Agnes Louisa Sowle was born on May 14, 1869, at Hagaman, New York, a small village not far from Amsterdam.[1] Duty and hard work were her early companions as she watched her parents, Isaac and Isabel Sowle, labor to remove indebtedness from the 90-acre farm Isaac had inherited from his father. Even as a child she dreamed of working with the poor. "Many were the visions that came to me of the good I might sometime be able to do," she later wrote. "Opening an orphanage" was about as specific as these hopes were, but they all centered on "gathering in the unfortunate ones of the earth." She attended the village school until she was 14, when she left to work at a knitting mill, adding her income toward eliminating the family debt. Her general aspirations became focused after she heard a traveling missionary speak. It seemed impossible, however, for her to enter the missionary field. Even if her parents could afford a preparatory school, they would not approve of her pursuing such a career.

Isaac and Isabel were not affiliated with any particular church during Agnes's childhood. When she was 12 the family joined the Dutch Reformed Church. For her, "uniting" with the church brought "no particular joy or religious experience" in itself. At her first communion, however, she felt a nearness to her Lord that intensified her missionary desires. She sought out other young people and found youth meetings at a local Methodist church. She wrote for a prospectus from Mrs. Osborne's Training School in Hackettstown, New Jersey, and broached the idea of missionary work with her mother. Isabel was not strongly opposed, but when Isaac learned of his daughter's plan he was set against it. Agnes asked if the objection stemmed from her "unfitness" or because they wanted her on the farm. With one voice they answered, "We want you to stay at home." And so she prepared to leave, having secured a scholarship donated by a Mrs. Houghton of Grace Church, Brooklyn.[2]

On Sept. 9, 1891, she said farewell to the farm and traveled to New Jersey where it soon became clear that others experienced religion more deeply than she did. Her fellow students would talk about "spiritual things," about "the power of God," and "the cleansing blood of Jesus." There was mention of "full salvation." "All of this was strange to me," she wrote, "and I did not understand what it meant." Her religious commitment grew incrementally, almost organically, the way fields of grain come to head or cattle mature or apples ripen.

"One night I was in a prayer meeting," she wrote, "and became under conviction for 'heart cleansing' or 'heart purity.'" She did not reveal this experience but went to her room and prayed for further religious conviction. "If there was anything more for me, I wanted it," she said. Not unlike classical mystics, she was willing to surrender everything to gain this purity of heart. Suddenly, "how I seemed to melt away to nothing and then I saw the Lord. Great peace and joy filled my heart." This experience, this cleansing from sin, being baptized with the Holy Spirit, as she understood the experience, transformed her life. From then on, service toward God was no longer a duty; it became the love that propelled her forward.

Agnes's training next took her to a "missionary farm" outside Hackettstown. She was strong and accustomed to hard work. She washed clothes, cooked meals, churned butter, and sewed clothing. The students rode to and from the school at Hackettstown in a horse-drawn wagon. Cooperation and support among them strengthened her confidence. The students held street meetings and public gatherings in the town. Agnes played her part in these although she would have preferred a role in the background. She wrote a poem in which she became the moon, serene, illumined and illuminating. The last stanza went:

> This time a woman is in the moon,
> Not a solitary man.
> Can you guess this woman's name?
> Will you tell me if you can?

Her final preparation was at the Union Missionary Training Institute in Brooklyn.[3] She had her eyes set toward Africa, specifically Liberia and the Congo, "the white man's grave." The institute, founded by Lucy D. Osborn after she returned from India, emphasized the "practical phases of soul winning." There were lectures on the Bible and warnings against fanaticism, extreme emotionalism, and faith healing. There were lessons on basic health and medical procedures during which Agnes took part in vaccinating inmates at a local half-way house. The institute encouraged students to participate in Christian work outside the school. Agnes taught Sunday school, visited jails, and assisted in other mission work throughout Brooklyn and New York City. The students would intervene when they thought they could lift someone from sin or misfortune. And once she took a tour of Hell.

Late one night, she and several classmates ventured into New York City's Bowery, "where all sorts of moral wrecks abound." They passed "parlors of iniquity" and went into beer saloons and dance halls. They saw "the masks of degradation and sin" on faces in opium dens. There could be no mistake about Hell. It was so hot, as the Brooklyn evangelist T. DeWitt Talmadge had pronounced, "that if a person was taken out and put in a red-hot caldron of potash he would freeze to death instantly." Agnes had been among the throngs who attended services at Talmadge's nationally famous Brooklyn Tabernacle. She was there on the Sunday when just as the service came to an end a large pipe from the organ crashed to the floor. There was an outburst of flames and within 15 minutes the building was consumed. An eight-story hotel next door also burned.

She graduated from the institute on May 29, 1895. A classmate described each graduate in humorous verse and characterized Agnes as "stout and fresh as a rose." "You've but to say 'blush' and the blood it will rush," the poem continued, "From the roots of her hair to her toes."

> She is quite healthy looking and good on the cooking
> And she washes and hangs up the clothes.

Because funds at the institute and at the WHMS were low, even Liberia and the Congo were closed to missionary work. Agnes returned to the family farm to wait for whatever field of service might open. She had made another discovery while at the institute: Albert Warren Newhall. He graduated with her, and, although she did not entirely approve of his prankish escapades, she agreed to see more of him. He accompanied her to the boat as she started up the Hudson River. Later that summer he visited. They became engaged, and he enrolled in medical school at the University of Vermont in Burlington.

.ˑ.

FOR SEVERAL MONTHS Mrs. H.M. Teller had urged John Tuck to move back to the states for the sake of his wife's health. In April 1895 Teller wrote Sheldon Jackson that Tuck refused to leave. Jackson suggested that one solution would be to transfer the Home to a different community and leave Tuck at Unalaska as the government teacher. Teller agreed, but she would have preferred to see him dismissed. "Of course," she wrote, laying this solution squarely in Jackson's lap, "we have not much to say about that."[4] Nevertheless, the society began looking for a replacement.

In August a letter arrived in Hagaman, New York, addressed to Agnes Sowle. The institute had given her name to Anna Beiler, and Beiler's letter was frank. She asked Agnes to become the matron at the Jesse Lee Home in Alaska. The Home was crowded. The island was remote. There was no physician for a thousand miles. There were only three or four white women in the town, none of whom was guaranteed to be congenial. It rained every other day. She would find witchcraft, polygamy, and immorality. Much was horrible, and she would have to embark in three weeks.

Agnes rushed into the barn to tell her father. "It seems to me," he said, "you'll have to consult someone else before you decide." She knew that Albert would not object. He would be busy for three years. She accepted the position by return mail. "My age is 26, my health is good, I do not know what it is to be sick," she wrote. "I was called to be a missionary when twelve years of age, but thought it was an impossibility because I was poor and had only a common school education." Now, she wrote, the time had arrived. She had a great many questions and couldn't even find the island on a map.

She had three weeks to prepare, pack, and get to the West Coast before the last steamer of the season left for Alaska. Her family scurried to sew such clothing as they thought she would need. She received money for clothes but spent $25 of it on medicine for the children. At the Simpson Church in Brooklyn, she attended a large prayer meeting. Her remarks reflect her passionate religious belief and an innate modesty.

> I realize I am going to a land of loneliness and privation. The picture is not one to encourage any but a soul saved by grace. I do not know where my feet shall tread, but my Master does, and He is going before me. I shall follow in His footsteps, and as He takes up His feet, I shall put mine in the path He has made. He will lead aright, and God helping me I will do the very best work I am capable of for Alaska. I need and ask your prayers.[5]

She visited the Union Missionary Training Institute where she was welcomed by Hester Alway, the acting principal, who later told a reporter:

> The medical training that we give here is almost invaluable to missionaries in their fields of work. One of our students has gone to Unalaska to take charge of a school of girls. There is no physician there except a ship's surgeon for a few months in the Summer.
>
> She has gone out there armed with a medicine chest, prepared for the purpose by Dr. Mosher, who was in that part of the country last Summer. A special study was made of the diseases of the country, so as to prepare the missionary for the exigencies of the place.[6]

Then, after quick farewells with hugs and hymns, she boarded a train for Chicago. Her traveling companion was Elizabeth Mellor of Brooklyn, who had been hired as an assistant teacher. She had also been recruited by Teller. The train crossed the Mississippi River and wound through Missouri, Kansas, and New Mexico before reaching San Francisco where the young women boarded the SS *Umatilla.* At Port Townsend, Washington, they transferred to the *City of Topeka* for a voyage up the inside passage of Southeastern Alaska. Agnes was seasick all the way. She was teased by men aboard the ship that the only reason a woman would go to Unalaska was to find a husband. She kept an eye on her trunks as they were unloaded and loaded again at different ports, but somehow one went missing. "It was the trunk I needed most, " she wrote. "In it were all my best clothes the home folks had made; all my underwear, overshoes, rubbers, medicines, etc." At Wrangell, Juneau and Sitka, she and Elizabeth visited missionaries who gave them advice. In Sitka she learned for the first time exactly what her job entailed.

> I learned that the people to whom I am going are very immoral and some have said that no white woman would go to such a place except to get a man. I mean to show them that such is not my case. I do not expect to achieve anything great, but I do mean to show what purity of life and character is. If I can save a few of the girls from a life of sin I shall never feel sorry that I crossed those waters. Some sailors from the Revenue Cutter *Rush* told me I would have to take the children to the Russian Greek Church. It seems the man who has charge of the Home is not conducting things as he should. I have to straighten out all the affairs of the Home, relieve the man of his position. Not a very enviable task in view and not a very friendly welcome awaits me.[7]

1. Material for this chapter came from the Newhall Manuscript and from interviews by Ray Hudson with Agnes Newhall's daughter Edith Drugg, Feb. 13, 1976, and her son, Chester Newhall, July 23, 1983.

2. *WHM*. February 1896:25.

3. For an account of the institute, see "Fitted As Missionaries," *The New York Times*, Nov. 8, 1895:9.

4. April 1, 1895. Teller to Jackson. PHS. RG 239. Reel 13, 1894-1897. Box 6.

5. *WHM*. February 1896:25.

6. "Fitted As Missionaries," *The New York Times*, Nov. 8, 1895:9

7. Newhall Manuscript, 120.

Departure of the Tucks

ON NOV. 1, 1895, JOHN TUCK WROTE TO William Hamilton at the Bureau of Education in Washington. His letter indicated a troubled state of mind if not downright paranoia. Agnes Sowle and Elizabeth Mellor had arrived on October 8. Tuck would later surmise that these two young women at first fell "into the hands of a band of conspirators." This may have been part of his thinking when he wrote Hamilton that "events have been occurring, some of them of a rather startling nature." He was vague in details. "Our opponents have tried to make things red hot for us and would have succeeded but for the interposition of Providence and the fact that we were on the inside of the fort and acting wholly on the defensive. More definite I can not be just now."

Agnes Sowle wrote to Albert Newhall that Tuck bluntly told her he would not turn over the accounts or the indenture papers for children living in the Home, nor would he relinquish his position as superintendent.[1] Michael Healy, as justice of the peace, prepared papers that acknowledged Agnes as the representative of the WHMS and as custodian of all the children living in the Home, 29 girls and four boys, ages 4 to 17. Agnes prevented Tuck from moving the structure that had been added to the rented facility onto the new building, and she refused to pay for food and freight that had arrived until he delivered all the records and accounts. This he reluctantly did. Although Jackson wrote in his 1895–96 report that Sowle had been appointed to take charge of the Home so that Tuck could "give his whole time to the Government school," it is clear that Tuck was being leveraged to resign.[2]

Mellor wrote that she and Sowle had found Mattie Short, now Mrs. Hastings, quite cordial. They soon learned, however, not to invite her to the Home as Mary Tuck would fall into hysterics if the woman came anywhere near. "Our policy has been to keep on neutral ground in this matter," she wrote," and we told both parties of our intentions to do so from the first."[3] The two women also had close contact with the Woodwards. After the storm that blew the school off its foundation, Sowle spent a few weeks living with the commissioner and his wife to relieve the crowded conditions at the Home.

During the winter of 1895–96 the staff at the Home managed a sort of truce. Tuck had been impressed by Sowle's composure during a chimney fire on Thanksgiving. Much of the work at the Home fell on her. Mellor worked two hours a day for her room and board but spent most of her time teaching school. By mid-December Sowle had decided to pay the transportation of another missionary to the Home, Sarah Rinch, a graduate of the Union Missionary Training Institute. Mary Tuck was able to do little. Her periods of erratic behavior increased. She would walk through the rooms, observe a child misbehaving, and then address Sowle with lengthy anecdotes interspersed with criticism of the job she was doing. She had "hysterical spells" that brought all work to a standstill. During the day, Tuck taught school "in the room under the bedroom" and Mellor taught in the crowded dining room. Sowle devoted herself to cooking, cleaning, sewing, business matters and correspondence. Every other evening, Mellor would take charge of the children so that Agnes could write personal letters. By the time the first steamer arrived on February first, she had more than 40 letters ready requesting much-needed supplies.

Sowle's first year was one of mistakes and triumphs, of self-doubt and inner rewards. Among the fondest memories that Aleuts would have of Agnes Sowle were her visits to their homes. Although she had been warned that the residents were immoral, her visits were free of self-righteousness. She went to bring food and medicine and to get away from the Home's noisy children and demanding adults. Only three months after her arrival she had won the respect and gratitude of several Native families. She had tried and enjoyed local foods, including fresh seal meat which she compared favorably with beefsteak. She salted codfish that were given to the Home and prepared barrels of salted seal meat. For Christmas that year she received three grass baskets and two embroidered wall containers sewn from seal throats, examples of the finest of Aleut handicrafts.

January 1896 brought a round of illness to the village. "Her knowledge and skill in sickness is a boon to this Home," a physician associated with one of the revenue cutters is reported to have said about Sowle, adding, "beside, she has such good common sense."[4] On January 10, after she visited several residences where people were ill, Sowle described the homes. "The native huts, or barabaras, are made of sod, and are built partly underground," she wrote. "They are very warm but there is only one room with one small window which admits the light but no fresh air." She found the atmosphere stifling. "Words cannot express what the peculiar odor is like!" According to Mellor's statement made two years later, there were only about a dozen barabaras still in use. In 1888 George Wardman had written that all barabaras had been "done away with."[5] In any event, only the poorest residents made use of the traditional Aleut home by the time Sowle arrived at Unalaska. The first of the wood frame cottages erected by the A.C. Co. had gone up in the 1870s at the time the company was building such houses in the Pribilof Islands. Sowle felt more at ease in these dwellings. "Some of the houses are one story frame structures with shingled roofs," she wrote. "They have three rooms and are quite comfortable." It was after visiting in such homes that she remarked in a letter, "I do not get away from the Home much, and it is such a relief that sometimes I half wish I did not have to go back."[6]

Her first Russian Christmas, the week beginning Jan. 7, 1896, saw the "star" come to the Home. Her description is important because it suggests starring was at this time restricted to men and boys. It is also a description that neither ridicules nor condemns the event as "pagan." Indeed, her early comments on Orthodox religious practices were

"RUSSIAN CHRISTMAS STAR," *displayed on the beach at Unalaska by a group of people whose names are not known. Courtesy of the Alaska and Polar Regions Collections, Elmer E. Rasmuson Library, University of Alaska Fairbanks (Charles E. Bunnell Collection, 73-66-50).*

remarkably free of overt criticism and avoided the rhetoric that permeated so many descriptions of Aleut life by other missionaries and that tinged her own later confrontations with the church.

> *Russian Christmas* comes thirteen days later than our Christmas. The night after Christmas groups of men and boys come around to the houses with beautiful revolving stars. The stars are made out of glass, tissue paper etc. on a wooden frame and in the centre of the star is a picture of the nativity. A group enters the house, form a line and sing or chant for some time. One boy carries a bag to receive donations of bread, apples, etc. They go about the village with the stars for three days and on the last night all the stars are carried in a procession of men and boys to the graveyard where they chant and pray. Following the three days of stars and chanting many persons go about from house to house in "masquerade."

By spring conditions at the Home were again in crisis. There had been another serious encounter with Mattie Hastings. Willard Hastings had stormed into the Home threatening to horsewhip Tuck if he did not allow the children to talk with his wife occasionally. Sowle intervened and quieted the confrontation. She was exasperated. "The idea of two girls coming up here to take the care and responsibility of 35 children and to get into such mixed up affairs," she wrote. "It needs a person as wise as Solomon, as patient as Job, and as consecrated as Paul or John. I feel ten years older than when I left home." A few days later Hastings and Tuck had words in the street and Hastings struck the missionary, knocking him to the ground. When Tuck entered the Home, nose bleeding and eye blackened, his wife went into hysterics. Hastings presented himself to the commissioner and paid the required fine for fighting. "He felt it was money well spent," wrote Sowle. After Tuck's fiscal irregularities came to light—he was admittedly not good at keeping accounts—Sowle wrote, "Everyone is angry with Mr. Z [as Tuck is referred to in her letters] and if he gets out of the place alive he will do well."

In the fall of 1895 Jackson wrote to Tuck that the Bureau of Education had decided to make a change in the staffing at Unalaska. Either the letter never reached Unalaska or Tuck ignored it, because in March Jackson again notified Tuck of his termination. "In closing your services for the government," he wrote, "I desire to express my great satisfaction with your work in the schoolroom and my appreciation of your ability as a first-class teacher."[7] By the end of April 1896, there could be no mistake. Tuck seemed baffled at the news. "*Even* in Dr. Jackson's letter of dismissal," he wrote to the commissioner of education, "there is only praise for my work in the school room."[8] Tuck wrote to Jackson that "dismissal will amount to condemnation in the eyes of everyone, and against this great wrong, I want to enter my earnest protest."[9] Tuck suspected Jackson had given in to the missionary society's aim of placing young women in the school who could double as missionaries.

The Tucks had no one to whom they could turn. Their old supporter Michael Healy had sided with Mattie Short. Even if he had wanted to help, he was unable. In January "Hell-Roaring Mike," the temperance crusader, had been accused and convicted of drunkenness aboard his vessel. His wife was frantically writing to Jackson to help restore her husband to command.

Commissioner Harris did nothing to counteract Jackson's decision. He replied to Tuck's letter that he considered him "a valuable man for certain environments." Then he tactfully described two invaluable qualities in successful "missionary-teachers."

> In order to accomplish the best results, a missionary-teacher should possess in a very marked degree the qualities of persuasiveness and attractiveness, thus overcoming opposition, subduing alien elements and building up a small work into a great one. In the settled civilization of the older States these particular requirements are not essential, but in the peculiar surroundings of the work at Unalaska these qualities are absolutely necessary.[10]

In the end it took a formidable representative of the Woman's Home Missionary Society backed by the subsequent arrival of Sheldon Jackson to remove the Tucks. Maria Freeman Gray—no relation to the A.C. Co.'s Nicholas Gray—had only recently been appointed to the Alaska Bureau and made a member of the committee on supplies. She arrived on June 3, 1896, and promptly scolded the two young women at the Home for the patience they had shown the Tucks. By June 11 Tuck was communicating with Mellor and Sowle only in writing; he would not speak with them directly. He contradicted their statements, but he turned over a check that was due to the Home. By the middle of June he and his wife were packing their belongings. On June 19 Sheldon Jackson arrived on the *Bear*. Five days later he "escorted" John and Mary Tuck to the steamship *Homer*. "A large number of friends, whom they had made among the natives," Jackson wrote, "were also at the wharf to bid them godspeed." Jackson mentioned none of Unalaska's white community there to say farewell, an indication of final strained relations. That evening Jackson held a communion service in the still temporary and still crowded Home.

Gray had absolutely nothing good to say about Tuck when she wrote to the commissioner of education in February 1897. "It was very unwise for Mr. Tuck to have planned such a bld'g for the Home," she wrote. It was "about twice as large as it need be."[11] The school also, she declared, was designed larger than required. (Both, however, would be crowded within a few years.) Gray was surprised that Dr. Jackson had approved such buildings. On the other hand, she found Lycurgus Woodward an "excellent Christian" who had "done a great deal to keep the Home from 'going to pieces' during the last year."

Gray's attack on John Tuck was not limited to the construction of buildings. She charged him with misappropriation of tuition funds, specifically those paid by the disgruntled Adolph Reinken. She attributed "deceit and dishonesty" to him "from year to year."

Elizabeth Mellor, *Unalaska. From Sheldon Jackson's* Education in Alaska, 1895–1896. *Washington, Government Printing Office, 1897.*

He had questioned Woodward's motives and had misrepresented Mattie Hastings who was, according to Gray, "an *honorable* [emphasis in original] woman and has proved beyond a doubt her remarkable fitness as a teacher." If any student showed signs of affection toward Mattie, Gray wrote, the child would be punished by the Tucks. This "caused her much trouble." (Sowle's letters give examples of students being reprimanded for this behavior.) Gray found the Alaska Commercial Company "friendly to our work and . . . interested in the success of our Home." If Tuck had only "conducted himself in an honorable manner in his transactions with them" the mission would be better off. Gray wrote a similar letter to Woodward himself who showed it around the village.[12] Mellor wrote to Jackson complaining about the commissioner's lapse in judgment.

Matrona Salamatoff had become acquainted with Maria Freeman Gray while she was in California completing her training. Gray encouraged *Woman's Home Missions* to publish Salamatoff's article "Women of Alaska" in June 1896, shortly after the Tucks had left. Unlike Gray, Salamatoff praised the Tucks for trying "to teach their girls to behave themselves better, to be truer to themselves and to lead purer and nobler lives."

Sowle was relieved by the departure of the Tucks. They had made her work difficult and delicate. The day they left she wrote, "The Lord has sent deliverance. Praise his name."[13] If there had been an institutional memory in the Woman's Home Missionary Society, however, John and Mary Tuck's final year might have received more than a sigh of relief from Sowle and two sentences in the yearly report of the society.

> After seven years of labor, Mr. and Mrs. Tuck have come home, and we are sure they needed the change and rest. We can only pray that Mrs. Tuck may be restored to health and strength, and they be enabled in some other field to accomplish even more than in the pioneer work they prosecuted in Unalaska.[14]

Faint praise, indeed. Sheldon Jackson was more lavish in his summary of their work. He provided a final glimpse of the missionary couple departing the island.

> This year completes the seventh year of service by Mr. Tuck. Too much praise can not be given him for his patience and self-denial and long continuance in the service in the face of great opposition and difficulties in maintaining the school. Nor is it too much to say that the unstinted praise which has been given of the progress of the pupils in that school is due to his superior skill as a teacher. The progress of the pupils under him has been so marked that Government officials in their public reports, desiring to secure better educational facilities for this or that community, have mentioned Mr. Tuck's school at Unalaska as the type desired. For a portion of that time the school was known as a contract school. The Woman's Home Missionary Society of the Methodist Church, and the ladies of that association, the Government, and all

friends of humanity owe Mr. and Mrs. Tuck a large debt of gratitude for what they have accomplished. In view of these things it was not strange that some of the native Aleut population came to the wharf to bid Mr. and Mrs. Tuck god-speed as they left Unalaska for their eastern home.[15]

The Tucks sailed from the harbor at three in the afternoon. Looking toward the village as the ship followed the curved shoreline out of the bay, they would have seen the uninhabited symbol of seven years of work. The Jesse Lee Home had been built, but the Eliza Jane Baker Chapel, the schoolrooms and reading rooms, the spacious kitchen and dining room, the dormitory rooms named and furnished in honor of departed children, stood empty.

NOTES

1. Excerpts from these are found in the Newhall manuscript.

2. Jackson, *Education in Alaska 1895–96*, 1445.

3. Mellor to Jackson. April 21, 1896. NARA. RG 75. Letters Received, 1883-1907.

4. Woman's Home Missionary Society. Reports from Bureaus. 1896–1897:107.

5. *Fur-Seal Fisheries of Alaska*, 30.

6. Newhall Manuscript, 131. Entry dated Jan. 11, 1896.

7. Jackson to Tuck, March 7, 1896. PHS. RG 239. Box 5, folder 24.

8. Tuck to Harris. May 14, 1896. NARA. RG 75. Letters Received, 1883–1907.

9. Tuck to Jackson. April 21, 1896. NARA. RG 75. Letters Received, 1883–1907.

10. Harris to Tuck, May 23, 1896. PHS. RG 239. Box 6, folder 5. Tuck later taught for many years in Chicago.

11. Gray to Harris. Feb. 18, 1897. NARA. RG 75. Letters Received, 1883–1907, entry 804, box 9.

12. Mellor to Jackson. May 17, 1897. NARA. RG 75. Letters Received, 1883–1907, entry 804, box 10.

13. Newhall Manuscript, 140. Entry dated June 23, 1896.

14. WHMS. Reports from Bureaus, 1895–1896: 106.

15. Jackson. *Education in Alaska 1895–96*:1436.

7

On Their Own

WITH THE REPLACEMENT OF JOHN AND MARY TUCK and the arrival of a stately and commodious building—although still unoccupied because of needed repairs—the Jesse Lee Home had a new beginning. Separate structures for the Home and the public school might have clarified the distinction between the two institutions if John Tuck's suspicions had not been true. The young women sent to teach in the government school were specifically selected because they were willing to serve as missionaries for the Methodist mission. Anna Beiler wrote in her 1895–96 report that the school at Unalaska was not a "secular" institution but "a Christian home and school" whose teachers claimed "allegiance to the King of kings." John Tuck's response to Woodward's call for an offensive against the deep Orthodoxy of the community suggested waiting until the Home had a building and a full cadre of teachers. After Tuck's departure, however, the staff for the next three years consisted of young women who were less interested in confrontation than in service to a growing number of girls. Agnes Sowle, Sarah Rinch, Elizabeth Mellor, and Matrona Salamatoff—the matron, her assistant, the teacher, and the assistant teacher—played distinct roles but were alike in their youthful idealism.

The mid-1890s saw several institutional developments at Unalaska in addition to the Jesse Lee Home. The Alaska Commercial Company began to reduce its widespread empire. A dramatic decline in the sea otter population was accompanied by the closure of most of the company's village stations. Chernofski, Kashega, Makushin and Biorka experienced greater and greater poverty. Their populations diminished as people moved into Unalaska. After securing the contract for the Pribilof Islands fur seal harvest in 1890, the North American Commercial Company built substantial headquarters at Dutch Harbor including a dock, store, company buildings and a hotel, under their general agent George R. Tingle. During the first years that Sowle was at Unalaska, the Dutch Harbor manager for the company was Joseph Stanley Brown. He had been a professional geologist and served as a special Treasury Department agent to inspect the fur seals in 1891. At the time he was at Dutch Harbor, he was married to Molly Brown, daughter of the late President Garfield. She became a supporter of the Home.

By 1890 the church that had been constructed under the direction of Father Innokentii Shaishnikoff in the 1850s needed major renovation. The parish began collecting funds.[1] Hunters donated sea otter pelts, other individuals made smaller monetary gifts, and the church received a first-class share in the Pribilof fur seal harvest. Father Nicholas

Resoff, who had become the priest at Unalaska after the death of Father Shaishnikoff in 1884, secured permission from the Holy Synod in St. Petersburg for construction of a new building. In 1893 he was transferred to St. Paul and his place was taken for a year by Hieromonk Mitrofan, who had come to Unalaska to teach in the Russian school. On June 2, 1894, Mitrofan signed a contract with Rudolph Neumann of the A.C. Co. for construction, using the same site as previous incarnations of the church. It fell to Father Alexander Kedrovsky, a graduate of the Vologda Theological Seminary in Russia, to oversee the actual construction. He arrived in 1894 and remained until 1908.

With three altars and a nearby residence for a bishop, the Church of the Holy Ascension was technically a cathedral. It rose over the landscape like a cathedral, with a primary nave over 37 feet wide and 63 feet long. Two auxiliary chapels off the nave gave the building its distinct cruciform shape. The chapel on the Iliuliuk River side was dedicated to St. Sergius of Radonezh and consecrated on Sept. 4, 1894. The chapel nearer the bay was dedicated to St. Innokentii of Irkutsk and consecrated on Jan. 30, 1895. The entire church was consecrated on Aug. 18, 1896. The entrance was beneath a bell tower that rose more than 50 feet at the western end of the building. Octagonal cupolas graced the bell tower and the pyramidal roof over the main chapel.

Since 1816, the church had been the paramount building in depictions of the village landscape.[2] The community took pride in its church, which symbolized the centrality of Orthodoxy to their lives. This is why the first engraving Sheldon Jackson used showing Unalaska was so strange. The double-paged illustration in his 1886 report included more than two dozen wooden buildings stretching from the dock in the west to the smallest Aleut cottages in the east. There were numerous A.C. Co. buildings: the store, the company house, and warehouses. But the Orthodox church was completely absent. Where the church should have been was a disorderly cluster of buildings. With the completion of the new church, the dominance of Orthodox Christianity could not be so easily drawn out of the picture. The energy that permeated the local parish could not be denied.

In 1895 Kedrovsky organized a Temperance Society. In 1898 a parish brotherhood dedicated to St. Panteleimon was formed under his leadership. He oversaw the operation of the Russian school, known as the Ioann Veniaminov Missionary School, and improved its curriculum. The attached boarding facility, known as the St. Sergius orphanage, continued to host boys from villages outside Unalaska. In 1899 there were 68 pupils at the school and 23 boys in the boarding facility. Kedrovsky held classes for adults to broaden their understanding of church teachings and practices. To assist in this effort, he encouraged the publication of several books in Aleut, including a reprint of Veniaminov's influential 1834 Aleut work *Indication of the Path to the Heavenly Kingdom*. Despite irreconcilable religious differences, Sowle praised Kedrovsky for his efforts and his exemplary moral character. However, the attacks against the Orthodox Church as a "foreign" church and a religion of form without spirit continued.

FATHER ALEXANDER KEDROVSKY, *Russian Orthodox priest at Unalaska, and his family. Courtesy of the Alaska State Library, Historical Collections (Michael Z. Vinokouroff Photograph Collection, P243-1-086).*

Agnes Sowle's position was clear: She was a missionary, the director and matron of the Home. She accommodated the wishes of Father Kedrovsky regarding Orthodox children. In June 1896 three girls at the Home died. They were buried from the cathedral. Molly Borenin, 12, had been ill for a long time but suddenly grew worse. She was visited by her father a half-hour before she died on June 2. "The old grandmother came in and washed the corpse," wrote Sowle, who assisted, "and after finishing the task she washed her own face and hands in the same water. The natives believe that such washing will keep away disease." Sowle herself washed her hands in "carbolized water." At the end of June, Melina Siftsoff died from "quick consumption" and Agnes was unable to attend the funeral because "another child was about to enter eternity." This was Mary Popoff, one more victim of tuberculosis. "It is dreadful to see anyone die of consumption," wrote Sowle, "for they die by inches." Before lapsing into a coma that lasted five days, Mary was visited by her father. Sowle had given her a booklet of religious verse, and the girl had translated one of them into Aleut for him. The month of June was sea otter hunting time, and Mary's father had to depart on the annual hunt. Left on her own, Agnes tried her best to prepare the child for death. Mary told the missionary that "she was ready to live with Jesus and the angels."

> I asked her if she wanted to go and be with Molly.
> She said, "Yes."
> "Do you know where Molly is?" I asked.
> Mary replied, "She is in Heaven."
> Then I asked if there was any message for her father, when he came home from hunting.
> She said, "Tell him—tell him." These were the last words she ever spoke.[3]

In addition to attending the dying, the women in charge of the Home became marriage brokers. Seeking good husbands for the girls had started with the Tucks, and it became a source of pride to succeeding directors. Sowle's first matchmaking was arranged for a Mr. Anderson, who arrived from Sanak on the mail boat in 1897. He approached her about the oldest of the girls, Ludmelia Prokopeuff, affectionately called Lutie, and apologized for his "blundering way." Sowle found it very amusing and couldn't help laughing. She introduced Lutie to him and the girl agreed to give her answer the next morning. He failed to show up, however, so Lutie went berry picking. She told Agnes, "Mama Sowle, if Mr. Anderson comes here, tell him I say yes."

The wedding took place three days later, but Sowle's record does not indicate whether it was performed by the U. S. commissioner or held in the Orthodox church, probably the latter. In any event, the wedding was followed by a supper. Nicholas Gray knew Russian customs and plied the couple with shouts of "*Gorka*" at which they had to "kiss each other in order to make things taste sweet."

THE RUSSIAN ORTHODOX CHURCH *of the Holy Ascension at Unalaska. Courtesy of the Alaska and Polar Regions Collections, Elmer E. Rasmuson Library, University of Alaska Fairbanks (Lulu Fairbanks Collection, 68-69-2367).*

Sowle was upset that the Home was not credited more for producing such eligible brides. She was, however, realistic about suitable partnerships. Mr. Peterson, a man in his sixties, was dissuaded from marrying one of the girls because, as Sowle told him, "he would end his days in grief." Courtships sometimes brought difficulties, too. The older girls would occasionally "escape" from the Home with a sailor or one of the village's young men, and Sowle and Mellor would enlist the help of the marshal to round up the culprits. In two cases the men were tried and found guilty of "abduction" and "seduction." The judge was inclined to let them go with a warning, but Sowle and Mellor spoke their minds freely and a more severe sentence was handed down. Things got so bad Sowle considered stopping sailors from attending worship services as some came only to see the girls and to pass them notes. "If it were not for the American flag," she wrote in December 1895, "this would be a (heathen) foreign country. Here I am surrounded by awful immorality. It is common for white men to live with the native women and not marry."

. .

AN INTERNATIONAL TRIBUNAL IN 1891 and 1892 had ruled against the United States in a dispute with Canada and Great Britain over pelagic sealing, the hunting of fur seals on the open sea. There had been a temporary absence of sealing schooners coming into port, but by the mid-1890s seal hunters were again at Unalaska each spring, waiting for the season to open. These vessels frequently carried hunting crews of Native Americans from the Pacific Northwest. "There were many Indian schooners anchored in the bay," wrote Sowle in July 1896. One day several Indians approached the Home, and a crowd gathered around them. Agnes went to investigate and learned the Indians were going to perform "a war dance."

> The Indians were dressed light and were in full paint and feathers. They went at it in real earnest. The tum-tum beat and they kept time to the music with their shouts and grunts while they kept up the leaping and stooping—all the movements peculiar to a war dance. It was exciting and we all enjoyed it. The very best kind of gymnastics it seems to me and with none of the evil influences of the white man's mixed dance. Some money was thrown to them but they did not want it and they gave it to me for the home. Well that is one way to raise money for missions. The Indians were pleased to give the six dollars for they like the Home.[4]

It was in mid-October of this year that Matrona Salamatoff, who had left Unalaska to pursue training as a nurse, returned to be the assistant teacher.[5] Living among Protestant missionaries was not a unique experience for this daughter of an Aleut Orthodox priest. She sympathized with the goals of both the school and the mission.[6] While he was at Unalaska in June, Sheldon Jackson wrote a letter and left it for Salamatoff's arrival. He wanted her to know that the entire school, including Salamatoff's classroom, was under the leadership of Elizabeth Mellor. She was not an independent teacher, but subordinate to Mellor. "Miss Short (Mrs. Hastings) when a teacher," wrote Jackson, "did not understand this and got into trouble." He also cautioned her against dancing and drinking wine. The latter was a common practice "among the better classes of Unalaska." Congress, he wrote, required government teachers to teach temperance, but example "is more powerful than precept." Curiously, Jackson ended his letter, which he had shared with Mellor, with the additional caution "that besides Miss Mellor, you take no one into your confidence, until you have seen me upon my return."[7]

The day after she arrived back in Unalaska, Salamatoff wrote affectionately to Sheldon Jackson thanking him for his kindness toward her. "Your letters I shall read over very often," she wrote, "and treasure them as I do my own dear father's."[8] She assured him that she agreed with his prohibition against teachers drinking wine. "I have seen the sad results of wine drinking," she wrote, "and will not be the one to approve of it."

Salamatoff identified with her mother's Russian heritage and not the Aleut of her Unangas father. The Orthodox clergy, according to Mellor, were initially displeased to find Salamatoff among the staff living at the Home. Their attitude changed, and by March 1897 they had accepted her as part of the school landscape. In April a letter arrived from the bishop requesting that Salamatoff teach English in the Russian school. She turned down this request and by June had accepted the position of teacher at Afognak on Kodiak Island.[9] Following her second year at Afognak, she wrote to Jackson that if all went well she would soon "be no more Miss Salamatoff. . . ."[10] She married Charles Pajoman that fall. In 1902 she wrote a personal note to Jackson in which she recalled her earlier years at Unalaska and told of her new life.

> It is a long time since you and I had a personal chat together. You do not come here, so the best I can do is to converse with you on paper, which is not half so satisfactory as seeing you. Perhaps it would interest you to know what else I do besides being a teacher. Of course I take care of my home and Mr. Pajoman claims my attention too. Quite often the sick send for me. I never refuse their call and am happy that my training in a hospital is of use to me now. I feel that God has been good to me all my life. Many a time I bless the dear kind friends who were good to me in my day of youth and trials. Many are dead now. (Poor Mr. Neumann and Capt. Hooper are among them). You too my dear I thank most sincerely for your interest in me. Even when I am married you are kind to me. May God bless you over and over my dear friend, and give you many years more to live.[11]

"Many Years! Many Years!"—*Mnogaya Leta! Mnogaya Leta!*"—was the refrain of one of the Russian Christmas starring hymns. At the end of her letter she added, "I like teaching very much. When I stop it, it seems something is amiss, so if agreeable to you, would like to do so another year." The report from the following year provides another insight into her character. She noted that a meeting had been held with several parents in which she stressed how parents and teachers must work together "in bringing up and educating the children; how they must be taught obedience first of all; how they are like seeds that grow badly and are choked with weeds if they are not watched and cared for." Among the graduates of her school was Alexandra Kashevaroff, who herself was now teaching English in the Russian school at Nushagak.[12]

Before applying to Sheldon Jackson for a position in Alaska, Elizabeth Mellor had substituted in a Brooklyn public school for two weeks and taught three private pupils for 45 days. She had also been the organist in a facility for tuberculosis patients. During her first year at Unalaska, as assistant teacher, she was paid $499.97 while Tuck, as teacher, received $900.00. The following year, when she assumed Tuck's position, she received $630, or 70 percent of his salary. Her assistant, Matrona Salamatoff, was paid $405.00.

Under Mellor and Salamatoff the school enrollment climbed to its highest since opening in 1889.

UNALASKA SCHOOL ENROLLMENT 1889-1897

Contract School

1889–90	30
1890–91	43
1891–92	35

Public School

1893–94	24
1894–95	39
1895–96	39
1896–97	48

In 1898 Mellor was asked why she had traveled to such a distant place to teach school. She answered that she had always liked mission work.[13] The distinction between her employment as a government school teacher and her service as a Protestant missionary was illusory at best despite her protestations that she kept the two vocations separate. Anna Beiler had been impressed by how Mellor's missionary zeal permeated her outlook. She found her "as interested in our work as if she was our own missionary, which she practically is."[14] Mellor lived in the Jesse Lee Home and taught school in the Jesse Lee Home. The great majority of her students were Aleut girls indentured to the Home. When she began, there were only seven pupils who came from the community. Her sister Ada, a graduate of the Baptist Missionary Training school in Chicago, arrived as her assistant after Matrona Salamatoff transferred to Afognak in 1897. Each morning both Mellors would join

Agnes Sowle and her assistant Sarah Rinch, who had arrived the previous year, for prayers, devotions, and Bible study.

Mellor's evangelical enthusiasm had sent a chill through the Orthodox community as the 1896–97 school year began. The parish was preparing for the August 18 consecration of the main altar in their new church. Bishop Nicholas himself would be present. Imagine the consternation of the clergy and the Orthodox community when a copy of *The Alaskan and Herald Combined* arrived from Sitka with her boast, "The Lord has blessed us and shown his approval of our work by the conversion of six of our girls." [15] Try as she might, Mellor never regained the complete trust of the community. [16]

Unalaska weather was wild throughout that autumn of 1896. Jackson was told that whalers who had visited the Aleutians for 46 years testified that this particular season would be known as "the Storm Season." Meanwhile, the women at the Home were working to restore calm in the community. Matrona Salamatoff, not yet off to Afognak, was adept at bridging factions. She and Mellor joined with Nicholas Gray to prepare a musical entertainment for Washington's birthday on Feb. 22, 1897. Gray, a vocal opponent of the Tucks, was attuned to nuances within the Orthodox community. As became clear with later decisions he made, he would not have cooperated with the Home had there been a general feeling against their work at that time. Mellor and Salamatoff were in charge of the "Philharmonic Society Chorus"—16 girls from the Home, Mr. Woodward, Mr. Hudson, Mr. Gray, and themselves. Gray was also the leader of the Unalaska Brass Band. The program was printed in English and Russian. There were pieces by the band, songs by the choir, comic sketches, a shadow pantomime, an accordion trio of three Aleut musicians, and a piano duet played by Mellor and Salamatoff. [17]

. .

HAVING BEEN IN SOLE CHARGE of the Home for more than four months, Sowle began to wonder "if the care of so many children is my real work, or whether God is letting me get a taste of my ambition to work for Him just to let me find out how incapable I am." She enjoyed the day-to-day activities. For relief she explored the islands. On a ride in a launch with Captain Hooper, who commanded the Bering Sea fleet, she had relished the lush summer scenery. "High mountains carpeted with the greenest moss and grass, their slopes ending in precipices which are close to the water's edge. . . . The wild flowers begin to bloom in June and they grow in great profusion." She made a visit to the Pribilof Islands to see the herds of fur seals. One afternoon she and Sarah Rinch climbed a mountain "so steep it seemed dangerous to descend." But starting down, Sowle realized that "imaginary troubles are worse than the real ones."

Nevertheless, doubts about her ability to direct the Home continued. "This place needs one more experienced," she wrote. "Sometimes my head just whirls to know what to do with some of the children; they are so bad. . . . There are no end of trials in this work.

I feel I am too young for this work."[18] She had not transformed life in the village, but she took comfort in the thought, "No doubt it is the same in all countries." She turned to books on the lives of missionaries. "It may help to know how other folks get along," she wrote. "Once it seemed strange to me that missionaries should toil so many years before much impression was made. It seemed as if something was wrong either with them or their doctrines but now I am trying it for myself."[19]

As spring arrived in 1897 and the end of the school term approached, Father Kedrovsky saw Elizabeth Mellor and warned her that her position was in jeopardy. Bishop Nicholas, upset over her printed comments about the conversion of six girls, had complained to authorities and asked for her removal. Kedrovsky extended some comfort by remarking on the slowness with which the government acted. She and the priest both laughed when she replied that she would be ready to leave anyway by the time they got around to her case.[20] Her annual report for the year reflected improved cooperation between the Home and the Orthodox church. By May school attendance had grown from 39 to 48. Boys from the Russian school were attending her classes when their school was closed for holidays. Improvement in both mathematics and reading was noted. "The work of the year has been very pleasant," she concluded, "and the outlook is most encouraging."[21]

NOTES

1. Information on the construction of the church is found in the National Register of Historic Places Inventory-Nomination Form, 1984, prepared by Barbara Sweetland Smith with additional material from Lydia T. Black.

2. See the two watercolors of Iliuliuk in 1816 made by Ludwig Choris during the Kotzebue voyage.

3. Newhall Manuscript, 138.

4. Newhall Manuscript, 144.

5. She is listed as part of the teaching staff in both the 1895–96 report and the one for 1896–97. However, she arrived back in Unalaska on Oct. 19, 1896, and taught only one year before transferring.

6. See her letter published in *Christian Advocate*, Oct. 25, 1893, where she writes, "Providence led me . . . [to become] assistant teacher in the Methodist mission school at Unalaska." Sheldon Jackson Scrapbook. Vol. 63. PHS. RG 239.

7. Jackson to Salamatoff, June 24, 1896. PHS. RG 239. Box 6, folder 6.

8. Salamatoff to Jackson, Oct. 20, 1896. NARA. RG 75. Letters Received, 1883–1907.

9. She died at Afognak in 1915. For a description of her see Jacobs, ed., *A Schoolteacher in Old Alaska*.

10. Salamatoff to Jackson. March 25, 1899. PHS. RG 239. Box 6, folder 20.

11. Matrona Pajoman to Sheldon Jackson, June 30, 1902. PHS. RG 239. Box 7, folder 2.

12. *Report of the Commissioner of Education for the Year 1903*, 2338.

13. "A Talk with Miss Mellor." Undated article, probably 1897. Sheldon Jackson Scrapbook. Vol. 63. PHS. RG 239.

14. Woman's Home Missionary Society. Reports from Bureaus. 1896–97:107.

15. *The Alaskan and Herald Combined*, Sitka, Alaska. June 20, 1896.

16. In "A Few Sketches of Jesse Lee Home" Mellor details the six students who she claimed had been converted. *WHM*, Nov. 1896, Vol. 13, No. 11.

17. NARA. RG 75. Letters Received, 1883–1907. Box 9. This copy of the program has a notation by Mellor.

18. Newhall Manuscript, 150.

19. Newhall Manuscript, 152.

20. Mellor to Jackson. May 17, 1897. NARA. RG 75. Letters Received, 1883–1907.

21. Education Report, 1896–97, 1606.

"MRS. ANNA F. BEILER, *Secretary Bureau of Alaska," from* Woman's Home Missions, *November 1899.*

8

The Secretary's Visit

No sooner had Alaska Bureau secretary Anna F. Beiler stepped into the still-rented Jesse Lee Home on May 20, 1897, than she delivered her first lecture: The staff needed their own dining room where they could digest their food in peace. "Nothing seems to suit Mrs. B.," sighed Agnes Sowle in a letter home. The secretary expected her to do things with nothing and with nowhere in which to do them. "Mrs. B. had no mercy on us and nothing suited. I am blamed for all things at every turn. I have to laugh to keep from crying, and sometimes cry to keep from having a back ache and sometimes all three come together."

How different was the account by Elizabeth Mellor that *Woman's Home Missions* published. She and Agnes met the ship at the dock, she wrote; although Beiler had been seasick and was relieved to get on shore, she soon took charge and delivered a talk on the book of John, chapter 14, at the Sunday service. Mellor thanked the women of the society for sending the secretary and concluded, "Her coming will be most blessed in its results." She referred to "Mrs. Beiler's own Christlike heart and wise head."[1]

Of her trip to Alaska, Beiler herself would write, "I have 'dwelt in the tents of wickedness.'"[2] The whole tone of the territory, she declared, was against Christianity. Missionaries were not welcome. For over a month she supervised completion of the Jesse Lee Home's new building. Neither the A.C. Co. nor the North American Commercial Company would give her an estimate for finishing the structure, so she hired two transient carpenters and employed Native men as laborers. The gold rush into the Klondike had begun, however. Freight prices had shot up, and her carpenters soon abandoned her for better-paying jobs. Still, within a month, the building was ready for occupation. Sheldon Jackson wrote, "The building that had been the eye-sore of its friends and the laughing stock of its enemies is now the admiration of all residents, and all join in hearty expressions of the skill with which it was managed by Mrs. Beiler."[3]

The move was complicated when the A.C. Co. again objected to the mission's land claim and fenced off the property. Undeterred, Beiler supervised Agnes and the other younger women who did the actual packing and carrying. "As there are no horses or wagons," wrote Sowle, "all must be carried in our arms or on wheelbarrows." They would sleep in the new building but operate during the day out of the old one. Despite the upheavals in living conditions, Beiler seemed intent on finding unclean corners and placing the blame on Agnes. Finally, Agnes offered to resign. "I told Mrs. B. that the work was too much for me," she wrote to Albert Newhall, "and that a more competent person should come." Agnes and Albert had tentatively planned to do missionary work in Africa after their marriage. Beiler wouldn't hear of her resigning, but insisted that Newhall himself should come north.

In June, author Alice Palmer Henderson visited Unalaska as part of a tour of the territory. At the end of a long day in the village she was, as she wrote, "tired almost to imbecility." Her published account reflected such a state of mind. It is in large part a hodgepodge of gossip and error. In it, however, are two astute descriptions. She wrote that Anna Beiler was "a woman of wonderful executive ability, fearless of everybody and everything." While not naming "the missionary teacher," she described Elizabeth Mellor as one

> who seems not only to be loved and admired by the pupils, but by all on the island. She is the sort that accomplishes something, being young, wide-awake, enthusiastic, and not by any means least, pretty. She has a lovely complexion and laughing eyes and is altogether good to look upon. She is a Brooklyn girl, yet says, and looks it, that she is quite happy and content in this dull little hamlet in the Northern Pacific. Instead of bursting rudely into a native's home, as I have seen so many "benefactors" do, she always knocked; and then, with a cheery word and smile, made herself genuinely welcome.[4]

Henderson found that the pupils did all the housework and cooking as well as sewing and knitting. They were advanced in their studies and read "with a musical and distinct enunciation." She met one girl who expressed a desire to study at the Carlisle Indian School toward becoming a teacher. Henderson had reservations, however, about the donated reading material she saw on the bookshelf. What, she wondered, had propelled people to send a "Report of the Department of Agriculture" or the "Official Catalogue of the World's Columbian Exposition" or "Nelson on Infidelity"?

From July 8 to September 4 the women at the Home had a brief respite while the abrasive secretary Beiler visited the "tents of wickedness" along the Yukon River. The Home's ownership of the land was established, and the A.C. Co. offered to sell the fence. Agnes purchased it—only to be scolded by Beiler on her return.

While Beiler was traveling up the greatest of Alaskan rivers, getting stuck on sandbars for days at a time, touring Dawson and Circle City, and finding apt comparisons between the rush for gold and the rush to salvation, Elizabeth Mellor prepared to leave Unalaska with six girls and one boy. For several months she had discussed the possibility of students attending the Carlisle Indian School in Pennsylvania. Sheldon Jackson had approved the plan and had earlier arranged for other students from Alaska to go there. Several Unalaska parents, however, objected to the idea. Nevertheless, as Beiler put it, the mission "must save the children, oftentimes *in spite* of the parents." Father Kedrovsky also expressed his reservations. Sowle said this was because "he doesn't want any of these people to be educated, get above living in barabaras and eating seal meat," but this was patently incorrect.

Kedrovsky had just asked Mellor to teach English to the boys in the Russian school the next September. He had seen how quickly impressionable girls could be swayed even while living in their own village. To be thousands of miles away, he felt, would make them extremely vulnerable to outside pressures.

A few days before Mellor and the girls were to leave on the SS *Portland*, Bishop Nicholas arrived from San Francisco. He sent word that he wanted a signed paper promising the return of the girls within a year. Mellor immediately consulted Captain C.L. Hooper of the Revenue Cutter Service, who advised her to get legal control over each child. Mellor spent the day rushing to secure these. Pelageia Tutiakoff (17) and Sosipatra Sovoroff (18) were of age under the laws of the Oregon Territory, the only laws then governing Alaska, and were able to write their own statements of intent. Eudocia Sedick was a 14-year-old orphan from St. Paul Island and Commissioner Woodward had her apprenticed to the Jesse Lee Home. Dora and Annie Reinken were daughters of the Adolph Reinken who had once removed his children from the Home. Sheldon Jackson had arranged for their brother John to enter Carlisle in November 1894, and permission for the sisters to travel was easily secured.

Parsha Block's case was unique. She was not headed to Carlisle but to a school in Chicago. Portus B. Weare, who owned the North American Transportation and Trading Company of Chicago, had passed through Unalaska from the Klondike gold mines. He had met Parsha and asked if he could pay for her education. Her mother came to the Home and agreed to her leaving. With Annie Shaishnikoff as interpreter, Parsha's mother, Martha Kalastrakoff of Attu, signed a statement in front of Commissioner Woodward. Parsha was enrolled at the Forestville public school as a third grader.[5] In 1902 she graduated from the eighth grade along with 1,200 other children. She was the head of the class and received a gold medal.[6]

The boy, 11-year-old Ivan Penkoff, was enrolled at "Mother Jewel's Home" in York, Nebraska. The Woman's Home Missionary Society had established this orphanage for boys in 1890 on a large farm. Mellor wrote that Ivan was from "another island or village" and that his father had abandoned him at Unalaska after the death of his mother.[7] He was brought to the Home by the commissioner. According to Sowle, he wanted to become an engineer so he could "take Mamma Sowle to Dutch Harbor in a steam launch."[8] His dream was not fulfilled. Ivan died of tuberculosis three years later, on June 13, 1900, and was buried at York.[9]

A final meeting between Kedrovsky and Mellor took place in Woodward's office. Mellor assured the priest that she had all legal papers in order and urged him to tell the bishop to "drop the whole matter and stop making a fuss." One way or another the children were going, and any opposition would only create hard feelings. Kedrovsky assured her he did not want to quarrel, and she agreed and "so we parted good friends."[10] The day she left, Bishop Nicholas sent word that he wanted her to teach English in their school the next fall. Mellor consented but asked Kedrovsky to agree that he would send the boys to her for an hour a day if that was the arrangement Sheldon Jackson wanted. Mellor's own preference, pending the move into the new school building, was to teach at the Russian school.

On July 8 Mellor and her charges sailed from Unalaska aboard the *Portland* at 7 in the evening. Excitement on the vessel was electric; it carried miners from the Klondike with more than $700,000 in gold.[11] On their way south, Mellor and her girls were asked to sing hymns for the men. Pandemonium greeted the ship in Seattle as more than 5,000 residents crowded the dock to witness the arrival of what was rumored to be a ton of gold. Mellor and the children were treated to a special luncheon, and after a few days they boarded a train for Chicago and Minneapolis. After dropping off Ivan and Parsha, Mellor took the remaining girls to Carlisle where they were enrolled on July 25. While there, Mellor showed samples of gold ore "given to her by the miners who were with her on the first famous boat that carried so many miners with their millions from the gold country to Seattle, this summer."[12] A student newspaper reported that in addition to teaching in the government school she assisted "the Presbyterian and Greek Missions, out of school hours." Mellor arrived in Brooklyn for a short visit with family and friends. She described Unalaska as "really beautiful and picturesque."[13] She said the Aleuts "are an intelligent people, and they seem glad to come to the school." Her characterization of adult Aleuts, however, was not complimentary: they were unattractive and unclean. When asked if they were religious, she replied, "Most of them are devout members of the Russian Church." She said she had studied Russian during the winter and enjoyed it. She said the girls that she brought to Carlisle would be trained to become assistant teachers in the government schools of Alaska. It was the rare student who would free herself from the role of "assistant" under a white head teacher to become a full-fledged instructor herself.

The staff at Carlisle were impressed with the Aleut children and found their English excellent. Mellor was encouraged by this reception and after her return to Unalaska began grooming another set of children for Carlisle. When she left for the last time, in the fall of 1898, she was accompanied by five girls and one boy: Irene Sovoroff (age 14), Helen Fratis (13), Marie McLeod (15), Kathryn Dyakanoff (12), Vasha Nakotin (14), and John Benson (12). Kathryn Dyakanoff continued her education at the West Chester State Normal School in Pennsylvania and eventually returned to teach at Unalaska, Atka, and other localities for 29 years. She became a well-known lecturer on Alaska. Marie McLeod became a missionary and teacher and would later return to work in the Home.[14] In Seattle these children were amazed by street cars moving on their own and by a frog hopping across a floor. They laughed to see Mellor talking to a black box, but soon each child tried the telephone. They visited schools and did recitations for the classes. Once again Mellor was interviewed and spoke highly of her students at Unalaska.[15]

When their train pulled into the Chicago station, they were met by Parsha Block, who greeted them with "a mixture of dignity and ill-concealed delight." "Dignity" because, as she had made clear to her classmates at the Forestville school, "she was of noble birth on her father's side." She "queened it" over the other students, according to a reporter. After welcoming her old friends, Parsha "escorted the party to the Great Northern Hotel, where luncheon had been prepared."[16]

In 1902 there were 10 girls at Carlisle, including the nine brought from Unalaska by Mellor, who claimed to be members of the Russian Orthodox Church. The girls' parents had sent a request to the bishop in San Francisco that a priest go to Carlisle to minister to them. The director of Carlisle, while willing to have the priest come to the school for religious purposes, wrote to Sheldon Jackson on the belief that some of the girls were "from the Jesse Lee Home and are Methodists."[17] Asked by Jackson to clarify the girls' religious affiliation, Mellor replied that although they had been given the option of attending Orthodox services at Unalaska "almost all of them showed evidences of being spiritually awakened"—that is, of renouncing Orthodoxy. The parents of Kathryn Dyakanoff and Sosipatra Sovoroff were particular about their children attending the Orthodox church, she said, and Sovoroff was "quite attached to it." The children of Adolph Reinkin were to attend Orthodox communion, but he was not "particular about regular weekly attendance." Mellor had a commonsense solution: "Were I asked for an opinion in the matter, I should say, 'ask the children themselves if they wish to attend Greek services.'"[18]

Mellor returned to Unalaska from the first Carlisle trip, accompanied by her sister Ada, in September of 1897—about the time Anna Beiler returned from her trip along the Yukon. Ada Mellor was set to begin her employment as assistant teacher. The first impression the young women had was that Beiler's experiences had softened her and made her more accommodating. All she needed, however, was a little rest and she was her driven self, finding fault with everything. "If I ask how to do things," wrote Sowle, "I am told to use my own judgment, and yet it is never right." Ada Mellor was told to fill the lamps. She asked where she should do this. Beiler replied, "Anywhere." After Ada had filled them on the kitchen table, the secretary commented, "Well, Miss Ada, I thought you had more sense than that."

And on it went. Everything carried to the new building was placed in the wrong location and had to be moved. The staff was driven from one chore to the next until late in the night. In their spare time, Sowle and Rinch were expected to paint and wallpaper all 22 rooms in the new Home. "Nails have been driven, wash boards and tubs fixed, pieces of wood fitted into the floor," wrote Sowle. "This work is taking the life out of me." The women reacted in opposite ways. Sarah Rinch carried a frozen smile regardless of the situation; Agnes wept. "Between Miss Sowle's tears and Miss Rinch's smiles," Beiler told Elizabeth Mellor, "I don't know what to do."

MISS M. ELIZABETH MELLOR AND HER ALEUT PUPILS NOW IN CHICAGO.

"MISS M. ELIZABETH MELLOR *and Her Aleut Pupils Now in Chicago," from the* Chicago Daily Tribune, *Oct. 24, 1898.*

"Mrs. B. makes me feel as if I am good for nothing," Sowle wrote. She did not want praise but disliked the continuous criticism. There was a bright side, however. When one of the staff was being scolded, the others had a break. Beiler told Sowle that if she maintained proper authority and arranged work correctly there would be ample time for rest. She demonstrated the technique. Several boys were called to clean the hallways of the wood shavings that had accumulated. Beiler gave them a severe talking to and each boy grabbed up an armful of shavings.

"Now boys," she said, "I am going to lie down for half an hour and when I return this work must be finished."

The boys stampeded down the stairs and Beiler retired to rest. A half hour passed. She came out of her room. The shavings still littered the hallway. The boys were playing at the lake. Agnes held her tongue. The next day when a drain had to be dug, Beiler assigned the task to the same boys and this time sat herself in a chair in front of them until the job was done.

In her published reports, Beiler called Sowle and Rinch "devoted missionaries [who] are doing valiant service." She wrote about "the noble force of workers on the field," and declared they "enjoy so much and suffer so much, for which no gold can pay."[19] It was Sowle's devotion to what she perceived as her Christian duty that enabled her to survive the last weeks of Beiler's visit. "I must confess I have worked hard and done my best," she wrote, "and yet have never been talked to so or scolded so much in my life." At last, on October 17, Anna Beiler boarded a steamer and left. She was physically exhausted. Society publications later referred to her "scars of service" and to the "severe illness" she had contracted in the Territory and to the "serious lameness" that followed as a result of "the exposure of her long and arduous journeyings in Alaska."[20] Sowle wrote that she was "twice glad, as the old saying goes." Glad the secretary had come to "set things right and get the new building in shape" and glad that she had finally left.

A few days later the women and students from the Home traveled across the bay to Dutch Harbor for the launching of the first paddle-wheel boat built for transportation on the Yukon. The Gold Rush had spurred the construction of these vessels, which were shipped in pieces to Unalaska and assembled. Elizabeth Mellor was asked to christen the *John C. Barr* with a bottle of champagne. She demurred even when the builders explained that she wouldn't have to drink what was left in the bottle. She wanted to use Apollinaris water, but the last vessel so christened had soon gone on the rocks.[21]

Although Anna Beiler had departed, a reminder of her paraded the halls of the new Jesse Lee Home. A girl called Baby May, perhaps seven-year-old May Dyakanoff, would hold her dress up to her knees and rush around looking for dirt and misplaced objects. She chastised children who happened to get in her way and hollered for Elizabeth, Ada, Sarah or Agnes—all played by other girls—and then scolded them severely. The girl pretending to be Sarah would laugh uncontrollably and the girl playing Agnes would wail until everyone burst into laughter. The pantomime went on for weeks.

For the first time in months, Sowle could relax. "I have rushed about doing a little of everything but, as it was all the wrong thing done, it was hard," she wrote. "Now I shall go to work systematically and get the important things done."

NOTES

1. *WHM*. August 1897:121.

2. Woman's Home Missionary Society. Reports from Bureaus. 1896–97:106.

3. *WHM*. January 1898:6.

4. Henderson, *The Rainbow's End: Alaska*, 23–24.

5. She was under the direct guardianship of Captain C.H. Barter and lived at his home at 4507 Forestville Avenue,

6. *Education in Alaska*, 1902, 1244. Jackson received this information from John Tuck, who attended the graduation ceremonies. Tuck to Jackson, June 9, 1902. PHS. RG 239. Box 7, folder 2.

7. *WHM*. August 1901:145.

8. Newhall Manuscript, 154.

9. E-mail, April 4, 2005, from Bridget Smale, Director of Communications, Epworth Village Learning Center, York, Neb. Additional information from Martha Murray.

10. Mellor to Jackson. July 22, 1897. NARA. RG 75. Letters Received, 1883–1907.

11. A few days earlier, the *Excelsior*, with miners carrying $400,000, had anchored in the port. It arrived in San Francisco three days before the *Portland* reached Seattle.

12. *The Indian Helper*. Indian Industrial School, Carlisle, Pa. Aug. 20, 1897, No. 45.

13. "A Talk with Miss Mellor." Undated newspaper article. Sheldon Jackson Scrapbook. Vol. 63. PHS. RG 239.

14. Her name was sometimes spelled "McCloud" and "McLoud." As an adult, she used "McLeod."

15. "Indian Children from Alaska Who Will Finish Their Education at Carlisle," *Seattle Post Intelligencer*, Oct. 16, 1898. The article carries a drawing of four of the girls.

16. "Miss M. Elizabeth Mellor and Her Aleut Pupils Now in Chicago," *Chicago Daily Tribune*, Oct. 24, 1898:10. The article contains drawings of all the students, Mellor, and Parsha Block.

17. R.H. Pratt to Jackson, Jan. 2, 1902. PHS. RG 239. Box 6, folder 36.

18. Mellor to Jackson, Jan. 31, 1902. PHS. RG 239. Box 6, folder 36.

19. Woman's Home Missionary Society. Reports from Bureaus. 1896–97:107, 108.

20. *WHM*. November 1899:216.

21. Mellor to Jackson. Oct. 21, 1897. NARA. RG 75. Letters Received, 1883–1907.

9

Burial and Separation

Aɴɴᴀ Bᴇɪʟᴇʀ'ꜱ ᴠɪꜱɪᴛ ᴄʀᴇᴀᴛᴇᴅ ᴀ ʟɪᴛᴇʀᴀʟ ᴄʜᴀꜱᴍ ʙᴇᴛᴡᴇᴇɴ ᴛʜᴇ Home and the Orthodox community, a grave in which the good will that had been developing between Mellor and Kedrovsky was buried. The Aleut community rose in a united front against the missionaries, who now openly defied the Orthodox Church. The Home was forced to articulate its religious and cultural agendas: the conversion of children to Protestantism and the eradication of most vestiges of Russian or Aleut culture. A fundamental change in the student population at the Home resulted as fewer Aleut children entered and more children from Yup'ik and Inupiat background were recruited. Harsh feelings continued for years on both sides. When the Russian ethnographer Waldemar Jochelson visited from 1909 to 1910, he observed, "In Unalaska there is a comfortable Methodist home for Eskimo and Aleut children. But even impoverished Aleut parents would not allow their children to live in this home."[1]

The immediate cause of this crisis was the death and burial of Mary Peterson of Sanak.[2] Mary's father had placed an older brother, William, at the Home in 1895. Two years later, after their mother Maria Ivanova died, Mary, John, and Aleck followed. Ill when she arrived, Mary had been carried to the Orthodox church several times for services where she received Holy Communion. She died of tuberculosis of the hip on Oct. 13, 1897. She was buried three days later, the day before Beiler's departure. The funeral was arranged by the women of the Home without the participation of Father Kedrovsky. According to Sowle, William Peterson had anticipated his daughter's death and had instructed the Home to conduct the funeral. He wanted his children to have nothing to do with the Orthodox Church. According to Kedrovsky, when Peterson returned from Atka and learned from the priest about his daughter's burial he denied that he wanted his children converted to the Methodist faith. He was outraged and removed his remaining children from the Home.[3]

In the past, the priest had been notified when a child died. Kedrovsky had learned of this death and had gone to the Home, where Sowle informed him they would conduct the funeral. She told him a child could be baptized by one church and buried by another and still go to heaven. With her matter-of-fact nature, she suggested he just add a note beside Mary's baptismal record stating she had died and been buried by the Methodists. Kedrovsky insisted that whenever a white man married a Native woman he agreed that their children would be raised Orthodox. Sowle, in effect, said, "Prove it." He could not produce a signed statement. He turned to Commissioner Woodward and the marshal but without success. Woodward wrote to the priest that he had "no jurisdiction over the con-sciences of Men. Every man has the right to worship God according to the dictates of his own conscience in the United States of America."[4] The priest revisited the Home shortly before the funeral was to begin at 9 a.m. and for two hours "Mrs. Beiler fought it out with him," wrote Sowle, "and made him understand that he was not in Russia."

The content of this exchange is unrecorded. Beiler's tongue was not particularly kind when dealing with her own missionaries. It was probably less restrained when she con-fronted someone she regarded as one of "the followers of the Czar," as she called the Orthodox residents of Unalaska in her report for that year. In this report she referred to the people as "priest-ridden" and berated them for their "prejudice" against all other denominations. The following year she referred to the Orthodox Church as "the State Church of Russia" and as "a Church of sterile forms and image-worship" whose members "are in the inmost depths of pagan darkness."[5] According to Kedrovsky, Beiler proclaimed, "I have planted a root here." To this he replied, "Where? In another's orchard."[6] To em-phasize her personal closeness to the government in Washington, D.C., she held two fingers together. "The President himself is a Methodist," she told the priest, "and all our officials are preachers."[7]

In the end, Kedrovsky retreated and the funeral went ahead. Commissioner Woodward led the singing and read the burial service. The small coffin was carried to the cemetery and buried just as an Orthodox deacon arrived with a signed order to deliver the body to him. It was too late.

The cemetery occupied a small hill and an adjoining slope. The Home, by mistake, had interred Mary in the consecrated or Orthodox portion rather than on the Protestant side. Beiler wrote to Kedrovsky that the cemetery was a village cemetery and any Amer-ican could be buried there. "We buried her in accordance with the customs in the United States," she declared. "If you have a title deed to the Cemetery and continue to feel uncomfortable about the matter we will consider the advisability of removing the body. It is possible it may be done anyway."[8]

"I am very glad that Mrs. Beiler was here," wrote Mellor to Sheldon Jackson, "so she could lead the movement and also have an opportunity to appreciate the state of affairs caused by such an action." Deliberately, neither Elizabeth Mellor nor her sister took any part in the funeral. Mellor was not present at any of the exchanges between the priest and the women from the Home. On the morning of the funeral, she began school at the usual time even though none of the students from the Home were present. Only eight students arrived from the village. In the afternoon, none of the boys from the Russian school returned. Kedrovsky later explained that he had been sending them to the public school without the bishop's permission and now felt he needed to secure this before they returned.

Mellor was at pains to portray the school as taking no sides in the dispute. That it had "no religious bias whatever," she said, would be realized by "the intelligent portion of the community." Nicholas Gray agreed and said he would speak with the bishop in San Francisco in December. While playing down its negative effect on the public school, Mellor acknowledged the change in policy that this burial announced.

> By a conscientious maintenance of the school as "neutral ground", where justice is shown to all, added to the fact that the boys *have been* here, I feel sure that, sooner or later, matters will adjust themselves.
>
> We all know now *why* Mrs. Beiler has been detained—it is much better for all concerned (and particularly for the Home) that she herself should take this first radical step.[9]

A few years later Mellor would refer to "the decided break from the church" that was made "by the Home."[10] Despite what she wrote about neutrality, at the close of her letter Mellor clearly identified with the women of the Home. "There is a dispute over the ownership of the cemetery," she told Jackson, "and we may remove the body to a plot of our own." Mellor's role, however much she might protest, was transparent to the community. Shortly after the burial, Aleut residents wrote that they would return their children to the public school when "there will be a teacher independent of religious sects, who will not labor to get more girls into the Methodist Home, there to entice them away from the Orthodox religion."[11]

That statement was contained in a remarkable petition sent to Father Kedrovsky on Oct. 18, 1897. It was signed by 40 residents—parents of children in the Home and other members of the Orthodox community. The first two who signed and perhaps wrote the petition were First Chief Vasilii Shaishnikoff and Second Chief Vasilii Salamatoff. Shaishnikoff was a son of the late priest Innokentii Shaishnikoff and a member of the most prominent Aleut family at Unalaska. Salamatoff was from Atka, either an uncle or a cousin of Matrona Salamatoff, the recent assistant teacher. Both men were literate in Russian and Aleut; Shaishnikoff was also literate in English. Others who signed the petition included the widow and other children of Father Innokentii Shaishnikoff, Emilian Berikoff (a prominent sea otter hunter), Nikeefer Dyakanoff (patriarch of an important family, who had grandchildren in the Home), Anfesia Shapsnikoff and Martha Sovoroff (widows with children in the Home), members of the Repin, Kudrin, Golodov, Sherebernikoff, Borenin, Gromoff, Prokopeuff, Krukoff, Melovidov, Resoff, and Kushin families, and, finally, Alexei Yatchmeneff, who would become the most important Aleut chief of the 20th century. These people formed the cream of Aleut society.

The petition affirmed Mellor's assessment that the Home had taken a "radical step" in its relationship to the community. The religious goals of the Woman's Home Missionary

INTERIOR OF THE CHURCH OF THE HOLY ASCENSION, *early 1900s. Courtesy of the Alaska State Library, Historical Collections (B.B. Dobbs Photographs, P12-185).*

Society had emerged into the open. The duplicity it had practiced for almost a decade was set aside. It is startling that in 1897 the Aleut community thought a "transformation" had just occurred in which "an annex to the Government's public school" had become "a Methodist institution." This belief was repeated several times in the petition. "When we placed our children in the Home, the managers explained to us that they would be taught the various branches in the public school, of which the Home was said to be an annex, while in the Home itself they would learn housework and housekeeping." The Home had portrayed itself as a "benevolent institution" where "no religious ends" would be pursued. The Home had even agreed that children would be allowed to attend the Orthodox church on Sundays and holy days. The priest had visited the Home at Christmas, Epiphany and Easter with the cross and holy water. Until 1896, the petition states, the staff at the Home generally agreed with these conditions although there were "a few occurrences which did suggest some doubt of their absolute honesty."

The petition noted that in 1896 Commissioner Woodward had begun to preach openly at the Home. On Sundays children were taken on excursions to Dutch Harbor so they would not be available for Orthodox services.[12] The petitioners wrote that children were kept from attending both Christmas and Easter services, and they were punished for asking to attend the Orthodox church or for making the sign of the cross.

Anna Beiler was specifically blamed for the burial of Mary Peterson. She had "ordered" it and had justified the burial with the declaration that "the Home . . . is a Methodist institution, and does not bring up children gratuitously, but works in the interests of Methodism." For Aleuts this meant "that the Home now takes in girls, and in payment for a bit of bread it gives our children, demands of them their souls." Aleuts also objected to the use of what was considered their cemetery by a religion intent on the destruction of the Orthodox Church.

Of further significance, the petition demonstrated that the Aleut community felt excluded from the American legal system. "We have no share in the protection of the law," it stated, "although, on other occasions, we are punished in the law's name. . . . The representatives of the law in this place, not only do not act in our behalf, but themselves partly abet" what Aleuts considered an abridgment of their rights. Commissioner Woodward was clearly allied with the Home, and Beiler had made a show of her close association with powerful people in Washington, D.C. The petition asked Kedrovsky to refer the complaints of the community to a higher court "which will not be influenced by anybody's close relations to Washington or acquaintance with officials of high rank."

The petition specifically asked that the contracts which had indentured children to the Jesse Lee Home be declared void because the Home had violated the terms. Sowle had offered to activate the clause about children attending the Orthodox church, but the Aleut community wanted the complete return of their children. The petition minced no words as it concluded, "Let the courts, the law, and the honor of the American people restore to us our children, taken from us by fraud."

Enrollment cards indicate that nine children left the Home during the next 11 months. None of them, however, were children from Unalaska. On the other hand, the school population dropped from 68 for 1897–98 to 31 for the following year. Jackson's annual report was mute on the upheaval that had caused this decline.

Kedrovsky referred the petition to Bishop Nicholas and it became part of a general complaint he made on behalf of Orthodox believers across the Territory. Kedrovsky also referred the matter to Deputy U.S. Marshal Blaine, emphasizing that Unalaska parents had given their children to a government school, not to a missionary home. Nicholas Gray gave a hint of the severity of resentment against the Home. When a flag and flagpole arrived for the Home and a dedication was planned for November 6, Gray said he could not ask the local brass band to play without compensation. Normally, because of the music instruction he gave the musicians, they would perform whenever he asked. The 12- by 20-foot flag, a gift of Mrs. Clinton Fisk, was raised to the band's rendition of "The Star Spangled Banner," and then it was put away. The captain of the cutter *Corwin* gave the Home a smaller, more practical flag for everyday use.[13]

However unpleasant Beiler's visit had been for Agnes Sowle personally, the secretary's fiery departure galvanized the young missionary to follow the strict orders given to her. Sowle immediately cut the relationship between the Home and the Orthodox community. She wrote to Kedrovsky that she would no longer allow children brought up in the Home to attend the Orthodox church. She would not honor any agreement signed by John Tuck. The only exception would be children sent from the Pribilof Islands or those whom she accompanied. If any parent wanted to withdraw a child, this could be done on payment of $50 for each year the child had lived in the Home. Kedrovsky, of course, pointed out that this condition was prohibitive as the parents who sent their children to the Home were among the poorest in the village.[14]

As a show of good will, Kedrovsky attended the Christmas program at the public school. The cover of the program for this event featured a drawing of the new Jesse Lee Home, symbolic of Mellor's allegiance to the mission. She made overtures to the community by visiting and delivering a gift to every child who did not attend the program. But on Russian Christmas, January 7, Mellor held school, and Orthodox children from the Home were not allowed to attend church. On Orthodox Epiphany, January 18, a girl prepared to leave school to attend services and Mellor forcefully removed her coat.

Father Kedrovsky was not silent. Several articles, blunt and accusatory, were published in Orthodox journals and newsletters. In February, an article titled "More Sad News" appeared in the *Russian-American Messenger*, a publication of the Orthodox Church. It contained both the October 1897 petition from Unalaska residents and a letter from

"RUSSIAN CEMETERY, UNALASKA, ALASKA." *Photograph by F.H. Nowell, published by Portland Post Card Co. for the 1909 Alaska-Yukon Pacific Exposition. From the author's collection.*

Kedrovsky. A few months later, another article began, "Will there ever be an end to the tribulations we suffer here in Unalaska from the illegal acts of the Methodists?" This article declared, "It is not perfectly clear that the public school annex home [i.e., the Jesse Lee Home] was nothing but a crafty, pernicious and unscrupulous trap set for us by the Methodists."[15]

The only reference to difficulties between the Home and the Orthodox church published by *Woman's Home Missions* was in a letter Sowle wrote on Nov. 19, 1897. She based the hostility between her institution and the Orthodox community on a case of child abuse and makes no mention of the burial of Mary Peterson. "I wish I might write a more encouraging letter as to the spiritual welfare of our Home. If I could look away down deep in the hearts of these people, perhaps I could see more than I think I see by outward appearances." She then related how a boy had been beaten by an intoxicated aunt. The U.S. marshal had brought the boy to the Home and the commissioner had assigned him there until he came of age. "This aroused the wrath of the Russian priest," she wrote. "He said it would have been better for the child to be beaten to death than to come under the care and teaching of our Home, because there was no heaven for any outside the Russian Church."[16]

By "the continuation of good deeds" she hoped to overcome the "animosity and prejudice" of the village "in the name of our precious Savior, who I am sure is looking on with deepest pity at these priest-ridden people." She then echoed a statement Sheldon Jackson made about the same time that a hospital should be established in connection with the Methodist mission.[17] "What we need now," she wrote, "is a medical missionary, one who cares not for money . . . but one who loves souls, and will tenderly care for the body." She went on to add, "If only a place could be fitted up for him, and the necessary outfit furnished. It would be the means of helping us to gain the confidence of these people; for, although they dislike us, they come to us when they are sick or in trouble." She happened to know just such a physician.

1. Jochelson, "People of the Foggy Seas," 417.

2. Information for this event comes from the Newhall Manuscript, from a letter from Mellor to Jackson (Oct. 16, 1897. NARA. RG 75. Letters Received, 1883–1907), and from a report from Alexander Kedrovsky (Oleksa, ed. *Alaskan Missionary Spirituality*, 328–329).

3. According to enrollment cards, William, John, and Aleck left the Home in May 1898. This would be about the time travel would have resumed between Unalaska and Atka.

4. Library of Congress, Manuscript Division. The Alaskan Russian Church Archives. D49.

5. Woman's Home Missionary Society. Reports from Bureaus. 1897–98:110.

6. *Russian Orthodox Messenger*. Vol. 5, No. 3:51.

7. *Russian Orthodox Messenger*. Vol. 2, No. 7:223.

8. Library of Congress, Manuscript Division. The Alaskan Russian Church Archives. D49.

9. Mellor to Jackson. Oct. 16, 1897. NARA. RG 75. Letters Received, 1883–1907.

10. Mellor to Jackson, Jan. 31, 1902. PHS. RG 239. Box 6, folder 36.

11. Petition, Oct. 6/18, 1897. *Russian Orthodox Messenger*. Dec. 13, 1897. *Alaska History Documents*, Archives of the Arctic and Polar Regions Collections of the Elmer E. Rasmuson Library, University of Alaska Fairbanks.

12. At the headquarters of the North American Commercial Company, they occasionally visited Mary Garfield Brown, daughter of the late U.S. president and the wife of the company agent, Joseph Stanley Brown. "She is lovely," wrote Agnes, "and has been very kind to the Home by her frequent visits."

13. *WHM*. February 1898:32–33.

14. *Russian Orthodox Messenger*. Vol. 2, No. 19:556.

15. Ibid.

16. *WHM*. March 1898: 47–48.

17. *WHM*, January 1898:6.

10

Albert Warren Newhall

THE GOLD MINERS WHO ARRIVED IN SAN FRANCISCO AND Seattle aboard the *Excelsior* and the *Portland* initiated a rush through Alaska that culminated in 1898 with tens of thousands of people clambering over various mountain passes into the Canadian Yukon Territory. A few thousand chose to go by water, along the coast of Alaska and up the Yukon River. Travel on the river was restricted to a few months each summer. Men (and a few women) congregated at Unalaska early in order to reach the river the moment it was navigable. As the Klondike rush was peaking, the first discoveries were being made on the Seward Peninsula. In October 1898 the Cape Nome Mining District was organized. The Nome gold rush exploded over the next two years and brought new waves of hopeful prospectors north. Ships left Seattle and other West Coast ports in May. After unloading freight at Unalaska, they remained until the northern ice had dispersed, usually in early June. The streets of Unalaska and Dutch Harbor were clogged with hundreds of men. At Dutch Harbor the North American Commercial Company operated a bar at "Ye Baranov Inn." A trail led from Dutch Harbor across Amaknak Island to where a ferry carried people to Unalaska for 50 cents. Halfway along this trail was a convenient saloon, while at Unalaska itself there were four more, "running wide open where unlimited quantities of rum are on sale with the implements for carrying on the various gambling games in plain view to the passer by."[1] None of the establishments were properly licensed.

Crowds stampeded from one fight to another. Men washed clothes and bathed in small freshwater lakes. The curious viewed a large octopus for 10 cents a look until an elderly Aleut arrived and claimed it as his. Commissioner Woodward opened his house and charged 50 cents for a home-cooked meal. The Orthodox church charged 25 cents for a tour and attendance at a service. Sophia Reinken's husband, Henry Swanson, had built a fine home near the A.C. Co. corral. It had a picket fence through which their son Henry, five years old in 1900, handed flowers he had picked and received a coin or two from the hopeful miners.[2] In late June 1900 it was estimated that there were more than 8,000 people on the beach at one time and that 5,000 people had watched a ball game on an improvised field.[3] On calm evenings music could be heard coming from vessels in the bay with the bugler from a revenue cutter occasionally joining in.

Dr. Albert Warren Newhall arrived in the midst of this activity.

He was born on Feb. 6, 1872, in Lynn, Massachusetts, to Nelson Allen Newhall and Hannah Breed. When he was nine the family moved to Stoneham where he attended public school. Bert, as he was called, quit school in his junior year to work at a tannery, then a shoe factory, and finally at a company where he was able to study chemistry.[4] As a boy he had reluctantly attended Sunday school at the Methodist Episcopal church, at his aunt's insistence. At 16, however, he asked to join the church. He kept his baptism a secret from his parents, who were not church-goers, but once they learned of it they voiced no objection. They also rarely failed to remind him of his new status whenever his behavior slipped a bit. He eventually became aware, as had Agnes Sowle, that there were others who "had an experience, a victory, a freedom, a blessing that was not mine." Shortly after a youth meeting, he found what he was looking for. He later wrote, "A work of grace, distinct from conversion, had been wrought in my heart."

In 1891 he began to do volunteer missionary service in Stoneham despite some opposition from his family and peers. This experience propelled him toward a vocation as a missionary and in 1892 he entered the Union Missionary Training Institute's program on the farm near Hackettstown, New Jersey. Life was divided between farm work and school at the Centenary Collegiate Institute in town. His classes included history, chemistry, astronomy, logic, psychology, Latin, rhetoric and English. In the evenings back at the farm there were lectures on "soul winning," Bible study, and "moral science."

Albert first met Agnes Sowle one morning when he chanced upon her sitting on the cellar stairs, busily stirring something in a glass jar. He had not slept well. His room above the kitchen regularly filled with smoke from green wood and the bed was infested with biting insects.

"What are you mixing up?" he asked. She evaded answering.

"Is it corrosive sublimate?" he asked, and she burst into tears. "Have you found anything?" she asked.

"Discovered anything! Why, they almost ate me up alive!"

They both laughed and before long he was put on the exterminating committee and "after a long fight the pests disappeared."

Agnes was not the first love of his life. When he was about 21 he proposed to a woman he had known since she was nine years old. She turned him down. Years later, in a letter to a former student who was having a similar experience, Newhall wrote, "A young man should never mourn because a girl does not accept him—he should rather be glad that he did not get one that did not like him above all others."[5]

Following a year at the farm, he spent two years at the institute's headquarters in Brooklyn. He volunteered on a canal boat that had been converted into a missionary post where seamen could spend time. He visited numerous vessels for religious services. He treasured an extensive collection of testimonials from "converted seamen." This early acquaintance with seamen proved valuable in Alaska.

After graduating from the missionary institute in 1895, he and Agnes briefly went their separate ways. He went home to Massachusetts, and she returned to her family's farm in upstate New York. Albert had an infectious appetite for life and loved to tease. Mary Winchell once wrote, "His greatest gift was a sense of humor."[6] He was, simply put, irresistible; shortly after his arrival for a visit at the Sowle farm he and Agnes became engaged. Before marrying, however, he wanted to become a physician. He enrolled at the medical school at the University of Vermont where several friends gave him financial assistance and provided free board. He lived in an attic his first year and then found lodging at the home of a Methodist minister whom he assisted. Agnes, of course, left for Alaska shortly after their engagement. They corresponded as regularly as the irregular mail service allowed.

Albert Newhall graduated from medical school on June 30, 1898. He and Agnes were married six days later, on July 6, at the home of her parents. His mother and father were present. The newlyweds were given a wedding supper, and they opened their gifts: assorted silverware, a china clock, a quilt and bedspread along with other bedding, towels, a gold breast pin, two handkerchiefs, and a paper cutter. The $115 in cash was especially appreciated. July was spent in Stoneham with his friends and relatives. They visited Maine and New Hampshire before returning to her parents' farm in Hagaman. On August 11 they left from Amsterdam, New York, for Boston where they boarded a train that took them to Montreal, across Canada, and down to Seattle. On September 15 they left on the SS *Roanoke,* and they reached Dutch Harbor on Sept. 22, 1898. The weather was good and they walked the trail across Amaknak Island until they faced the A.C. Co. dock. A rowboat took them across to the village.

When the Newhalls arrived at the Home, they found Carl J. Larsen and his son visiting. Larsen was presiding elder of the Alaska District for the Western Norwegian-Danish Conference of the Methodist Episcopal Church. He was on his way home after a trip through Southeastern Alaska, a trek over the Chilkoot Trail, and a boat ride down the Yukon River to St. Michael. During the three days he was with the Newhalls he appointed Albert "a local preacher" under a special missionary rule. Larsen was impressed by the doctor and wrote, "He is a very earnest Christian man and will undoubtedly be of great service."[7]

Dr. Newhall began working as the assistant school teacher. When Elizabeth Mellor resigned and Mary Mack took her place, Dr. Newhall was pleased and wrote that she was "sent of God." Not quite. She had been dismissed by the board of Moravian missions for "gross moral delinquency" as a result of her involvement with a fellow missionary.[8] Before long Dr. Newhall was writing that she was a great trial, "an unsaved woman with no interest in Missions, no interest in anyone but herself." She was "like a thunder cloud most of the time and does us much harm in the village by her venomous tongue." Mack did not return for the 1899–1900 school term and her place was taken by Frances Mann. Although Newhall appreciated having the assistant teacher position, he preferred to concentrate on work at the Home once school ended in the spring of 1899.

ALBERT WARREN NEWHALL. *Courtesy of the Unalaska City School District (Clara Cook Collection).*

For the first time since the Woman's Home Missionary Society had been placed in charge of the school, a public school teacher did not live in the Home. Mann found lodging with the Alaska Commercial Company. She was exactly what the school needed, and Sheldon Jackson recognized this. He commended her to the commissioner of education and remarked that the Orthodox community was now well-disposed toward the school and had sent their pupils back.[9] School enrollment climbed to 76. Relations between Mann and the Newhalls remained cordial.

Anna Beiler, apparently unaware of Mann's aversion to missionary work, wrote, "I am glad to say the Greek priest has consented to allow his whole school to attend the public school one half day, in order that they may learn English. This is a great victory, for there they will hear gospel hymns and catch the spirit of Christian teachers, and it means much to the people of the Aleutian Chain."[10] She was especially happy to have a doctor in residence at the Home.

Newhall's outlook toward the Orthodox Church would eventually change, but initially it was influenced by Beiler's negativity. "The Greek Church is a dead letter," he wrote in 1898 or 1899, "and losing its grasp on the coming generation."[11] He found the work at Unalaska "hard and perplexing." A child would be added now and then, but the village was essentially closed as a source for students. A dozen children from Yup'ik or Inupiat communities were expected to fill the void, but none arrived until October 1899. The pelagic sealing Indians who had entertained Agnes Newhall with a dance and contributed to the Home made occasional visits. Albert recalled one visit where the men identified as Methodists and joined in a series of hymns. "At the close the leader put his hand upon his heart," Newhall wrote, "and said, 'Fine, make heart feel good in here.' Then we bade them God speed on their journey. Since then several groups of Indians have called 'to have a sing.'"[12]

In an article published in February 1900, Newhall challenged the church to meet the needs of Alaska.

> The Esquimaux have no definite religion, and their minds are open to the gospel call. . . . The Aleut tribes . . . have been under the dead formalism of the Greek Church for over a century. Although loyal to the church and wholly under the sway of the priesthood, they are ignorant, superstitious and grossly immoral. The natives want their children educated and Americanized, but fear the opposition of the priest. . . . The Indians of Alaska are worshippers of the Great Spirit with all the superstitions of that system. . . .
>
> The discovery of gold has brought thousands of miners to these regions. All classes are represented. All are bent on the accumulation of wealth. They sacrifice home, friends, health and even life itself in the search for treasure. The

trials and temptations that beset the miner are many. Without the restraint of civilization, sin and corruption are rampant. . . . The effect of such a condition of society is demoralizing both to the white man and the native.[13]

He drew parallels between religion and patriotism.

The missionary work has much to do with the molding of the future character of this people. The religion of the people and loyalty to the stars and stripes should go hand in hand. Many are kept in ignorance of this country by influences wholly foreign and in opposition to the principles of American independence. Protestantism overcomes this. We teach loyalty to our country and to God. The opportunity for mission work in Alaska has come.

Newhall was clearly reflecting the attitude of the church at large. Anna Beiler continued to solicit support for the Home by leveling spurious accusations against the Orthodox Church. She charged its clergy with corruption and with an "absolute" hold over the Native people. "Even the more intelligent among the Alaskans," she lamented, "are more loyal to the foreign church than to the United States government. To the public schools and the missionary societies we must look for the only influence that can break this thralldom, and in time elevate the people into good citizenship."[14]

Albert Newhall's initial missionary work gave little promise of surmounting the barriers the Home had erected between itself and the Aleut community. He took his role as a preacher seriously and saw a sharp distinction between his church and the Orthodox Church. It was "them" and "us," "truth" and "error," the "true faith" and "superstition." Luckily for him and for the community, everyone bled in exactly the same way. His skills as a physician would gradually bring the community closer to him. He, in turn, would slowly come to appreciate the strengths and deep faith that resided within the Aleut community. This process, however, would take years and involve epidemics and personal losses.

NOTES

1. H.H. Roberts, Captain, U.S. Str. *Manning*, to Secretary of the Treasury, June 24, 1900.

2. Swanson, *The Unknown Islands*, 4.

3. Moser, J.F. "Report on the Steamer Albatross operating from Japan to Unalaska, March 4, 1900–June 30, 1900." Page 44. NARA. RG 75. Letters Received, 1883–1907.

4. Newhall, Elmer. Undated letter about the life of Albert Warren Newhall. Lowder, *The Great Physician*, 193.

5. A.W. Newhall to Simeon Oliver, Dec. 4, 1924. Copy provided to Ray Hudson by Simeon Oliver, May 1979.

6. *WHM*. November 1929:11.

7. Shepard, *Have Gospel Tent Will Travel*, 23–25.

8. Fienup-Riordan, *The Real People and the Children of Thunder*, 229.

9. Jackson to Harris. May 30, 1900. NARA. RG 75. Letters Received, 1883–1907.

10. Woman's Home Missionary Society. Reports from Bureaus. 1898–99:107.

11. Woman's Home Missionary Society. Reports from Bureaus. 1898–99:108.

12. *WHM*. February 1900:30.

13. Newhall, Albert W. "Alaska." *WHM*. February 1900:30–31.

14. *WHM*. November 1899:215.

The Doctor

ALBERT WARREN NEWHALL WAS A CONSCIENTIOUS PHYSICIAN and a devout missionary. Perplexed by his initial cool reception and puzzled by the general attitude toward the mission, he turned to practical activities. He made repairs and improvements to the building. He taught boys to mend shoes. He and the students planted a garden with seeds from Sitka. Lettuce and turnips were excellent. Kale, carrots, onions and parsnips did nicely. Peas did not do so well. A silo was built to help maintain the two cows, Patience and Alaska, and two calves. He led worship services and conducted Sunday school.

No work, however, was more gratifying for a doctor than tending the sick and injured. When he arrived as physician to the community, the port of Unalaska provided him with an abundance of patients. The Klondike and Nome gold rushes were seen as providential by Anna Beiler, who looked forward to increased evangelical work. She wrote that the Klondike fields were yet to be fully developed while at Nome "the ocean shore is graveled with gold." On the mainland of Alaska, copper waited to be mined. Unalaska itself was about to see "one hundred men at work . . . opening up the limitless sulfur mines at Mt. Makushin" and developing a quartz mine a few miles outside the village. Despite her optimism, local mining operations never materialized. The Huntsville quartz mine had first been located in 1887 with subsequent relocations in 1904, 1913, and finally in 1916.[1] It was never a paying operation. The sulfur on Makushin remained in the ground. The injured and sick from Nome and the Klondike, however, did provide Newhall with more than enough patients for the facilities available to him. Relaying stories he heard, he described conditions in Nome in a letter to Beiler.

> The lowland, covered only by the deep and swampy growth of moss has proven a hot-bed of disease, and the unsanitary condition of affairs has added to the spread of the disease. Cape Nome fever is rife and has taken away many lives. [Newhall described this as "a form of typhoid, generally mild in its course."] The country is devoid of timber. The supply of coal is small, likewise provisions. As a result the miners have overcrowded the steamers in order to leave the country. Many will be unable to get out and much suffer-

ing will result. The death rate is hushed up mostly in order that the ship companies may lose no trade next spring. Two hospitals have been erected, but have not met the demand.[2]

Newhall described several of his cases in an 1899 letter and in his unpublished memoir from around 1918.[3] There are some discrepancies between the two accounts.

- Alec Allen was good-natured and patient but objected to his liquid diet: "You might as well kill me as starve me to death." He recovered after a month's stay.

- Josiah Reed (an Englishman in 1918; a Canadian from Toronto in 1899) had his spiritual ups and downs. In 1899 Newhall wrote that he "has been led to a consecration of his life to God. . . . The Lord has touched his heart with the healing power." But in 1918 he recalled, "We were glad to be rid of him as he was morally untrustworthy."

- Thomas Owen was "an old crank" (in 1918; age 24 in 1899) with typhoid. Never satisfied with the food, he would groan and declare his heart had stopped until the other patients asked the doctor "to knock him in the head or chloroform" him. Once recovered, he was grateful.

- Edward Hall had abandoned the Christian training of his youth. Very ill and near death, he was frequently delirious. Newhall felt obliged to tell him the end was near and did so during a period of lucidity. He "made an earnest prayer, confessing his sins and imploring God's mercy and pardon." On November 13 Newhall wrote that he would not survive long, and he died shortly afterward. Over a year later Newhall met his parents and comforted them with an account of their son's return to faith.

- Another miner, Edward Liebeck, age 38, ill and delirious with typhoid, recovered and went to work at the Huntsville mine. He had promised Newhall that he would send money to his wife but gave in to drink. Newhall found him dead drunk one Sunday afternoon on the beach. A bartender chanced by and offered to take him home, but some hours later Agnes and Albert discovered him almost frozen in an empty shack. They again nursed him back to health and he left, as Newhall wrote, for the "north seeking gold—and neglecting his family at home."

- Several other men died and were buried in the hillside cemetery. Among these was a Mr. Girling of London, a wealthy English mining official. In 1899 Newhall wrote, "The service was held on Monday evening at eight o'clock. The room was well filled with officers from the SS *Roanoke*. The choir composed of Esquimaux, Aleut and Creole. In the darkness of the night, with the wind and

rain to wail their mournful dirge, the procession wended its way to the hillside,
where the remains of Mr. Girling were laid to rest."

· Horace Marshall had almost gotten over a bout with typhoid when he had a
relapse and arrived at the Home on a stretcher. He died on October 27, shortly
after arriving, leaving a wife and six daughters in Wakefield, Massachusetts.

· Anfine Anfinsen (a Norwegian in 1899; a Swede in 1918) "was a good man"
whose experiences in Nome "had brought only trouble to him. However, he
sought the Lord and found peace of mind and heart" (1918). In 1899 Newhall's
recollection was similar. "Since coming to the Home he is rejoicing in the Lord.
In the place of unrest and condemnation, peace and joy and trust in a heavenly
Father."

Anna Beiler set to work on establishing a hospital as soon as Newhall arrived. During
the first year of her campaign, $10,000 was appropriated provided it could be raised. By
1898 she had secured $2,051. The WHMS received $300 toward the hospital fund by rent-
ing beach land immediately in front of the Home for construction of a Yukon river boat.[4]
The Home collected $150 as payment for boarding local children and this also went into
the hospital fund. By 1900 about $3,000 was on hand. Beiler asked Dr. Newhall to design
a modest facility, a "cottage hospital," that could be built for $3,500. No sooner had she
written to go ahead and start building than she received news from him that a marine hospital had arrived aboard the steamer *Homer*.[5]

The Revenue Cutter Service had operated its own medical facility at Unalaska beginning with the navigational season of 1896. From June 26 to Sept. 17, 1897, it used a building
supplied by the North American Commercial Company at Dutch Harbor. In 1900 the
company supported Captain C.L. Hooper's recommendation that a permanent revenue
cutter facility be established to help control the spread of disease from Nome to the thousands of men waiting at Unalaska.[6] This hospital, in a building rented by the N.A.C. Co.
and staffed by assistant surgeon Dunlop Moore, was a disappointment to the company. It
acted as a quarantine station for vessels heading from Nome to prevent smallpox being
carried ashore to infect the 7,000 gold-seekers crowding Amaknak Island.[7] However, it
provided no services to the community. "The officer in charge," wrote Newhall, "would
take only marine cases. He would not take natives, travelers, or even the sick at the company's houses or attend them."[8]

The need for a general hospital facility at the Home was greater than ever. With no
room for isolating the sick, Newhall had to refuse cases that he felt might be infectious. He
made house calls to the village and to the company residences and treated children at the
Home. From mid-1900 to the spring of 1901 a series of epidemics swept the region. On
May 15, 1900, Annie Benson of Morzhovoi died after an acute illness. When Dr. Newhall

asked her if she thought she would get well, she answered matter-of-factly, "No. I am going to be with my mother."

On the Fourth of July 1901 an elaborate celebration was held on the A.C. Co. wharf. Tables were set with all sorts of foods and sweets, especially enjoyed by the village children. There were foot, pie, and greased pig races; a Home boy, Adloat, won $6 in a race. Children from the Home sang and the teacher read the Declaration of Independence. That afternoon an English steamer came into port and the commissioner, R.H. Whipple, ordered its British flag lowered and the American flag raised. The skipper refused and the marshal was told to make the exchange, which he did. A few days later, an English cutter arrived and the insult to the British flag was reported. The commissioner was forced to apologize and the marshal was ordered to raise and lower the British flag three times, "while at each dip" the commissioner "touched his hat to the flag." Newhall commented, "Of course, he choked back his wrath while the onlookers smiled."

The staff at the Home remained on the alert to protect their older girls from unwanted advances by men—locals and itinerant sailors and fishermen. At least once, Dr. Newhall pressed charges against three young men, fortified by whiskey sold to them by the cook at the A.C. Co., who were discovered loitering around the Home. They were each fined $60. One of the young men was a reader in the church; the priest paid his fine but then deducted it from his wages.[9] Newhall occasionally addressed sexuality with lectures on "young manhood, young womanhood, maternity, and venereal diseases." The content of these talks is unknown but they were open to village residents as well as the older students in the Home.[10]

As a "local preacher" Dr. Newhall was occasionally asked to perform weddings at the Home or at one of the company hotels. On May 30 he and Agnes went to the N.A.C. Co. hotel at Dutch Harbor where he married a man from Texas and a woman from California. A lively supper followed during which the embarrassed hosts discovered they had nothing for the missionaries to drink except water. The Newhalls retired early.

NOTES

1. Record. District Court of Alaska, 3rd Division. I (No. 79574), page 16a.

2. *WHM*. February 1900:31.

3. Newhall to Beiler, Nov. 13, 1899. *WHM*. February 1900:31–32.

4. *WHM*. February 1900:29.

5. Strobridge, *Alaska and the U. S. Revenue Cutter Service, 1867–1915*, 134–135.

6. *Annual Report of the Supervising Surgeon-General of the Marine-Hospital Service of the U.S.*, 1901:618, 620.

7. Ibid., 620.

8. *WHM*. August 1901:146.

9. Newhall Manuscript, 205.

10. Woman's Home Missionary Society, Report from Bureaus. 1905–06:127.

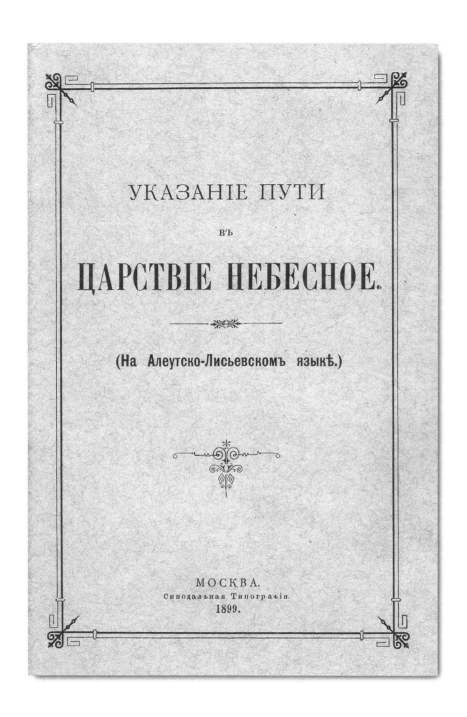

УКАЗАНІЕ ПУТИ

въ

ЦАРСТВІЕ НЕБЕСНОЕ.

(На Алеутско-Лисьевскомъ языкѣ.)

МОСКВА.
Синодальная Типографія.
1899.

THE COVER IN RUSSIAN *to the 1899 reprint of the Rev. Ivan Veniaminov's* Indication of the Path to the Heavenly Kingdom, *which was written in Aleut. From the author's collection.*

12

Deaths and Theology

Bᴇɢɪɴɴɪɴɢ ɪɴ ᴛʜᴇ sᴘʀɪɴɢ ᴏꜰ 1900 ᴀɴ ɪɴꜰʟᴜᴇɴᴢᴀ ᴇᴘɪᴅᴇᴍɪᴄ accompanied by measles and smallpox covered much of Alaska. Termed "The Great Sickness," it "struck with lightning force and within days whole villages were sick or dying."[1] As many as 2,000 people died throughout the territory, with some villages losing between 25 and 50 percent of their residents. Dr. Newhall wrote that at Unalaska "it was introduced by a boy from St. Michael." This was true for the influenza, but the measles arrived later, probably off a vessel from the south.

The epidemic reached Unalaska on August 20. Tuberculosis, pneumonia, and a later outbreak of whooping cough increased the mortality rate. The exact number of deaths remains unknown. Newhall wrote that about one third of the Native population in the whole territory died. A report from the Woman's Home Missionary Society stated that he treated more than 70 cases at Unalaska and that there were 30 deaths in the village.[2] Schoolteacher Frances Mann mentioned a fall and winter epidemic of measles "and its sequel" that "caused the death of about one third of the population." Mortality rates at the smaller villages on Unalaska Island—Makushin, Chernofski, Kashega—were also high. At Kashega, one third of the residents died.[3]

During the course of the epidemic, on September 27, 13-year-old Irene Tetoff died of tuberculosis. She died at the Home and was, essentially, buried secretly by the Newhalls while the Orthodox community was attending the daily church service. Adlooat, a 15- or 16-year-old Eskimo boy from Wales who was living at the Home, built her coffin.[4] Dr. Newhall's account of Irene's death and burial is circumspect regarding the Home's obligations toward children of the Orthodox faith. He had told Irene that she could not live and had asked her if she was afraid to die.

> "Not if I was sure of heaven." We had prayer and she prayed earnestly for salvation. That day she wanted us to read the Bible every time we came in. The next day she was very happy for peace had come to her heart. She was ready to go and all fear of death had gone. The day she died, she asked Agnes to have a service in the chapel and for all the girls and boys to carry her to the Protestant graveyard. We asked if she wanted the priest. She said no. Irene repeated this request to Miss Darling and Judge Whipple. Irene had been trying to be a Christian for over a year and she did not attend the Greek Church nor go to confession. She died trusting in Jesus, and we buried her on the hillside.[5]

The day of the burial, Kedrovsky and another priest visited the Home to discuss a different matter with the schoolteacher.

> We were met by the husband of the Matron; he seemed agitated, scared. We did not then know why the sight of us threw him into such a state; but later we learned that on that very day, while we were celebrating the divine Liturgy, they had buried Irene Titoff, a girl from St. Paul's Isle, whence the government agent is in the habit of sending children to the Home, to be educated, but with the express condition that such children shall be permitted to attend our church, and shall not be enticed into any other religion. It is clear from this that their action in the case of Irene Titoff was dishonorable. The deceitfulness and bad faith displayed by the managers of the Home are outrageous.[6]

Kedrovsky had not forgotten the events of 1897. He stated that Irene had received confession and communion at the Orthodox church in 1900. His response to what he perceived as another in a series of affronts was to write to Agnes Newhall on October 16. He expressed his bitterness at the Newhalls' action and requested permission to visit the Orthodox children in the Home for religious instruction. The letter was angry. Do you think your deeds "are agreeable to our Lord Jesus Christ?" he asked. Apart from abandoning her pledge to refrain from interference with the children's religion, she and her husband had confused them with a false distinction between an "American" and a "Russian" religion. "I only know that there is a Christian religion," he wrote, "to our misfortune divided in two: one orthodox; and the other unorthodox." Children, he said, were impressionable and would never want to contradict or go against the wishes of adults who did them kindnesses. He asked her to reflect on her actions and to consider if they were examples of Christian teachings.

Agnes gave herself a month to cool down before answering. Her reply on November 12 contains a concise statement of the aims and purposes of the Jesse Lee Home at the beginning of the 20th century.

> The Jesse Lee Home is an institution under the Woman's Home Missionary Society of the Methodist Episcopal church.
>
> Its objects—the advancement of Christ's Kingdom and the uplifting of fallen humanity. Its special interest and work lies in the children of Alaska. The children placed in our care are clothed, fed, cared for, educated and their moral and spiritual welfare carefully guarded. We assume complete charge of the children while under our care. . . . No children are admitted to the Home with the privilege of attending the Greco-Russian Church. To be sure, four Seal Islands [Pribilof] girls and two others are allowed to attend said church

when, according to *our* judgment, the weather and their condition of health will permit.

In case of death, services and burial are conducted by the Home management except in such cases as *we* shall decide otherwise. Interference in these respects will not be tolerated. It is our aim and prayer that these children may be led to become true Christians.[7]

In her annual report Anna Beiler remarked about Irene's death and one other: "One of the girls, thirteen, passed on triumphantly, and made an especial request that no priest should come. She wanted to go from the Home to the grave, while the children sang gospel hymns. One of the boys went home while repeating the Lord's Prayer. They die well. *It does pay.*"[8]

Agnes Newhall refused Kedrovsky permission to visit the Home for religious purposes. She, as her husband and Anna Beiler before her, characterized the Orthodox Church as one that gave lip-service to Christ but was little more than a religion of "form and ceremony." She decried the moral condition of people in the village, calling "most of their homes veritable brothels of sin." Finally, returning to Irene Tetoff, Agnes wrote, "Hers was a triumphant death such as the children had never witnessed and can never forget."

This letter must have been hard for her to write to someone for whom she had personal respect. "Your character and daily life are an example," she wrote, "such as the people have not often had before them during the past." In conclusion, she wrote: "May God's blessing be with you and make you a blessing in this place."

Kedrovsky answered two weeks later and addressed Agnes as "respected Matron" and "most worthy Matron." He revisited the case of Irene Tetoff and the religious guarantees in the agreements when Orthodox children were indentured to the Home. He referred to the "moral ugliness" that fouled the work of the mission. At the end he called for a truce: "May Christ's love and peace take up their abode between us!" Preceding that, however, were several pages of theological hardball.

He explained that the penitent made confession to God, not to the priest, and that the priest was there as witness "to the penitent's sincere and profound repentance at heart." He discussed the importance of "external worship" being the result "of the worship that is within the heart." He disagreed with her assessment of the moral condition of Aleuts and chided her for exaggerating to make a point. Regarding local homes as brothels, he wrote, "In the literal sense, there are, by the mercy of God, no such houses as those you speak of—excepting the saloons, the owners of which are 'outside of our pale.'" Besides, he said, the sins of the flesh, the sins that are easiest "to detect, to be horrified at," are also those easiest to correct with God's help. The smaller sins, the less noticeable, are even more dangerous

Southwest Alaska and Part of Aleutian Islands. These Islands Extend 1,500 Miles West of Unalaska, and are Methodist Territory.

COVER OF *February 1900* Woman's Home Missions *showing locations reserved for specific religious denominations. "Gr. Cath." refers to locations where there were Orthodox churches or chapels.*

and "eat into our hearts like rust." As a matter of fact, he declared, some of the sins she accused Aleuts of committing did not exist among them at all.

He was not intimidated by her declaration that interference would not be tolerated. He would interfere whenever the Home violated the terms of agreements. He wrote that he was not attacking her personally. He understood that she was acting on the orders of others.

Kedrovsky referred to an observation made by the first and greatest priest to serve among the eastern Aleut. In 1833 Veniaminov had written about the purity of the Aleut heart contrasted with that of Westerners. Kedrovsky said the Aleuts' "outward religiosity . . . is the fruit of an inward and sincere disposition. And that is why"—here he almost directly quoted Veniaminov's address to Aleuts—"they may enter before us into the Kingdom of Heaven." Kedrovsky had been studying Veniaminov's Aleut work *Indication of the Path to the Heavenly Kingdom* which had been reprinted in 1899. In the preface, the early priest compared Aleuts with Russians and wrote to his Aleut parishioners, "You journeyed on the road before them."

> The road pointing towards God's Kingdom is hard and narrow and uncertain. You will be tempted to live like other people, but I see how you suffer poverty, cold, and tribulation and are not troubled by these. You are eager to learn about God. I see you are closer to the road and it is not hard for you to travel along it.[9]

Irene's sad history continued after her burial. An Aleut man went to the cemetery and placed an Orthodox cross at her grave. He left to get material to construct a fence. Before he returned, Adlooat built a fence around the grave but excluded the cross and set a headboard over her grave. In July 1901, Irene's sister, Sophia, left to attend the Carlisle Indian School where she, too, succumbed to tuberculosis.

During the death and burial of Irene, Agnes was busy with a 10-month-old infant of her own. On Nov. 26, 1899, she had given birth to a daughter who was named Isabella. Frances Mann had been a great help as the doctor was busy with illnesses at the Home and in the village. Isabella was healthy and walked when she was 13 months old. She was good-natured and delighted everyone. By the outset of winter in 1900, however, she was failing. She had contracted iliocolitis and this was worsened by measles. On New Year's Day, 1901, Dr. Newhall wrote that she was declining rapidly. "From the human standpoint there is no hope," he wrote. "Yet God is able to raise her to health again." On January 4 she showed signs of recovery, but the next day the fever returned. At four that afternoon she died.

The Newhalls hired a visiting carpenter to construct a coffin, but he got so drunk he passed out. Three village friends, including a saloon-keeper, finished the small casket. The funeral was held in the parlor of the Home, and the child was buried in the cemetery at the base of what was soon called Mt. Newhall. Both Agnes and Albert were shaken by their daughter's death. Friends and children at the Home did what they could to comfort them. The missionaries hesitated to call their child's death "cruel"—a suggestion, Newhall wrote, from Satan—but there was no answer. "We feel deeply the loss of our little one," he wrote to Sheldon Jackson, "and are led to wonder why but God knows best. We feel to say, 'Thy will be done.' The Lord is good. A very present help in time of trouble."[10]

In the spring of 1901 another round of illness struck the village. Three children at the Home died. On March 14, Alexandra, the infant daughter of Zakhara and Preskilla Shemakensky, died.[11] Alexander Kedrovsky was not in town, and the assistant priest, Vasilii Kashevaroff, went to the Home with his parish vital statistics book. There was disagreement over the child's paternity, and Agnes Newhall refused to deliver the child's body even after Kashevaroff showed her where the child had been recorded as being Orthodox. Words were exchanged. The priest accused the Newhalls of being "unfair and un-Christian." Agnes slammed the door in his face. Anna Beiler's account of this confrontation was equally blunt. It began, "The ignorance of the priesthood in regard to our polity, manners, and customs is lamentable. Yet they are the teachers, the leaders of the people. The forms of their worship feed the superstition of the people."[12]

Alexandra Repin, 14, died on April 6. During her last illness, Kashevaroff was able to give her the sacraments. He consulted with Alexei Yatchmeneff, then the second chief of the village. Yatchmeneff got Alexandra's mother to go to the Home and request that the priest be allowed to visit. At first the Newhalls refused, but the mother was persistent and they finally conceded. When Kashevaroff arrived, the missionaries had absented themselves and no one was present except Alexandra and her mother. After her death, her two brothers removed the body and she was buried from the Orthodox church. The name of the third child was not recorded.

At the time Kashevaroff made his report to Kedrovsky in April 1901, word was circulating through the village that the Newhalls had resigned and were leaving that summer. The rumor was true. Agnes was physically and emotionally exhausted. In October 1898 her father had died, and the following January her sister had died in childbirth. Agnes longed to be with her mother. The Newhalls had submitted their resignations shortly after the death of Isabella, but they expressed the intention of returning in a year. "We are sorry that a change must be made," Agnes wrote. "The Home is just rising above past prejudices, and is winning the respect of the people. Great wisdom must be exercised."[13] Ella Darling arrived in March 1901 to assist Agnes. She had attended the Folts Mission Institute in Herkimer, New York. Work on a hospital building was put on hold although Beiler continued to solicit funds for the project. The Newhalls left Unalaska aboard the *Portland* on July 9, 1901. With them were five girls bound for the Carlisle Indian School: Annie King, Annie Vereskin, Sophia Tetoff, Olga Reinken and Vera Wagner. Adlooat also went with them. Albert and Agnes had developed a special fondness for the young man and had invited him to visit their families and friends on the East Coast.

NOTES

1. Fortuine, *Chills and Fever*, 215–26.

2. Woman's Home Missionary Society, Reports from Bureaus. 1899–1900:114.

3. Kashevaroff, Vasilii to Aleksander Kedrovsky. April 17/4, 1901. Russian Church Collection. Library of Congress. A translation of this letter was supplied by Euguenia Anichtchenko.

4. *WHM*. August 1901:146.

5. Newhall Manuscript.

6. "Report from Rev. Priest Alexander Kedrovsky of Unalaska, Including Correspondence with Mrs. Agnes Newhall, to Bishop Tikhon, 11 November 1900" in Oleksa, ed., *Alaskan Missionary Spirituality*, 328.

7. Ibid. 331–32. Emphasis in the original.

8. Woman's Home Missionary Society. Reports from Bureaus. 1900–01:123.

9. Based on translations from the Aleut by Anfesia Shapsnikoff and Ishmael Gromoff in possession of Ray Hudson.

10. Newhall to Jackson, Jan. 18, 1901. NARA. RG 75. Letters Received, 1883–1907.

11 Kashevaroff, Vasilii to Aleksander Kedrovsky. April 17/4, 1901. Russian Church Collection. Library of Congress. A translation of this letter was supplied by Euguenia Anichtchenko.

12. *WHM*, August 1901:146.

13. Woman's Home Missionary Society, Report from Bureaus. 1899–1900:116.

THE BEAR, *woodcut by Adlooat from* The Eskimo Bulletin, *Vol. V, May 1902.*

Adlooat

THE TALENTS, INITIATIVE, AND CHRISTIAN DEVOTION OF ADLOOAT, the first Inupiat to live at the Jesse Lee Home, made a deep impression on Albert Newhall.[1] As one of the few male residents, the older teenager was like a younger brother to the 27-year-old doctor. Newhall never tired of retelling Adlooat's story. His life was the perfect morality tale.

A year or two before coming to Unalaska, Adlooat made woodcuts for *The Eskimo Bulletin*, a small publication produced by the schoolteachers at Kingegan, on Cape Prince of Wales. He was then 14 or 15. The July 1898 issued carried one with the descriptive title "Herd, and Trains of Supply Sleds Crossing the Divide at Head-waters of the Kevudlena, Kookpuk, and Pitmegea Rivers." In it four parallel rows of people in sleds follow a herd of reindeer. The animals, distinct in the foreground, gradually merge into a vast throng. The horizon curves down on the left in a series of three low triangular hills. It is a powerful and effective portrayal. A smaller work, "The Belvedere in Winter Quarters" appeared that same year in Volume 4. A more complex print, probably dating from the same year, appeared in the final issue of the newspaper, May 1902, as an illustration for a contest to guess when the *Bear* would anchor at Cape Wales. The *Bear* fills the center of the woodcut from side to side. Its masts and rigging are fine lines in the upper half of the picture while the lower third consists of horizontal lines of water. Both works were signed in the block. They show an artist of strength and originality.

These two illustrations may seem to represent diverse worlds: that of traditional Eskimo subsistence and that of western law and culture. However, the Kinugmiut Eskimos were traditionally whalers, not herders. Domesticated reindeer had been introduced to the Seward Peninsula in 1892 by Sheldon Jackson and Captain Michael Healy. The animals were brought from Siberia aboard the *Bear*. A year earlier Jackson had turned 16 reindeer loose on Amaknak Island, but they did not survive for long unattended. Wales received its first herd in 1894. After an apprenticeship with Siberians and Lapps, Eskimos were given herds. By 1901 there were approximately 4,000 reindeer on the Seward Peninsula. The Alaska Reindeer Service was incorporated into the Bureau of Education, and reindeer became a source of food, clothing, and employment.

When Adlooat was about 10 years old, he accompanied his parents and brothers to trade in Siberia, 55 miles across the Bering Strait. Returning home, they were caught in a storm that almost swamped their umiak. Adlooat remembered having heard from a visiting white man that God was in Heaven. He turned his face upward and his fear left him.

Hours later the family reached the Alaskan shore. Convinced that God had spared him, Adlooat lived in a state of grace, gladness, peace and joy for over three continuous weeks.

"Some years after this," Newhall wrote, Adlooat was living in Wales when the school-teacher was shot to death by three adolescents. Harrison Thornton had gone to Wales "to teach them about God and his love," according to Newhall's account. He was murdered by boys "who were angry because they were reproved for stealing grub from the storehouses." Newhall's version is partially correct. In 1890 Sheldon Jackson hired Thornton and William T. Lopp as the first teachers at Wales. Thornton had a history of severe depression and premonitions of death. He always carried a revolver. His first three years in the village were difficult. He traveled back to the States briefly and returned in 1892 with a wife and another woman teacher, Ellen Kittredge, who soon married Lopp. A strict disciplinarian, Thornton had frequently reproved one of the village boys for theft and mischief. On Aug. 19, 1893, this boy and two others knocked on his door late in the night. As Thornton approached the door they fired a whaling gun they had removed from a wrecked vessel. The shell passed through his body and exploded against the hall paneling.

Two of the boys were captured immediately. In accordance with Eskimo justice of the time, they were executed by their elders on the beach.[2] Their bodies were stripped and left in the open for dogs to devour. The third boy escaped for several weeks. When he finally returned to the village his uncle took him to Thornton's grave. There he was given three choices: death by strangulation, stabbing, or shooting. He selected to be shot. "Adlooat was there," wrote Newhall, "an eye witness to it all."

By 1899 the Lopps were still at Kingegan although the school was a marginal affair. That year, while his parents were on a trading expedition to Kotzebue Sound, Adlooat left his uncle's home where he had been living.[3] He persuaded Captain Jarvis of the *Bear* to give him passage to Unalaska. Adlooat scrubbed decks, cleaned the brass, and washed dishes. He also carved ivory. He arrived at the Home on Oct. 17, 1899, practically an adult. Newhall asked him why he had come. In his broken English he replied, "I come—learn about books little bit—God more." He was 15 or 16 years old.

His arrival delighted and encouraged the missionaries. Albert found him "an earnest Christian of unusual moral strength. Very conscientious but somewhat sensitive, but as we understand him better we appreciate him more." Their appreciation grew as he adapted to life at the Home. He built the fence around Irene Tetoff's grave. He played with the Newhalls' daughter Isabella and felt her death very strongly. In a letter to Anna Beiler, in which he thought he was 16 years old, he detailed some of his activities at the Home and said that he would send her an ivory scrimshaw work.

Beiler brought the scrimshawed ivory piece to the annual meeting in 1901. It was described as "a walrus tusk, carved with animals, and an illustration of the revenue cutter *Bear* and the legend, 'My native home.'"[4] She declared it "really a work of art."

Unalaska, Alaska, May 15, 1900

Mrs. Beiler—My Dear Friend: I am going to tell you a few words. I am glad to write you a letter. I love God, and I came Christian when I was little boy about ten years old, and I have been Christian about six years, and I would never turn back from God. I will love God forever. I think to-day I am sixteen years old; I am not sure. I like to learn how to read and write and how to talk English. Dr. Newhall is going to teach me next winter. I came from Cape Prince of Wales, and I came to Unalaska on the Bear steamer. I am going to tell you about Jesse Lee Home. I milk the cow and feed her, give some hay and feed the calf every morning and every afternoon, and I feed the hens. When I hear you care for the Jesse Lee Home I am very much please. I am going to make for you ivory, and I carve picture on it. You will see it how I will make a good one. … We must love God forever and ever. And who makes those good things? God makes those good things. … I hunt all the time, only Sunday I didn't hunt, because holy day, and we must rest for Jesus and sing to him. ... Pray to God for me, and I will stand for Jesus and read the Bible, and God bless you and save you from all sin. I suppose you love God very much.

Your truly friend,
Adlooat [5]

Knowing they would be gone from Unalaska for only a year, the Newhalls invited Adlooat to accompany them east. Their time together cemented the closeness of their relationship. After the sea voyage to Seattle, they boarded a train. "When Adlooat first entered the train he was filled with wonder," Newhall wrote of their departure on July 20. "As the train was slowly pulling out through the lower city, he said, 'Are we going fast yet?' In a few moments however the train began to go fast and then he only smiled."

The temperature rose to 109 degrees as the train crossed Montana into North Dakota's badlands. "The air coming in the windows was like that from a hot air furnace," Newhall wrote. "Adlooat slept in a top bunk, clad only in 'nature's garments.' In the morning he thrust out his head from behind the curtains and said, 'O my! it is very like a hot stove.'"

He and Albert took several excursions together, one time dashing out to see steamers on the Mississippi River. The Newhalls took him to Niagara Falls and to museums in Boston. They went to Philadelphia and New York City. During part of his stay, he worked on the farm owned by Agnes's parents at Hagaman. While there, he was baptized in the Methodist Episcopal Church on Dec. 22, 1901, and took the name Warren Adlooat Sowle. From the farm he wrote to an Eskimo student at Carlisle that he would like to live like the American people do when he returned "to his poor country."[6] He stayed with the Newhalls at Stoneham, Massachusetts, and was there for the Newhall family reunion at the end of the year. In January 1902 he wrote Sheldon Jackson a letter expressing his thanks for the help Jackson had given to the people of Cape Prince of Wales. The letter is full of ardent Christian sentiments.[7] He was with the Newhalls when, on March 8, Agnes gave birth to a son who was named Chester Albert Newhall. He met the widow of Harrison Thornton who, according to Newhall, had "recovered her health and spirits" and was "an earnest Christian worker." He visited numerous churches, wearing his parka with a wide white fur ruff. He would sing with Dr. Newhall but usually did not speak himself as he was unsure of his command of English and did not want to be ridiculed.

While traveling with the Newhalls, Adlooat occasionally told them about life at Wales. His uncle and two cousins had been traditional healers, or, as Newhall recorded his expression, "witch doctors." Newhall set down Adlooat's comments on these healers.

When it is very stormy this man who wants to be a witch doctor takes off nearly all his clothes and goes out in the cold and darkness. He stays out a long time, and comes back unharmed. Now, it is so cold if you stay out long with nothing on it will freeze you. He says the soul of a dead whale, or walrus, or seal has come, and takes the place of his soul.

After this if any one is sick they call the witch doctor, and he will sing. He has a drum made of seal intestines. The witch doctor will take a skin coat, and hold it between his knees, and he is set down and seems to go to sleep.

Something strange will happen. His soul will go away off, and from away off the soul of a dead polar bear, whale, or seal will come. The people will watch him. His lips and his throat do not move, yet beneath that skin coat is heard the snarling and growling of the polar bear, the blowing of the whale, or noise of the seal. When they catch whale they will not work for five days, and when anybody dies they will not work. The witch doctor says if they do the whale's soul {or} the dead man's soul will kill them. After they take the body to the hillside they begin to work.[8]

And then Newhall attributed to Adlooat the following conclusion: "The young people believe in God now. They call the witch doctor an old cheat and a liar."

On April 10, 1902, Adlooat left from Boston to return to Cape Prince of Wales, where he found Hugh J. Lee in charge of the American Missionary Association. Years passed before the Newhalls again heard from their namesake. By 1910 he had married a woman named Stella (Ong-nak-luk). They were living at Cape Prince of Wales with three daughters, Agnes (Oo-ne-a-tok-ok, born in 1904), Helen (Oo-gwo-ke, born in 1907), and Siskana (eight months old in February). In 1911 Adlooat wrote thanking Dr. Newhall for his letter and things that had been sent. He mentioned Mrs. Thornton and called her "a lovely woman," adding that "her prayers and yours are keeping me well and strong." In this letter he mentioned a daughter Isabel (Ta-o-kan-na) and 2½-month-old Chester (Se-ko-won-na).[9] Adlooat was working with the village cold storage project and acting as a custodian for goods left behind by the schooner *Redfield*, a vessel owned by Captain McKenna that had wrecked nearby. He continued to practice subsistence hunting.

Adlooat wrote again in June 1913 thanking the doctor for a box of goods that he had sent. His daughters were enjoying the dolls. He promised to send a photograph of himself and his children. Apparently, he had become something of an authoritarian himself.

> We are trying to clean this village since I came back but you know the people are not willing to do any thing until now. Everybody have to clean his house and bury dead dogs. This winter we were starting a village club, which is call, "Wales improvement club." The younger people are glad to start it but I don't think the older people are glad of it, but they will have to do what we say or else get into trouble.

That letter was signed "Warren S. Adlooat," suggesting his Eskimo name had resumed prominence. Indeed, his descendants carried that surname. He and Stella eventually had seven children. Newhall wrote that Adlooat had built "an American house" and that he acted as an interpreter for the missionary. He played the organ at church, led singing, and taught Sunday school. The organ had been given to him by people in Southport, Long

THE BELVEDERE in Winter Quarters *(above) and* Herd, and Trains of Supply Sleds Crossing the Divide at Head-waters of the Kevudlena, Kookpuk, and Pitmegea Rivers, *woodcuts by Adlooat from* The Eskimo Bulletin, *Vol. IV, July 1898.*

Island. Using a loan from the captain of a revenue cutter, he had opened a small trading store which had been successful enough for him to repay the loan the following year. He also served as the official translator for the *Bear*.

Adlooat was a participant in traditional subsistence activities. In 1916 he killed the first whale caught there in 10 years. "Warren furnished enough fresh meat to feed every family at Wales for a month," *The Eskimo* reported.[10] In 1917 he was appointed assistant teacher at Wales, working under Arthur Nagozruk. One of the largest schools in Northwest Alaska, it was taught entirely by Eskimos. The following spring he was elected to the village council and served as secretary. However, that summer he was transferred to Shishmaref as assistant teacher.[11]

Dr. Newhall returned to Adlooat's story in 1918. The influenza pandemic struck coastal Alaska with fierce intensity. It eventually reached Kingegan through, according to Newhall, the dead body of a mail carrier whose funeral attracted almost the entire village. Before long, villagers fell ill and many died. Among the dead was Adlooat's mother, Wey-ak-k-nieu, who had not converted to Christianity. Adlooat himself was teaching school and assisting in mission work at Shishmaref. He had left his wife and children with wood, food and supplies for the winter. When news arrived of the influenza outbreak, he returned home to his family.

Newhall's account is filled with suppositions, imagined thoughts and conversations. What it does, almost more than anything else, is to reveal Newhall's own outlook on adversity.

> Adlooat was on the way—sad but anxious to reach his home. He found the village deserted—all was so still—as still as death—Yes death reigned in the place.—Had his loved ones gone with the rest—No they were spared to him yet but oh how ill. How he worked to save them. No efforts were spared and little by little they were getting better. A little babe was born but it passed away shortly. Those were busy days and anxious ones for Adlooat but he prayed to God for his loved ones, and believed that all would come out for the best. How he did rejoice to see his loved ones again & what a pleasure to care for them.
>
> But the time came when the aching bones, the fevered brow, the chills— the weakness were his portion. Not able to keep up longer Adlooat went to bed a victim of the dreaded flu. Now who would help to care for his family and for him.
>
> There was the promise "I will never leave thee nor forsake thee." His faith was in God, and he would trust him. The superintendent of schools at Nome heard of the illness at Kingegan and sent a good hearted Christian woman to

their help. Mrs. E.W. Tashner was a nurse in the mission hospital at Nome and when the call for help came she was more than glad to go to Kingegan and lend a helping hand to the needy and so the journey was made to the village of Kingegan. From igloo to igloo wended the steps of this good woman and to the house of Adlooat. How he did rejoice at her coming. What a load was lifted from his heart. How gentle her ministrations — how faithful the efforts and soon the wife and children were on the road to health but Adlooat grew worse and went down into the dark, dark valley.

Adlooat dictated a letter to Tashner in which he reviewed his life and thanked those who had helped him. He prayed that his life would be spared for the good of his family. "The shadows gathered," Newhall wrote. "The summons came and Adlooat passed on to the life beyond."

Dr. Newhall felt his friend had sacrificed his life for those he loved. For more than 16 years he had labored for the good of his people. Newhall acknowledged Adlooat's limitations and understood that other Inupiat men excelled his friend in various ways. Nevertheless, he compared Adlooat with the person he admired most. After Agnes Newhall died, the children of the Home and her friends erected a monument over her grave with an inscription that the doctor wrote might equally apply to Adlooat:

> Without the village of Kingegan, beneath a grassy mound, lies Adlooat asleep until the resurrection day. No monument marks his resting place but could there be erected there a remembrance in carved stone how fitting would be the inscription as a tribute to that earnest consecrated Christian life, "He hath done what he could."

Newhall kept in occasional contact with Adlooat's eldest child, Agnes. In 1920 she wrote that she had two sisters and three brothers. She was married. A letter written after that mentioned that she had two children, Frank K. Adlooat, born July 11, 1921, and Ernest Enowseak, born Feb. 20, 1923. She signed the letter Agnes O. Kiome.

Among Newhall's papers is an incomplete document, five pages, in which he copied something apparently written in part by Adlooat. If this is Adlooat's last testament, perhaps dictated to the nurse, it is remarkably coherent and detailed. He reviews his efforts to lead his people into a Christian life. When discouraged, he would remember the words of "my friend Chester — 'You can do more good by being good than any other way.'" This Chester was Dr. Newhall's brother whom Adlooat would have known in the east, and not Newhall's son who was an infant when Adlooat returned to Wales. Adlooat's reflections indicate that some people resisted accepting his message. "I find some who try to do me injury are of my own people," he said, "and I remember my Lord was the same way when he lived upon the earth that He was despised by some of his own people so I am not wondered on that account. As long as I tries to do right I will not care what other people may say against me." He tried to remember the saying, "Revenge not yourselves."

The last three pages were clearly written by Newhall himself. They tell of a religious revival that spread among reindeer herders "the second year after the arrival at Kingegan." [Perhaps 1904 if "arrival" refers to Adlooat's return home.] This was initiated by Sit-a-rang "who was an earnest Christian and had been in the Jesse Lee Home." Educated in the States, he also had returned to work among his people. As the herders went from place to place seeking better moss for the reindeer, they carried their religious enthusiasm. Eventually they arrived at Kingegan, where meetings were held in various homes. "Many people young and old were converted and started to live the new life. Ad-loo-at was happy—that was just what he had hoped and prayed for. He played the organ which the friends in Southport L.I. had given him, he led in the singing and interpreted the Word of Life to his people. He was glad for he knew that this would make them a strong people."

Dr. Newhall had been impressed by Adlooat's sincere endeavor to lead a deliberately open life as a Christian. The other Inupiat and Yup'ik children who came to the Home deepened his appreciation for these northern people. He eventually chose to spend the last five years of his life at Barrow, the Alaskan community in the heart of the region that had been the home of many of his students. On his way from Unalaska to Barrow, Newhall was unable to visit Cape Prince of Wales. At Savoonga he met a young man "whose smiling face and sturdy Christian character" made him think of Adlooat. In Nome he preached through a translator. "And was it not strange," he wrote, "that he should be a brother of Adlooat who lived with me for several years and this many years ago."[12]

1. Material for this chapter came from the Newhall manuscript and letters. Newhall later wrote a longer account (12 chapters) about Adlooat's life. This was reprinted by Norma Lowder, *The Great Physician*, 101–186.

2. Ray, *The Eskimos of Bering Strait, 1650–1898,* 214–20.

3. *WHM.* June 1902:104.

4. *WHM.* December 1901:225.

5. *WHM.* August 1901:147.

6. Annebuck, Oct. 18, 1901. NARA. RG 75. Entry 804, Letters Received, 1883–1907.

7. Adlooat to Jackson, Jan. 16, 1902. PHS. RG 239. Box 6, folder 36.

8. *WHM.* June 1902:105.

9. There is reportedly a cover photograph of Adlooat and his family in an issue of "The Work at Home," published by the Woman's Home Missionary Association of the Congregational Church of Massachusetts and Rhode Island. I have not located a copy of this. —R.H.

10. *The Eskimo.* September 1916:6

11. *The Eskimo.* July–August 1918:8

12. Newhall. "The Trip—Unalaska to Barrow. 1925." Alaska State Historical Library. MS 106. Folder 5.

14

Furlough and the Next Five Years

WHEN THE NEWHALLS AND THEIR YOUNG CHARGES LEFT UNALASKA in 1901 aboard the *Portland*, they had a good view of Priest Rock, the sentinel guarding the eastern entrance to Unalaska Bay. Shortly afterward, the vessel entered a deep fog bank that lasted for three days during which Agnes and Albert meditated "on the ups and downs of life." The *Portland* kept out at sea, bypassing the Inside Passage, until reaching Cape Flattery. At Port Townsend quarantine officers came aboard to check for smallpox. Here Sophia Tetoff first saw telegraph wires and remarked, "O my!! What for do they have their clothes lines so high?"

After dropping the girls off at Carlisle, the Newhalls and Adlooat continued on by train to Philadelphia and New York City, then north to Amsterdam and Hagaman. Agnes's mother was delighted to see them. Trips to Boston, Buffalo, Niagara Falls, and other places followed until early January when the Newhalls rented rooms in Stoneham, Massachusetts. Agnes was now seven months pregnant. In early February her mother arrived, and a month later Chester was born.

During the year in which the Newhalls were recovering their strength, renewing acquaintances, and welcoming a new member to their family, the work at the Home was managed by Elizabeth Schwab, Harriett L. Barnett and Ella A. Darling. Schwab, a graduate of the Union Missionary Training Institute of Brooklyn, sailed to Unalaska in July 1901. She was described as a person with "a beautiful spirit" and as someone who could be thoroughly relied on. Her salary was paid by the New York East Conference of the Methodist Church. She remained until early in the summer of 1905 when she left to take a medical course at Northwestern University. Schwab was joined in August 1901 by Harriett Barnett, who had been working in Utah although she was originally from Massachusetts. The WHMS noted that Barnett was "an experienced missionary, with the wisdom and scrupulous neatness acquired in a well-ordered New England home." She would spend most of the remainder of her life at Methodist missions at Unalaska and Nome. Ella Darling continued on the staff, holding kindergarten for the younger children and teaching cooking to the older girls—and perhaps having a local waterfall named after her.[1] The enrollment at the Home rose to 38 children. There were 92 in the public school.

The devastation caused by the influenza epidemic along Alaska's western coast had left hundreds of orphans. Mrs. Beiler called for the erection of another sizable building. "It is absolutely necessary," she wrote, "for the best interests of the Home, that we have another building, for boys. We have an eye to this as soon as it is practical."[2] Beiler also reported on increased expenses at the Home. A change in management at the North American Commercial Company resulted in the loss of the Home's usual 20 percent discount.[3] Oil was $40 a barrel and coal was $15 a ton. Nevertheless, she wrote, "We are there and intend to remain."

The staff at the Home initiated weekly get-togethers with village women. "We take our work and sew, and knit, or crochet," Schwab wrote. "We call it the Pleasant Afternoon Circle." Well-intentioned, the afternoons were another attempt to "win the confidence" of the local women "and lead them to Christ, and only in this way can we get so near them. . . . We must be careful not to arouse the antagonism of the priest."[4] The three women worked well together and enjoyed Unalaska. One of them wrote to Beiler:

> Here at Unalaska . . . the restless waters of Bering Sea are ever dashing their cold waves at our feet. Far too cold for bathing purposes at any season of the year, our only enjoyment of the sea lies in looking out upon it, and occasionally going boating. The mere word "Alaska" brings a shiver to ordinary mortals, but I have found that this Aleutian peninsula [sic] is an exception to much of the country. The warm ocean current that sweeps around the point equalizes the temperature, and were it not for the piercing winds the climate would be comparatively mild. There is a much longer rainfall here than is desirable, the wholly clear days being few in number, but when the sun does appear it is a signal for a general holiday. Regular duties are laid aside whenever possible, and then away to the hills, or out upon the water—anywhere to be in the rare and delightful sunshine.[5]

The saga of John and Mary Tuck's relationship with Unalaska also ended in 1901. Mary had died on Feb. 10, 1899, three days after undergoing surgery. "It is probable that my wife carried with her to Alaska the trouble that at last resulted fatally," Tuck informed Sheldon Jackson when replying to a letter of condolence.[6] "Her increase in size and weight about a year after going there was doubtless due to a considerable growth of the tumor." The last 2½ years of her life were comparatively comfortable. They had moved to Chicago where John was teaching school. As she assembled a scrapbook about Alaska, Mary expressed an interest in returning to missionary work. After her death John gave the scrapbook to the society. They used a number of her clippings in subsequent publications, noting "though dead she yet speaketh."

By late 1900 or early 1901 Tuck decided to challenge the treatment he had received from the missionary society. He thought Maria Freeman Gray, Lycurgus Woodward, and Mattie Short (Hastings) had maligned him, and that Lydia Daggett had done nothing to defend his reputation. When his "exceedingly modest claims" for reimbursement of expenses were ignored, he wrote again adding as many claims as he could think of that stood any chance of success during arbitration. The total came to over $2,000. The society was horrified, even when he explained that he would donate every cent back to them as a memorial to his wife.

Delia Williams, corresponding secretary for the board of directors, wrote to Jackson for help. Apparently no contract had ever been signed between Tuck and the society. Many of those who could have clarified the situation were now dead. Tuck insisted that "the verbal contract entered into had reference to conditions of labor and responsibility radically different from those we encountered." Worst of all was Tuck's threat to expose what he called the "crookedness in the business dealings between the Government and the Woman's Home Missionary Society, which we would be much embarrassed to have him expose."[7]

Jackson may have advised the society, but he did not directly intervene. In 1902 the society sent Tuck a check for $300 and a receipt for a gift of $2,000. He wrote Jackson that he would add to the $300 by the sale of curios and "the set of very valuable sable furs" he had brought from Alaska, and would use the money as "the nucleus" of a memorial to his wife.[8] He maintained an active interest in Alaska and collected all the published reports on education in the territory. He continued to teach in Chicago, living with his mother and then taking in boarders after her death. For his part, Jackson was relieved a settlement had been reached; the controversy had been "exceedingly unpleasant" to him as he was "a warm friend of both parties."

·˙·

THE NEWHALLS REMAINED IN THE EAST until May 24, 1902, when they departed Boston for a long trip back to Unalaska. Leaving was always difficult, and this farewell was especially poignant because Albert's father was feeble and they did not expect to see him again. They traveled through Vermont and New York, where they saw Buffalo Bill's parade in Troy, and on through Pennsylvania. At Carlisle they picked up Annie King, who was to live with her uncle. In San Francisco they boarded the A.C. Co.'s steamer *St. Paul*, which took them all the way to St. Michael and Nome and finally, after a sea voyage of 22 days with a newborn infant, to Unalaska on September 5. Dr. Newhall had purchased a dozen Plymouth rock chickens in San Francisco. He had forgotten to purchase grit for them, but they survived as far as St. Michael. There a husky aboard the ship slipped its chain at night and in the morning only "a few feathers were left to tell the tale." A year later a dozen live chickens arrived at Unalaska as a gift from the A.C. Co. Before long the flock had grown and there were so many eggs that some could be sold to the community.

A Mrs. Springer traveled from Nome to Unalaska with the Newhalls. She visited the mission for a day while the vessel was coaling and recorded the names of various rooms: The chapel was named for Eliza Jane Baker; Harriett Barnett's room had recently been repainted and was named for the Rock River Conference; the Newhalls' room was called after Frances Negus, Northwest Iowa Conference; and the dining room bore the name

New England Conference. She noted that the library, parlor and hall were carpeted. Dr. Newhall told her how the weather attacked even the best built structures. "Boards are carefully arranged under the windows to carry off the water," Springer wrote, "but it comes through even where there are no windows."[9] On stormy days, Albert and the older boys hauled pails of water from various leaks around the building. Springer was told that within four hours during one stormy night the doctor carried 21 pails of water from four windows.

Dr. Newhall resumed his role as superintendent. Agnes took no official position. As Anna Beiler put it, she would do "what she may feel able to do in the hospital and in visiting among natives."[10] She was, however, perpetually active. In the fall of 1902 she made a quilt into which she worked the names of each of the 85 children who had been in her care.[11] She bought a thousand salmon at a penny each and prepared them for the winter. "I do not know what we should have done without Mrs. Newhall," wrote Ella Darling in July 1903. "There is so much to do. Nearly everything that comes in barrels and boxes needs some change or repair." Both women were busy converting old dresses into shirts for the boys and old raincoats into trousers. There were few older girls in the Home at this time and so "the medium-sized girls have to be classed as big girls, which of course they like, except for the work."[12]

Agnes was pregnant again and on Oct. 22, 1903, she gave birth to her last child, a daughter who was named Edith Marguerite Newhall.

. .

WITH THE RETURN OF THE NEWHALLS, a period of stabilization began in which staff positions were clearly defined and the complex relationships with various segments of Unalaska society were gradually articulated. People who reside in the Aleutians long enough learn to live with earthquakes. The violent rupture between the Home and the Orthodox community gradually closed. The Home and the school became distinct institutions however much they might share attitudes and goals. Agnes and Albert Newhall began to raise a family of their own. They refined their missionary goals and deepened their ties to the community at large. These are the years that children at the Home and in the community remembered with fondness and thanksgiving.

The Home's Sunday school had 44 enrolled; in 1903–1904 it received 111 visitors. All staff members assisted with classes. The overt demonizing of the Orthodox Church ceased as the Newhalls came to know and appreciate the members of the local clergy. The missionary society, however, continued to excoriate Orthodoxy in statements such as one in 1904 which referred to the Home's "efficient" work "built out of the waifs discarded by the Russian-Greek Church."[13] Another, from the following year, referred to "the superstitious and gross heathenish practices inculcated by the Russian Greek Church" and how these made it "more difficult to reach the Aleutes than if they had never heard of Christ."[14] The Orthodox Church was blamed for regional poverty, as though it were responsible for the dramatic over-hunting of sea otters. Agnes and Albert Newhall generally remained aloof from this uncharitable rhetoric. They began to understand what was appropriate and what was not when dealing with their neighbors. As a result, adults and children from the community began to visit the Home. When a child at the Home had a birthday, village children attended the celebration and frequently impressed the staff with their behavior. Among Aleut children in the Home were Henry, Sophia, and Agnes Swanson of Unalaska, and Charles and Polly Dirks of Atka. Peter Kashevaroff, son of the Orthodox priest at St. George, was a frequent visitor. He was a clerk at the A.C. Co. and was courting one of the older girls at the Home, Eliza Gould. Henry Swanson recalled those visits.

> Eliza Gould was just like mama to me. I was there at the Jesse Lee Home when Peter was courting her. I was about ten or eleven years old and I used to bother them a lot. I thought, "Gee, whiz! That crazy Peter coming up from the store in the evening and sitting with a damn girl! That girl is supposed to be out here playing with us." Of course, she was a grown-up woman. I was just a kid. So I used to go in there and pester them. I'd stand in front of them until Peter gave me some candy. This was every evening. One evening I went in there and he had no candy. He was nervous there, picking his fingernails with his pocket knife. I said, "Okay. I'll take the knife." So he gave it to me![15]

Plans for a hospital were now incorporated into those for a boys' dormitory. Materials arrived and construction began in June 1903. The projected building was valued at $5,000.[16] Newhall oversaw the construction, which progressed on schedule although he had to use his own salary to pay the final bills. (The society eventually reimbursed him.) The new dormitory went into service that fall and the doctor was pleased with its construction and design.[17] It was east of the main Jesse Lee Home, and a boardwalk ran between them. Although the Home had gone through various surveys and property disputes, no clear record was kept of title to the land. In 1906 the society wrote to Jackson confessing that neither it nor the Methodist Church could find a clear title. "No doubt Mrs. Beiler had information upon this point," wrote the corresponding secretary of the board, "but no one left seems to know about it."[18] The writer assumed the Home sat on government property.

The Newhalls moved into a new room and were in charge of the boys' dormitory. Dr. Newhall read to them in the evenings. After listening to *Pilgrim's Progress* for a while, one of the boys was seen walking around with a large flour sack filled with rags strapped to his back. "It's my burden of sins," he answered when asked. As soon as the supper bell rang, however, he found deliverance. During the winter of 1904–1905 Newhall read from *Youth's Companion*, a monthly periodical. "The last story was of great interest," he wrote, "about a young American making a trip from the States to Sitka, and across Siberia to Saint Petersburg. How the boys and girls crowded up to me on the benches as I read it aloud! I could scarcely move my elbows." In the middle of the story, the subscription ended.

JESSE LEE BOYS *on the beach at Unalaska. Courtesy of Alaska Children's Services, Anchorage.*

Newspapers were passed from house to house, from saloon to store to house to Home. "How eagerly I read about the election of Roosevelt in February," Newhall wrote, "almost time for his inauguration!"[19]

The doctor and his wife established an efficient hospital ward. In 1904 Newhall had 32 patients from the Home and 195 from the community or from visiting ships. He made 609 home visits.[20] In 1905 he had 32 patients from the Home and 190 from outside. He made 457 visits within the community and 158 at the Home. He extracted 52 teeth.[21] Agnes began spending more and more time assisting in the hospital.

A generous gift of a thousand dollars was earmarked for improvements to living conditions in both buildings. With this money a laundry room was completed, freeing the dining room in the girls' building from the drying clothes of 40 people. A water pump was installed along with pipes leading from the lake to the boys' dorm and hospital. The Newhalls had a dresser in their bedroom and each of the staff women had a comfortable chair in her room. Shades for the windows were ordered.

On Feb. 10, 1905, Agnes Newhall answered specific questions from Lavinia Wallace Young, now the secretary for the Alaska Bureau. She began by describing activities in the original Jesse Lee Home.

> Miss Schwab has charge of the cooking, laundry work, and the care of rooms on the first floor—parlor, reception room, hall, kitchen, teachers' dining room, students' dining room, and pantry. She also conducts the crocheting class, and mends the boys' working clothes.
>
> Miss Barnett has charge of the second and third floors, which include the sewing room, two dormitories, storeroom, and the teachers' sleeping rooms. She looks after the drying and ironing of the clothes, the bathing of the girls, and the many duties connected with getting fourteen girls off to school at nine o'clock each weekday morning. Such time as is left after attending to these duties is spent at the sewing machine.
>
> My duties are as follows: I have charge of the boys' dormitory and hospital, care of the sick, the drying and mending of thirty pairs of stockings each week, the knitting class one hour each day, the making of all the new clothing, the care of the boys' Sunday clothes, and the getting twelve boys off to school each school day at nine o'clock. . . .
>
> The doctor's duties are so numerous I do not know where to begin. He has charge of the mission, all of the business, of the outdoor work, which means the care of thirty chickens, two cows, the garden, fishing and haying in summer, mending shoes, repairing buildings and fences, in addition to his regular medical work, which means a good deal, since he is the only physician in the place.

Then, most important of all for all of us is our religious work. We try to keep this uppermost at all times. With so many young bodies to care for, we sometimes fear that we are spending more time upon them than upon their souls, but we do try to teach them to love God and to keep his commandments.[22]

Young was new to her job and turned to Sheldon Jackson for advice and information. He sent her copies of reports and gave her specific information about ways of transporting missionaries to the territory. Looking toward further development, she asked if there were any other location within "Methodist territory" where a mission should be established. She also inquired why their work at Unga had been stopped. The energy with which she pursued the Alaska work ground to a halt when, after November, weeks went by without mail arriving from Unalaska. March came and still nothing. She feared there was truth in the rumor about the loss of the *Dora*, the stout little "workhouse of the Aleutians" that carried mail between Unalaska and Valdez. As it turned out, the ship had left Kodiak on Dec. 28, 1905, and been swept out to sea in a terrible storm. It drifted without power for more than 2,000 miles, finally arriving in Port Angeles, Washington, on March 2.[23]

The Newhalls became adept at balancing the various factions within the village. Two major commercial companies were still vying for a declining business: the long established Alaska Commercial Company in the village and the North American Commercial Company at Dutch Harbor, which had operated since 1890. In addition, there were smaller stores and independent businessmen and vessel owners. Relations among these competing parties were frequently hostile.

Nicholas Bolshanin was among the Newhalls' friends. Born in Sitka around 1875, he was involved in numerous economic developments at Unalaska and served as deputy U.S. commissioner for several years. In 1903 he built a 17-foot rowboat for the Home. It was named *The Perchment*, after the man who gave $35 for its construction at one of the annual meetings of the missionary society. Materials cost $23 and Bolshanin donated his labor. It was a graceful boat, white with a green saxboard and bottom, with "Jesse Lee Home" in green at the bow. It took three pairs of oars to operate. With this Dr. Newhall and the older boys were able to secure cod and salmon. The boat was also used for trips to the store at Dutch Harbor or when the doctor's services were required there. In 1907 Bolshanin taught ivory carving to the boys.[24] In 1910 he married Olga Reinken, who had lived in the Home and attended school at Carlisle. She was a sister of Henry Swanson's mother.

Nicholas Gray, whom John Tuck had counted among his foes, now supported the work and even gave the Home a discount on purchases. Gray acted as deputy U.S. commissioner before Bolshanin took the post, although the agent at the N.A.C. Co. at Dutch Harbor thought this created a conflict of interest. Gray and Dr. Newhall worked together to get the local saloons closed in 1904. According to Newhall, people "became disgusted" as it was now "unsafe for respectable women to be out alone in the village, especially at cer-

NICHOLAS GRAY, *born in Russia and fully bilingual, began his long career with the A.C. Co. as a schoolteacher at Unalaska in 1880. After teaching several years at St. Paul in the Pribilof Islands, he became a bookkeeper at Unalaska and gradually rose to the position of store manager. His attitude toward the Home changed from antipathy to full support. Courtesy of the Alaska State Library, Historical Collections (Michael Z. Vinokouroff Photograph Collection, P243-2-181).*

tain times."[25] According to the agent at Dutch Harbor, however, Gray decided to close the saloons after the town's jailer lost his money gambling in one of them. A petition was circulated and the saloon keepers boycotted the A.C. Co. Gray made a distinction between the village—"a native town"—and Dutch Harbor—"a white man's town."[26] The closure was short-lived and the saloons soon reopened. Then on Sept. 24, 1905, a sailor from the *Bear* was discovered unconscious along the boardwalk that ran from the A.C. Co. store to the dock. There were at least two saloons along this boardwalk. Dr. James White, ship's surgeon, worked on him for an hour, but the sailor died and was buried on the 26th. The captain wrote to the saloon owners that he would pursue the forfeiture of their licenses. In 1891 the government had claimed the first 1,000 feet of land from the wharf as a government reserve. In the spring of 1906, the marshal received instructions from the court at Valdez to order all white men living or doing business there off this property. Only the A.C. Co. was allowed to remain, because of its historical claim to the land. The saloon owners moved into locations outside this reserve.[27] By then there was little money at Unalaska to support the saloons anyway. No ship had arrived from Nome for two years, and the locals had little work.

Visitors from out of town would occasionally drop by the Home. When callers arrived, as Harriett Barnett wrote, "one of us, sometimes two, must spend an hour or more in the parlor. We want people to get a good impression of the Home, and this is perhaps our best advertisement."[28] In 1903 there was a visit from U.S. senators from New Hampshire, Vermont, Minnesota, and Colorado during a tour of the territory. On another occasion, the captain of the *Marblehead* loaned the ship's phonograph to the Home for an evening of music. John and Edith Kilbuck stopped in May or June 1904 on their way to Point Barrow. They had worked among Yup'ik people of the Kuskokwim River region since 1885. Mr. Brevig of the Teller Mission and Mr. Henrickson of the Swedish Evangelical Mission at Golovin also called at the Home.

Ella Darling left in the spring of 1904 and soon married a Mr. McCurdy. She wrote that the continuous work made service at Unalaska particularly difficult. "We get no intermission from our labor here, which makes the care and nervous strain greater. I am sorry that we are not a stronger generation, so that we might without impunity take years of toil upon us without the fear of breaking!"[29] In the 1908–09 annual report a similar complaint was expressed. After stating that three children had died from tuberculosis that year, the report said, "While our missionaries do not have tuberculosis, they do become worn and nervous, and it is decided by the Secretaries and Boards in charge of work in Alaska that three years [instead of five] is as long as any worker should remain in the field, there being no chance for vacation or change without returning to this country."[30]

In September 1904 Agnes's mother arrived for an extended visit. She was an immense help to her daughter. She mended clothes and knitted 35 pairs of stockings before leaving in the spring. With her went Elizabeth Schwab, who had worked at the Home for four

From the original caption: "A VIEW OF THE TWO-STORY METHODIST MISSION CHURCH *with a bell tower in Nome, Alaska, with a dog lying on the boardwalk in the foreground, 1920." Courtesy of the Consortium Library, University of Alaska Anchorage, Archives & Manuscripts Dept. (Wilson W. Brine Papers, 1919–1926, 1938, UAA-hmc-0074).*

From the original caption: "NOME, ALASKA, JULY 4TH PARADE, *1918. Lomen Bros., Nome," P.S. Hunt (1866–1917), photographer. Courtesy of the Alaska and Polar Regions Collections, Elmer E. Rasmuson Library, University of Alaska Fairbanks (John Zug Album, 80-68-255).*

years. Schwab's replacement, Rebecca Wunderlich, arrived later in the summer of 1905 from Sandy Hook, Connecticut. She had taught three years in country schools. In Seattle she met Mabel Benedict, from Los Angeles, who was also heading to Unalaska. They sailed on July 16. In Valdez they transferred to the *Dora*. Dr. Newhall sent authorization for them to take custody in Chignik of a 16-month-old child whose mother had died. They arrived at Unalaska on August 9. Agnes was at the dock expecting to welcome only one new worker. She wept for joy on discovering that two young women had arrived to assist her. The letter telling that Mabel Benedict had been recruited arrived on the boat with her.

A week later Wunderlich wrote enthusiastically about Unalaska.

> I am enjoying my work immensely. . . . Much of Mrs. Newhall's time is spent at the hospital. On Wednesday afternoon a party of twenty of us went out for a ramble. One cannot really walk here without climbing a hill, but we found beautiful flowers, blue flags of different shades of blue, wild geraniums, daisies, delicate yellow meadow rues, and blue grass plants. We also found the blue moss berry and the salmon berries, which are nearly ripe. In a few days we expect to gather enough of these for a treat for our family of forty-three people, including twenty-one girls and fifteen boys. From the hill we could see nearly the whole town. The Home buildings make quite a little settlement on the east end. There are about twenty-one white people here, and one white woman outside the Home, a Mrs. Harmon. Several white men have married Russian or part native wives. . . . Our garden gives us spinach, radishes, and lettuce. The rhubarb crop promises an abundance in the future, and we expect that October will bring us a fine crop of turnips.[31]

A letter from Mabel Benedict, written the same autumn, confirmed Wunderlich's optimistic impressions. She wrote, "We were sorely needed, for I do not know how two women [Agnes Newhall and Barnett] kept everything going as these did. They certainly had it too hard. Miss Wunderlich and I think ourselves very fortunate in having such pleasant surroundings. The children are clothed comfortably and nicely, and have good fare. There are nice soups and puddings for the little ones; in fact, they have the same kind of food we do. It is all cooked together, and there is an abundance. Mrs. Newhall and Miss Barnett are capable and economical. The children are nicely trained and very affectionate."[32]

Benedict wrote that the father of two boys, George and Innokentii, had made arrangements for them to be brought to the Home after his death. Their mother moved to Unalaska to be near them. Benedict found the girl children in the Home and in the village to have "a delicacy and refinement in their features. . . ." She also noted that Agnes Newhall was soon to go to the Home's summer camp where she would pick and dry berries for the winter. Some of the boys would accompany her to pick berries. "She needs a rest," wrote Benedict, "and looks forward to the quiet." Benedict collected Native baskets; when Henry Dirks came to visit his children she was able to purchase two large baskets from Atka "for the bargain counter price of six dollars."[33]

When Benedict left Unalaska in September 1908 she took five girls from the Home: Anna Gould, Nellie Tilton, Alexandra and Stepinita Oustigoff from the Pribilof Islands, and Sophia Swanson, Henry Swanson's sister. According to an annual report, Benedict had adopted Sophia, "who had so entwined herself around her heart that she could not bear to leave her." When the ship came in sight of Puget Sound, Sophia asked, "Miss Benedict, is that a piece of the states?" Benedict had leveled charges against sailors, including men on the revenue cutters, accusing them of "debauching the natives of the Aleutian Islands." The *Seattle Post Intelligencer* reported that she had left Seattle for San Francisco for the start of a tour of the United States when she was subpoenaed to appear before a federal grand jury at Valdez on November 24.[34] However, she was able to attend the annual meeting of the missionary society in Philadelphia at which Sophia Swanson and Nellie Tilton sang for the assembly. The Oustigoff girls were placed in a school, and Benedict took Sophia and Nellie to her home in Ramapo, New York.

Harriet Barnett, who had filled the position of matron for five years, left for a year's leave in 1906. Margaret Powell of Portland, Oregon, filled that position until June 1907, when she accepted an appointment as a schoolteacher for Sinuk, a community near Nome. The Newhalls had found her a person of "excellent spirit, never outwardly ruffled amid the cares and trials incident to a life in such a large household." They were sorry to see her go.

The Methodist Church had opened the Hilah Seward Industrial Home and Orphanage in Sinuk (also known as Sinrock) in July 1906. It was associated with the introduction of reindeer to the Seward Peninsula. Margaret Powell's sister and her husband, M.A. Sellon, were in charge of the mission in 1907. Nellie M. Cramer, M.D., and Inez Walthall worked at Sinuk for many years and the mission flourished. In 1911 the Lavinia Wallace Young Mission was established at Nome under the leadership of Harriet Barnett. In 1913 W.F. Baldwin arrived, and gradually more and more facilities were built at Nome, including a church, parsonage, workshop, gymnasium, and the Maynard-Columbus Hospital, in 1917. In 1919 the children living in the Hilah Home were moved to a newly established orphanage in Nome.

NOTES

1. As a boy in 1907 Henry Swanson wrote about hiking to Darling Falls. The name is unknown today.

2. *WHM*. August 1901:147.

3. Woman's Home Missionary Society, Reports from Bureaus. 1900-1901:122.

4. *WHM*. June 1902:103.

5. *WHM*. May 1903:82.

6. Tuck to Jackson, April 5, 1899. PHS. RG 239. Box 6, folder 22.

7. Delia L. Williams to Jackson, March 7, 1901. PHS. RG 239. Box 6, folder 32.

8. Tuck to Jackson, June 9, 1902. PHS. RG 239. Box 7, folder 2.

9. *WHM*. May 1903:85.

10. *WHM*. June 1902:103.

11. *WHM*. May 1903:85.

12. *WHM*. April 1904:64.

13. *WHM*. April 1904:63.

14. Woman's Home Missionary Society, Reports from Bureaus. 1904–05:110.

15. Swanson, *The Unknown Islands*, 19.

16. Newhall, Albert. Fragment of a letter to William L. Distin, Surveyor General, Sitka, Alaska, late 1902, as part of an application for an official survey of mission property. Hudson, ed., *Cuttlefish: Volumes One, Two & Three, Stories of Aleutian Culture & History*, 240.

17. *WHM*. April 1904:66. Henry Swanson said both this building and the marshal's home and office, built about the same time, were constructed by a McCurdy.

18. Delia L. Williams to Jackson, May 1, 1906. PHS. RG 239. Box 7, folder 23.

19. *WHM*. July 1905:134.

20. Ibid.

21. Woman's Home Missionary Society, Reports from Bureaus. 1904–05: 109.

22. *WHM*. April 1905:68.

23. "Steamer Dora is Safe," *The Alaskan*. March 3, 1906.

24. *WHM*. October 1907:185. He died Dec. 4, 1957.

25. *WHM*. April 1904:65.

26. North American Commercial Company Log Copy Book, May 10, 1904-Aug. 11, 1905. July 7, 1904. Alaska Commercial Company Records. Archives of the Arctic and Polar Regions Collections of the Elmer E. Rasmuson Library, University of Alaska Fairbanks.

27. Applegate to "Friend Ross." Aug. 1, 1906. Alaska State Historical Library. MS 0003.

28. *WHM*. May 1903:84.

29. *WHM*. April 1904:61.

30. Woman's Home Missionary Society, Reports from Bureaus. 1908–09:140.

31. *WHM*. October 1905:191.

32. *WHM*. January 1906:247.

33. In 1911 Benedict sold 52 baskets from Alaska and Canada to the American Museum of Natural History in New York City for $565.

34. *Seattle Post Intelligencer*. Oct. 14, 1908.

WALKING FROM THE BOYS' HOUSE, 1912. *On the back of the original photo is written: "The Boys as they look coming over to dinner. Theodore Nutbeam, Daniel Sipary, George Porter, Fred Chipitnoi, Nicholi Peterson, Paul Morton, Peter Saposnikoff, Peter Golivin, Innokenti Peterson, Simeon Oliver, George Peterson, James Palatoff, Charles Lee, Nick Hanson, Johnie Saposnikoff, Teddy Peterson, Cecil Waln, Baby Nick Peterson. Superintendents' house and Mt. Newhall and Miss Winchell and Mrs. Newhall and Edith. Taken June 18, 1912, from Clara Cook." Courtesy of the Unalaska City School District (Clara Cook Collection).*

15

Children from the Arctic

By 1902 the Home had been expecting Yup'ik and Inupiat children from the North for several years. They would fill places vacated by Aleut children who had been removed by their parents or who had left the home for marriage or employment. "We are expecting a dozen Esquimaux from the North, and others from the mainland next summer," wrote Beiler in her 1897–98 report. Mixing her metaphors, she continued, "These will be entirely virgin soil, and we feel more can be accomplished with these than with those who have been kept under the bondage of superstition. Yet we intend to do all we can for those on the Aleutian Chain. Especially are we anxious for moral and spiritual growth, that comes only with the spirit of 'Him who went about doing good.'" The following year, however, she had to report, "The Esquimaux, whom we anticipated coming from the Arctic, have not yet come to us. We trust this is only a temporary delay."

Adlooat had arrived and left before the first group of Eskimo children appeared in late 1902. Harriett Barnett recorded their arrival.

> On November 17, 1902, the children rushed into the house shouting, "The *Bear* is coming! the *Bear* is coming!" Of course all ran to the windows—not to see a hungry bear descending from the hills upon our little settlement, but the white and graceful revenue cutter *Bear* entering the harbor from Bering Sea, on her last trip from the North for the season. We were hoping she might bring us some of the children of whom rumor had reached us from time to time, and lo, she had.

> Word soon came that seven Eskimos had arrived, all to become inmates of the Home. Soon the procession was seen coming up the street, and a droll one it was to eyes not accustomed to the native costume. The parkas (coat and hood combined) covered the person nearly to the knees, and with the girls were even longer. And the *mukluks*, or covering for the feet, were long boots made of the skin of the hair seal. . . . The little party were soon seated in the parlor, their impedimenta in an irregular heap in an adjoining room, and the work of getting acquainted with their names and with them begun. Only two could speak much English. . . . They had come to us to learn, and wanted to go to school. They had never seen a piano, and that instrument impressed them very much, having, as we afterward learned, an ear for music, and all good voices.[1]

Five of the children were from Golovin Bay: Oscar Ungeuk (age 16), Samuel Simooluk (16), Garfield Nutakiuk (15), Molly Shitukanuk (15) and Edward Owkan. Two others were from Unalakleet (Unalaklit): George Segauk (10) and Annie Aneeuk (12).[2]

Aneeuk was a foster child of Mary Antisarlook Andrewuk (Changunak), widely known for her work with reindeer. She was the wealthiest Native woman in the north and extended her protection to numerous children. Aneeuk was soon diagnosed with tuberculosis. Harriett Barnett felt the warmth of her hand when first meeting her "and glancing up observed the pink flush upon the cheek, and marked the quick rise and fall of the chest. 'Ah,' I thought, 'consumption has marked this child for its victim.'" Aneeuk gradually grew weak and was eventually bedridden. She died on December 30, 1902. The staff had communicated with her through an interpreter. The boys made a rough coffin and covered it inside and out with white muslin. She was buried in her arctic clothing, in "her snowy robe" on the last day of the year.[3]

Segauk Antisarlook, known in English as George Walker, had been adopted by Mary Antisarlook Andrewuk (Changunak). George was the son of a Portuguese sailor and the African-American cook aboard a whaler. After his mother died, Mary adopted him and in 1902 sent him to the Home.[4] Harriett Barnett wrote that one child was "a bright and interesting little fellow of ten—a mixture of Negro and Portuguese."

At least two of the new boys were old enough to work for the North American Commercial Company at Dutch Harbor for two weeks in June 1903. They took their earnings in clothing from the company store. Later that summer they dried salmon near Wislow Island at Reese Bay, west of Unalaska, for the Home's winter use.[5] On Oct. 4, 1903, Molly Shitukanuk left to attend Carlisle Indian School. A month later three of the boys—Oscar Ungeuk, Garfield Nutakiuk, and Edward Owkan—sailed on the *Bear* to attend the same school.[6] Perhaps they arrived in time to watch Nikifer Schuchuk play center for the Carlisle football team. Although there is no record of him attending the Home, he was described as "an Eskimo. . . . from the Aleutian islands, on the American side of the frigid Bering sea."[7]

"One time there were five young men in the Jesse Lee Home," Dr. Newhall later recalled the first Eskimo boys. "When prayer meeting night came all the boys would sit on low benches—the five Eskimo and the rest Aleut." The Eskimo boys took turns praying in their own language—apparently at some length. "When they would finish," Newhall wrote, "all the other boys would be laid out around on the floor asleep and snoring."

Other children from the North followed; among them were several who became among the best known Jesse Lee Home alumni. Eleven-year-old William Baylies (Catua) arrived in October 1903. Simeon Oliver (Nutchuk) and Dick Hansen (Owchoouk or Aughoouk) came in 1904. Oliver was two and Hansen was 18. Hansen stayed one year; Oliver, 17. According to the April 1905 issue of *Woman's Home Missions*, four Eskimo girls had also joined the Home. They had actually arrived on Oct. 21, 1904: Nellie Tilton

(Alagoona), age 9; Leila Norwood (Iriluk), 11; Mary Ann Hopson (Unukseruk), 9; and Lucy Leavitt (Pupkena). Two years later Jennie Alexander (Abuk) arrived. George Porter (Oslooluk), age 12, joined the Home in 1907. In 1910 Akawanna Seymour, the wife of William Seymour, arrived with her daughter Margaret (Aganuksuk) from Herschel Island. The next year Akawanna returned to her husband leaving Margaret at the Home. Mary (Turagana) and John (Nanoona) Carpenter were brought from Herschel Island in 1912.[8]

Several of these students came from the Canadian arctic. The ships that carried them sailed from Herschel Island, but the children themselves may have been from villages on the mainland. Herschel Island—which author John Bockstoce has described as "a wide brown lens on the horizon"[9]—lies just west of the Mackenzie River and 50 miles east of the Alaska/Canada border. The island was a resting place for whalers who would sometimes spend the winter in Pauline Cove. Among the children known to have come from there are Jennie Alexander, Lucy Leavitt, Nellie Tilton, Mary Carpenter, Margaret Seymour, William Baylies, and John Carpenter.

Henry Swanson, renowned in later life as a storyteller and expert on the islands, remembered the whalers coming into port. "There was about a dozen whaling boats came up here," he said. "*Belvedere* was one of them. Let's see, there was *Belvedere, Karluk, Gayhead, Jeanette, William Baylies,* and *Alexander.* That's six of them, but there was more. Of course, Dutch Harbor was going full blast in the whaling days. That's where the whalers stopped to pick up coal and everything."[10] He said that at least two of the children were named for the vessels that brought them to Unalaska. William Baylies arrived on the steam bark *William Baylies* in 1903 and stayed until 1911 or 1912 when, according to Henry, he returned to the north.

Jennie Alexander was named after the *Alexander*, a vessel that made 10 whaling voyages between 1894 and 1905. Jennie was 11 when she arrived at the Jesse Lee Home. She was born somewhere around the mouth of the Mackenzie River in 1895 and given the name Abuk. Her mother, Ewana, died when she was an infant and she was raised by her grandmother until she was old enough to live with her father, Kaniya. She hunted seals with him and they sold the skins to whalers. When he was absent on long hunting trips or worked for one of the whaling captains, she stayed with her uncle, Kalalul, and his wife and daughter. After her father's death, her uncle took her to Herschel Island, but he sickened and died shortly after they arrived. Abuk was taken in by one of her father's friends. When Captain Benjamin Tilton arrived he brought her aboard the *Alexander*, explaining that Kaniya had given him permission. On Aug. 13, 1906, the *Alexander* was traveling under steam and sail in thick fog when the voyage ended abruptly at Cape Parry, some 500 miles east of Herschel Island. Jennie Alexander herself wrote the story around 1912.

One morning early most of us were in bed sleeping. Only those who had to stay and run the ship were up. The first thing we knew we were on the rocks!

We had to get dressed as quickly as we could and get off the ship because it was leaking very fast. There were nine boats full of people, and each boat took with them one sack of flour and canned fruits and crackers and some other things that do not have to be cooked.

There was a crazy man who was on another whaler. The captain of that whaler did not want him on board, and so he put him ashore, and Captain Tilton took him on his whaler and was going to take him down. When the ship was wrecked there were two cats and two squirrels on board. This crazy man took care of them himself. He used to feed them with his own food. When it was raining, he would take them under his coat. Sometimes he would put me under his raincoat, too, and keep me dry. He used to talk to himself most of the time. When we got to Baillie Island we went ashore to stay over night. And this crazy man took the two squirrels and let them go, and took the cats and tied string around their necks. And after all the care he had taken of them, he threw them into the lake and they were drowned.

That same day the cook made pancake dough and did not have anything to fry it in. So, one of the men went along the beach and brought a flat stone, and the cook fried them and we ate them all. When we Eskimos eat whale blubber, the white men always make fun of us because we eat it. But after while they ate it with us in the boat and never made fun of us again.

The next day we started for Herschel Island. It was a long way. It took us nine or ten days to get there. We did not see land any of the time anywhere. Every time when the boat went down I thought we would sink. The waves were so high. I used to cry most of the time, but Captain Tilton would tell me not to cry. He used to tell me not to look at the sea. But even if I did not look at the sea, I would feel when the waves were going up and down.

After we got to Herschel Island we were glad that Captain McKenna's schooner was there. We were going down in the sailing boats if it had not been there. As soon as we got there, we went to the schooner and ate supper and slept there. The next morning they heard that my uncle was going to get me, but Captain McKenna said he was going to start early in the morning so we were gone when my uncle got there. And that's how I came to the Jesse Lee Home.[11]

She had not been at the Home too many months when Lucy Leavitt and Nellie Tilton joined her. Lucy was the daughter of Captain George Leavitt who had a long career in the western Arctic whaling business. While at the Home, she too wrote an account of her childhood in the Herschel Island area. Although Lucy spent the rest of her life in the

LUCY LEAVITT. *Courtesy of the Unalaska City School District (Clara Cook Collection).*

Aleutians, George Leavitt had a number of sons who remained in the North and established families. About Nellie Tilton, Henry Swanson once said:

> Captain Tilton had a daughter in the Home—Nellie. I saw her in New
> York in 1917 when I was in the Navy. They called her father "Big Foot" Tilton
> on account of him coming overland when all the whalers were stuck up there
> that one winter. They drove a herd of reindeer up for 'em, but he came all the
> way across Alaska. Took him quite a while. Everything was all over with by the
> time he got down to Kodiak or somewhere down there. Well, he was a big
> man, and he also had big feet.[12]

The problem with this particular story is that "Big Foot" Tilton was George Fred
Tilton, third mate of the *Belvedere,* one of nine ships Henry refers to that were trapped in
the ice in late 1897. Nellie's father was Captain James A. Tilton of the whaling steamer
Herman. Nevertheless, Nellie had her own adventure. Captain Tilton sought permission
from Captain Henderson of the revenue cutter *Thetis* to take his daughter to Unalaska. He
explained that he had "two other children" living at the Home who had Eskimo mothers.
Henderson told Tilton he would need written permission, and Tilton promised to apply
for this. Henderson was scandalized by the relations between whalers and Native
women—especially after another whaler, William Mogg, asked for transportation for himself and the unmarried mother of his three children to *his* ship, the *Olga,* at Barrow, where
they promised to marry. Henderson said he would marry them after he took the *Thetis* to
Teller to obtain water.

Not wanting to wait for his permit—or for the ice —to arrive, Tilton left with Nellie,
Mogg and Mogg's fiancée. The lawbreakers, as Henderson considered them, had a six-hour
headstart, and he might have given chase if he had known the *Herman's* destination beyond
the vague "somewhere along the Siberian coast." Tilton, as it turned out, dropped the couple at Barrow where a Presbyterian missionary performed the marriage.[13] He then continued to Unalaska where Nellie was left at the Home.

Simeon Oliver (Nutchuk) was about two years old when he arrived. Eventually he
became a pianist, author and lecturer who did more than any other resident to make the
Home known. His father, James Holveg, was from Oslo. His mother, Kueuit, was either
from St. Michael or from a village in the Kuskokwim River region.[14] Oliver's account of his
parents' meeting on a frozen lake near Chignik on the Alaska Peninsula is full of drama
and romance. After rescuing Kueuit from death by freezing, Holveg left her with friends
at Chignik. She was a teenager and was sent to the States for education. After she returned,
she and Holveg were married. She was 18 and he was 45. He had changed his name to
Oliver by this time. Simeon was born at Chignik in the summer of 1903. Kueuit died two
years later following the birth of a daughter, Christine. James Oliver took his daughter to

the Baptist Mission at Kodiak where she died at the age of nine in 1915. Only after her death did Simeon learn he had a sister.[15] While Oliver was taking Christine to Kodiak, Simeon was sent by himself to Unalaska. When Dr. Newhall met the steamship, he found a boy dressed in a thick undershirt, a once-white cotton dress that came almost to his knees, and red leather boots with copper toes. His hat had blown away. His face, arms, and legs were tanned and hardened by the wind. Dr. Newhall, writing in the third-person, recalled the boy's arrival.

> He came across the deck a-smiling—until he found that he was to leave the boat—he had made friends and loved those good hearted men and seriously objected to being taken ashore. The doctor took him in his arms and up the beach line he went a mile or so to the mission with that little feller a-kicking, using his little fists vigorously and screaming with all his might. In the home there [were] many little children about his age and soon the little boy was playing with them and as happy as all the rest.[16]

Within a year, according to Mabel Benedict, Oliver was speaking good English and showed signs of the independence and energy that would characterize his later career as a professional musician.[17]

Whether arriving as infants, children or teenagers, all these children were welcomed into a growing family. They were outside the tensions that still existed between Unalaska's Aleut residents and the staff at the Home. In many ways, in fact, they mitigated the estrangements that had developed during the late 1890s and helped to create bridges between the Home and the community. A photograph of Mary Prokopeuff Lavigne with eight girls from the Home illustrates this. Originally from Attu and a superb Aleut weaver, Lavigne was hired to teach basketry in the school. In the photograph she stands with Aleut and Inupiat girls. Each girl, including Jennie Alexander and Lucy Leavitt, holds an Aleut basket that she has been working on. This basketry is a source of well-earned pride among Aleut people. It ranks among the finest grass weaving in the hemisphere. Many in the Aleut community would have been pleased that Eskimo girls at the Home had taken the time to learn this art.

1. *WHM*. May 1903:84.

2. Dr. Newhall frequently hyphenated these names between each syllable, but he was not always consistent. Outside of direct quotations, the hyphens have been removed.

3. *WHM*. May 1903:85.

4. *WHM*. April 1904:62. This article called her "Igloo Mary," but her full name was given in the April 1905 issue where her photograph is on the cover. More information about her is found at http://library.thinkquest.org/11313/Early_History/Native_Alaskans/mary.html

5. North American Commercial Company. Log Copy Book, May 31, 1903–Sept. 16, 1903. (June 27 and July 23.) Alaska Commercial Company Records. Archives of the Arctic and Polar Regions Collections of the Elmer E. Rasmuson Library, University of Alaska Fairbanks.

6. *WHM*. April 1904:66.

7. "Eskimo Center and Two Other Members of the Carlisle Football Team." *Chicago Daily Tribune*, Nov. 23, 1903:10.

8. John Carpenter wrote that his father enrolled him in the Home. John Carpenter to Philemon Tutiakoff, Aug. 14, 1978.

9. Bockstoce, *Arctic Passages*, 78.

10. Swanson. *The Unknown Islands*. 1982:17.

11. Hudson, ed., *Cuttlefish: Volumes One, Two & Three,* 149–53.

12. Swanson, *The Unknown Islands*, 17. For the three Tiltons see Bockstoce, *Whales, Ice, & Men*.

13. Strobridge, *Alaska and the U. S. Revenue Cutter Service, 1867–1915*, 158–59.

14. Oliver, *Son of the Smoky Sea*, 7–10, 15–18. Earlier he gave a slightly different account in a letter to Myrtle C. Hatten which was published in the October 1931 issue of the Jesse Lee Home newsletter *Ku-eu-it*.

15. Simeon Oliver has an account of visiting her grave in *Son of the Smoky Sea*, 207–08.

16. A.W. Newhall. "Simeon Oliver." Ms. dated Feb. 10, 1926. Alaska State Historical Library. MS 0106. Simeon's published account is similar to this one and both describe him as a "Kewpie" with his chubby legs and face, "as plump as a roll of butter" in Newhall's words.

17. *WHM*. January 1906:247.

16

The Public School

By 1900 the population of Alaska had reached 63,592, having doubled in a decade. Gold rush publicity had opened the territory to closer scrutiny, resulting in more legislative acts. Local communities began to incorporate, with seven-member city councils and three-member school boards. A legal code was adopted, and new judicial districts were formed. To the dismay of Sheldon Jackson, the prohibition on alcohol was repealed. In 1905 the territorial capital was moved from Sitka to Juneau, which had become a bustling mining town. Public school teachers were no longer expected to be missionaries.

At Unalaska, the staff at the Jesse Lee Home remained keenly interested in the school and worked to maintain "the most cordial and sympathetic relations" with teachers. The teacher from 1901 to 1902 was Clara Gwin. Ann Mann was her assistant. Mann's sister, N. Frances Mann, had taught from 1900 to 1901. Unfortunately, as Sheldon Jackson reported to the Commissioner of Education, Frances had attended "all the balls and dances, many, if not the majority, of which were of low character."[1] Jackson went on to say that "among these half civilized people it is necessary for the moral welfare of the pupils that the teacher should set an example free from all possible reproach." He also noted that he had promised "Mrs. Clara Gwyn" the position of principal teacher. The spelling of Clara Gwin's name gave everyone trouble. An article she wrote was published in *Woman's Home Missions* in 1903 under the name Clara Given. In this article she described the Home as "a busy hive" with 42 children. Most of her students came from the Home and from the boarding school run by the Orthodox church. She found her students made fair progress in everything except arithmetic. She taught handiwork to the girls on Fridays for an hour; the boys practiced mechanical drawing, until the supplies ran out.[2]

Gwin began school in the fall of 1902 facing opposition from the local school committee on which Dr. Newhall served. She and Ann Mann had apparently experienced difficulties controlling the rowdier boys, although her report had said nothing about unruliness. The committee wrote to the Commissioner of Education describing "the peculiar geographical position of Unalaska" that resulted in transient miners and other men "who have not profited by the rising influences of Ladies society." These men exhibited "a certain freedom of speech and actions, which is decidedly characteristic of the frontier," and the "morals and general deportment" of children at school were being shaped by contact with such men. What the school required, the committee concluded, was a "strong *masculine* arm and mind to cope with such difficulties as present themselves in the attempt to properly control children, that have been [affected] by such evil influences." Gwin sub-

WILLIAM AND MARY DAVIS, *schoolteachers. Photo in the author's collection from E. Pelagia McCurdy, who wrote on the back, "Were very strict."*

mitted her resignation to Sheldon Jackson on Oct. 13, 1902. The doctor's brother, Chester Newhall, was offered the position at the doctor's suggestion, but he declined. Ann Mann continued teaching with what help she could find in the community until William A. Davis arrived at the end of April.

Clara Gwin moved to Kodiak where in 1904 she married Albert C. Goss, a long-time employee of the Alaska Commercial Company. A decade later, as Clara Goss, she would become one of the most ardent supporters of the Home.

Davis had served as principal of the Bennett Academy in Clarkson, Mississippi. "Owing to the resignation of the principal teacher [at Unalaska], a number of substitute teachers taught periods of one and two months each until my arrival," he wrote. There were about 75 students, and the attendance was excellent. Father Kashevaroff, the priest in charge of the Russian school, "arranged his services at the mission so as to have the children in his charge attend school each afternoon and he assures us of hearty co-operation in the future." Davis had taught for 21 years and in all that time had never found students who excelled the Aleut children in reading, writing, and spelling.[3] Ann Mann was his assistant until she left in late June; her place was taken by William's wife, Mary S. Davis. Mary organized an after-school sewing class for girls and women.

This peaceful year was remarked upon by the Commissioner of Education, who was at Unalaska as part of a tour of the territory. "The change from the condition of affairs in the old days," wrote Hamilton to Sheldon Jackson, "when the village of Unalaska was a hot bed of strife is very gratifying."[4] He stayed at the hotel at Dutch Harbor. Ironically, the only saloon on the island that had survived the mass closing initiated by Newhall and Gray was "The Baranoff Wine Rooms" at his hotel.

Davis's tenure was marked by a series of charges he leveled at the local community beginning shortly after his arrival. He accused "white men with native wives and . . . mixed breeds" of selling and buying impoverished girls from Attu to work as servants. It was a charge that quickly made the rounds of newspapers. "Girl Slaves in Alaska" was on the front page of *The New York Times* in 1903,[5] while the *St. Louis Republic* headlined, "Declares Human Slavery Under the American Flag Still Exists in Alaska."[6] In the St. Louis article Davis is quoted as saying that in 1903 he had found, "to my horror and disgust, eight little girls, ranging in age from 6 to 12 years, in slavery." Two years later there were still six girls "in bondage as servile as that of the blacks before their emancipation. . . ." On Aug. 4, 1905, the Secretary of the Interior asked the governor of Alaska to investigate these charges.[7] In 1907 *Woman's Home Missions* published a poem by Davis called "The Alaskan Slave Girls." It began, "God pity native orphan girls whose lot/ Is cast upon Alaska's western isles!" They were lured aboard schooners "upon whose mast waves/ Our dear old flag" to find "their lives at morning pass into eclipse/. . . No merry shouts nor laughter from their lips. . . ." "In this great age," the poem asks at its conclusion, "shall their cry be unheard,/ And their emancipation still deferred?"[8] Davis went so far as to make the accusation that the Orthodox Church was in "strenuous opposition" to Aleuts bettering their lives.[9]

Each summer during school vacations, Davis panned for gold along the beach and streams of the island. A small creek north of the village off the beach toward Summer Bay is still known as Gold Creek. He never had the slightest success, but he had "succumbed to the gold fever," as he later expressed it. On June 8, 1905, he left Unalaska for Seattle. At every port along the way he listened for rumors of gold. In Ketchikan he learned of the recent strike at Atlin, British Columbia. Hooking up with two partners, Jackson Shepard and Ole Quean, he headed into the mountains.[10] Eventually the three men found a lode-bearing stream. Davis recovered a 52-ounce nugget worth $800. They filed a claim and over the next two years made $8 a day—"Which to me is a much better proposition," he wrote, "than teaching school."[11]

. .

IN HEARINGS IN Washington, D.C., in March 1904, Sheldon Jackson was asked about the effect of government schools on church schools. He replied by referring to the case at Unalaska, blurring some of its recent history.

> When the public school was started the mission orphanages closed their schoolrooms and sent their children to the public school. For instance, at Unalaska the Methodist Church built up an orphanage and home and the Russian Orthodox Church had a parochial school. When the Government established a public school the Methodists closed their schoolroom and sent the children to the public school. The Russian Church closed their school at noon and sent the pupils in the afternoon to the public school. Both churches continue to feed, clothe, and train in the industries the children in their orphanage or home, but for literary training they come to the Government school. The children of the Methodist orphanage and the Russian orphanage all come to the Government schools for their book learning. . . . There is no conflict and no competition. The work is harmonious between the missions and the Government teachers.[12]

Until 1905 there had been no distinction between Natives and non-Natives in terms of federal education.[13] In 1905 Congress passed the Nelson Act, which differentiated between schools in villages for Native children, operated under the Secretary of the Interior, and those for white children and for "children of mixed blood who lead a civilized life," operated by the territorial government. The children at Unalaska clearly fell into the second category. To form a territorial school, a community with 20 eligible children could petition for establishment of a school district. Funding for the school would be the responsibility of the territorial governor.[14] Unfortunately, the petition required signatures of

12 adults who were citizens and 12 such persons supposedly could not be found at Unalaska.[15] That difficulty testifies to the way the white minority in the Aleutians viewed Aleut people who, in fact, had been considered citizens under the Treaty of Sale in 1867. Nicholas Gray at the A.C. Co. had become a supporter of the Home. He and Dr. Newhall were at a loss when Unalaska's school was closed by the secretary of the interior. Gray said he would watch over the school building while Dr. Newhall arranged for half-day and evening sessions at the Home.[16] Mabel Benedict assisted with the teaching, and this may have been the occasion when the Orthodox priest taught in the public school. "They didn't have any teachers that winter for some reason," recalled Henry Swanson, "so they got local people to teach. He [the priest] was a good teacher, too. He was real fierce."[17] The annual report of the WHMS referred to the Nelson Act as "an unrighteous law passed by the last Congress."[18]

In May 1906 Newhall consulted with a member of the former school board and with Father Kedrovsky. All agreed they wanted the school reopened under Sheldon Jackson. This would mean asserting that the community had enough full-blooded Native children to warrant a government school. Once re-established, the school perhaps could then admit "creole" children. The community would face too many difficulties in trying to establish a territorial school. Hiring their own teachers would be next to impossible, and they were unable to find anyone willing to give a bond, as required, "for twice the amount of money handled." Newhall discouraged any notion of having teachers live at the Home. "They lived in the mission at one time," he wrote, "and the priest thought it was only a scheme to proselyte his flock."[19]

After being closed for a year, the school reopened under the Department of the Interior in late autumn 1906 when James J. Potter was appointed as the teacher with M. Abbie Vinton as the assistant.[20] Dora Reinken had been offered the assistant teacher position but had to decline as she had married.[21] During the school year the staff at the Home found Miss Vinton more congenial than they did Mr. Potter. By spring, there was a move to have Vinton replace Potter. She herself wrote to the commissioner of education on April 28 saying that she understood Potter wanted to be transferred to Unga and that she would happily take his place. To reinforce her request, Dr. Newhall sent the commissioner a petition asking that she be made principal. Vinton, according to the petition, was "a woman of ability, of sterling character, an excellent teacher, with an influence over the children that has been only for good." It was signed by all the staff at the Jesse Lee Home; C.C. Harman, the deputy U.S. commissioner, and his wife, Inez Harman; Nicholas Gray of the A.C. Co.; the sea otter hunter and fox farmer Samuel Applegate and his wife, Martha Meidell Applegate; Adolph and Alexandra Reinken; and Mae Wagner.

A counter-petition was sent simultaneously. This was written by Fr. Alexander Kedrovsky, and was signed by himself, Leontii Siftsof, Chief Alexei Yatchmeneff, Second Chief Philip Tutiakoff, and 20 other residents. "This petition is sent in because of another which is being circulated," wrote Kedrovsky, "and we consider the same as taking undue advantage of the present teacher."

> The opposing petition is intended we believe to displace Mr. Potter because he does not favor the Home and disregard the Russian elements. The village children are at least three fifths of number in school and should be treated as equal to the Home children.
>
> The writer has visited the school and seen the circumstances while nearly all the signers of this petition are interested by having children in school. The signers of the other petition are those teachers in the Home and men who have no families and have never been inside the school room. Furthermore the Russian element of the village do not want a missionary as the principal of the school. There is already an agreement signed among the village people that if a missionary is made principal the village children will not attend the Government school at all.

Kedrovsky went on to say that Vinton "can be called nothing else than a missionary as her teaching is largely religious work." Newhall had said much the same when writing to Hamilton. "Teachers are like missionaries," he had told the commissioner. Lavinia (Mrs. R.H.) Young, the secretary of the Alaska Bureau of the WHMS, had written to Hamilton on April 24 recommending Mrs. J. C. Healy as an assistant teacher to Vinton. She said that Healy was the widow of a Methodist minister. She didn't mention that Healy was also her sister.

On May 17, Siftsof wrote to the commissioner emphasizing the need for a balanced school staff. One teacher [M. Abbie Vinton] already, he wrote, lived and taught at the Jesse Lee Home. "Our wish is that this school may continue to be one, where in all are treated alike and taught in a way that will best promote the interest of all and every pupil there in, but not confine its work to a favored few or any religious class." The letter was cosigned by Chief Alexei Yatchmeneff and Second Chief Philip Tutiakoff.

In the end, Potter returned as principal teacher for the 1907–08 term and Vinton was his assistant. The following year found an entirely new staff in the school. The Orthodox community and the Jesse Lee Home staff found agreement about the new principal teacher. They both disliked him.

NOTES

1. Jackson to Hamilton. June 20, 1901. NARA. RG 75. Letters Received, 1883–1907, entry 804, box 13.

2. *WHM*. May 1903:86. There is no record of a Clara Given teaching at Unalaska.

3. William A. Davis to Commissioner of Education. June 15, 1903. NARA. RG 75. Letters Received, 1883-1907.

4. Hamilton to Jackson, July 18, 1904. PHS. RG 239. Box 7, folder 12.

5. *The New York Times*, Dec. 19, 1903:1. In this article he accuses "a German," "a Scotchman," and "a Russian priest."

6. *St. Louis Republic*. July 31, 1905.

7. On hearing this, Sheldon Jackson asked the commissioner of education to investigate a similar incident at Afognak. Jackson to W.T. Harris, Nov. 7, 1905. PHS. RG 239. Box 7, folder 9.

8. *WHM*. October 1907:186.

9. *WHM*. December 1907:225.

10. Ole "O.K." Quean had been a prospector for years. He settled at Unalaska where at different times he ran several establishments including the Fair Pool Room and Restaurant, Quean's Fish Saltry, and Quean's Store, on land leased from the Orthodox church.

11. Davis, William A. "Dream Reveals Gold Mine; True Story from Far North." *Chicago Daily Tribune*. March 10, 1907:E5.

12. Statement of Dr. Sheldon Jackson, of Alaska, Tuesday, March 10, 1904. House of Representatives. Hearings before the Committee on the Territories. Volume II. Washington. Government Printing Office. 1904:820.

13. Case, *Alaska Natives and American Laws*, 6.

14. Ibid., 60, 199.

15. William Hamilton to Sheldon Jackson. June 20, 1905. NARA. RG 75. Letters Received, 1883–1907.

16. Woman's Home Missionary Society, Reports from Bureaus. 1904–05:109.

17. Swanson, *The Unknown Islands*, 14.

18. Woman's Home Missionary Society, Reports from Bureaus. 1904–05:109.

19. Newhall to Jackson, May 9, 1902. PHS. RG 239. Box 7, folder 23.

20. Captain O.C. Hamlet to William Hamilton. Nov. 16, 1906. NARA. RG 75. Letters Received, 1883–1907.

21. Adolph Reinken to Sheldon Jackson, Nov. 18, 1906. PHS. RG 239. Box 7, folder 25.

The Camp at Summer Bay

THE WINTER OF 1905–06 WAS ONE OF THE MOST SEVERE IN MEMORY. It dragged on and on, delaying the planting of the Home's garden. The weather and the work exhausted Agnes. Albert feared for her health. In March 1906 Mrs. R.H. Young, responding to a report from Elizabeth Mellor about starvation in the Aleutians, suggested to Sheldon Jackson that reindeer be introduced to the islands. "I think Dr. Newhall could manage the new department with success," she wrote.[1] But in early May he submitted his resignation effective September 1907. "We have learned to love this work," he wrote to Young, "and it will be very hard to leave it." He was giving 15 months notice in order for the society to find a suitable replacement. He reflected on his eight years and his wife's 11 years at Unalaska.

> This work does not need a man given to special evangelistic work so much as a steady faith in God and a patient continuance in well doing. The work is largely in training the children under our care. One also has to use great tact and wisdom in getting along in a Russian Greek community especially where a number of priests are liable to misjudge one. During the past years I have tried to do my best work for the Mission and the cause of God. . . . No doubt that there are others who could have accomplished more. . . .
>
> During the past 12 years there has been progress in the work. The mission has won respect of the people. Personally I do not think I am just the one most suited to the place. I am not a farmer, nor even the son of a farmer, and in the outdoor work, farming, etc., some one more skilled would do better. The same thing applies to carpentering. I can care for the sick, teach and conduct meetings (though I am not a preacher) but on some other lines I am not a great success. I know we have won the confidence and respect of the people, and if Mrs. Newhall cannot stand the strain of living with so many children, I think I had better stand aside and let others take up the work. I am not discouraged or down hearted at all, for the work is in better shape than at any time since we came here.[2]

Realizing that in the interim his wife needed rest away from the Home, Dr. Newhall decided to construct a retreat at Summer Bay, a wide sandy beach about two miles north of the village. During previous summers, he and Agnes had pitched a tent in order to spend a little time away from the Home. A visitor in September 1905 had found them with "a wash tub full of berries," and commented, "They were enjoying their camping out as it made a change for them."[3] At Summer Bay, a salmon stream flowed with the tides in and out of a large lake separated from the bay by shifting sand dunes. Two smaller bays, Humpy Cove and Morris Cove, lay just north of Summer Bay. A fishing couple, Mark and Justina "Annie" Moriss, lived at Morris Cove for most of the year.[4] Chester Newhall, the Newhalls' son, recalled that Mark Moriss was Croatian. As a boy Chester watched the Morisses fish for salmon. After they pulled in a full net together, Mark would give Annie a hug and say, "Good girl, Annie!" They'd take the fish to their camp and he would go to bed, leaving Annie the task of cleaning all of them.[5] The Newhalls and the Morisses became friends. Mark and Annie would occasionally visit at the Home during the winter when they lived in the village.

In addition to Mark and Annie's home, there were a few summer barabaras used by one or two Aleut families. Today a road built during World War II meanders from the village along the shore, but in 1906 the route was over a series of rocky landslides and along a pebble-strewn beach. A pinnacle rock, Little Priest Rock, marked the corner where the shoreline curved into Summer Bay. The preferred way to get to the bay was by schooner or skiff, but landing at Summer Bay took skill. It was, as Newhall wrote, "a place where it is difficult to land owing to the heavy surf which comes up often if the wind chances to be north or northwest."

In May 1906 materials for two camp houses were received from an old schooner, the *Marguerite*. Captain Lee had agreed to deliver the lumber, seine, luggage, and one ton of coal. Unfortunately, because of a big sea running, the coal had to be landed a good distance from the camp. "With much difficulty and more swearing the kind hearted captain got it ashore," wrote Newhall. About a week later the doctor and 11 boys including 3-year-old Chester arrived at the bay. They erected a 6-by-9 tent and started work on the first cabin. At night they slept like sardines in the tent, and young Gabriel, on the far end the first night, rolled out into the rain. It took three days to get the outer walls of the 10-by-15-foot cabins erected. The buildings were in no danger of blowing into the sea. The walls were only four feet high, and adapting the semi-underground barabara technique so frequently disparaged in publications of the mission society, the side walls facing the sea were anchored two feet down in the sand. Before returning to Unalaska, Newhall and the boys were able to roof one shack and cover it with tarpaper. When completed, it would serve as the kitchen and boys' bunkhouse for nine crowded beds. The kitchen section had two tables, a stove and a coal container. The second cabin was designated "the teacher's" and held bunks for the girls and for Mrs. Newhall.

The first outing to Summer Bay took place the next Wednesday. There was quite a crowd: Dr. and Mrs. Newhall, Chester and Edith, and of the Home children May, Feofan, Gabriel, William, Charles, Henry, Daniel, Theodore, John and Fred. Eliza Gould arrived a few days later. "The schooner ride was not without excitement for the weather was rough," Newhall wrote. "Edith was seasick and cold. The cabin was a box like arrangement where one could sit down, but if he stood up he must stick his head out the hatch. The craft was only 25 feet long and with every gust of wind lay over to the water well. A landing was made at 4:30 p.m. and not much could be done ere night was upon us."

Agnes slept with Edith on a cot surrounded by luggage of all sorts. The other girls slept on the floor. The wind started blowing, creating a downdraft in the smoke stack until everyone had nearly choked to death. The sand on the roof dried from the heat and drifted through cracks into their eyes and ears. Then it rained and the roof leaked. In short, "It was a terrible night."

Gradually the cabins were put in shape and the business of eating, sleeping, and catching fish, dressing them, and packing them to the Home was in full swing. "Agnes does not think it is wholly a picnic," wrote Dr. Newhall, "to be feeding fourteen boys and girls." Fresh water was found on a hillside spring as salt water from the bay backed up into the lake at high tide.

After they had seen the *Dora* depart one day, Dr. Newhall hiked into town from Summer Bay for the mail. While there he picked up a pail of butter and placed some hard candy on top. He was given a ride back with Mark and Annie Moriss. The wind was strong but Newhall had confidence in Moriss's sailing abilities. Mark wanted to smoke and asked his wife to light his pipe. She tried and tried, but the wind was too strong. "I held my coat around her head," wrote Newhall, "and she pulled her shawl close about her. Even then it took ten minutes to get it going." Then he added with good humor, "Not exactly missionary work, but it was lending a helping hand in time of need. A pipe is a sailor's source of contentment and happiness." Williwaws swept across the bay. The sea was rough. The sandy landing at Summer Bay was too treacherous, so Moriss dropped his wife and Dr. Newhall at Little Priest Rock. After a trek to the camp the doctor delivered a small pail of butter and candy crusted with sand.

Newhall described the fishing technique used at Summer Bay:

> A boy usually goes on the hill and watches the surface of the water for salmon. When the fish jump there is excitement. The net is loaded on the boat. Two boys go in it; one to row and the other to set the seine. A boy on shore holds a line which is [attached] to the seine. The seine is set and they row ashore keeping off from the shore. Then two groups of children begin to pull the net in and when it nears the shore there is great excitement for the fish jump and lash the water into a foam.
>
> We seine for red salmon but often get other things in the net, trout, herring, flounders, pogies, jelly fish, star fish. Once in a while a cod or halibut.
>
> Some of the fish is dried "Ucala"; some is smoked "baleeka", but most of it is salted.[6]

[ABOUT A HIKE *to Summer Bay*]

Eliza and I started "o'er cobbled beach, o'er crag and torrent stream," beginning the journey at 3:30 P.M. I was arrayed in a cap, jacket and mackintosh, and Eliza wore a blue gingham apron, black jacket, and a wide head shawl. We labored, and after three miles heavy walking we decided that we were tired and sat down to rest and refresh ourselves.

As we sat looking out upon the wide waters and the hills we saw a boat coming toward us from Dutch Harbor. At first Eliza thought it might be the doctor, but soon we remembered that it might be some men off a schooner which came in that morning. We hurried along the beach much troubled in our minds. Water lay to the left, and the rocks almost perpendicular for a hundred feet or more, and that boat with three strange men was close among us.

Well, they drew near the shore just ahead of us. One said, "Good evening," but I was too frightened to reply. He then asked if we could tell where the village was, and said that he wanted a doctor, as one of the men had a sore hand. I told him the doctor was in Summer Bay, and he asked if we would go with them and pilot them to the doctor. I frankly answered, "No," but he replied, "Oh, I understand, you need not be afraid. We will take you safely to the doctor." By this time I saw that the man had a good face, and they stepped out of the boat and allowed us to sit in the stern side by side.

We reached the camp at 6 P.M. They were on the beach to meet us but did not expect to see us in a boat with three men. The doctor soon lanced the man's finger and received payment therefor. It was decided that I should return with them to Dutch Harbor, which I did. When we reached the schooner the whole crew of twenty-one men were out on deck. The captain asked Mr. Potter how he got to Summer Bay and he replied, "This lady piloted me." Then I told them all how kind Mr. Potter was to me.

I was very thankful that I came back with them, for the next morning one of our dreadful storms was upon us, which lasted two days in full fury.

Rebecca Wunderlich, June 1, 1906
Woman's Home Missions, November

On July 4 of that summer of 1906, the children hiked to town where a community celebration was hosted by the A.C. Co., a visiting ship, and William Hamilton, the commissioner of education from Washington, D.C. While the children were gone, the adults had hoped for a quiet day of rest. Salmon were seen jumping, however, so with the help of four Aleuts who were spending time at their fish camp nearby, the seine was set. One hundred thirty-eight large red salmon were taken and divided among them all.

The time at camp was never dull. One evening Chester was playing with his bowl of food and Agnes said, "Chester, stop playing and eat." He moved his bowl but it toppled off the table and Agnes cried out. At her shout, a cat came flying from somewhere and landed in a dish of pickles. "Over went the dish, the cat, [and the] pickles and numerous tins from the shelf went rattling into the coal box." Chester's clumsiness was instantly forgotten in the burst of laughter that enveloped the room.

Chester would put a few salmon roe into a small pail, go to a shallow corner of the lake, and tip the pail down so a little water could run into it. Along would come a few tiny minnows. "The kittens," Newhall wrote, "have many a feast from his fishing."

Once while straining brine at the lake, Dr. Newhall watched one of the boys who was washing out a cloth. He spread it on the water where it floated. "Daniel," said the doctor, "climb on it with both feet and have a sail." Daniel did and promptly sank.

On another day, when only Agnes and two of the girls were at the camp, five deserters from a schooner made their way to Summer Bay. They were "a hard looking crowd" and broke into an empty barabara to find a place to sleep. Two of the men came up to the Home camp to learn whether anyone was looking for them. As they approached the cabins they saw a steam launch anchored in front. They raced back to warn their companions, and all of them ran toward the lake straight into the search party. Two of the deserters had revolvers and escaped, but three were captured. The next morning Mark Moriss was able to force the remaining two to surrender.[7]

After eight weeks it was finally time to pack up and leave. The older boys loaded the luggage into the skiff built by Nick Bolshanin. They started pulling toward Unalaska, leaving the rest of the campers for a promised ride aboard a small steamer. The time set for departure came and went. No steamer. Dinner time passed, but no one dared to unpack to prepare a meal. The evening was calm and the mosquitoes were thick. The younger boys started to get restless. "The bay began to get rough," Dr. Newhall wrote. "Our hopes fell. And then the steamer appeared, whistled and anchored some two miles off shore."

Mark Moriss loaded everyone into his new codfishing dory and after a long hard pull they were out among the whitecaps. "So rough was it that when the dory rose up on a wave," wrote Newhall, "the folks on the steamer could see half the bottom of it. Then the bow would fall with a splash into the trough of the sea, and mount another wave." Moriss was about to quit as the perspiration poured down his face. Agnes was seated on the bottom of the dory in the stern. The doctor squatted a little to the front. Polly Dirks was in the bow holding tightly to a cat. As they neared the steamer they could make out children from the Home, tourists, and crew. "Oh, what a sight we must be!" Agnes exclaimed. "Of all the vehicles I have ever traveled in—parlor cars, tourists, electrics, carriages, farm wagons, hay racks, stone bolts, lumber wagons with boards for seats and no springs, steamships, river steamers, schooners, launches, row boats, rafts—and here I am on the bottom of a cod fishing dory. It beats them all!"

A gang plank was readied, but it was tricky getting aboard. "When the dory rose up on a wave," Newhall wrote, "one had to grasp the iron rod at the foot of the stairway—jump up, climb up—hang on for dear life until someone pushed your feet on to the lower step." The moment Agnes reached the deck, she collapsed in a heap and burst into tears. In a few moments she had recovered and after a short rest in the captain's quarters she was herself again. On reaching Unalaska, after a stop at Dutch Harbor, she was welcomed by everyone as though she had been gone for many months.

The Home received a new seine and that was first used in Margaret Bay, on Amaknak Island, shortly after the group returned from the camp at Summer Bay. The first haul on Saturday, July 21, brought in 171 salmon. The second resulted in 101 fish. Monday and Tuesday they caught no fish, but on Wednesday an entire school of fish was taken: 1,058 salmon. Newhall wrote that it was a big job to dress them and hang them under the steamer to dry.

That December children from the Home took part in a school entertainment held on December 21 at the A.C. Co. hall in the upstairs of the three-storied laundry building. On the 25th the Home presented a Christmas program featuring the "Cantata of Joseph" and another titled "Seeking the King." On February 22 the children participated in a community program at the A.C. Co. hall for Washington's birthday.

· ·

ON MAY 7, 1907, Dr. Newhall wrote to Mrs. E.T.C. Richmond, a supporter of the Home in Toledo, Ohio, that the work was progressing well. "Just now we are busy making our garden. We plant it about the end of June and raise a number of vegetables such as kale, cabbage, lettuce, radishes, etc. There are 43 children in the Home both Aleute and Eskimo." He mentioned that he expected to leave Unalaska in the middle of the summer. He did not know who his replacement would be. "My prayers and interest will still be in the work," he wrote, "although I think our call is to the homeland. Twelve years of service entitles Mrs. Newhall to a rest I think." On Aug. 5, 1907, Albert and Agnes Newhall left Unalaska. With them went three older Home residents: Polly Dirks, her brother Charles, and Eliza Gould. Peter Kashevaroff, unwilling to see Eliza go off without him, arranged to join the group.

[Excerpt from a letter *to Phil and Flora Tutiakoff from John Carpenter, Jan. 7, 1980, after receiving a photograph of Summer Bay*]

I recognize the slopes of what we used to call "Mt. Craig," because of its craggy top overlooking Summer Bay Lake. How often I hiked that trail across the spit & over the beach to the pinnacle (which was usually topped with nesting bald eagles) where we climbed a rather steep & arduous trail to the top where we could look to see the two cabins (owned by the J.L.H.) situated across the river outletting that beautiful lake. ... Summer Bay Camp ... was a retreat for vacationing teachers, during the summer months, to get away from us pestiferous kids at the "Home." I loved it when it was my turn to hike that trail with a heavy pack of baked beans, loaves of freshly-baked bread, pickles, butter, etc., and notes (from the boys & girls) and whatever mail may have arrived on the "Dora." It was an unforgettable experience for any one of us who hiked that trail! Teachers (usually, two together) & privileged (by virtue of best behavior) boys or girls usually spent two weeks there. There was, of course, the other retreat (two cabins) in the other direction, over at Huntsville where teachers could also rest, refresh their thinking, hike along the beaches, or, into the back hills (beautiful cranberry hill just above, on that trail leading into the mts. beyond) or, catch up on their correspondence to friends & relatives outside.

The right half of this photograph is often reproduced on its own. The full version appears in The Fisherman's Son, *by the Rev. Peter Gordon Gould (Peter Golovin at Jesse Lee). His caption reads:* "FOUR BOYS OF THE JESSE LEE HOME (1912): *1. Henry Peterson, fox farmer and hunter's guide; George Peterson, Father Hubbard's guide; 3. [Simeon] Oliver, first Eskimo to become a concert pianist; 4. P. Gordon Gould." Photo from the girlhood album of Annie Swanson Hatch, courtesy of the Hatch family.*

In Seward they saw Harriett Barnett, who had arrived from Seattle after a year's furlough. They waved goodbye to her as she boarded the *Dora* for the voyage to Unalaska. There were 37 Japanese workers headed to one of the salmon canneries along the Alaska Peninsula, and the decks were piled high with crates of food, coal, mail bags, and assorted freight. Harriett was the only woman aboard.

NOTES

1. Young to Jackson, March 14, 1906. PHS. RG 239. Box 7, folder 21.

2. Newhall to Mrs. R.H. Young, May 9, 1906. PHS. RG 239. Box 7, folder 23.

3. Churchill, Frank C. *Journal No. 3: Alaska-Siberia*. Sept. 1, 1905. Hood Museum. Dartmouth College.

4. Although Morris Cove was named for them, the spelling was altered. Newhall consistently misspelled it.

5. Personal conversation with Chester Newhall, Burlington, Vermont, July 23, 1983.

6. Newhall Manuscript, 224–25.

7. It may have been events such as this that prompted Dr. Newhall to purchase the pistol which is now with his granddaughter and her husband, Donna and Rodney Larrow.

18

Two Interim Doctors

HARRIET BARNETT ARRIVED BACK AT UNALASKA SEVEN DAYS AFTER Makushin volcano had erupted and covered the village with half an inch of ash. "Notwithstanding the unsettled condition of things terrestrial," she wrote, "I am glad to set foot once more on the shores of Behring Sea. It seems like coming home, and everyone is so effusive in welcome."[1] Among those greeting her were the Newhalls' replacements, Dr. Frank H. Spence and Jessie S. Spence of Fairgrove, Michigan. They had arrived a few days earlier, on Aug. 5, 1907, after a 22-day voyage from Seattle. Dr. Spence had been seasick most of the way. "The old Pacific slapped us in the face with a strong head wind," wrote Jessie, "and washed our decks with her waves, and proved a great leveler of the human beings on board. Nearly everyone was very sick, the doctor desperately so, also some sailors."[2]

The Spences in their turn had been welcomed by Mabel Benedict, Emma Supernaw, Rebecca Wunderlich and, briefly, by the Newhalls, who had left a month earlier than expected, on the same vessel that brought the Spences to Unalaska. Emma Supernaw had arrived in July to replace Benedict.[3] Frank and Jessie Spence, married for 27 years, were described as "capable, cultivated, and earnest" and having "the true missionary spirit."[4] He was 52 and she was a year older. Barnett was optimistic about the new doctor. "Dr. Spence is doing his best to get things in repair for winter," she wrote. "He is not accustomed to such flimsily built houses as we have in Alaska, and is quite disturbed over the rain beating in around the windows. I think he is going to be excellent at keeping things repaired and in order. We are having our few summer days now in September and were obliged to let all the fires go out except in the kitchen."[5]

When Dr. Spence saw materials for repairing the Home off-loaded from the November 1908 boat, he said he felt like singing the Doxology. A typewriter also arrived, donated by women in Philadelphia.[6] He bought a small building for use as a carpentry shop and asked the society for more tools.[7] This shop had its own convoluted history: Spence purchased it for $50 on Oct. 8, 1908, from Ivan Olgin after George King, who had moved the shop onto land that was owned by the Home, released any claim to it.[8] During the summer of 1909 good weather allowed the doctor and the older boys to dip 35,000 shingles using two barrels of shingle stain.

According to Simeon Oliver, Jessie Spence was a registered nurse. She was a frequent contributor to the WHMS publication and made requests for various improvements. In October 1906 she asked for a small organ. "The boys are musical, and as they have no instrument," she wrote, "it would be a great up lift to them spiritually, and, as you know, every way."[9] She also requested rubber stair silencers for the sake of patients in the hospital room as the carpet was "of no practical use"[10] when it came to muffling the sounds of all the boys. The silencers were donated by Mrs. Perchment, whose husband had given money for the skiff. A new carpet for the parlor was another need. "I had the parlor carpet taken up and cleaned last week," wrote Wunderlich, "and we wore our fingers patching and darning it. May we hope for a new one?"[11] They were also looking for someone to donate a bell that "could be heard in the village."

The water pump that had so pleased the Newhalls a few years previously was now inadequate. "It is a crime to have fifty or more people depend upon a small hand-pump for water in such a windy country, where the danger of fire is imminent all the time, and in cold, stormy weather this pump will freeze in spite of all precautions; then all the water has to be carried from the river through a biting, cold wind, which makes this part of the work a sore trial to the Superintendent and teachers. Three hundred and fifty dollars would give us a good little pumping engine that would put water on both floors of the buildings and give a much better fire protection, and later, with a few more dollars, give light in the Home instead of the dangerous lamps now used."[12] A new gasoline pump was installed in 1911 or 1912.

Joseph L. Brown became the schoolteacher in 1908. He and his wife, Sophia R. Brown, lived at the Applegate house as the Applegates had gone to California for the winter. In January 1907 Martha Applegate had given birth to their first child, a boy named Meidell. The Applegate house, located along the front beach at the center of the curved bay, was a large home that locals nicknamed "The Bird Cage" because of its ornate decorations. Brown was an enthusiastic teacher. He developed a sizable school garden at Margaret's Bay on Amaknak Island for which the North American Commercial Company loaned a team of horses and a plow. He added a tool shed to the school property. Brown was also a strict moralist and complained to Harlan Updegraff, chief of the Alaska Division for the Bureau of Indian Affairs, about the character of the men who ran the post office, the A.C. Co., and the Russian school. He objected to the dances provided for men off the revenue cutters, especially because children attended until late at night. "This makes them almost unable to do any work on the following day," he wrote.

The supply agent in Seattle for the Department of the Interior, quoting Captain V.E. Jacobs, wrote, "Mr. Brown has done wonderful work at Unalaska among the natives there, and is doing one thing that tends to make the natives feel that they are a part of the United States, and that is he will allow them to talk nothing but English—in fact, punishes them if they talk any other language." Jacobs himself wrote, "This place is peculiarly under the old Russian spirit of domination. . . ." A strong school, he felt, would reduce this foreign influence.

In his record sheets for 1908–09 Brown listed 15 boys and 14 girls from the Jesse Lee Home, 7 boys from the Russian "Mission School," and 7 girls and 2 boys whom he named as "so called slave children." In addition there were 13 girls and 27 boys from the village. One other girl had died of tuberculosis during the year. Altogether there had been 35 girls and 51 boys, a total enrollment of 86.[13]

On Jan. 15, 1909, Kathryn Dyakanoff, who had just graduated from the State Normal School in West Chester, Pennsylvania, wrote to Updegraff for a teaching position. "If I am appointed to a school," she wrote, "I should like very much to teach at Unalaska, as I was born there, and my family will expect to see me there, and as I have been away so long I should like to be with my people again."[14] When Updegraff learned that Brown had discouraged her from returning to Unalaska (because he wanted a Mrs. Harmon as the second assistant teacher), the chief of the Alaska division explained to him that the department's goal was to place Native girls as teachers. Olga Reinken, who had graduated from the Carlisle Industrial School in April 1909, had also applied. She was given the position. "My father was very much surprised to see me," she wrote to Updergraff. "I would like to teach elsewhere in Alaska if it were not for the fact that Father is growing very old so I feel it my duty to be as near home as possible."[15] Joseph Brown had Olga Reinken substitute for him "while he was away visiting the destitute natives to the westward."[16] In 1910 she married Nicholas Bolshanin, the deputy collector of customs.

Brown managed to antagonize almost the entire community. In his 1909–10 report he wrote that village children had almost perfect attendance. In a turn-around of the usual situation, he scolded the Home for a poor turnout. "Our irregularities [in attendance] are nearly all due to the children of the Jesse Lee Home, who would be just as interested in school but are kept out on many occasions." This statement did not please the missionaries. In 1909 Dr. Spence had written an endorsement of Brown's work. On Feb. 25, 1910, he withdrew that approval in a letter to Dr. Romig of the Bureau of Education, Alaska Division, in Seward. He accused Brown of manipulating regulations until the marshal was able to secure a girl from the Home to serve as his hired maid. "In many other ways has he showed his spite against the superintendent and the Home," Spence wrote.[17]

According to the 1909–10 report, Brown had secured the cooperation of the Orthodox priest and reduced the number of church holidays until there were only about five days that interfered in any way with school attendance. However, in February 1910 the new priest for Unalaska, Father Alexander Panteleev, wrote to Romig complaining about Brown and asking for his removal. This letter was, in effect, a petition and was signed by 31 villagers and Dr. Spence. Brown was accused of a number of acts including:

· Working against the Jesse Lee Home by declaring the contracts between children and the Home to be void.

· Forcing girls to stand in the wind without coverings on their heads to have their photographs taken.

· Taking children climbing in the hills when they should be in school.

[To Mrs. E. T. C. Richmond, of Toledo, Ohio. *Undated, but around May 7, 1907*]

Dear Friend,

I will tell you about Christmas we had the cantata of Joseph. A cave was made and it looked like rocks with snow sparkle on it in it was a Santa Clause who moved his head candy was given to all.

This is the month for clams we take some bags and hoes and we dig in the beach at low tide sometimes it is dark and it is hard to find clams.

One day we went to Darling falls for a picnic we climbed a mountain till we saw water on both sides the Pacific ocean and Bering Sea and another island we had prayer meeting there when we were coming home it rained hard and we walked about five miles and when we reached home we had ginger tea and went to bed.

I like to read books about history and animals This Christmas I received Arabian Knights and I liked the story of Aladin or the wonderful lamp.

I hope you will answer this letter I have written to you now I will close.

Henry Swensen [18]

[To Mrs. E. T. C. Richmond, Toledo, Ohio. *May 16, 1907*]

Dear Friend.

I am eleven years old and I am in the fourth reader. My father was a fisherman and hunter hunted ptarmagin he would put on white clothes so that he would look like snow then he could come near them and shoot them. when he comes back he sells them sometimes he would catch foxes and take the skins off and sell them.

when he went out fishing he would stay all day and come home in the evening but one day he was lost at sea and was drowned and his schooner sailed home with the sails up and no one on board. We have prayer-meeting every Thursday night we all pick out a song and a verse from the bible I go to school and like to read very much.

From
Henry Swensen

· Slapping children until their faces were swollen.

· Compelling children to spy on their parents for him.

· Refusing to allow children to attend the Orthodox church on holy days, saying "Saturday and Sunday is enough to go to church."

In July Dr. Romig visited Unalaska to investigate the charges. "Mr. Brown and assistants have done good work," he concluded. "Mr. Brown has made error in the matter of not upholding the Home Contract as fully as he should but on the whole has done good work." He recommended, and Brown concurred, that he be appointed to another school the next year. In the fall of 1910 Brown began teaching at Kenai.

That year, 1910, Romig also investigated a case involving Henry Swanson, then 15 years old. On Sept. 1, 1900, during the measles epidemic, Henry's mother, Sophia, had returned to the Home with Henry and her two daughters, Agnes and Sophia. Her husband had drowned a few months earlier, and she had just given birth to a daughter, Ruth. She was overwhelmed. On September 8, Ruth died from complications of her birth and of measles. Once Sophia herself had recovered, she left to work as a cook at Dutch Harbor, leaving her children with the missionaries. Henry was a favorite of Dr. Newhall's. On May 7, 1907, the doctor had written to a supporter of the Home in Toledo, Ohio, enclosing a letter from Henry along with this description: "Henry . . . is a bright boy. His mother is a half breed, German Aleute and his father was a Swede. His father was a hunter and fisherman but was lost in the sea. Henry is very studious and likes to read. Above all the children he is the one you will find absorbed in some kind of a book."

On April 1, 1908, Sophia married Captain Christian T. Pedersen, a widower with several children. He was a well-respected captain and was able to provide a good home for her and their combined family. In 1910 they approached Dr. Spence with a request to take Henry back into their home. His two sisters were attending school in the States. Dr. Spence refused to release the boy. Captain Pedersen waited until the next day and went to the school where he asked Henry to come home with him, which Henry did.

Dr. Spence was alarmed when Henry failed to return to the Jesse Lee Home. The next day he had deputy marshal W.J. Morton bring the Pedersens and Henry to the school, with Brown now wearing the hat of deputy U.S. commissioner. Spence produced a contract, but Sophia denied signing it. She said Dr. Newhall had promised her she could have Henry when she was ready for him to rejoin her family. According to the deputy marshal, "The Commissioner after considering the evidence that had been offered by both sides refused to take action for want of jurisdiction and was unable to find wherein any crime was committed." Henry, matter-of-factly, "walked out of his own free will with his parents."

"The Home expects to take up the matter with District Judge when the Court Officials arrive here," wrote the marshal, "and Captain Pedersen has given bond to return here and submit the case to the Judge. The boy's parents have at no time coerced the boy nor tried to secret him. In fact they sent him to school and told him to go back to the Jesse Lee Home if he wanted to do so. Captain Pedersen and his wife have at no time during the controversy acted with any criminal intent."[19]

Before long Henry was aboard the *Elvira* on a sea otter hunt to islands around the Alaska Peninsula and Kodiak. The vessel was owned by Fred Schroeder and skippered by Captain Pedersen. Pedersen had promised that Henry could attend the Chemawa Indian School in Oregon. After the *Elvira* returned on September 2, Henry and three younger boys from Unalaska, Walter Reinken, Sergie Shaishnikoff and Leonti Anderson, sailed for school on the Coast Guard cutter *Manning*. Henry's Jesse Lee Home enrollment record ends with the single word, "Abducted."[20]

Another glimpse into the personality of Dr. Spence has come from Peter Gordon Gould, who entered the Home as Peter Golovin in 1908. He and several other young boys were once given a lesson by Dr. Spence on how "if you are going to be a person living in a society of persons you must give heed to the law of obedience to authority higher than yourself."[21] The boys wanted to go berry picking but Dr. Spence told them not to leave the premises that afternoon. The boys sat on the porch, as Gould recounted the story, like a local church committee discussing the question "Resolved, that our pastor has outlived his usefulness in our parish." They decided to ask Mrs. Spence for permission. Before long the boys were picking and eating berries by the handful. Simeon Oliver arrived with word that Dr. Spence wanted to see them. They returned and the doctor took them upstairs.

"Dr. Spence was a very precise man," wrote Gould. "He lined us up in a row in the attic, got a box, sat down on the box and called the first boy, who was Jimmy Polutoff, laid him over his knee, straightened out the wrinkles of his britches, and made contact." As soon as Jimmy let out a tiny grunt, the doctor stopped. Now, for some reason, it was Simeon's turn. Simeon braced himself and took a few whacks before his grunting stopped the punishment. "I figured that since the paddling stopped as soon as the grunt was produced on two occasions, there was no need to think that it wouldn't stop on the third time. So I timed the descent of the paddle." His genuine yell immediately sent him off the doctor's knees.

"So it was during my stay at the Jesse Lee Home," wrote Gould, "that in one way or another we were taught that if you are going to grow up to be a person living in a society of persons you must learn the law of obedience to that which is greater than yourself."

Medical matters kept Dr. Spence in town during the summer of 1909. Among other cases, a sailor who had been operated on for appendicitis in the Pribilof Islands was sent to Unalaska when his case worsened. The annual report for 1909–1910 also said that six children had died during this period, five of them from tuberculosis.[22] While the doctor stayed in town, Jessie Spence took the boys to Summer Bay for fish. They filled eight barrels with

October 1915

Dear Mrs. Young:

The report of the mission at Sinuk you sent me came safely to hand. I was glad to hear from you. I am sending you a picture of myself, my husband and my daughter, taken last year. When I have little Martha's picture taken by herself I will send you one. I am proud of her, for she is the only child I have. I have adopted a little girl to be her playmate. The mother of this little girl is always sick and has four other children besides Helen. So I have taken her to care for and clothe and bring up. I would like to write Mrs. F. H. Spence, but do not know her address.

When I visited Unalaska in 1912 I met Dr. and Mrs. Newhall and their daughter. I heard of Mrs. Spence going up North from Mrs. Applegate's and that on the way they took with them as far as Unalaska Chester Newhall. Chester was just a little boy when he was at the Home with his father and mother. He must be a big boy now. My sister Nellie's little boy was one year old the 3d of this month. He is such a cute little boy!

Wishing you a Merry Christmas and a Happy New Year, I am yours truly,

Alexandra P. Bourdukofsky

salmon, about 350 fish, and caught a thousand herring. She was very pleased with the *Perchment*. "Our eight boys are like ducks," she wrote, "and are excellent rowers."[23]

In the summer of 1908 Peter Bourdukofsky of St. Paul in the Pribilof Islands arrived at the Home asking for a wife. He told Dr. Spence that he had a home and would be a good husband. The doctor consulted with the women on the staff and they decided to ask Alexandra Petersen, who had entered the Home from Morzhovia in 1902 with her brother and three sisters. She agreed.

> The children of the Home gathered wild flowers and decorated the chapel. Miss Wunderlick found material for a white dress in her trunk, and with this and pretty ribbons the bride was very attractive. The guests included several officers from boats in the harbor, one of them a member of the United States navy. "It was a very pretty wedding," said Captain Daniels. . ..[24]

Alexandra wrote to the Home from St. Paul in 1909. "I am home here with my husband. He is good for me," she said. "Everybody respects him because he takes good care of his old father. . . . I am happy with my husband." She came back to Unalaska in 1912 and visited the Newhalls, the Applegates, and others. In 1915 she wrote to Lavinia Young, of the Alaska Bureau, telling her she had adopted a girl to be with her own daughter.[25]

When Noah and Clara Davenport arrived at Unalaska as the new teachers on Aug. 30, 1910, they were met by Dr. Spence. Their rooms at the school needed work and the doctor invited them to stay at the Home until the rooms were ready. While Noah unpacked, Clara was shown around the village by Mrs. Spence and Miss Robinson, the matron at the Home. They saw 39 Japanese prisoners, the crew of a seal poaching vessel, carrying lumber from the government warehouse for a project. There was mutual good will between the Davenports and the staff at the Home although the teachers never affiliated themselves with the Home. "The government teachers in Unalaska this year are good Christian people," reported the missionary society later in the year, "and the children have made better progress than ever before."[26]

The Orthodox priest Alexander Panteleev was also new to the community, and he paid a call at the Home bringing the Davenports a large dish of salmonberries. "We are still at the Mission and will stay on there until our rooms are in order," the teachers wrote on September 5. "They ask us to stay as long as we will. The Mission, Methodist Episcopal, is a large one and they are keeping about 30 native children. Everything is kept in the best condition and they seem to be doing a lot of good. They treat us most cordially and we are made to feel very much at home." The teachers remained at the Home another nine days.

Dr. Spence learned in 1910 that his mother was ill, and he asked to be replaced by fall. He wrote that it took "grit, grace, and grumption" to do this work on the firing line in Alaska. On the requirements for a superintendent, he was very specific: "He must be a preacher, teacher, Sunday school Superintendent; a fisherman with knowledge of boats, traps, and seines, salting, drying, and smoking the fish; be a carpenter, a blacksmith, build fences, paint houses; be a pump man, physician and surgeon, village counselor, a farmer, know something of law, an accountant and business manager; visit boats in the harbor; plan work; be storekeeper, and also many things too numerous to mention. He must have a wife that is sweet and agreeable, who must visit in the village, look after sick babies, make blouses for twenty boys, darn stockings, drill children for special occasions such as Easter and holidays."[27]

The Spences were praised for their work. "Dr. Spence and his wife have been indefatigable workers, and the new flooring has been laid and painted, and many improvements about the Home speak of their thrift and energy."[28] As she was preparing to leave Unalaska, Mrs. Spence gave Clara Davenport a number of beautiful potted plants, among them a "splendid . . . rose" and "a beautiful begonia in full bloom."

Dr. Newhall's absence was still considered permanent, so the society looked for another physician willing to venture into the Aleutians. On Oct. 3, 1910, Dr. Henry Klopper, his wife, Mabel, and their young son and daughter arrived on the *Dora*. He had been in private practice in Oregon. It was a cloudy day with a heavy sea bringing large swells onto the beach. Snow had covered the higher hills. The next morning the Davenports were among the large crowd at the dock to see the Spences depart. "They have been here three years," the Davenports wrote, "and will be missed by many if not all."[29] Among the other passengers were the 39 Japanese prisoners who crowded the decks of the *Dora* on their way to jail in Valdez. In 1916 the Spences went to Nome where he served the Presbyterian church until 1921.

On a beautiful moonlit night, October 14, the Home held a reception in honor of the Kloppers, with parlor croquet, much laughter, and delicious refreshments. Dr. Klopper stayed only one year, and little is known about his work. He appeared to enjoy Unalaska. The Davenport diary recorded several times that he arrived at their door with the gift of a duck or ptarmigan. On the last day of 1910 his wife gave birth to a daughter. It may have been this that shortened their stay. With that vagueness endemic to the society's publications, he was said to have "found the work more difficult than he anticipated and desires to return." According to the monthly magazine, "Dr. Klopper is an excellent man, honest and faithful, but many things have transpired to render the work difficult, and hence the change will doubtless be for the best."[30]

Dr. Newhall heard from the new secretary for the Alaska Bureau, Mrs. J. H. Parsons of Tacoma, Washington, that Klopper was not suited for the work, had instituted unwise policies and had shown a lack of tact and poor financial management.[31] Parsons' information came in large part from Miss Robinson, who had left in March 1911. From the beginning she and Dr. Klopper had not agreed on much.[32] Parsons told Newhall that all the

DR. HENRY AND MABEL KLOPPER *and children. Courtesy of the Unalaska City School District (Davenport Collection).*

teachers were leaving because of unhappiness with Dr. Klopper. This was not true. Supernaw and Barnett left on planned furloughs and Parsons had not found replacements. The remaining teacher, Clara Cook, described conditions as more pleasant after Robinson left. "We get along better than we did when the Matron was here," she wrote.[33] The annual report for 1910–11, however, describes Unalaska in a way that suggests it was written by someone who felt antipathy for its storms and isolation. It may well have been influenced by a letter or report from one of the Kloppers.

> Alaska is a most difficult field, where for months the workers do not hear from the outside world in the winter time, and at most but once a month: where the coming of a boat closes the school and all the town goes to the wharf, hurrying to get their mail, to quickly read and answer, if possible, the most important letters, because the boat is there for only a short while, sometimes not more than two hours.
>
> These islands are bleak, bare, dark, gloomy, and wind and rain-swept for nearly every day in the year, and the roar of the sea is scarcely ever still.[34]

Clara Cook would describe Unalaska differently. She had been aboard the *Dora* when the trusty vessel docked at 11 a.m. on Oct. 28, 1910, a beautiful late fall morning. For the first two and a half weeks she lived in the boys' dormitory, which also held the superintendent's quarters. "I never seen a better behaved home of boy's," she wrote in her slightly irregular English, "and so polite and so ready to help me and wait on me."[35] After Dr. Klopper asked her to move to the main building and assist with the girls, the older boys would escort her over the long boardwalk between the two buildings after dark. "It is awfull dark and stormy some nights," she wrote, "but we have had a few beautifull moon light nights. I don't think I ever saw the moon so beautifull." In November, she remarked, the sun only struck the Home in two places but she could see it illuminate the western slopes of Mt. Ballyhoo rising above Dutch Harbor. Cook described a well-ordered institution, busy, caring, and run with an established routine. It is the Jesse Lee Home of popular tradition.

1. *WHM*. January 1908:8.

2. *WHM*. October 1907:185.

3. Woman's Home Missionary Society, Reports from Missions. 1907–08:130–31.

4. *WHM*. October 1907:183.

5. *WHM*. January 1908:3.

6. *WHM*. March 1909:11.

7. Ibid.

8. Hudson, ed., *Cuttlefish: Volumes One, Two & Three*, 240.

9. *WHM*. January 1908:3.

10. Ibid.

11. *WHM*. October 1907:134.

12. Woman's Home Missionary Society, Reports from Missions. 1910–11:182–83.

13. NARA. RG 75. General Correspondence. Unalaska. Brown noted that one student "married after 25 days of English school" but did not include this student in the list.

14. Dyakanoff to Upergraff. Jan. 15, 1909. NARA. RG 75. General Correspondence. Unalaska.

15. Reinken to Updergroff. Aug. 14, 1909. NARA. RG 75. General Correspondence. Unalaska.

16. Brown to Updegraph. Nov. 5, 1909. NARA. RG 75. General Correspondence. Unalaska. Another name that gave spellers trouble.

17. Spence to Romig. Feb. 25, 1910. NARA. RG 75. General Correspondence. Unalaska.

18. Candace Waugaman Collection. Alaska State Historical Library. MS 156. As an adult, Henry always spelled his last name "Swanson." The 1908–09 school term record spelled it "Swensen."

19. Undated entry. *Correspondence Copy Book, 1903–1910*. Pat Locke Archival Collection. Museum of the Aleutians.

20. Alaska Children's Services. Jesse Lee Home Archives.

21. Gould, *The Fisherman's Son*, 19–20.

22. Woman's Home Missionary Society, Reports from Missions. 1909–10:147.

23. *WHM*. October 1909:4.

24. *WHM*. October 1909:11.

25. *WHM*. February 1916:8.

26. *WHM*. July 1911:7.

27. Woman's Home Missionary Society, Reports from Missions. 1909–10:147–48.

28. Ibid., 1909–10:148.

29. Davenport, *Unalaska Days*.

30. *WHM*. July 1911:7.

31. At this time the Bureau of Alaska had two branches, one serving Unalaska and the other focusing on Eskimo regions. Mrs. R.H. [Lavinia Wallace] Young had been appointed secretary for the bureau in 1904. After the bureau was divided, she concentrated on work among Eskimo people, primarily on the Seward Peninsula. She retired in 1917. Mrs. J.H. Parson was appointed for work among Aleuts in late 1909 or early 1910.

32. This is reflected in Clara Cook's letter of Jan. 16, 1911.

33. Clara Cook letter, April 17, 1911. Robert Collins Collection.

34. Woman's Home Missionary Society, Report from Bureaus. 1910–11.

35. Clara Cook to "Dear Sister and all the dear ones," Nov. 19, 1910. Robert Collins Collection.

19

Clara Cook

CLARA COOK WAS LIVING IN HILLSDALE, MICHIGAN, WHEN SHE accepted the job at Unalaska in 1910. She was 39 years old. When she arrived, the staff consisted of Dr. and Mrs. Klopper along with the matron Miss Robinson, Emma Supernaw, and Harriet Barnett. Cook referred to herself and the other women as "teachers." Her first 10 months saw a dramatic reduction in the staff. Supernaw left in early December. Barnett's failing health had led her to tender her resignation as early as the summer of 1909.[1] When she returned to Alaska the following year, she worked in Nome three years before coming back to Unalaska briefly. Robinson remained until March 6, when she departed to take a position in Tacoma. The atmosphere at the Home improved. Although the staff was reduced by one, "I don't half to work any harder than I did before," Cook wrote, "and things goes on more pleasant." As her duties multiplied, Clara gained an intimate knowledge of the complexities of running a home for more than 40 children. She was an extraordinarily hard worker completely devoted to the children under her care.

Her surviving letters and scrapbooks are invaluable records of the Jesse Lee Home from 1910 to 1914.[2] If we are to believe Lavinia Young, secretary of the Alaska Bureau, the period from October 1910 to September 1911 was a period of crisis because of the inept management of Dr. Klopper. Cook's letters covering those months, however, show a well-organized and successful operation. Granted, the Home may have been coasting on the momentum established during the previous decade by the Newhalls and the Spences. And granted, with three young children and a husband who liked to absent himself to hunt ducks and ptarmigan, Mrs. Klopper could easily have found life in stormy Unalaska difficult. But for Clara the Home was also a happy place.

Here, culled from Clara Cook's letters, are some impressions from her first year. Certain details have been amplified with comments from the diary kept by schoolteachers Noah and Clara Davenport. Sundays began with breakfast at 7:30, followed by Sunday school at 10:30. Clara had eight boys and five girls in the youngest class. Dinner followed at noon. At 3:00 there was a service with preaching. Clara enjoyed Dr. Klopper's preaching and missed it when he was called out on medical duties. After the service she was responsible for 18 girls until supper at 5:30. She usually stayed in the children's dining room to lead them in saying or singing grace and to keep order while they ate. "They never leave the table without asking me to excuse them," she wrote, "and if one comes in late they ask to be excused." There were four tables in the children's dining room for the 39 students.

The teachers had their own dining room with three large windows whose light allowed a collection of houseplants to thrive. Even in November (1910) two roses opened. The tables were set with white linen and china dishes. The older girls took turns each month learning how to cook and to wait on the tables.

The diet was varied. There were potatoes (five dollars a bushel), onions (five dollars a bushel), beans, and rice. The dozen or so hens gave from six to 11 eggs a day. The only cow was no longer giving milk so they used 12 cans of Carnation condensed milk a week. For meats and fish they had canned roast beef, dried beef, salt pork, corned beef, codfish, salmon, and even whale blubber. There were fish chowders and many other kinds of soup. Sweets included cakes, cookies, doughnuts, tarts, puddings, and pies. Among vegetables were fresh radishes and peppers from the Home's garden. They had canned cabbage, corn, peas, and lima beans. Apples, pears, dried apricots and peaches were on hand. (The Methodist church in Tacoma sent a barrel with 45 quarts of canned fruit in it.) There were blueberries, salmonberries, and cranberries. Each day 30 to 50 loaves of bread were baked.

On Monday mornings Clara oversaw nine boys and five girls doing the laundry in four washing machines and nine stationary tubs. The clothes were soaped, rubbed, rinsed and starched. The boys carried the wet garments up to the third story in the girls' dorm where they were hung to dry. On Monday afternoons, Clara darned socks. On Tuesdays she sewed until school was dismissed and then she went to the laundry to oversee the ironing. This occasionally occupied girls until bedtime. She would sew all day on Wednesday and Thursday and on Friday mornings. Sewing involved patching clothes, making new garments, and frequently altering donated clothing to fit the children. She noted in November that during one week, for only the boys, she darned 68 pairs of socks and mended 23 pairs of pants, 16 shirts, 5 "overshirts," and 7 nightshirts. She made two underwear suits "out of webbing." While she lived in the boys' building, she had a constant stream of buttons to sew on or rips to repair. After she moved to the girls' dorm, the boys' clothing would arrive in a bag all at once for her to mend.

She sewed again on Saturday mornings until 10 when she supervised the bathing of 18 girls. That generally took two hours. After lunch, meetings of the Junior League occupied the children from 3:00 to 4:00 after which Clara went back to her sewing. Bedtime came at 7 for the younger girls and an hour later for the older ones. Girls would come to her room in the evening for prayers and to read their Bibles and receive a goodnight kiss.

Clara's room was large and had a closet, a folding bed, a commode, a bureau with a mirror, a corner seat made of cherry wood with two pillows on it, a center table with a lamp, a rocking chair, and two sets of bookshelves also of cherry. She had a rag rug on the floor and a "stove as big as a ten quart pail with a four inch pipe." There were a total of 17 stoves in the two buildings and the coal for them cost $105 a month. Coal oil lamps provided light in the evenings. She soon decorated her room with a throw on the bed and trinkets on her dresser along with four photographs. She kept a washbowl, pitcher and soap dish on the commode. Her brush and combs sat in the center with her Bible, two other books, and an Easter lily bulb in a glass dish. One of her bookcases was filled with books. The other, covered with a silk curtain, was used to store her writing materials. On the window she hung curtains brought from Michigan. She had her own bedding and feather bed, "so it seems like home."

Clara enjoyed the mix of people. She found the children "very affectionate." She learned to appreciate the Eskimo children and the occasional Eskimo adult. When she arrived there was an Eskimo woman, tattooed in traditional fashion between lower lip and chin, whose husband had sent her from Nome to learn western ways. Clara soon came to feel very close to the woman. She found the local children had an unusual "brogue" and expected that she would soon be talking like them.

"I am as happy as I would be anywheres," she wrote, "so I thank and praise God every day that he sent me here. I don't find it lonely or desolate here. I never tire looking at the snow covered mountains. They are grand." But then she added, "The only thing I don't like is the awfull storms and wind. We have had three since I was here. We are only about 100 feet from the sea and when the wind comes from the north the waves splash up 10 or 20 feet where they hit the banks. And the rain comes in the windows in spite of all we can do it will come with such force. It has rained most all day today. I have my north window packed with clothes to soak up the water." She didn't mind the cold and wore "heavy winter clothes" to combat the chilly winds. When out in a boat, she wore a dark blue cape with a plaid edge and fringe that Harriet Barnett had left behind. "We haven't had any real cold weather," she wrote in January 1911, "and only a little snow. If it is not any worse than so far the climate is grand." She found beauty everywhere she looked. At 9:30 on the night of January 16 she wrote, "This is a beautiful night. The sky is full of stars and the moon is grand." When storms and high tides sent salt water up the creek and into the lake that supplied their fresh water so that the Home had only salt water for three days, she wrote, "I found it was good for chapped hands."

Always when the mail boat arrived came the mad rush to read incoming letters and add finishing touches to outgoing ones. On December 1, Clara received 14 letters and two cards. She dashed off answers to questions, but Harriet Barnett was leaving on the boat and Clara had to assume cooking duties for the Home. A month later she had 12 letters and 17 cards to read when the mail was delivered at 11 a.m. She was halfway through replying when the "half hour" whistle blew so she just signed her name to each of the rest of the incomplete letters and ran to the dock with four of the girls. This was the last boat until March. When the *Dora* arrived on March 6, another flurry of 25 letters, some more than 10 pages long, came for Clara. This mail day was complicated by the departure of Miss Robinson and the fact that the washing was only partly hung up to dry when the boat

Sisters Annie *(left)* and Helen Swanson. *Courtesy of the Unalaska City School District (Clara Cook Collection).*

arrived. One young girl was sick in bed, and when one of the older girls, who had also been sick, tried to help Clara, she fainted in the teacher's room

During the Christmas season in 1910 community members crowded into the chapel for a program on December 23. The Russian school loaned chairs to the Home. Clara Cook found Father Panteleev and his assistant, Leonti Sifsof, very friendly. The A.C. Co. and the N.A.C. Co. provided oranges, apples, nuts and candy. The Home was also given a roasting pig for the holiday. Served with the pork were dressing, gravy, potatoes, turnips, and mince pie. Clara had baked 11 pies, 100 fancy cookies, and 100 doughnuts. The day before, she had baked 73 loaves of bread. For Christmas, the teachers ate with the delighted children. Besides the gifts of oranges, a handkerchief, a pin cushion, and boxes of candy, Clara received three works of Aleut crafts. One was an embroidered wall bag of gut and another was a woven grass card case. In addition, she received "a string of white eggs from St. Paul's island." This consisted of four or five blown eggs (often strong seagull eggs) strung vertically with decorative yarn placed between them.[3] The oldest Inupiat boy at the Home, William Baylies (Catua), gave her an ivory breast pin in which a pure white heart was suspended from a straight piece of gray and brown ivory.

Mrs. Klopper did what she could to relieve Clara's workload, but the birth of her daughter in December meant she had three small children needing attention. In March, after Robinson left, she moved into the matron's room so that Clara would not be alone in the girls' dormitory. She carried her 3-month-old infant and oversaw the girls at their tasks.

Having assumed cooking duties after Harriet Barnett left, Clara soon learned to try new recipes. She cooked seal meat, which "don't taste as bad as it might." She made Russian pie (*pirok*) with rice, onions and salmon. Older girls assisted—or tried to. When it was Margaret Seymour's turn, Clara remarked, "She don't know a platter from a soap dish," or what it meant to peel potatoes. Margaret (Aganuksuk) had arrived from Herschel Island in 1910. Clara found that she would sometimes do the opposite of what she was asked to do, "but we get along nicely. She will kiss me and jump to wait on me, but has an awfull temper when roused." Clara also continued to supervise the washing and ironing. And the sewing never ended. Eight suits of clothing for the little boys, 7 to 9 years old, were made along with bibbed overalls and long johns. For all her work, her health was excellent and she was even gaining weight, up to 136 pounds from 126 when she had left Michigan.

On January 17 she felt five light earthquakes rumble through the village. Doubling the actual number, she wrote that the island had two active volcanoes. "Now don't be frightened," she reassured her sister, "for the Lord will take care of me, and it is just as near Heaven here as any place if he sees fit to take me." Two and a half months into her job, she wrote, "Realy I believe I would shed some tears if I had to leave here now, as many or more than I did for leaving Hillsdale." Late on February 1 or during the early hours of Feb. 2, 1911, the village was covered with ash. Noah and Clara Davenport had noticed unusual amounts of steam or smoke issuing from Makushin Volcano since January 25. Cook was up writing that evening and became aware of a strong gassy smell. In the morning "the mountains looked like ash heaps." When damp, the ashes smelled like sulfur.

Washington's birthday was celebrated with an entertainment sponsored by the Unalaska Brass Band, directed by Leonti Sifsof. The Home loaned its chairs for the lengthy program. Teacher Noah Davenport gave an address as did Father Panteleev and Dr. Klopper. There were comedic sketches including "No Law Suits in Heaven" and "The Competing Railroad." Songs in English were interspersed with ones in Russian. The Russian school choir sang a new song in Aleut. The great storyteller Isidor Solovyov, now approaching the last year of his life, gave a presentation on "Aleut Home Life and Song," assisted by his wife. Scattered among all these were performances by the "Unalaska Royal Brass Band," as Clara Davenport called the ensemble of 17 instruments, adding that they "ought to be suppressed." "And oh, that Band!" she noted in her diary. Edith Newhall Drugg remembered the band's music for all of her long life.

> They used to practice above the old laundry there at Unalaska. And, oh! The sounds that would come forth were perfectly horrible! So when we'd hear something that was horrible outside we'd say, "Sounds like the Unalaska Brass Band!" And the children would all laugh. . . . We'd be walking by, maybe going down to the dock or the A.C. Company and we'd hear these horrible sounds coming forth with the Unalaska Brass Band practicing up there. It was terrible.[4]

Nevertheless, the Davenports had a great time at the entertainment as did Clara Cook and the rest of the community.

On Monday, March 20, 1911, 11-year-old Onita died after two months of suffering. It was the coldest day of the winter, with the temperature dropping to 10 degrees. Clara was relieved that the child's agonies were over. When Clara had first arrived, Onita was ill with diabetes and was expected to die any day. She had survived five months longer. "The night before she died," Clara wrote, "she was singing Safe in the arms of Jesus. She died smiling without a struggle." The older boys built a coffin and dug a grave. The coffin was lined with white cloth. Geranium leaves and a fuchsia blossom were placed in the child's hands. A calla lily and asparagus ferns adorned the coffin's lid. The Home's flag was lowered, and the bell was tolled. Dr. Klopper conducted the service and preached a sermon.

The children's health was always a concern. Nellie Holmberg, 11 years old, was also ill, and Clara was worried. Nellie had a bad cough and was being kept home from school, but she survived. Clara encouraged her and the sisters Annie and Helen Swanson to write to her friend Clara Stevens. Nellie and Stevens maintained a correspondence for many years.

March 31, 1911

Dear friend Clara,

I am going to write you a few lines and tell you how I am getting along here. We have such good times here. I go to school and I can read pretty well. One night the ashes fell and the mountains and hills looked very queer to me because this was the first time I saw the ashes fall. The ground and the mountains are covered with snow and the sun is shining. Sometimes it is very cold. We are practicing for easter. Our program is called Our Lord Triumphant. Please tell me when your birthday comes and how old you are. My birthday comes in May 21 and my age is 10 years. I'll be 11 years old this year. I have two brothers and two sisters. I had more than two brothers but they are dead now. I came to the home 1909 in Sept.

From Nellie Mabel Holmberg

March 31, 1911

Dear Clara Stevens,

I thought I would write to you. I go to the republic school and I am in the geography and hygiene. I was ten year old the 3rd day of March. I can talk English very well. I was in the home 10 years. I like Miss Cook very well. I am well and happy and I hope you are the same. The doctor [Henry Klopper] has three children. I had a for-get-me-not chain from My dear friend Miss Barnett. I had a dolly and a game of cars and a drawing book, a story book. My dolly name is Alma she has blue eyes and brown hair. I haven't seen my Mother since I was a baby. I have a sister her name is Annie E H Swansen. She is writing to you.

With love remain
From Helen Edith Hattie Swansen

March 31, 1911

Dear Clara Stevens,

I thoughtt I would write to you. I am going to Government
school and I am in Hygiene and Geography. I am 11 years old
and my sister is 10 years old and her birthday come's March 3
and mine come's May 15. My father come's once a year to see
me and my sister. My Mother never came to see me since I was
a baby. I am very happy and I hope you are the same. I was in
the Home for 8 years and this make's my 9th year. We had a nice
Christmas. Are teacher[s] are very nice. I like my school teachers.
My doctor's name is Mr. and Mrs. Klopper they have three
children. Your friend

Annie Edith Hattie Swansen

August 25, 1912

My Dear Clara,

I thought I would write a few lines to you. Please excuse me for not
writing to you. I did not have time to write to you because [I] had to
help Mrs. Goss. We are all having a good time and I hope you are too.
I was very glad to see my mother and so was Helen. She came to see us
this year while papa went down to Seattle. One day we went out to pick
some salmon berries. We went to san[d]spit to get them and we got
quite a lot. Our silo is nearly full of hay now. … We are having nice
weather now a days. I think I will close with

love from your friend
Annie Swanson [5]

On April 13, a Thursday, a terrific storm bombarded the village. At noon, just as the children arrived home for lunch, the unfinished riverboat *Colonel McNaught*, abandoned years before on the beach in front of the boys' building, burst into pieces. Cook estimated the vessel at 150 feet long and 30 feet wide. The ship's cabin disintegrated and pieces went flying. The deck broke into three or four sections and sailed 200 to 300 yards before lodging in the ground. A 12-inch mast, 20 feet in length, sailed over the boys' dorm. Five-inch iron pipes, 14 to 16 feet long, hurled through the air. Dr. Klopper was standing near a window when a timber crashed through. Cook wrote that the chimney on the boys' building was knocked off, some of the roof was torn off, timber was stuck through into the interior of the building, and the side wall was knocked in. There were six or seven holes in the room, some of them eight inches across. Somehow, no one was injured.

Dr. Klopper rushed to the school and asked Noah Davenport to photograph the wrecked ship. The A.C. Co. owned the vessel and had been asked several times to remove it after it was abandoned. Its presence was one of two things that Agnes Newhall had objected to because it had blocked the Home's view of the bay since 1900.[6] (Her other complaint was the lack of an adequate boardwalk between the boys' and girls' dormitories.) The company assumed responsibility for repairing the building and removing the wreckage. In the meantime, the boys camped out around their dormitory in various dry locations. Whenever storms appeared after this one, Mrs. Klopper would dress herself and her children for a quick escape should the building begin disintegrating. "So do you wonder I am a little nervous, too," wrote Clara, "when the house shakes like a leaf nearly." She wrote that once the house shook so much that one of the girls got seasick in bed and vomited.

Stormy April quieted down. On April 28 the *Dora* arrived with a new teacher, Mary Winchell.[7] She was by far the best writer ever to live at the Home. Her two books are jewels and reflect the great love she developed for Unalaska and the people.

Mary Winchell was born in 1878 in College Springs, Iowa, and began her professional career as a teacher in that state. However, from her childhood she had wanted to be a missionary. She attended Amity College in College Springs and later spent two years at the University of Southern California, during which time she volunteered in a Japanese mission. She had teaching jobs in Idaho and Colorado, and then, during a year off, she applied to the missionary society for a position in Puerto Rico as she spoke some Spanish.[8] Lavinia Young wrote asking if she would consider Alaska instead. Help was badly needed at the Jesse Lee Home. In a week Winchell had left Loveland, Colorado. She arrived and was welcomed by Dr. Klopper and the boys from the Home. Mary found Clara Cook a cheerful presence. While out for a stroll that evening, Winchell saw the school and went inside "to the pleasing sight of desks, black-board, erasers and chalk." She opened a door by the blackboard and discovered she had intruded into private quarters where two young people sat at a table. She and the Davenports became friends for life.[9]

THE WIRELESS STATION *at Dutch Harbor. Photograph from E. Pelagia McCurdy, in the author's collection.*

Mrs. Klopper acted as matron until mid-July when the job was assigned to Clara Cook. Clara found it less physically demanding than cooking, but there was more "governing" of students. She continued to oversee the drying and ironing of clothes, sewing and mending, and keeping the second and third stories of the main building clean. On July 20, she and eight girls cleaned more than a thousand herring and 26 salmon one day and expected the boys to arrive from the camp at Summer Bay with another load the next day. Calm weather brought out hordes of mosquitoes. The Davenports took her over to Amaknak Island and she came home with her arms full of wildflowers.

In late May or early June, Martha Applegate moved into the Home. Her son was born on July 14. There had been worry over the pregnancy, but everything went well. On the Fourth of July the staff and children were invited aboard the Japanese man-of-war *Naniwa* commanded by Captain Hara. By mid-August most of the winter's supply of fish had been salted: cod, salmon and herring. The storeroom was filled with 250 50-pound sacks of white flour in addition to graham, corn meal, and whole wheat, plus seven barrels of sugar. Clara had the school clothes almost ready. She had cut out and sewed 14 pairs of overalls and altered 19 pairs. She had made 10 undergarments, three dresses, and three aprons. She had even started to learn how to pick and prepare wild rye grass used in Aleut basketry. "I have started a basket," she wrote, "don't know when I will get it finished." Mary Prokopeuff Lavigne, from Attu, was teaching basketry in the public school. Clara was now perfectly at home. "I like this climate so well," she wrote, "I may want to spend my remaining days here."

The wireless station on Amaknak Harbor was completed in August. The project had first been presented to the secretaries of the Navy and Treasury in 1908 as "a great convenience for the Nome and Bering Sea fleet, permitting them to keep in touch with the land in this section of their route."[10] The station would relieve vessels from calling at the port of Valdez, a trip usually considerably out of their direct course. Construction on the wireless station started about the Fourth of July. It was located a short distance from Dutch Harbor at a place facing Unalaska and known in those days as Chy Town. The flashing lights from the station could be seen at night. Once it was operating, Clara wrote, "We felt quite city-fied." Each day personnel from the wireless station would post a couple of typewritten pages of news at the A.C. store. One great service provided by the wireless was advanced notification of the arrival of the *Dora* and other vessels. On October 16 a storm toppled both towers, but service was not interrupted for long; the men at the station used a kite with a very long wire to receive and send messages. "They say it worked beautifully while the wind lasted," wrote the Davenports.[11] In November, in fact, one of the operators came to the Home and offered to send Christmas greetings for the staff free of charge.[12] The Newhalls, who were back by then, were able to send one to their son Chester.

On August 21 a fire started near the chimney in the attic of the girls' dorm. When Clara rushed up the steps she found it blazing away and immediately began throwing water to keep it contained. Dr. Klopper and the older boys came running and climbed onto the roof. "I thought for a while the house would go," she wrote. "I guess I threw 25 pails of water. I was as wet as if I had been dipped in the sea hair and all." The girls pumped water on the third floor and carried it up the stairs. Once the fire was out they immediately began "to dry up the water without being told." An older girl had corralled the younger children and kept them away from the Home. The day after the fire Clara was so lame and sore that she could hardly roll over in bed. Dr. Klopper took it upon himself to extend the water pipes up to the attic and install a faucet.

Five days later the *Dora* once again came into port. Dr. and Mama Newhall, with their daughter Edith and Emma Supernaw, had returned.

NOTES

1. *WHM*. October 1909:4.

2. Unless otherwise noted, quotations from Cook letters in this chapter are all from the Robert Collins Collection. Three scrapbooks assembled by Cook were given to the Unalaska City School in 1978 by Stephen and Kathie Assenmacher after they purchased them from an antique dealer in Hartland, Michigan. These formed the basis of the student publication *Cuttlefish Three: Home on the Bering* (Unalaska City School, 1978-79).

3. See Hudson, ed., *Cuttlefish: Volumes One, Two & Three*, 63, for an illustration of one of these.

4. Personal conversation with Ray Hudson, Feb. 13, 1976.

5. All four letters are from the Robert Collins Collection, Unalaska Historical Commission.

6. Winchell, *Where the Wind Blows Free*, 44. Although she would have seen the wreckage and heard the story, Winchell's chapter "Blessed Be the Wind" is highly fictionalized. She arrived two weeks after this storm and the Newhalls were living in Massachusetts at the time.

7. In *Home by the Bering Sea* Winchell gives an incorrect date for her arrival. Both the Davenport diary and the Cook letters confirm she arrived on April 28.

8. *WHM*. October 1935:13.

9. Recounted in Winchell's inscription in Davenport's copy of *Where the Wind Blows Free*. Davenport. *Unalaska Days: A Diary*, appendix.

10. *Seattle Post Intelligencer*. Jan. 16, 1908.

11. Davenport. *Unalaska Days*, 52.

12. Clara Cook, letter, Nov. 27, 1911.

20

A Trip on the Dora

Aᴌᴛʜᴏᴜɢʜ ʙʏ 1911 Dʀ. Nᴇᴡʜᴀʟʟ ʜᴀᴅ ᴇsᴛᴀʙʟɪsʜᴇᴅ ᴀ ᴘʀᴀᴄᴛɪᴄᴇ ɪɴ Stoneham that was growing each month, he and Agnes agreed to return to Unalaska. Edith would have to leave her school and their young son Chester would stay with the family of one of the doctor's brothers. "When one gets the spirit of mission work upon her," Agnes wrote about their decision, "if she stops she is like a fire horse laid off from service—when the alarm rings she is ready to spring to the work."[1] Dr. Newhall told how they were persuaded to retrace the long voyage to Unalaska.

> We had returned to the states, never expecting to return to Alaska again but there seemed to be urgent need for us to return. Mrs. Parsons of Tacoma, Wash., wrote us about conditions. How that a man not adapted for the work had by his unwise policies, his lack of tact, poor financial management, etc. had almost run the institution into the ground. [In her published report, Parsons referred to Klopper as "an excellent man, honest and faithful."] Only two teachers were left and they would not stay. Would we return?
>
> Miss Barnett, then in Canaan VT. wrote stating she thought we were the ones to set things right. Mrs. R.H. Young of Long Beach, Cal. wrote us asking us to go and later wrote that she had asked too much.
>
> After much prayer and many tears we agreed to go. It was during the "World in Boston" that the final telegram came. Aunt Ruth, Agnes, Miss Supernaw & Miss Barnett were in the kitchen. All lifted up their voices and wept while I fled to pick some rhubarb in the garden.
>
> To say it was hard to make the decision and to pull up stakes, is to put it mildly. We thought it best to leave Chester, our boy at home, and that was hardest of all.[2]

In his reply to Parsons, Newhall wrote, "No one knows more than we do what the discouragements are, and how much truth there is in the reports of workers as to the uselessness of such work. . . . Jesse Lee Home stands as a beacon light in a dark land, and it has been a blessing to many. . . . It has seemed to us that the Lord might be leading us back. Our decision looks easy on paper, but it has caused many prayers and more tears."[3]

The four years on the East Coast had gone quickly. On Oct. 2, 1907, they had arrived in Little Falls, New York, where Dr. Newhall came down with typhoid. He was hospitalized into November. On Thanksgiving Eve, Peter Kashevaroff and Eliza Gould were

Hashevaroff –

"PETER" AND "ELIZA"

Once boy and girl in Jesse Lee Home; now
heads of a happy Christian home
in Vermont

Courtesy of Alaska Children's Services, Anchorage.

married by the Rev. C.E. Dotey at Dr. Newhall's brother's home. From November 1907 until August 1908 the Newhalls lived at 169 Cherry Street in Burlington, Vermont, where Peter and Eliza lived with them as did Polly and Charles Dirks. Peter was employed as head clerk at George H. Mylkes on Church Street, a store specializing in interior decorating supplies including fine china, wallpaper and souvenirs. Eliza gave birth to a girl in October 1908 and the next year the little family moved to 125 Elmwood Avenue. This son of an Orthodox priest was in charge of the Alaska exhibit at the annual meeting of the missionary society in Brookline, Massachusetts, "where he won golden opinions for his intelligent courtesy."[4] In 1908 the Newhalls moved to Stoneham, Massachusetts, where they purchased property at 20 Pine Street on which to build a home. They were visited by Mr. and Mrs. Applegate and Nick Bolshanin from Unalaska. On October 1 they moved into their new house. Two weeks later, on October 16, Agnes's mother died.

Dr. Newhall traveled around the northeast and gave a number of talks on Alaska and on his missionary work. In February 1910 he visited the Kashevaroffs in Burlington before speaking in Montpelier. The New England Conference of the Evangelical Church was held in Stoneham in March and the Newhalls opened their home to visitors. A large missionary exposition was held in Boston in 1911. Agnes, Harriet Barnett and Emma Supernaw took turns giving talks every day at the Alaska exhibit. Chester and Edith Newhall visited the exhibit on Saturdays and sang the "Russian Lullaby" every hour. Dr. Newhall helped build a model of Unalaska village including the Orthodox church. He helped with a display of the cliff dwellings on King Island. His brother Chester made a "fine water color panorama of mountain scenery—Unalaska."

Peter and Eliza Kashevaroff left Vermont to return to Unalaska sometime in 1910. By November Eliza was established in her own home and had given the Davenports "a fine lunch of duck stew."[5] Before long Noah Davenport and Peter became great friends.

Albert, Agnes, and Edith departed Stoneham on July 29, 1911, taking a train from Boston's North Station where many folks gathered to see them off. The crowd included the former marshal Willard Hastings and his wife Mattie Short, along with Polly Dirks and her brother Charles.[6] Emma Supernaw joined the Newhalls in Montreal. She had traveled there from her family's home in West Chazy near Plattsburgh, New York. They traveled across Canada and down to Tacoma and Seattle. The *Portland*, their old standby, was no longer in service.[7] They took passage on the *Alameda* for a trip up the Inside Passage to Seward, stopping all along the way. Dr. Newhall described Cordova, in Prince William Sound, as "a typical mining town, electric lights, and plank walks. The Copper River and North Western R.R. starts here. . . . What impressed us most were the mosquitoes, millions of them." And about Valdez he wrote: "This town is built on a glacier bed and had recently had a freshet. Many houses were overturned, and debris was scattered about. Mrs. Newhall bought some yarn to knit stockings so she was happy." At Seward the Newhalls boarded the *Dora*, the indefatigable *Dora*. "The SS *Dora* is not a commodious ocean liner,"

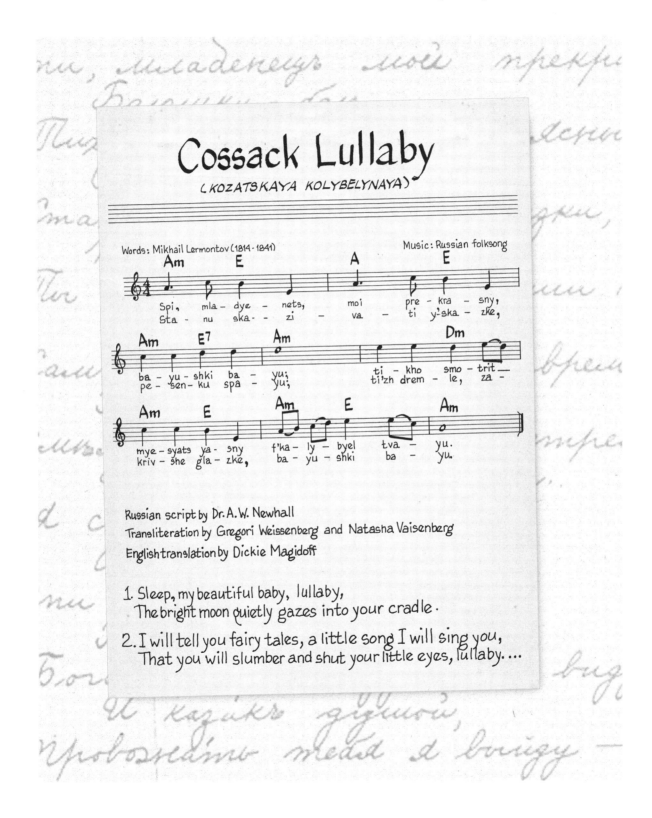

Cossack Lullaby
(KOZATSKAYA KOLYBELYNAYA)

Words: Mikhail Lermontov (1814-1841) Music: Russian folksong

Spi, mla - dye - nets, moi pre - kra - sny,
Sta - nu ska - zi - va - ti y'ska - zke,

ba - yu - shki ba - yu; ti - kho smo - trit
pe - sen - ku spa - yu; ti'zh drem - le, za -

mye - syats ya - sny f'ka - ly - byel tva - yu.
kriv - she gla - zke, ba - yu - shki ba - yu.

Russian script by Dr. A. W. Newhall

Transliteration by Gregori Weissenberg and Natasha Vaisenberg

English translation by Dickie Magidoff

1. Sleep, my beautiful baby, lullaby,
   The bright moon quietly gazes into your cradle.

2. I will tell you fairy tales, a little song I will sing you,
   That you will slumber and shut your little eyes, lullaby. ...

Newhall wrote, "and looks very small beside the SS 'Alameda.' I must confess that my heart sank at the thought of taking a voyage in such a craft."[8]

> She has little room for freight and less for passengers. Her decks were so loaded with freight that there was little room to walk round and no place to sit down except on the edge of a batch and in a life boat, fastened to its davits and the latter was the favorite seat. Four small staterooms and six berth apartments are the first class accommodations. Passengers slept on the seats in the dining and smoking room. I went aboard with Edith and as she groped her way down the narrow stairway to the deck below, she exclaimed, "Misery and me! What kind of a boat is this?" Yet with all her limitations the 'Dora' is a staunch sea craft, having weathered the Alaskan gales for the past 31 years. In fact, after getting used to our quarters, we came to feel quite at home on her and it was a happy company of travelers.

They stopped at Port Graham, Seldovia, Homer and Iliamna and arrived at Kodiak "just as the Greek church bells were ringing, and by a coincidence at the same time that we arrived at this place four years ago. . . . All along the line, we hear that we are coming, and all seem to be glad." The ship stayed only one hour and was off again. On Sunday evening a group sat in a corner of the dining room and sang familiar hymns and other songs while from the cook's sleeping quarters came the "rang-a-tang-tang" of a phonograph. "It was a medley, but it helped to pass away the time."

Before long, they were in strong winds.

> Oh dear! The Dora is not much of an ocean greyhound, for when she has a fair wind and does her best, she makes only 6 or 7 knots. Crossing the Shelikoff Strait!!! We were a forlorn looking crowd. A northeaster was raging, an old timer that would make an 'old salt' grit his teeth – – – Well!! We grit ours before the day was through—and the following night as far as that went.

> When in sight of Karluk, the steamer blew three whistles, (good bye) and steered out into the face of the gale to cross the strait. Such a day as we put in. Miss Supernaw was in bed sick, her diet, an occasional hardtack. Agnes, Edith and I were on deck most all day. Seated on the floor of the after deck, up against some freight, we braced our feet and held on. How the vessel rolled. Sails were set to steady her and yet when the big ocean swells would rise up, she would rise up too—and then roll down the other side—down - down - down, until the edge of the deck would seem to touch the water. Then up - up - up on another crest—and then another roll down the other side. Not once in a while, but every few moments. It was a wonder how we could come right side up again. By night the gale had increased and a driving rain was added to it.

Such a night. We three were conquered and crawled into bed, clothes and all, feeling wretched and miserable. We bumped and pitched about in the bunks with every lurch of the vessel, and how she pitched and rolled. Wave after wave would hurl itself in all its fury against her. Now a pitch and then a lurch. The boat would seem to poise in the air; shiver and tremble; then a big wave would hit her 'kerbunk' and she would careen over, over, over, right herself and then go in for another stunt. Once in a while something would get loose on deck and jump about, and then the pots and pans in the galley would dance a jig. All night the crew worked hard to keep the deck freight from going overboard. We could not make Cold Harbor.

There were kittens aboard and a mate said Edith could have one if she didn't get sea-sick. If she did, the kitten would go overboard. "All through the storm Edith kept up, for fear the kitten would go into the sea. The next day the mate said he would excuse her." They spent eight hours at Chignik. At Belkofski an Aleut man came aboard. He smiled at Dr. Newhall who asked, "You know me?"

"*Aang* [yes]," the man answered. "You Doctor Newhall, you go Unalaska." He told the doctor he was glad and that the people at Unalaska were happy when they heard he was returning.

"Well, I always tried to be good to you," the doctor said.

"We know it," the man replied.

On the 18th day of their trip they rounded Priest Rock and reached the wharf at 9 a.m. on August 26. Among the crowd welcoming them was Mark Moriss. "He was so anxious to see if Chester was on board, that he climbed right over the railing on to some freight. He thinks a lot of our little boy and so does Nanna his wife. The children at the Home were glad to welcome us back. Altho it was *very* hard to leave our home, friends, and for a time the boy, yet we feel that we were needed here at this time."

The Newhalls had a day or so with the Kloppers to catch up on the status of the Home. The Kloppers paid a farewell visit to the Davenports before leaving on the *Homer* at four in the afternoon on August 28. It was, as on the day they had arrived, a rainy unpleasant day.[9]

Thwaites.   *S. S. Dora, The "Bull Terrier" of Alaska.*

"THE S.S. DORA, *the 'bull terrior' of Alaska," by John E. Thwaites, mail clerk aboard the* Dora *from 1905–1912. Thwaites' photographs of coastal Alaska appear in many collections; this portrait of the* Dora *is from Annie Swanson Hatch's album, courtesy of the Hatch family.*

1. *WHM*. January 1912:7.

2. Newhall Manuscript, 252.

3. *WHM*. July 1911:8.

4. *WHM*. January 1909:6. This issue also carried a photograph of the Kashevaroffs with their child.

5. Davenport, *Unalaska Days,* Nov. 9, 1910.

6. Charles shot himself to death in Newton, Massachusetts, in 1911. Polly continued to live in Stoneham until 1914 when she returned to Alaska.

7. The *Portland* had been approaching Cordova in a heavy blizzard the previous November when it struck an uncharted rock near the mouth of Controller Bay. The captain ran it ashore about two miles farther on. All the crew and passengers got off safely, and much of the cargo was saved. The vessel itself was eventually beaten to pieces by succeeding storms.

8. Newhall Manuscript, 260–64.

9. The Methodist Church appointed Henry Klopper as the minister to Smith River Indian Mission in Napa, California, in September 1911.

21

A Home to Itself

THE NEWHALLS AND EMMA SUPERNAW HAD DECIDED IN SEATTLE that one of the first things they would do on reaching Unalaska would be to give Clara Cook and Mary Winchell a short vacation at Huntsville, the shallow cove about two miles from the village on the eastern side of Captains Bay.[1] During the gold rush, riverboats had assembled at the foot of the truncated valley that rises in a series of scalloped hills from the shore. Towering above them is Pyramid Mountain. At its base and about a quarter of a mile from the beach, a stamp mill for gold-bearing quartz had briefly operated. The A.C. Co.'s plan to invest in the mine was thwarted by the 1906 San Francisco earthquake, which destroyed the company's headquarters. By 1911 the machinery was covered with moss and rust. A derelict cabin stood by the shaft, and a ton of dynamite was stored nearby. Boys from the Home would occasionally be caught dragging sticks of the explosive through the tall grass. Close to the shore, the Home had built a cabin where Cook and Winchell were sent for a two-week rest. "We are as cozy as kittens in a cottage 10 by 15 feet square, four feet high at the edge 8 feet in the peek," wrote Cook. "It is lined with white muslin, and two caribou rugs, two cot beds, cupboard, cook stove, table, two chairs, an organ, has two windows. A little mountain stream runs past the cottage on its way to the sea where we get lovely water to drink." Later, a lean-to was added that contained two additional bunks and an extra wood box.

Winchell also enjoyed her stays at the cove. "Huntsville was a delightful place," she wrote, "and we who loved to go there found it very comfortable." However, not everyone cared for its rough accommodations. One woman said to Winchell, "Why walk three miles to sit on a box in a shack when you can sit at home and be comfortable?"[2] After Mrs. J.H. Parsons, the bureau secretary from Tacoma, visited and discovered the walk to Huntsville required wading through water even when the tide was low, she referred to the retreat as a "miserable little cabin, scarcely high enough to stand upright in" and called it "a leaky old shack."[3] No place, however, could have been lovelier in the eyes of Mary Winchell. "Thank the Lord for Huntsville," she wrote.

Every day someone came to check on them. On September 10, Dr. Newhall arrived with 26 children, but usually the women had the day to themselves to rest, read, and explore. Wading through high grass, Cook found heaps of tin cans and piles of broken crockery where shipbuilders' tents had once stood. These remains gave her pause to consider the transitory nature of life. "Many lost their lives and all here," she wrote, "and where are the rest that are alive? Life is so uncertain." Actually, no one had died there, but a man from Biorka had been killed the week before while helping the A.C. Co. remove the wrecked riverboat from the front yard of the Home.

Clara had been working harder than she realized. On returning to Unalaska she had trouble sleeping, and her nerves were upset. Dr. Newhall didn't prescribe medication, but he did reduce her workload and suggested she try doing something completely different. She began taking piano lessons from Clara Goss, doing more fancy work, and going outside more. She pinned a motto up in her room:

> Build a little fence of trust around today.
> Fill the space with loving work and therein stay.
> Look not through its sheltering bars upon tomorrow.
> God will help thee bear what come of Joy or Sorrow.[4]

These sentiments were reflective of what was happening to the Jesse Lee Home itself. With two fine large buildings, with about 30 children, and with a full component of experienced missionaries, the Home built a fence around itself. It was independent of the community. It no longer needed to recruit students from Orthodox families. Needy or orphaned Aleut children were usually absorbed into local families; new children entering the Home more frequently came from northern parts of the territory or from the Alaska Peninsula region.[5] The staff concentrated on their own work; they stayed inside their own perimeter. It is not entirely true to say they never left "its sheltering bars." Indeed, the outreach to both Aleuts and non-Aleuts in the community became more effective as their overt proselytizing decreased. Independence created an identity that could then be integrated into the wider community. This was especially true of Dr. Newhall's medical work. The missionaries no longer measured success solely in terms of conversions from Orthodoxy. They were content as never before with whatever came their way.

.   .   .

WHILE THE HOME STABILIZED, communities in the Aleutians underwent profound changes. During the years from the initiation of the Jesse Lee Home in 1889 to the arrival of Dr. Newhall in 1898, sea otter hunting had remained central to Aleut lives. The otter population had steadily declined, however, and commercial firms and individual fur traders looked for new sources of wealth. The Klondike and Nome gold rushes profited the A.C. Co. and the N.A.C. Co. along with local saloons and smaller stores. Aleut people had little share in this boom, and their poverty mounted as sea otter hunting came to its slow but inevitable end. On July 7, 1911, the Treaty for the Preservation and Protection of Fur Seals was signed in Washington, D.C., and sea otter hunting was outlawed for the next 15 years. Blue fox farming had been introduced but so far had failed to make up for the loss of the otter. Villages throughout the chain experienced deepening poverty.

The publications of the Woman's Home Missionary Society had always tended to exaggerate hardships. The more desperate the orphans, the swifter the flow of contributions. This time, however, the missionary ladies got general conditions correct even if they skewed some of the details.

> On the Aleutian Islands the condition of the natives in some cases is deplorable; they are fast dying of starvation, disease, and a general hopeless inertia. On one of these islands there remain only thirty-six or thirty-eight souls, half starved and thinly clad, more or less afflicted with disease, and unless something is done very quickly they will be past early help. It is with the greatest difficulty these natives keep from starvation; their only food being fish. In the past the fur-bearing animals were depended upon for food and clothing; they traded the furs and received shoes and clothing. The blue and white fox and seal otter [sic] are fast becoming exterminated, and unless something is done at once the native population of these islands will be extinct. The Government has provided schools, but has done nothing to aid the natives along industrial lines whereby they might earn a means of livelihood.[6]

Much of the society's information came from reports by officers of the U.S. Revenue Cutter Service, which after 1915 became the U.S. Coast Guard. "Attention has been brought repeatedly to the wretched condition of the natives of the Aleutian Islands," wrote D.P. Foley in 1911. He was senior captain of the Revenue Cutter Service and commander of the Bering Sea Patrol Fleet headquartered during the summer at Unalaska. "There is nothing much to add to the reports previously made concerning them, except, if possible, their wretchedness is greater, and of course will increase year by year until the Government does something for them, or until they are wiped out of existence by disease and starvation."

The solution he proposed was to concentrate everyone in a single settlement at Unalaska, beginning with the most destitute villages of Attu, Chernofski, Biorka and Kashega, about 36 families with 153 individuals. Unalaska had enough land to accommodate the newcomers. "The Alaska Commercial Co., in addition to occupying the [government] reservation and inclosing a large pasture field near the lake, has a corral about one-third the size of an average city block within the limits of the village. It should vacate this latter piece of ground." He appreciated the work of the Home but wrote, "The Jesse Lee Home, a missionary school, has inclosed about six times as much land as it will ever have use for." (In 1917 the society claimed title to 160 acres.) This resettlement would cost about $25,000 initially, Foley wrote, with $10,000 more for a suitable water project for the village.[7]

Foley had made this proposal before. In 1910 he acknowledged that villagers were opposed to the idea. "Like other people," he wrote, "they have a love for their native places

"IN BACK OF THE BARN." *Back row, from left: 3, Dolly Smith; 4, Agnes Shapsnikoff; 5, Charlotte Smith; 9, Dora Balamatoff. Front row, from right: 2, Annie Pomian; 3, Kalissa Peshnikoff. Courtesy of the Unalaska City School District (Clara Cook Collection).*

and are moreover remnants of tribes that once waged bitter warfare against one another and some of the old animosities still live though the war spirit is dead. . . ."[8] He respected Aleuts and wanted them freed from poverty and dependence on charity. "This is but little to ask of the Government in the name of humanity, and these people are most deserving. They have never cost the Government anything, except for the establishment and maintenance of two schools, one here [Unalaska] and the other at Atka, and these of necessity benefit but a very small percentage of the school population." Aleuts "have never cost a dollar for soldiers to keep them in order, as have the Indians of the plains; perhaps if they had they would not have been so long neglected. They have never had any continued medical care or treatment; no treatment at all in fact, except what could be given by the surgeons of the revenue cutters in their occasional flying visits, and yet it is known that they are suffering, not as individuals but as a people, from some of the most dreadful known diseases. They are simply being allowed to rot away because of them."

Despite his regard for Aleuts, Foley thought of them as "children [who] need to be taught and controlled, and shown new ways of earning a livelihood. . . ." To replace hunting and fishing, he suggested they be shown how to grow vegetables and raise poultry. Fishing on the open sea would be available to them if they had a schooner. They needed a store where they could get fair prices for fox furs. They needed regular employment.

"The exploitation of these islands by hunters and traders who go about them in winter in small schooners and sloops is a growing evil which should be abolished," he concluded. "Some of these hunters are accused, and justly I believe, of poisoning the foxes and bartering whisky with the natives for furs."

His recommendations were echoed in the missionary society's reports. "It is hoped that the Government will gather the few natives on the farther islands of the Aleutian chain and put them on one of the larger ones, probably Unalaska, and there provide some kind of industrial work for them and establish a hospital or some means whereby their health can be cared for."

Conditions were better at Unalaska, but even here the loss of the sea otter meant increased poverty. As early as 1909 a visitor to Dutch Harbor found the North American Commercial Company complex almost deserted. Business generated by Alaskan and Canadian gold fields had vanished. "Only here and there one sees a human being in the settlement," wrote a visitor, "of which some stray horses, dogs, pigs, and fowls seem to have taken possession; we feel as if we were in a fairy tale; we are in a city of the dead."[9] The last manager was Fred Schroeder, who owned the *Elvira*, the vessel on which Henry Swanson accompanied the sea otter hunters. In 1910 the government ended its policy of leasing the Pribilof Islands to private companies—since 1890 that had been the N.A.C. Co.—and assigned management to the Department of Commerce and Labor. When the company effectively shut the door on its hotel at Dutch Harbor, the grand piano that had graced the lobby was moved to the Home. After its battering during the gold rush days and subsequent constant use by children, Mary Winchell found "its keys were yellow, weak of action, and it gave forth a thin, tinkling sound."[10] The N.A.C. Co. began selling off the inventory at its Dutch Harbor store in the spring of 1914. The Home bought four or five dollars' worth of Coats sewing thread at four cents a spool. Before long, the company closed down completely and Billy Moran was hired as a caretaker.

The Alaska Commercial Company continued to operate in the village of Unalaska itself. A 1901 reorganization and merger with other firms had produced two companies: the Northern Commercial Company and the Northern Navigation Company, the latter exclusively for transport. At Unalaska, however, the firm continued to operate under the original Alaska Commercial Company name.[11] The Northern Navigation Company owned the riverboat *Colonel McNaught* that had disintegrated in front of the Home. When the man from Biorka was killed during the vessel's removal, the A.C. Co. initiated a series of letters and coded telegrams trying to minimize its liability. The company went so far as to deny any involvement with the vessel, despite the fact that the two firms had the same 310 Sansome Street address in San Francisco. In the end, it settled with the man's family for a payment of $750.[12]

There is an abundance of information covering the years from 1911 to 1916. This is the period Simeon Oliver wrote about in *Son of the Smoky Sea* and Mary Winchell in *Home by the Bering Sea* and *Where the Wind Blows Free*. Reminiscences from other former Unalaska Home and community residents were generally based on this period as well. Some of Clara Cook's extensive correspondence has survived along with two of her scrapbooks containing copies of reports and articles by Dr. Newhall. Official reports and monthly magazine articles from the Woman's Home Missionary Society round out the picture.

The staff at the Jesse Lee Home was remarkably constant for these five years. Dr. Newhall was the superintendent, assisted by Agnes Newhall, whom everyone in the Home and village now called Mama Newhall. They lived in the boys' dormitory. In the girls' building, Clara Cook, Mary Winchell, and Emma Supernaw were in charge of different aspects: cooking, sewing, acting as matron. In January 1912 Mary Winchell was the matron, Emma Supernaw was the cooking teacher, and Clara Cook taught sewing. The women shared tasks, however, and assisted each other when the work piled up or when one of them was ill. Although Mama Newhall spent more and more of her time assisting with medical work, she frequently took all the socks to wash and mend. She also came to the girls' dorm every Wednesday to help Cook darn clothes. This camaraderie, this warmth and mutual support among the staff, was felt by the students.

Of the three women, Emma Supernaw is the least known. This is strange because next to the Newhalls, she spent more years working at the Home than any other missionary. She had first arrived in July 1908 as a replacement for Mabel Benedict.[13] Efficient and something of a disciplinarian, she was known as Miss Emma. A short, stout woman, she was a prolific knitter and an excellent cook. Bluntness and rigidity masked a generous

Deputy U.S. Marshal Ross *prepares for an outing with children from Jesse Lee. Courtesy of the Unalaska City School District (Clara Cook Collection).*

VISITING THE DOCK *at Unalaska. Courtesy of the Unalaska City School District (Clara Cook Collection).*

heart. The most personal glimpses of her were provided by Mary Winchell, but even these are brief. Once when the staff was discussing a project involving the community, Winchell heard her remark, "Better send a notice to the priest also. He feels that the natives belong to him."[14] Supernaw never took center stage but worked steadily to keep the Home running smoothly.

> Miss Emma was in the kitchen making soup from salt beef that came to us in barrels from the States. We always had plenty of good fish, but seldom had meat. When the beef was cooked, Miss Emma lifted it out to make room for the potatoes and onions. She cut the meat for dinner, but bits of beef and gristle always stuck to the bone. The children loved to chew this, and Miss Emma always saved the bone for them. She opened the door now, and called out, "Who wants this nice big beef bone?"[15]

Mary Winchell, vivacious and energetic, admired the Newhalls deeply. In 1911 she was 31 years old. The other missionaries referred to her as their "really truly missionary."[16] Like Emma Supernaw, she was short in stature. In 1921 one of the young girls asked her how old she was and she replied, "Forty-one." "My, how old!" exclaimed the girl. "But you're not very big yet."[17] Staff and children enjoyed hearing her read aloud and she did this for an hour or so every evening. After three years, she left on June 25, 1914, for a furlough. "When I stop to think what life will be here with Miss. W. gone," Clara Cook wrote, "I can hardly keep the tears back. She and I have been such close friends for over three years." The day Winchell departed, Clara was so upset she couldn't collect her thoughts enough to read the letters that had just arrived. Harriet Barnett came back for yet another year to take Mary's place. Winchell returned in 1915, sailing from Seattle on July 7 with the Newhalls' son Chester aboard the SS *Alameda*. Chester wrote this account of their arrival:

> After a run of about three hours [from Akutan] we passed Priest Rock, at the entrance of Unalaska Bay, and now you can believe I was excited, and kept my eyes open to catch a glimpse of the village. At first it seemed as if there was nothing but mountains, but soon an opening appeared and I saw Summer Bay ahead, a place where we used to camp to seine salmon. Then we passed Dutch Harbor and the village came in sight, and first of all the two large white houses of the mission with their bright red roofs, and that was the place I was interested in for mother, father, and Edith were there. I was anxious to get a sight of them and perhaps they were anxious to see what I looked like. Almost all the village folks were on the beach front, hurrying to the wharf. Miss Winchell and I stood on the upper deck in order to get a better view. We passed the buoys and the reef of rocks and made for the wharf. There were several vessels

tied up there—SS *Patterson* (a survey boat) and three cannery boats—SS *Glenwood,* SS *Virginius*; and also SS *Red Feather.* As we neared the wharf I spied the robust figure of my dear mother, standing out against the horizon, and my sister holding on to her mother. The gang-plank was soon out and it was steep to go down. Folks kept hollering up to me their greeting, and my old friend "Morriss" the fisherman was excited and said he was waiting to take me cod fishing. It was a good trip. I would like to take it again, but it does seem good to be here with my mother and father and sister.[18]

Clara Cook, steady and devoted to her work, left on her own furlough in late 1915. In preparation, she had ordered a new fur coat in 1913. She had been using one that had arrived in a donated clothing barrel and was now "only fit for the hills." By leaving in August 1915 she planned to avoid the heat in the States and to be back by June 1916 when the Newhalls themselves would leave on furlough. Returning that early would mean she had less than a year's vacation, but she didn't mind. She truly loved Unalaska. "This has been a lovely summer," she wrote in August 1914. "The older inhabitants here never remember such a summer. Two months without a hard rain or wind storm and lots of sunshine." The berries were plentiful. There was excitement on the last day of August when the dynamite abandoned at the Huntsville mine was detonated. A new company had started to work the mine and wanted to get rid of the unsafe explosives. "It is two miles from here with big mountains between," wrote Cook, "but when it went off we thought something struck the house, and every window rattled. We are wondering how our camp has stood it."[19]

Ole Quean, with whom schoolteacher William Davis had panned for gold in British Columbia in 1905, had a small general store at Unalaska. He received walrus tusks from the North as the last ships departed the arctic before winter set in. Once he sent word that his shipment had arrived and the women at the Home could have first pick. Simeon Oliver and Mike Berikoff were working in the store after school when Emma Supernaw and Clara Cook arrived. It was a blustery winter day and as they came in their glasses steamed up. The two women made their way to a table at the back of the store where Quean stood with the tusks. Supernaw was a bit nearsighted. She picked up an oosik and asked, "What kind of a tusk is this?" On being told, in Quean's blunt no-nonsense vocabulary, she dropped it and the two ladies departed quicker than they had arrived.[20]

In addition to the paid staff, the Home had the benefit of a devoted volunteer, Clara Gwin Goss. Clara's son, Cecil, was about the same age as Henry Swanson. Her husband, Albert C. Goss, had worked for the A.C. Co. in Kodiak since the early 1890s. In 1904 she and Albert were married there.[21] He ended his formal association with the company on May 1, 1912, and moved his family to Unalaska to try fur trading on his own. At Unalaska, they initially lived in a suite of rooms in the company house, but they eventually built a

CLARA GOSS AND STUDENTS *in the Eliza Jane Baker Chapel. Henry Swanson is standing at the far right. Courtesy of the Unalaska City School District (Clara Cook Collection).*

home along the front beach. One afternoon Chester Newhall was standing with A.C. Goss on the wharf when the bay was flat calm. "I was a little kid," Chester later wrote, "and I thought that his remark as he looked out over the bay 'as smooth as a school-marm's leg' was very naughty!"[22]

Relations between the Jesse Lee Home and the company—and agent Louis Strauss—were strengthened because of the close ties Clara Goss had with both of them. The missionaries were occasionally invited for special dinners such as the one Clara Cook described as "a five course dinner. It was fine, and served up in fine style." Again, for Christmas 1911, people from the Home were among the 15 guests the A.C. Co. hosted for a dinner "served up in grand style with finger bowls." From Sept. 15, 1913, to April 29, 1914, Clara Goss was at Atka with her husband. "As soon as the Mission people knew I had arrived," she wrote on returning to Unalaska, "the ladies all came down in a body to see me, and made such a fuss over me that it has almost turned my head. It seems like getting home." She visited the Home later that evening and was given her Christmas boxes. Mama Newhall had made her "one of the loveliest homemade sweaters I ever saw—navy, and very heavy."[23]

In August 1912, Clara Goss decided to live at the Home during the upcoming winter while her husband wintered at Attu Island. She was in poor health and wanted to be near the doctor. While there, she taught needlework and music. In his report for 1912–13, Newhall wrote that more than 16 of the children could play the piano or organ. Fred Chipitnoi had a natural talent, and Simeon Oliver, age 10, was fast on his heels. A baby organ in the boys' sitting room was constantly in use.

These five years saw the student population at the Home grow gradually from 34 in 1911 to 48 in 1915. Occasionally girls were married or left for training or work. Children died, primarily of tuberculosis. New children arrived. Nanoona, known later as John Carpenter, was brought to the Home from Herschel Island by his father in October 1912. His mother had perished while a member of a hunting expedition. He would remain until May 1925 when he went to work for Henry Swanson's stepfather, Christian Pedersen, and moved permanently to California. In 1928 Dr. Newhall received a letter from Nanoona, who was getting along fine in Oakland. He was now driving a car. "I don't know as I would want to drive with him," wrote the doctor. "He is such a jumping jack."[24] Later in life John Carpenter recalled that contact with the people in the village was minimal and occurred either at school or on special events such as the Christmas programs. Mary Winchell recognized the separateness of the Home and the village. "See," she told an interviewer, "the Jesse Lee Home . . . didn't have very much to do with the village. We had no authority that way."[25] There were still factions within the village that were hard to reconcile. "We all loved our island home," Winchell wrote. "We were anxious together if any were out in a storm; excited together, once a month, on mail-boat day; and happy together at Christmas. But for the different racial, religious, and economic factions to be held together in an organization was another matter."[26]

August 30, 1978

To the Students at the Unalaska School,

I was glad to hear from you and glad to receive a copy of *Cuttlefish Two*. It brought back fond memories of my years in Unalaska. ...

In the picture of the Jesse Lee Home the pump house is shown near the home. When I was there the pump house was by the river. I used to run the old Old's pump during the flu epidemic of 1919. I was the only one at the Jesse Lee Home that did not get the flu. The Coast Guard did the cooking and took care of the sick. I saw many coffins go by the Home to the cemetery during the flu epidemic, being too young to know how many people lost their lives at that time.

I remember the old Japanese schooner beached at Margaret Bay, caught for poaching seals and otters. We used to explore it as a boy.

I remember the trees at Expedition Island where we had picnics while at the home.

I remember Chief Alex Yatchmenoff used to run the donkey engine to pull the cars off on the tracks to the coal yard from the *City of Sydney*, the six-masted steel sailing ship which brought the coal from Fremantle, Australia.

I remember the tracks that ran from the wharf to the Alaska Commercial Company store, also the flag pole and old Russian cannons.

The Jesse Lee Home had a summer cabin at Huntsville where some of the children in the Home would stay a few days with one of the teachers. There was an old abandoned stamping mill for gold ore near by and the boys found dynamite sticks and were dragging them around and through the grass. The Coast Guard collected all of the old dynamite and exploded it on the beach one night. We heard and felt the explosion at the Jesse Lee Home.

I remember the ferry-man Semmie Bean. He ran the ferry between Unalaska and Dutch Harbor. I remember his house burned down one winter and he lost all his money and possessions. He tried to jump in the house to save some of the things but the flames were too strong. ...

John Carpenter

[EXCERPTED FROM A LETTER *reproduced in* Cuttlefish: Volumes One, Two & Three, *2005:249*]

CITY OF SYDNEY *delivering coal to Unalaska. Photo in the author's collection, from E. Pelagia McCurdy.*

The Home's physical plant was now extensive. The two large dormitories were connected by a boardwalk. Nearby were the pump house, a laundry, a chicken coop, a barn and a silo. In 1912–13 a new kitchen range was installed and the teachers were provided with a bathtub of their own. Water was piped to the dormitories. Toilets were installed along with a "run to the sea" for sewage. The chapel, a large warm room just across from the kitchen in the girls' building, was repapered and painted. Mary Winchell, for one, was glad they didn't have a separate chapel building because the girls could come and go to services without having to venture out into stormy weather.[27] By 1914 half of the barn roof had been reshingled. The exteriors of all the buildings were painted and five interior rooms were painted and papered. Linoleum was laid in the second hall, dining room, and dispensary room, and in Mary Winchell's room.

Much of this work was done by the residents. A new gasoline-driven water pump arrived on the *Tahoma* on May 18, 1912, along with lumber, dishes, stoves, and carpets, curtains and dry goods. Installation of the water system, indoor plumbing, and sewer line became the work of that summer. Gordon Gould described the process.

> Under the guidance of Dr. Newhall we dug the ditches, laid the pipe, did all the plumbing to install the bathrooms and such other facilities as were necessary in such an institution. It was a long summer of hard work. But when it was finished Dr. Newhall invited an engineer from one of the Revenue Cutters to come to the Home and inspect the works. You can just imagine how our chests puffed out when this engineer pronounced the job well done. Then after explaining the significance of the different pressure gauges he started up the engine. It was wonderful to see the pressure rise in the tank and realize that we had really done a significant job.[28]

Newhall then created a new job: running the pump engine. This was conferred only on the most responsible of the older boys and was a coveted position.

To help pay for many of these improvements, the women and girls began selling needlework and other handicrafts. Thursday afternoons were set aside for knitting, crocheting, and doing other types of fancywork. The teachers often carried their projects on into the evenings. Schoolteachers Noah and Clara Davenport were invited to the Home for an evening meal on Oct. 11, 1911. After a fine dinner, Dr. Newhall escaped to the boys' dormitory while "the ladies drew a table to the center of the room and began on their perpetual fancy work. Passing remarks between knitting needle changes or needle threading about different members of their little flock." Noah Davenport felt captive sitting with his wife "on the lounge while our hostesses did fancy work around the table." The teachers soon made their escape.

Clara Goss suggested the first summer bazaar. She organized the work, making sure that each girl had specific projects: scarves, napkin rings, doilies, pillow covers, collars,

CHLDREN AND STAFF OF THE JESSE LEE HOME, *c. 1912. Courtesy of the Unalaska City School District (Clara Cook Collection).*

baby blankets, sewing bags, needle cases, whisk broom holders, and a host of other items.[29] The boys, not to be outdone, made necktie racks and other items from brass. The first sale was set for three days in June 1912 when the revenue cutters would first arrive back in port. In addition to fancy work, the women planned to sell ice cream, cake, coffee, and home-made candy. Eighty pounds of candy had been prepared. Edith Newhall Drugg, using a report from her father, wrote about what happened next.

> Alas!!—Old volcano Katmai suddenly exploded and without any warning sent its ashes across the Shelikoff Straits and covered the villages of Kodiak, Afognak, Wood Island, Ouzinkie, Katmai, etc., some 100 miles away. All the Revenue Cutters were called to the scene of the disaster—and thus ended the prospects of selling what the children had made. As the fishing season was at hand and some of the teachers must be away [to Summer Bay], the sale could not be long delayed.[30]

The eruption at Katmai was the largest volcanic eruption of the 20th century. "If such an eruption should occur on Manhattan Island," wrote Robert F. Griggs, "the column of steam would be conspicuous as far as Albany. The sounds of the explosions would be plainly audible in Chicago. The fumes would sweep over all the states east of the Rocky Mountains. In Denver they would tarnish brass. . . ."[31] Word reached Unalaska through the newly installed wireless station and on June 22 the Coast Guard cutters *Bear* and *Thetis* arrived with details. Clara Cook wrote to her sister:

> It is not as bad as first reported. The ashes is all the way from one to ten feet deep all over that Island. The first foot is hard almost like stone. It was 48 hours falling and was as dark as night they went around with lanterns then could only see a couple of feet away. And the sky was ablaze some of the time and set the wireless station afire, and when the ashes came down the mountains like a land slide it turned some houses clear around and buried them in ashes. The Capt of the Bear said just the top of the trees stuck out in places. The people was panic stricken, and 400 rushed onto the Revenue Cutter Manning which was at the dock. One old barge there they took off 150 ton of ashes after it was over. They have gone back to their houses to live now, but all vegetation is killed and many of the people will leave there.[32]

Dr. Newhall spoke with men aboard the *Dora,* which had been in Raspberry Strait, between Kodiak and Afognak islands, when the eruption occurred.

> On the SS *Dora,* the darkness was so intense the ocean could not be seen from the deck. Ashes covered the decks and sifted in everywhere. As the com-pass was affected by the electrical display or storm, the course was made for the

open sea to avoid rocks and when the Dora reached Seward, she looked like a phantom ship.

At Kodiak the fall of ash varied 1 ft.-10 ft. deep. A few houses were crushed & other damage done. The wireless station was struck by lightning and burned . . . Jesse Lee Home offered to take the "Wood Island" Baptist Mission Children but their home was not destroyed. The natives at Katmai village were removed to another place which was named "Perry."[33]

Men from the *Bear* and *Thetis* came to the Home and purchased a number of goods prepared for the sale. Shortly afterward, on a Saturday, the U.S. Army Transport Service *Sheridan* arrived with more than a thousand passengers. Although Saturday was scrubbing and bathing day, the staff and children set up a sale in the parlors. A notice was posted on the front yard gate and down at the wharf. A boy was sent to notify the village. Although it was a stormy and windy day, people began arriving in late afternoon. Edith Newhall continued with her father's report:

There were numerous tables about the rooms. Miss Winchell looked after the fancy aprons, dresser scarves, etc.; Miss Cook, calendars, brass work, pillow covers, etc.; Mrs. Applegate, pin cushions and nick knacks; Miss Supernaw, work baskets, towel racks, match boxes, etc.—also sold candy and looked after the milk. Mrs. Newhall gathered in the shekels while "your humble servant" [Dr. Newhall] kept the phonograph reeling off nice music, or meandered around smiling on the folks. A soldier suggested that we sell milk, and he said that all the men would like some. We were going to sell it at ten cents per glass but he said that was too cheap, two glasses for two bits (25 cents) was cheap enough. How they did drink!!! Some men would drink four glasses of milk at one swig. They brought empty canteens to have them filled with milk. Miss Supernaw attended to the milk, stirring the cream into the milk as the pans set to raise. At one time the front hall was well filled with men waiting for the cow to be milked.

Our cowboy was working on the wharf, and so Daniel [Sipary] was dispatched to milk the cow, but "Diana" did not like the new order of things and Daniel said that she kicked him with all four feet at the same time. Theodore [Nutbeem] arrived and saved the situation.

The sales in 1912 brought in over $250. This success ensured there would be others in subsequent years even when Clara Goss was not in town, and about $300 was made annually to pay for improvements. The children were able to send donations to the missionary society for use at other locations. Clara Cook gave money she made "sewing for the white folk in town" to this fancywork fund. In June 1912, for example, Martha Applegate was suffering "a nervous collapse" and the women in the Home cared for her 11-month-old infant. Cook altered a suit for Mrs. Applegate and agreed to make her two nightgowns and some additional clothing.

For some of the girls, however, adding fancywork to the regular chores of darning socks and mending clothes was too much. "Work!" remarked Helen Swanson Malcolm. "We worked all the time. Every day we had to knit. We had to knit for an hour every day. . . . then Thursday we had an embroidery class, or like that, which they sold. We worked them and they sold them, and"—she added with a laugh—"we got a tenth of what they sold them for."[34]

There were good times for all, however. Two letters from 13-year-old Nellie Holmberg, originally from Sanak, provide abundant examples.

The girls and teachers also created a number of quilts. Edith Newhall Drugg recalled one that Clara Cook owned. This was donated to the Museum of the Aleutians by Stephen and Kathie Assenmacher in 2006.

> The red and white quilt, I practically became nostalgic over that. . . . I remember it well. In fact I'm quite sure I made some of the blocks, but don't remember if my name is on it. The Mission had fancywork classes two evenings a week. We girls sewed while Miss Winchell read aloud good books to us. This gave the girls some spending money, as they sold the embroidered pieces to the Revenue Cutter men . . . and also to passengers aboard ships which came into port. Another reason that I became nostalgic was that I had a red and white quilt of my mother's, with all the names of the children in the Mission and the main Jesse Lee Home building embroidered in the center. In my many moves I decided, at the time, I wasn't using it any more, it was out of style so I let it go. I should have *saved* it for History and memories. . . . Land only knows where it might pop up one day.[35]

[A LETTER *to Clara Stevens*]

December 26, 1913

My Dear Friend,

I thought I would write to you while I had some thing to say. We had a very nice Christmas. We are having our Xmas Vacation yet. We are having for two days Vacation this Xmas because we did not go to school for a month. [School started late that year because the teacher had not arrived.] If I had the program I would send one to you but I did not get one this time. They were all gone when I came to take one. We have our Xmas presents in flower sack instead of our Stockings because the flower sacks were bigger. So I will tell you what I had in my flower sack. I had three dolls, a book. The name of the book is The Story Christ. I had three Handkerchiefs, two yd. of hair Ribbons, A string of blue beads, an apple. A toy Village. Two Christmas cards and a pair of side combs from Miss Cook. (and a pencil) We went down to The Marshall Mr. Hasting's house and had part of the program because He could not come up to see the program on account of his feet. I had a happy Christmas and I hope you had. Our school teacher's Wife Mrs. Scott came over to see our Xmas presents and she brought her dear little baby Helen Scott. I cannot think of anything to say so I wish you A Merry Xmas and A Happy New Year.

Your Friend,
Nellie Holmberg [36]

February 29, 1914
[Note—*This was not a leap year.*]

Dear Friend Clara,

I am beginning this letter early because I haven't anything to do after I studied my lessons, so I thought I could start a letter to you. I don't think there will be any more skating this winter because it rained a long time and the ice melted. The fourth reader is reciting right next to me so I cannot think of much to say. Our school teachers are going away on the March boat so we have to quit going to school before vacation.

Peter Golovin [Peter Gordon Gould] the boy that sits in front of me moves around in his seat so much that I can't write straight.

It is time for our class to recite now so I have to stop till after dinner.

Here I am back to school. We have language today instead of spelling because we have to go upstairs everyday to sew. We Jesse Lee Home girls are sewing for the poor girls of the town. I made two pairs of bloomers and I am making an apron now. I enjoy sewing very much. I am very fond of reading too.

Yesterday we went clamming. Three girls, one teacher and six boys went. I will tell you our names, of the boys. Daniel Sipary, Fred Chipitnoi, Henry Peters, Simeon Oliver, Nick Peterson and Peter S. ["Saposnekoff" in Home records; "Shapsnikoff" in current spelling] I did [not] know how to spell the last boy's last name so I did not write it down. We dig the clams up with hoes and shovels. It's hard work digging clams but I like to dig clams very much. I ache all over today from digging clams. Miss Winchell gave a bag of peanuts to the one that got the most big clams and a smaller sized bag to the one that got the next most big clams. Daniel Sipary got the first bag of peanuts and Fred Chipitnoi got the smaller sized bag.

Doctor Newhall reads every Sunday and Wednesday night to the boys and two of the teachers, Miss Cook and Miss Winchell has just gone over and I am in Miss Winchell's room copying this letter. I can hear the girls laughing in the reading room—And Amelia [Peterson] playing on the mouth organ. The older girls are playing games in Miss Supernaw's room. Well it is time for me to go to bed and I am glad of it. So good bye. Your friend,

Nellie Holmberg

NOTES

1. Before getting to Huntsville, a hiker reached Agnes Beach, where today a bridge spans the water from Amaknak Island to Unalaska Island. This small cove was named after Agnes Newhall. (Chester Newhall, letter to Phil and Flora Tutiakoff, Dec. 3, 1978.)

2. Winchell, *Where the Wind Blows Free*, 132,128.

3. *WHM*. June 1920:6.

4. Clara Cook, letter, Nov. 27, 1911. Robert Collins Collection.

5. Mary Winchell, interview by Shirley Hook for Dorothy Jones in Pasadena, Calif., Nov. 11, 1967.

6. Woman's Home Missionary Society, Report from Bureaus. 1910–11:181.

7. Foley to Secretary of the Treasury. Oct. 9, 1911. NARA. RG 26, File 611, Box 1835.

8. Foley to Secretary of Treasury. Oct. 20, 1910, p. 58. NARA. RG 26, File 611, Box 1834.

9. Niedieck, *Cruises in the Bering Sea*, 180.

10. Winchell, *Home by the Bering Sea*, 217.

11. Kitchener, *Flag Over the North*, 46, 129.

12. Correspondence, "Accidental death of employee at Unalaska." Stanford University. Special Collections JL006.

13. A November 1916 article in *WHM* stated she was completing her 16th year at the Home. However, the annual report for 1907–08 said she arrived in July 1908 to replace Mabel Benedict and "has already won a place for herself"—suggesting this was her first year at Unalaska. (Woman's Home Missionary Society, Reports from Bureaus, 1907–08:130–31). *WHM* for October 1908 (p. 192) noted that she had left on the July boat for Unalaska.

14. Winchell, *Home by the Bering Sea*, 99.

15. Winchell, *Where the Wind Blows Free*, 68.

16. *WHM*. April 1912:22.

17. Mary Winchell, letter, April 10, 1920. Robert Collins Collection.

18. Chester Newhall, letter to Uncle Frank, Aug. 5, 1915. Copy in possession of Ray Hudson. Chester's friend Mark Moriss died in 1921 after he went out from his fishing camp at Morris Cove to hunt geese. It was a very windy day, blowing southeast. When he didn't return, search parties walked the shoreline but no sign of him was found. About two weeks later, part of his arm washed ashore near Summer Bay.

19. Clara Cook, letter, Aug. 31, 1914. John Carpenter recalled that it was the U.S. Coast Guard that collected and detonated the dynamite on the beach.

20. Simeon Oliver, tape recording with Henry Swanson, Unalaska, May 1979. An oosik is the penile bone of a walrus or other sea mammal.

21. After A.C. Goss died in 1935, Clara Goss moved to Seattle, where she died on Aug. 30, 1952.

22. Chester Newhall, letter to Phil and Flora Tutiakoff, April 1, 1979.

23. Clara Goss, letter, Oct. 15, 1913–May 2, 1914. Archives of the Arctic and Polar Regions Collections of the Elmer E. Rasmuson Library at the University of Alaska Fairbanks.

24. Newhall to Friend Mary. Dec. 12, 1928. Alaska State Historical Library, MS 0106.

25. Mary Winchell, interview by Shirley Hook for Dorothy Jones in Pasadena, Calif., Nov. 11, 1967.

26. Winchell, *Home by the Bering Sea*, 99.

27. Mary Winchell, interview by Shirley Hook for Dorothy Jones in Pasadena, Calif., Nov. 11, 1967.

28. Gould, *The Fisherman's Son*, 23-24.

29. See Hudson, ed., *Cuttlefish: Volumes One, Two & Three*, 179, for a more complete list.

30. Ibid., 181–83.

31. Griggs, *The Valley of Ten Thousand Smokes*, 1922:1.

32. Clara Cook, letter, June 23, 1912. Robert Collins Collection.

33. Newhall Manuscript, 272.

34. Helen E. Malcolm in McClanahan, ed., *Our Stories, Our Lives*, 177.

35. Edith Newhall Drugg, letter to Ray Hudson, March 24, 1977.

36. Both letters are from the Robert Collins Collection.

· 22 ·

The Hospital Wing

Dr. Newhall's medical work never slowed. Tuberculosis continued its persistent attack as did pneumonia. Added to these were "fractures, burns, poisoned wounds from fishing, gunshot wounds, etc. . . . eye troubles, hernia, Bright's disease, gasoline burns" and the occasional "epidemic of grippe." And, of course, boys would be boys and managed to produce an assortment of cuts and sprains. Death and illness were regular intruders into the life of the Home. Mary Winchell ended a letter full of the bustle of an ordinary day with, "Today we had a Memorial service. Had the chapel decorated. Tonight is Communion and tomorrow we have washday and also must line a casket and make wreaths and have a funeral for a sailor who died of heart failure today."[1] The Home contracted with the Treasury Department for medical services to the revenue cutters as a second-class hospital. In 1909 Newhall wrote that for services, including fresh milk, eggs and meat when available, the fee was $4.50 per day for each patient plus $1.50 per day for nursing services.

The hospital wing in the boys' building had two private rooms, a ward with five beds, and a dispensary. Even so, the facility was occasionally overcrowded. In the spring of 1916, with several beds already occupied, six new patients suddenly arrived, forcing Agnes and Albert to sleep in the attic for two months while their bedroom was turned into a temporary sickroom. Quarantine was a necessity when contagious diseases appeared. In 1918 three cases of diphtheria arrived on the SS *Roosevelt*. Dr. Newhall kept those patients in temporary quarters at Margaret Bay, across the narrow passage from the A.C. Co. wharf, where, according to Winchell, they got along nicely except for their tempers.[2] When illness struck, things could get comically ugly at times, as Clara Cook illustrated in one of her letters.

> I will try and write you a few lines to let you know we are alive and kicking and there is a lot kicking just now for all the Children has just got up from an epidemic which struck us last week and they are as cross as can be. I know how to pity them for I am going through the same. I have had a splitting headache for three days, and cant sleep nights for chills and pains and sore throat. Last Friday 20 was in bed, and of all the groaning, crying, vomiting no one got any rest and has not yet. Every Girl has had it and 15 of the Boys, and Dr. and Mrs. Newhall. Miss Winchell and Supernaw has escaped thus far, and laughed at us. Well I had to laugh myself. Such a mess as we did have to clean up. For some of the little ones vomited in bed, and the floor was nearly covered

The following is a list of some of the diseases and conditions treated during the past year. It will give a general idea of the work:

—abscess (face, fingers, hand, leg, scalp, etc.), adenoids, amennorrhoea, amputation (finger, leg, toes), Bright's disease, blood poisoning, bruises, burns (fire, gasoline), cellulites (leg), circumcision, club feet, confinements, conjunctivitis, constipation, coughs, cyst, diarrhea, dislocation (shoulder), dropsy, dysentery, dyspepsia, eczema, erysipelas hives, fauves [favus], fractures, frostbite, gangrene, gonorrhea, grippe, headache, heartburn, heart disease, hemorrhage, hemorrhoids, hives, hysteria, indigestion, inflammation, impetigo, itch, lice, lumbago, neuritis, otitis, piles, ptomaine poison, rheumatism, sprains, syphilis, tapeworms, teeth (extraction, filled), tonsillitis, tuberculosis (lungs, hip, etc.), ulcer (cornea, leg), wounds (poisoned, fishbone, gunshot, hooks, insect, knives, stones, etc.)

[A.W. NEWHALL, *Medical Report 1914*]

we could not furnish basons enough. Oh it was awfull, while it lasted. Everybody in town had it. It does not make any difference with color, or race, or age. This is wash day, and Miss W. and Miss S. went over and helped rub. I could only hold my head up so I looked after the little ones and washed dishes. The Children all went to bed as soon as supper was over tonight so it is quiet only for the wind and sea, which is in a foaming mass.[3]

Newhall's medical report for 1914 is the most complete we have.[4] That year older boys earned a little extra money by assisting with the sick while older girls did special cooking and took care of the hospital laundry, for which they also were paid. Newhall's list of diseases and conditions reads like a medical dictionary from A to W.

Of the 21 cases Newhall described in this report, most were people who had arrived by ship or skin boat with infected wounds. They had been accidentally shot, mauled by machinery, or stabbed. Two Japanese men, survivors of eight from a schooner that had wrecked off Nunivak Island where they spent the winter of 1913, were brought to the Home by a passing whaler. They had extreme frostbite. Simeon Oliver recalled that Captain Louie Lane of the *Polar Bear* once "brought a cargo of frozen Japanese to the Mission."[5] Newhall named two of them.

> Y-sho-ki-ti was a young man, 19 years old. He was a fine young fellow and free from all bad habits. He was cheerful and very appreciative of the kindness shown to him. He had all his toes amputated.
>
> Tan-da-ji-de was an older man and was rather surly in his makeup. He lost all the toes on one foot, having only a stump of a foot left. They attended services on Sunday and enjoyed them. It was amusing to see the bigger boys pack these "toe cases" on their backs to church. Folks smiled to see them come to church riding pig back. These men made good recoveries and were not very lame as a result of their misfortunes.

Two shipwrecks of historic importance brought patients to the Home in 1914: the *Karluk* and the U.S. revenue cutter *Tahoma*. For both of these Newhall wrote detailed accounts. In June 1913 Vilhjalmur Stefansson embarked on the Canadian Arctic Expedition with Captain Robert A. Bartlett in charge of the *Karluk*. This ship was familiar at Unalaska because as a whaler it had been in and out of the port for years. Entering the Beaufort Sea on its way to Herschel Island, it was caught in pack ice and carried west until it was crushed and sank near Wrangel Island. Eight men had died by May 1914 when C.T. Pedersen, Henry Swanson's stepfather, rescued the captain and the Eskimo guide who had gone for help. In September the remaining survivors were found by a trading schooner, the *King and Winge*, transferred to the cutter *Bear* and taken to Nome.

All this happened hundreds of miles from Unalaska and Dr. Newhall would have played no part except that a member of the scientific staff became gravely ill in Nome. The *Bear*'s physician decided the Scottish magnetician and meteorologist William Laird McKinlay needed to be seen by Dr. Newhall. On October 1, McKinlay was carried unconscious into the Jesse Lee Home. As he recovered, he amazed the missionaries with his tale of loss and survival. Newhall typed the story, omitting the patient's name, and enclosed it with his reports and letters. Copies were also shared with the staff. The doctor understood that whatever he sent out might later appear in one of the missionary publications and so he added a request, "Out of fairness to the patient, this narrative must not be allowed to be published."

In 1978 high school students at Unalaska were working on a publication based on Clara Cook's scrapbooks. They decided to use the *Karluk* story despite its caution. Unknown to the class, two years earlier McKinlay had published *Karluk, The Great Untold Story of Arctic Exploration*.[6] Eventually a copy of the student publication, *Cuttlefish Three: Home on the Bering*, was sent to McKinlay, who wrote he was "enchanted . . . with their accomplishment." Commenting on Newhall's request, he said, "I can see no reason why the writer should have thought it would have been unfair to me or anyone else if it were published. On the contrary, it seems to me that Dr. Newhall merited all publicity in acknowledgment of the magnificent work he was doing in these days. For myself, I think it is no exaggeration to say that I probably owed my life to him, for I was indeed very ill. . . . the *Bear*'s surgeon was completely baffled. But my recovery under Dr. Newhall was rapid and complete."[7] Twelve days after being carried into the Home, McKinlay was climbing Mt. Ballyhoo on Amaknak Island. He shared this excerpt from his diary for October 12 with the students: "Climbed Ballyhoo with Kendal [one of the *Bear*'s officers] and joined the Ballyhoo Club by signing the book placed on top. Height 1640 feet. Snow and fog prevented us seeing any distance."

In another letter McKinlay described regaining consciousness in the Home.

> Dr. Newhall and the ship's doctor took turns looking after me during the night. In the morning, Dr. Newhall installed a little Aleut on a chair by my bedside, with instructions to call him immediately I showed signs of recovering consciousness. The little fellow was named John Shoposhnikoff, and as soon as I opened my eyes, he was down from his chair and off to bring the doctor. When the doctor left, John remained on watch, and his first words to me were: "Do you have Jesus in Scotland?"[8]

John Shapsnikoff had entered the home from Unga at three years of age in 1909. He lived until Nov. 25, 1915, when he died, according to his enrollment card, from "asphyxiation ether." Perhaps he was undergoing surgery.

JOHN SHOPOSHNIKOFF *(Shapsnikoff): "Do you have Jesus in Scotland?" Courtesy of the Unalaska City School District (Clara Cook Collection).*

In his diary McKinlay wrote how on the night of Sept. 20, 1914, after the men from the *Karluk* had been taken aboard, the *Bear* rushed to the assistance of the revenue cutter *Corwin*. This ship had run aground near Cape Douglas while part of the rescue effort. As they hurried to help that vessel a distress call arrived from another. "We picked up an S.O.S. call which was being broadcast by Revenue Cutter *Tahoma*," McKinlay wrote, "which had struck an uncharted rock, somewhere to the west of the Aleutian Islands." The loss of this cutter meant the disappearance of the finest vessel in the service. Since its construction in 1908 it had been in and out of Unalaska. While at Unalaska in 1909 Dr. Friench Simpson aboard the revenue cutter *Perry* visited the "roomy and beautifully finished" new vessel. The woodwork was in oak and maple and the rooms were large. It was said to have been "awfully comfortable in a sea way."[9] The Davenports had admired it anchored in the bay, lit up at night with "Taps" wafting from somewhere on the decks. They went aboard for a visit in 1911 and enjoyed hearing the "fine player-piano."

In September 1914 the *Tahoma* sailed to Atka, Kiska and Attu. After leaving Attu early on the morning of September 20, the vessel approached the wrecked schooner *Trilby* on Alaid Island. Conditions were against salvaging anything for the owner, A.B. Somerville, and the *Tahoma* continued west. It stayed 28 miles away from a charted danger but about nine in the evening struck a mile-long submerged reef 33 miles south of Buldir Island. Today the reef is called the Tahoma Reef. Twenty hours later, as the ship was listing to starboard and filling with water, the 87 people aboard climbed into seven small open boats. Among the passengers were Anna Golley of Atka and her four children, along with U.S. deputy marshal Willard Hastings. Over the course of several days, all were rescued.

"Most of the men suffered from swollen feet and pains in the limbs," wrote Newhall in his medical report. "Jesse Lee Home did what it could to relieve and help the ship-wrecked men." Hastings had been suffering for some time from neuritis and a badly burned foot. While he recovered, Newhall visited him repeatedly and gradually heard the story of the wreck. The marshal told how he had sat in the lifeboat "with his leg wrapped in a blanket, but in salt water."

> One dark night, along towards morning he sat half dozing on the seat. He had sat in this uncomfortable position for more than a week, day and night, and as he sat there half asleep or benumbed with the cold, hungry, wet, miserable, thinking of home and loved ones, he pushed the wet blanket from his face and peered out into the darkness. He thought he saw a glimmer of light far out on the waves, but too many times had such a false hope been raised, so with a sigh of despair he tried to doze off again.
>
> Still that glimmer troubled him, and in a few minutes he looked again, and joy—a bright light glimmered for a moment on a far off swell and disappeared. With a glad heart, he roused the next man who was worn out and half asleep

at the oar and they looked and lo a light shone bright and clear in the distance. Only a moment—but it was light and it meant their salvation from a grave in the deep.[10]

On September 30, McKinlay noted in his diary that the last of the *Tahoma*'s passengers had been picked up by the revenue cutter *Patterson*. The Home loaned bedding for the men and supplied them with fresh vegetables from the garden. Medicine was furnished to the ship's doctor. When men from the *Tahoma* attended church on Sunday, Newhall saw their gratitude. "They went away with the feeling that they, indeed, had much to be thankful for," he wrote. "Jesse Lee Home had lifted up many prayers for these men and may this experience be sanctified to their good, leading them to turn away from sin and unbelief, and to trust in God and serve Him as they never have before."

Of the sailors who participated in the events surrounding the *Tahoma*, two would soon die at sea. Coxswain George Demarco from the wrecked ship joined the crew of the Coast Guard cutter *Manning* at Unalaska. A week or so later he went ashore with the ship's assistant surgeon to attend to a sick lighthouse attendant at Cape Sarichef on Unimak Island. Returning to the *Manning*, their lifeboat capsized, drowning the surgeon, the patient, and four of the boat's crew including Demarco. James Miller was the captain of the *Patterson*, which had found the last of the *Tahoma*'s passengers. Returning from a vacation in Europe the next spring, the young and personable captain was standing at the rail of the *Lusitania*, watching the coast of Ireland recede, when a torpedo struck. His body washed ashore and he was buried at Ennistymon in County Clare, two miles inland.[11]

"Never pity the dead," Dr. Newhall once told Simeon Oliver after the young teenager had assisted him in an unsuccessful attempt to save a gunshot victim. "They are safe. Keep your tears for the living."[12]

NOTES

1. Winchell, Mary. Letter, May 26, 1918. Alaska State Historical Library. MS 0003.

2. Ibid.

3. Cook, Clara. Letter, Nov. 25, 1912. Robert Collins Collection.

4. Hudson, ed., *Cuttlefish: Volumes One, Two & Three,* 199–203.

5. Oliver, *Son of the Smoky Sea,* 207, 88–89.

6. McKinlay, *Karluk: The Great Untold Story of Arctic Exploration.* See also Jennifer Niven, *The Ice Master: The Doomed 1913 Voyage of the* Karluk. Hyperion. New York. 2000.

7. William L. McKinlay to Ray Hudson, May 24, 1979.

8. William L. McKinlay to Ray Hudson, May 3, 1979.

9. *French Simpson Private Log.* May 21–October 1909. U.S. Coast Guard Historian's Office, Washington, D.C.

10. Newhall, "The Wreck of the Tahoma." Hudson, ed., *Cuttlefish: Volumes One, Two & Three,* 225–26.

11. NOAA History, A Science Odyssey. www.noaa.gov/cgsbios/biom14.html.

12. Oliver, *Son of the Smoky Sea,* 95.

23

The Government School

Now that the Jesse Lee Home was clearly an institution by itself, its relationship with the public school varied from year to year, in large part determined by the personality of the teachers. There was considerable turnover in the teaching staff. From 1910 to 1912 the teachers were Noah and Clara Davenport. They were followed in the fall of 1912 by Robert D. Scott, for two years, with Effie Scott as his assistant. From October 1914 until May 28, 1915, the teacher was Wilke Wilson. His assistants were Mrs. Alma Wilson (from October to February) and Kathryn Seller (from February to May 28). Joseph W. Coleman taught from 1915 to 1918. There was little continuity among these teachers because the new one always arrived weeks after the previous one had left.

The principal teacher during all these years was always a man. His wife frequently became the assistant responsible for the younger children. Clara Davenport and Effie Scott, however, gave birth while at Unalaska, and this reduced their activities in the school. Mary Winchell, with her experience as a teacher, was able to assist. She taught reading for an hour each day and usually managed to get her pupils through the first reader.[1] This relieved some pressure at the school, which grew increasingly crowded. In 1915 the enrollment was 76.

Noah and Clara Davenport balanced visits at the Home with visits to the Orthodox priest and his wife. Occasionally, people from the Home accompanied the Davenports to Orthodox services. On Jan. 6, 1911, the Davenports and Miss Robinson went to Christmas services at the invitation of the priest.

> The church is large and splendidly decorated with holy pictures. We were surprised at its gorgeousness, chandeliers, candles, robes and other paraphernalia. There were no seats except for visitors and during two hours not one of the parishioners sat down, although there were young girls who carried babies all the time. The service was in Russian and most formal. We wondered how they could read or chant so rapidly, the words coming in an unbroken string until the reader was through. A great number of attendants waited on the two priests, some cared for the many candles which required constant attention. We were somewhat startled when they lit the great chandelier of candles. The wicks were connected by some sort of fuse and when they lit it a man simply touched a light to the bottom end. The fuse flared and burned out instantly

leaving all the candles lighted. We were astonished at the beauty of the singing—full rich chorus, full of harmony.[2]

Despite its beauty, the church service impressed the Davenports as "an ancient idolatry." On the other hand, Clara and Noah found the missionary folks a bit dull though congenial. They felt closer to the Protestant church as a religion but enjoyed the company of the Orthodox priest and his wife more. Once they had invitations to both the Home and the Panteleevs, on the same evening. After dinner at the Home, the women began what Noah called their perpetual fancywork. "Some time I am going to sit down and write my impressions of the missionaries," he wrote. Unfortunately, if he did the account has been lost. After a suitable time, the Davenports excused themselves and went to the priest's home where they spent "the most pleasant evening calling since we came here." Here, too, "fancy work" was brought out, "but in a far different way from our last experience." Mrs. Panteleev showed them "some rare, old pieces of hand work, some hand wove, which she owns. One piece was done by her great grandmother. It looked rich even to me. Our general conversation went to subjects worth discussing and we felt greatly benefited by our call here." Guests that evening also included the commissioner Nick Bolshanin and his wife, Olga, a former Home girl.

The Davenports had a relaxed attitude toward Orthodox holidays. On January 19, the observance of the baptism of Christ, the town children were absent from school. So, "it being a fine day," they took the other children for a walk along the beach toward Summer Bay. The Davenports, like Dr. Newhall, had a sense of humor. "In school this morning," wrote Clara Davenport on Lincoln's birthday, "the teacher, smiling engagingly said, 'Now, children whose birthday is this?' Chorus of Aleuts—'*Willie Siftsoft*'s.' Teacher collapsed."[3] They became friends with Peter and Eliza Kashevaroff, and the two couples often visited each other. On one occasion, the Davenports went to the Kashevaroffs' home to listen to their new Victrola. Clara wrote in the diary, "They, or rather he, is 'quite musical.' He owns a violin, cornet, Victrola, guitar, and having exhausted the possibilities of these instruments, he has now sent for a violincello."[4] Once when Mary Winchell and Emma Supernaw visited Clara, she laughed as she told them how two local boys had made the sign of the cross when she approached them in school the day before. She may have thought they were giving her special recognition; more likely, they were seeking protection *from her* for some minor indiscretion.

On May 14, as Clara Davenport's due date approached, she went to see the Newhalls. Agnes and the doctor thought they should be on hand that evening, and they were given the spare room at the school. "They are extremely kind and were glad to stay right with us," wrote Noah. "Alaska has advantages in some respects." Their son Howard Tarte was born at 10 the next night after 12 hours of labor. "The doctor and wife stayed on all night and in the morning he brought a beautiful bouquet of six tea roses and ferns from Miss Supernaw

LEARNING GARDEN WORK *behind the government school. Courtesy of the Unalaska City School District (Davenport Collection).*

for the little mother. How happy they made her!" Agnes continued to tend Clara for several days. A little over a month later, the Davenports prepared to depart. They were invited to spend their last day or two at the Home. Kathryn Dyakanoff Seller stopped by and presented them with a basket from Atka for the baby.

During the tenure of Robert Scott, relations with the Home continued peacefully. Medicines issued to the school were turned over to Dr. Newhall, who gladly saw to any needs. Scott sided with the doctor in a dispute over sending children to the boarding school at Chemawa, Oregon. Those who returned after several years of absence had a difficult time finding employment and had lost fishing and hunting skills. The teacher prohibited the use of the Aleut language in the school so as to reinforce competence in English, an attitude approved by the Home. As at the Home, students in the school learned a variety of manual skills from carpentry to sewing. Scott had a good opinion of the local people, whom he called "very peaceful and law abiding." Homes were regularly given a thorough cleaning, he said, and people took pride in the village. The Scotts left in the spring of 1914, closing school early. Effie Scott had given birth in October or November. In addition, her own father had recently died.

The next teacher, Wilke Wilson, had not yet arrived by August 31. When school did begin, manual training and gardening along with basketry were continued. Plans were made to collect and prepare grass during the summer for classes the following winter "if they have the advantage of a basketry teacher again."[5] Sewing classes were coordinated with Harriet Barnett at the Home and Kathryn Seller. Mama Newhall taught knitting to the school girls two hours once a week. Wilson was less sympathetic with the local people and made a habit of visiting homes to inspect them. "I have helped these people in every way that I possibly could," he wrote, adding that he had "certainly had opposition."[6]

He stayed less than a year, but his successor remained for three. Joseph Coleman found children from the Home an indirect help in teaching English. Many of these students were Eskimo and did not speak or understand Aleut. Village children were thus forced to speak English if they wanted to communicate with their peers, during play as well as academic work. "The rivalry among the Home children and their eagerness for excelling," he wrote, "spread very rapidly among the village children and now it is a common thing to see them striving side by side often dividing honors in their work."[7] Coleman praised the work of the wife of the deputy U.S. marshal. Mrs. Buckley was a trained nurse and helped with two women who were severely ill. He reserved his greatest praise, however, for the Home.

I cannot speak too highly of Dr. Newhall and his assistants for the refining influence on the 47 children under their care and the hearty cooperation they extended to us in the school, not only in instilling the correct attitude toward the school, but in encouraging habits of study and willing submission to discipline. They also teach the children politeness, respect, and good manners; beside which each boy is taught the art of making a living and the things necessary for a man to know in the making of a home. Each girl is taught to sew, cook, and perform necessary household duties.

Coleman wrote that the Home received 12 newspapers and magazines and that about 30 books had been read to the children during the year. Because of this exposure to literacy and a healthy diet, Home children were about two years more advanced in their studies than children from the village. The teacher gave more emphasis to academic studies than to "manual training" because, as he put it, "the parents, white and native, seem to desire at least the rudiments of an education in the English language for their children." The last year he taught, from 1917 to 1918, Coleman emphasized "the citizenship and patriotic side" of the curriculum. He had become something of a crusader with goals not unlike those of the Home. He strove "to inculcate qualities of thrift, frugality, and loyalty to country; our ultimate object always being to better the child's living conditions, to create a desire for better things and show the way to attain this desire, to develop as far as possible a decent, law-abiding child in order that a useful citizen can be added to our country."[8]

Edith Newhall Drugg wrote about attending school during these years.

It was a good-sized building with half of it used for classrooms and the other half for teachers' living quarters. . . . The downstairs room was heated by a large pot-bellied stove. Coal was used for fuel which was shipped in from Nanaimo, British Columbia. It had to be hauled to the school by wheel barrow or on sleds in those days.

There were a couple of rows of double desks and seats in the school, which did not work out too well as to discipline! All desks had open inkwells and one day one of the girls dipped my braid of hair into the inkwell. Such a mess! In later years I corresponded with Anfesia Shapsnikoff and she said she was the one who did it. We remained friends. It just added a little spice to our school days.

The upstairs room was used for basket weaving and sewing. I believe it was Mrs. Lavigne who instructed us in the weaving classes. . . . In sewing class it came time for us to make our own aprons with long sleeves which we wore over our warm dresses. I was so proud of my work until I found out I had sewed the sleeve to the *neck* of the garment. I was crushed to have to rip that all out and start over again.

There was an old organ in the main classroom and they usually let us sing during the opening exercises. At that time I could play easy tunes and would accompany the singing. Once in a while they'd let the students select the songs and they would always choose the same old things, "Santa Lucia," "Juanita," and "The Soldier's Farewell." I never could figure out why they enjoyed these particular songs so much. I sure got tired of playing them.

The teacher lived in the other half of the building, but as the student-body grew, more teachers were needed so the government built a cottage next door to the school for the teachers' living quarters. The whole school building could then be used for classes. When the fierce storms came and the winds blew so hard, it was difficult to make one's way from the Mission to the school. The smaller children would hold hands and the older boys would be on each end of the line to keep us from blowing into the sea or the creek, depending on which direction the wind was coming from.[9]

In January 1912 the Davenports noted in their diary that Agnes Newhall had been to their home for a visit. "Mrs. N is going to take her daughter out of school," wrote the teachers, "—afraid of Aleut influence." This may have been shortly after Anfesia Shapsnikoff had been unable to resist dipping Edith's long blond braid into the inkwell. The Newhalls knew that Anfesia worked for the Davenports after school. Edith stayed in the school.

In 1915 Newhall tried to transfer administration of the school from the Department of the Interior's Bureau of Indian Affairs to the territory of Alaska. He corresponded with the district court which delayed a decision while consideration was given to objections by Leontii Sifsof of the Russian school and Dr. Schaleben, the administrator for education in western Alaska.

Asked once whether any friction existed between the Home and the school, Edith Newhall said, "The only friction we had . . . was between my father and one of the school teachers there. I don't know whether it was me that did it or whether it was the friction between him and the school teacher. . . . But, anyway, I was the only white child in school and he [the teacher] said he wasn't sent up there to teach white children. I don't know if I caused a scene for him or what. I really don't. My father never told me, but there was some kind of friction. So my father took me out of school and taught me the last two and a half years I was up there."

Edith said her father was "a pretty good teacher" in all things except mathematics, which both of them disliked. "It would have been just as well if my father wasn't teaching me mathematics," she said, "because I would be stubborn and I didn't even want to think of it. My mind would go blank and that was it and I wasn't going to do it. Fractions, you know."[10]

Her schooling under Dr. Newhall would probably have been for the years around 1918 to 1920. In 1919 Newhall once again inquired about creating a school district outside of incorporated towns in order to develop a territorial school. The commissioner of education wrote that such a school "would necessarily have to operate entirely separate from the mission and [be] subject to the same regulations as all other schools of the same class."[11]

NOTES

1. Mary Winchell, interview by Shirley Hook for Dorothy Jones in Pasadena, Calif., Nov. 11, 1967.

2. Davenport, *Unalaska Days,* 22.

3. William (Vasilii) Sifsof was a son of Leontii Sifsof, the deacon at the Orthodox church and a principal assistant to the ethnographer Waldemar Jochelson in 1909–10.

4. Davenport, *Unalaska Days,* 69.

5. Wilke Wilson. Annual Report, July 1, 1914 to June 30, 1915. NARA. RG 75. Box 75A.

6. Wilke Wilson, Annual Report 1914–15. NARA, RG 75, General Correspondence.

7. J.W. Coleman. Annual Report 1915–16. NARA, RG 75, Incoming Correspondence.

8. Coleman, Joseph. Annual School Report. NARA, RG 75, Alaska Division, General Correspondence. Unalaska, FY 1917–18.

9. Edith Newhall Drugg, "Some Notes from Earlier Days in Unalaska," in Hudson, ed., *Cuttlefish Volumes One, Two, & Three,* 10.

10. Conversation with Ray Hudson, Feb. 13, 1976.

11. Lester D. Henderson, Commissioner of Education, to Newhall, July 24, 1919. Jesse Lee Home Correspondence, Unalaska City School (copy received from Steve McGlashan).

UNALASKA, C. 1912. *On the back of the original photograph is written: "Unalaska showing the Jesse Lee Home bldgs and the Lake back of the Home. The Russian Greek Catholic church the second largest one in Alaska." Courtesy of the Unalaska City School District (Clara Cook Collection).*

24

Church and Native Culture

BETTER RELATIONSHIPS DEVELOPED BETWEEN THE PROTESTANT and Orthodox residents of Unalaska as prominent members of both groups came to know and appreciate each other. Peter Kashevaroff, as mentioned in earlier chapters, had married Eliza Gould, who was raised in the Home. The Kashevaroff family was a large and distinguished one that produced priests, scholars and administrators. Peter's father, the Rev. Peter Kashevaroff, was a deacon at Belkofski for 12 years before his ordination as a priest in 1897. Peter had accompanied his father on trips to Unalaska. In 1898 the priest and his family moved to St. George in the Pribilof Islands where he served until his death in 1930. The younger Peter was working at Unalaska as early as June 1903.[1] At that time another Kashevaroff, Vasilii P. Kashevaroff, was an assistant priest under Father Kedrovsky and an instructor in the Russian school.

Peter Kashevaroff had a remarkable ability to span cultural differences. Fur trader Samuel Applegate, who Henry Swanson said always wore a suit even when hunting sea otter on his schooner, was impressed by him. "Peter . . . is probably the most gentlemanly native Alaska has ever produced," Applegate wrote in 1916. "He has been employed by the Alaska Commercial Company as clerk in the store for many years."[2] Mary Winchell once remarked about his patience in the store when a crowd of girls from the Home arrived to make their giggly purchases. Peter and Eliza had a comfortable small home not far from the mission. As their family grew, he was interested in economic possibilities beyond clerking. Papers filed with the district court that year indicate he was involved with the mining claim at Huntsville. He also leased Ulak Island in 1916 for fox trapping.[3] Planting blue fox on the islands was a promising development, and he seems to have been in the forefront of this effort. He was equally respected by the Aleut community. Despite his marriage to Eliza by a Protestant minister while living on the east coast of the United States, he remained a member of the Orthodox Church. He was elected president of the Iliuliuk Club, a service and recreational organization of Aleut men.

Peter impressed the Newhalls just as he had the rest of the community. Through him they saw the variety and depth of Orthodoxy and Native culture as championed by the church under Father Alexander Kedrovsky. The Newhalls were living in Massachusetts when Father Kedrovsky left Unalaska in July 1908 after 14 years of productive ministry. He, his wife, and their five children were returning to Russia. "The father is very highly respected by all who know him," wrote a reporter for the *Seward Gateway,* "whether Aleuts,

Russians or Americans. He is a strong advocate of temperance and has done a noble work among the nations of his field of labor. He intimates that he may return to the United States to bring up his children as Americans."[4] Father Kedrovsky had seen the Home emerge from its façade as a government school into a full-fledged Protestant institution. After several painful confrontations involving Orthodox children in the Home, he and the Newhalls had never fully reconciled. Dr. Newhall was always willing to attend Kedrovsky's children when they became ill, and the priest gave the Newhalls a fine Russian tea set for Christmas one year. Nevertheless, there was at most a respectful but distant truce between them.

The priest who succeeded Kedrovsky was able to start a new relationship. Alexander A. Panteleev, born 1874, arrived at Unalaska in 1909 and served the community until 1912 when he was transferred to Pittsburg, Pa. A highly capable administrator, he eventually rose to become bishop of Alaska. He reached out to the Newhalls, visiting them at the mission and inviting them to the home where he lived with his wife and daughter. On April 10, 1912, Agnes and Albert visited the Panteleevs. They brought along Edith.[5] "Mr. & Mrs. Applegate; Mr. & Mrs. Goss, and Mr. & Mrs. Hastings were present," wrote the doctor. "About one half hour was spent in singing hymns—then we went upstairs and saw lantern slides. A lunch followed consisting of tea—bread—macaroons, meat cakes, etc. A very pleasant evening." Then he added, "I am studying Russian with the priest and I am teaching him English."[6] Newhall included in his manuscript the Lord's Prayer in Russian as well as a lullaby, a "Kossack Cradle Song." Edith recalled accompanying her father when he went to the Panteleev home for his lessons; she would play with the priest's daughter, Lubova, during the lessons and looked forward to the tea and "piroke" that were served afterward.[7]

Winchell said that the mission and the Orthodox church "got along well together." She recalled, "We would attend occasionally and they would bring out chairs for us. It was cold. No fire and no seats, that's the way Russian churches are."[8] John Carpenter (Nanoona) recalled the Orthodox Christmas star coming to the Home,[9] and Edith Newhall Drugg remembered attending Russian Christmas programs in the community hall above the A.C. Co. laundry. "We had a very good spirit going back and forth," she said. "There was never any animosity. Very good feeling. But the Russian Greek people of the village went to their church, you know, and we had our own services up at our place."[10] This good relationship was also evident in Chester Newhall's recollections of the beautiful sounds of the Orthodox church bells. "I remember being on the hills," he wrote, "and hearing the church bells ring—a blessed sound!"[11]

The Home adopted the Orthodox custom of baking a special bread for Easter. "The making of *kulech* [*kulich*] was a custom of old Russia," wrote Winchell, "and a very good custom it is."[12] Recipes vary, but the Home version was a sweet dough to which were added raisins, more sugar, and slivers of sliced almonds. Emma Supernaw baked kulich in regular bread pans rather than in the round ones customarily used in the village. (Tradition calls for a dome-shaped loaf, echoing the dome of the church.) She would frost enough for breakfast on Easter, and the unfrosted loaves would be used the following day. Kulich was featured in all the homes visited during the Easter period. Winchell recalled visits to Chief Alexei Yatchmeneff's home and those of John Peters and Father Panteleev. The women from the Home called on Elena Newman, daughter of Father Innokentii Shaishnikoff, in "her neat house with its nice, old-fashioned furniture." Winchell was impressed at how "she served *kulech* and tea with quiet dignity." Village women sometimes brought a decorated loaf of kulich to the Home.

"Rev. and Mrs. Pontalaief are striving hard to learn English," wrote the Davenports in their diary. "He comes and reads with the children every day in school and she comes twice a week. Though belonging to the soulless church that they do, they are individually greatly interested in the Aleuts and are doing all they can to help them. He goes about in summer to every village in this district—a territory 800 miles in length—and holds services with them. He also takes their confessions. While we couldn't by the wildest stretch of imagination believe in his church yet we find in them personally congenial and interesting people."[13]

Simeon Oliver has left two accounts of interaction with the Orthodox church. Once he and Charlie Lee snuck out of the Home to accompany Mike Tutiakoff to a crowded Christmas Eve service. The boys were horrified to discover two of the missionaries holding candles among the women worshipers. When the Orthodox members knelt, the two Jesse Lee Home boys dropped to the floor like lead weights to blend in with the crowd.[14]

Oliver also witnessed the blessing of the water, conducted by Panteleev. "Though we were so friendly with Father Panteleev," he wrote, "he became a different and unknown person the day of the great procession to the lake." The mission boys lined up on a bank to watch the event and to wave at their school chums. "Father Panteleev, waving his scepter and making the sign of the cross," noted Oliver, "turned abruptly when he came to the Mission grounds and made a tactful detour to avoid treading on them." Oliver said Dr. Newhall was amused that the boy in charge of the water pump, after the priest had blessed the lake, "always hastened to fill our tank with the holy water."[15]

In Newhall's 1912 report there appeared to be a softening of the usual harsh tone toward Orthodoxy. He referred to work among the Eskimo people as being Protestant. "As far as the Aleuts are concerned," he wrote, "the work is in a Greek Catholic field." He made no direct attack on the Orthodox clergy. Rather, he cautioned against expecting change too quickly. When he addressed what he saw as "the demoralizing condition among the people," he did not refer to the Orthodox Church. Instead, he blamed "immoral and degenerate white men, the use of intoxicating drinks, gambling, and the mixed dance. . . ."

Clara Cook wrote about the Panteleevs' final departure from Unalaska. The priest and his family sailed in September 1912. Before leaving, Mrs. Panteleev gave Clara a blossoming

THE BISHOP'S HOUSE *and the Russian School as they appeared shortly before World War II.*
Photo by Ted Elmore, August 1941, in the author's collection.

rose plant. "The whole town turned out to bid them farewell," she wrote, "and the band played. All we teachers went and our 32 Children. They was like by all. There is no Priest here now."[16]

In the fall of 1913 Father Demetrius Auchef arrived.[17] He stayed only a short time and made little impression on the folks at the Home. Father Dmitrii Hotovitsky, who came in 1915, supported the school and urged people to learn English. He was another of those exceptional men who served Orthodox communities in the Aleutians. He had come to the United States in 1908, working first as a song leader at St. Nicholas Cathedral in New York. He was ordained a priest in 1909 and subsequently lived in Colorado, New Jersey, and Pennsylvania. He arrived at Unalaska in 1916. In 1920 he moved to Belkofski where he became actively involved in economic developments. He served there until his death in 1952.[18]

The staff at the Home now worked hard to create bonds of friendship with the people in the village. The annual report for 1913–14 stated, "Our teachers try to make Jesse Lee Home the social center where the village folks can come with their joys and sorrows, and find love and sympathy."[19] This was the relationship that Anfesia Shapsnikoff remembered.

> Everything that we had we made and was given—including the Russian School and the Jesse Lee Home with Dr. Newhall and Mama Newhall. Fixing up things for the community as well as the Jesse Lee Home children, the Russian School done that very thing. . . . The chief [Alexei Yatchmeneff] and the second chief lived the same way as Dr. Newhall and Mama Newhall did. He took care of the widows and people that were needing and nobody was ever left out. . . . But yet, Dr. Newhall made it nice that he came and shared with the Russian School and seen to [the] needy. He was a doctor and a father to children that were here from all over Alaska, up north as well as southeast and the Aleutian Chain. It was a big loss to go and have him move away from here. . . . Mama Newhall knew everyone. By the time the baby was born until we went to school she knew them all, and so she outfitted a child that was in need. And so you never found anyone without anything.

Anfesia recalled gatherings at the Home.

> Christmas Eve we always went and had a community Christmas program at the Jesse Lee Home. That combined the Russian School boys who went and had a share in there and anything that they done was done in Russian. And, 'course, the Jesse Lee Home had the whole program and the pageant of Christmas. Dr. Newhall was at the organ and Simeon Oliver and Edith Newhall was at the piano and Dan Sipary and Fred—from Chignik—were the two fiddlers. Mr. Applegate—he was a trader from here to Nikolski—had a

boat by the name of *Lettie*. He used to trade in foxes. He was one of the three fiddlers. The whole community, over 300 people, would gather up in the Jesse Lee Home there.

I think there are some pictures of the big building. There was one room up in the front corner there that they used for entertaining. It was the girls' dormitory. . . . During the entertainment there Dr. Newhall would get up and he would tell of the Christmas story. Then he would have Father Kedrovsky come up and tell it in Russian. And then Leontii Sifsof—he was a reader of the church—he would come up there and interpret all that in Aleut. And so everyone that was there understood what they were saying and what they were doing. If there was someone who didn't understand what they said it was asked and Dr. Newhall would ask someone to interpret and Leontii Sifsof was always available to do that. And so we had entertainment in Aleut, Russian, and English.

William Ermeloff remembered that he and other boys from the village played with boys from the Home. Sometimes the two groups would have battles with (and over) toy boats on the lake.[20]

"As to poverty among the village people," Mary Winchell wrote, "there was fish in the sea, clams, some berries and some work on boats during the summer, though boats were few. But the marshal, Chief Alexis, [and] Jesse Lee were there to help, and the Alaska Commercial store would help also. So no one was destitute, I think."[21] However poor a family might be, the parents resisted surrendering their children to the Home. As noted earlier, Jochelson in 1909-1910 had found "even impoverished Aleut parents would not allow their children to live in this home." He added, "Orphans placed there by the American authorities would return to the Russian Church after they had grown up and had left the home."[22]

"I never lived at the Jesse Lee Home as my mother, bless her, would not stand to be alone no matter how poor we were," wrote Bill Brown. His mother was from Attu. He went on to say that his association with children from the Home took place at the government school. "We attended the Sunday School classes we enjoyed at the Jesse Lee Home," he said, adding, "I dare say no one can say but good for Dr. and Mrs. Newhall, wonderful people."[23]

Stability within the Aleut community was supplied by the church, Chief Alexei Yatchmeneff, and a village council. "The chief was always very good," Winchell said. "He was a fine person." Both the chief and the council worked to keep the village clean and to diminish alcohol abuse.[24] Yatchmeneff had become chief in 1902 and would remain in office until his death in 1937. On January 14, 1917, the community held a celebration of his 15th anniversary as chief. Joseph Coleman, the schoolteacher, has left this account:

The leading natives of the town and the priest made talks concerning this noted man and his influence on the history and welfare of the village. The main address on this occasion was given by the chief himself. He spoke of his own humility, how he had tried to serve his people, and had thought that since the United States had government officials to administer the affairs of the village, that he would relinquish his office as chief. Yet he had felt as a father to his people and thought that they would feel lost if he did so. He urged his subjects to be law-abiding and to always remember that they were natives and not to try to pass as white. . . .[25]

His insistence on maintaining Aleut identity is significant given the harsh economic conditions of the time and the persistent pressure for Aleuts to blend into the non-Native community. Even after he had taught manual training to 17 boys at school and they had built benches, shelves, two dories, and other useful articles, a schoolteacher, Agnes Danford, wrote about Aleuts at Unalaska, "Our government should make real American citizens of these Russians instead of permitting them to follow the manners and customs of their own country so far away."[26] The chief and the leaders of the community had an uphill battle to preserve their traditions and way of life.

Aleut basketry was an art that non-Natives appreciated. "We have long had an ambition to have the girls in Jesse Lee Home taught the rare basket weaving done by the natives of the Aleutian Islands," the annual report for 1908-1909 said, "but as necessarily some of the teachers would have opportunity to learn the art, too, no native woman was willing to give lessons, this being their one exclusive art. But at last a teacher was found, and samples of the work done by our girls are in the Alaska exhibit." The exhibit was the Seattle Exposition of 1909. The teacher was Mary Prokopeuff Lavigne, from Attu. The school-teacher Wilke Wilson wrote that she "is considered the best basket maker among the Aleuts, and seems to have been very satisfactory as a teacher."[27] Edith Newhall recalled the basketry lessons.

The upstairs room [in the school] was used for basket weaving and sewing. I believe it was Mrs. Lavine who instructed us in the weaving classes and sometimes we got a little bored and played around a bit. All of a sudden she'd notice we weren't paying attention to our work and she'd call us out by name in a loud, impressive tone—"*Weave* your basket!!"

Clara Cook also studied basketry with Mary Lavigne. Purchasing a basket was beyond her financial means. "The curios one could buy here would cost a small fortune," she wrote. "A nice native basket costs from five dollars up and they can sell all they can make to tourists in the summer. I have one that was given to me. It is not a fine one, but I am glad to have it." She had no idea when or even if she would ever complete her own basket.

THE BOARDWALK *running from the dock to the Alaska Commercial Company. Photo by J.E. Thwaites,
from a private collection.*

Again as mentioned earlier, Cook was always willing to try Native foods. Although traditional whaling had long since disappeared, commercial whalers were in and out of the port. Once a whale that had been harpooned but not recovered drifted to shore. People at the Home used their binoculars and could see "it was a mammoth thing." A group of local men went out and butchered it. A barrel of whale meat was given to the Home. "Salted it is fine," wrote Cook. "When the fat is pickled it tastes like pickled-pig-feet I love it. The lean is almost like beef."[28]

At Huntsville or Summer Bay, Mary Winchell would take children along the beach to find sea urchins and blue mussels. They cooked the mussels on the stove in the cabin and enjoyed traditional Aleut food with them.[29]

On occasion Dr. Newhall invited storyteller Isidor Solovyov to entertain the children. Solovyov was paramount among Aleut tradition bearers. His tales, transcribed, translated and published in 1990, form the core of a national treasure for Aleut people. The children and adults were transfixed by his performance. Mary Winchell described the climactic moments.

> As the song continued, his voice rose in volume, expression, and energy. Then, suddenly, this feeble old man crouched down. He beat his drum wildly, his feet keeping quick time to its rhythm. He sprang high into the air.
>
> We looked at each other in utter amazement. What were the words of this song, to so strengthen and inspire him?

Simeon Oliver wrote his own account of those evenings. He described how Solovyov's "music became louder and more exciting. Suddenly, . . . [he] sprang to his feet and began to dance the ancient festival dance of his people. Faster flew his feet, faster the tempo of the drum. He sang and shouted at the top of his lungs, kicking and leaping in the air. At last he dropped exhausted."

Anfesia Shapsnikoff has supplied additional information about Solovyov. She was not a resident of the Home, but like other Aleut children she went there frequently to visit friends or occasionally to have a meal. Unlike Oliver or Winchell, she could understand the words to the songs and stories. She remembered them and as an old woman retold them to other children. It is significant that she heard these stories in the Methodist orphanage and boarding school, with the Methodist doctor, his wife, the girls' matron, and other teachers as part of the audience. Only a few years before, there had been a general outcry against the Home by the Aleut community. It is also significant that only Anfesia remembered the story-teller's name. When Oliver and Winchell wrote their reminiscences, they got it wrong and called him "Feodor Selokoff" and "Old Andrea." But then, they were observers of the culture. Anfesia was a part of it.

1. North American Commercial Company, Log Copy Book. May 31, 1903–September 16, 1903. June 27, 1903. Archives of the Arctic and Polar Regions Collections of the Elmer E. Rasmuson Library, University of Alaska Fairbanks.

2. Samuel Applegate to A.K. Fisher, Bureau of Biological Survey, April 12, 1916. Alaska State Historical Library. MS 0003.

3. *Record*. District Court of Alaska, 3rd Division, I (No. 79574), p. 16a.

4. *Seward Gateway*. 18 July 1908.

5. Edith Drugg was living in Sitka when Panteleev became Bishop of Alaska. He was delighted to meet her and recall the early days at Unalaska. (Conversation with Ray Hudson, Feb. 13, 1976.)

6. Newhall Manuscript, 266.

7. Edith Newhall Drugg, letter to Ray Hudson, March 30, 1978.

8. Mary Winchell, interview by Shirley Hook for Dorothy Jones in Pasadena, Calif., Nov. 11, 1967.

9. Carpenter, letter to Philemon Tutiakoff, Aug. 14, 1978.

10. Edith Newhall Drugg, interview with Ray Hudson, Feb. 13, 1976.

11. Chester Newhall, letter to Phil and Flora Tutiakoff, April 1, 1979.

12. Winchell, *Where the Wind Blows Free*, 123.

13. Davenport, *Unalaska Days*, Oct. 27, 1911.

14. Oliver, *Son of the Smoky Sea*, 96–101.

15. Ibid., 101–02.

16. Cook, letter, Oct. 13, 1912. Robert Collins Collection.

17. A.W. Newhall, "Christmas 1913" in Hudson, ed., *Cuttlefish: Volumes One, Two & Three*, 189.

18. Black, *The History and Ethnohistory of the Aleutians East Borough*, 94–95.

19. Woman's Home Missionary Society, Reports from Bureaus. 1913–14:196.

20. Personal conversation with Ray Hudson. Sept. 1, 2005.

21. Mary Winchell to Dorothy Jones, Sept. 22, 1967.

22. Jochelson, "People of the Foggy Seas," 417.

23. Bill Brown to Steve Assenmacher, June 22, 1973.

24. Mary Winchell, interview by Shirley Hook for Dorothy Jones in Pasadena, Calif., Nov. 11, 1967.

25. Coleman, Joseph. Unalaska. Annual Report, 1916–17. NARA. RG 75. General correspondence.

26. Agnes Danford, Annual Report Unalaska, June 30, 1919. NARA, RG 75. Entry 806, Box 103.

27. Wilke Wilson, letter Nov. 10, 1914, NARA. RG 75. General correspondence.

28. Cook, letter, Oct. 13, 1912. Robert Collins Collection.

29. Mary Winchell, interview by Shirley Hook for Dorothy Jones in Pasadena, Calif., Nov. 11, 1967.

25

Scenes of Childhood and Beyond

"THE LAKE HAS FROZEN OVER AGAIN," WROTE CLARA COOK on March 14, 1914, "and the wind is blowing awfull hard." But from her window she could see the boys had made themselves sails and were flying across the ice on skates. "The children all love the wind," she wrote, "and we have lots of snow now." Children arrived at the Jesse Lee Home under traumatic circumstances. Often one or both of their parents had died or the family was destitute from illness or misfortune. To greater or lesser extents, the children must have been bewildered. They were frightened and alone. Then, with the resiliency of youth, they adapted; they built themselves sails. They flew across the icy lake.

When Simeon Oliver was 77 and Henry Swanson was 84, they were asked what their fondest memories were of childhood. "As I look back on this," Simeon said, "the isolation we had—we were always alone, we were by ourselves, and the rapport between the Native people and the white people was marvelous. We were all one people. . . ." He recalled the shared festivities between the Home and the Russian church. "Those were very wonderful days. I was young then and very impressionable and I look upon those days as very happy days. . . . We all attended school together; we were like brothers and sisters. . . . No problems whatsoever."

"That was the good part," Henry agreed. "There was no problems. And the people here lived off the land a lot, you know. So nobody was ever hungry. They didn't have much money, but they didn't need much money."[1]

Neither of these men was a Pollyanna; both had lived through difficult times, but when they spoke about the Home, they did so with affection. Simeon recalled Saturday afternoons when the children could leave the Home and go into the village. He and other boys would go to the dock and visit ships. The four-masted schooner *Holmes* was tied up once and they climbed all over it and were treated to cookies. He remembered the large summer garden where rutabagas, turnips, lettuce and radishes were raised. There were 50 half-barrels placed out in the garden area for rhubarb. The rutabagas and turnips, stored in a partially underground and sodded cellar, would last all winter. Radishes and lettuce were occasionally sold to officers aboard the revenue cutters. Dried fruits arrived from the States. Fresh meat came from beef on Sanak, purchased from parents of children in the Home.

There were occasional parties for the children. Dr. Newhall would hunt in the pantry for prizes—a piece of cheese, a cookie, a handful of figs. And each summer there were trips to beautiful sandy Summer Bay. The staff took turns there or at Huntsville. During the two weeks Clara Cook spent at Summer Bay in 1912 with Mary Winchell and six older boys, they caught only 130 salmon and 1,000 herring. The day they came home Dr. Newhall and the boys got 156 salmon in one haul with the net at Margaret Bay. The cabins at Summer Bay were much as when first constructed, but now the "teacher's cabin" had a carpet on the floor, an oil heater, and an organ. While there Cook explored two springs. The water in one was "as hot as you could bear your hand in" while in the other the water was ice cold.[2] This cold spring may have been at Morris Cove. It was there, according to her description, that they took salmon from "a pretty fresh water lake a few rods away with mountains on three sides." Staff and children explored the abandoned, or not so abandoned, barabaras at Morris Cove and Summer Bay. Clara Cook, according to Mary Winchell, "never approved of prowling."[3] However, Cook herself once wrote about just such activity:

> Years ago there used to be a half doz families of natives live there, but now all that is left is the empty Barabaras and the tomb stones. I visited all the Barabaras, and got a little Greek cross from one for a curio. They have their holy corner in all the native houses or Barabaras. This one had a picture of Jesus one side of the cross and the virgin Mary the other side, and a bottle of holy water hung beside them. We had to hunt around in the tall grass to find the Barabaras they are mostly underground and sod roofs. Every little raise in the ground we would hunt all around it to find an entrance.[4]

There was also time for serious study. Once after picking a large salmonberry, Dr. Newhall took it apart and counted 75 individual seeds.

Of course, discipline permeated the Home. Caroline Mabel Nielsen was four when she arrived from Sanak in 1911. She recalled that soon she was "just as mischievous as the rest" of the children. Once when she was not feeling well, she was allowed to rest in Mary Winchell's room. Caroline noticed the matron take a small bottle of perfume from the windowsill near her bed and put some on her dress. A few days later, Winchell again allowed Caroline to nap in her room after taking a bath. Tucked into the bed, Caroline shut her eyes but the moment the matron left, she sat up. She recovered the damp bath towel from the foot of the bed and took the bottle of perfume. The stopper was tight so she chewed at it until it came off. "I poured all of the perfume out of the bottle onto my towel," she wrote, "and then rubbed it all over my head."[5] A noise outside the door sent her scrambling back under the covers. An older girl had arrived to help her get dressed. Caroline panicked and pretended to be unconscious. The girl called for Mary Winchell who soon discovered what Caroline had done. "After she got through with me," Caroline wrote, "I thought I would never like her again." Caroline lived at the Home until she graduated from eighth grade in 1927.

"There were times when I was in the Home," wrote Simeon Oliver in 1931, "that I tho't it was a mean place but since I've knocked about a bit I've come to realize what the training has meant. I do not have any desire whatsoever to smoke or drink or use tobacco in any form."[6] Oliver recounted an episode with Mama Newhall that illustrated the limits of discipline. He had gone to Summer Bay with her and a group of children. For some reason, she had brought along "her own cherished set of exquisite china."

> One night I accidentally broke one of the beautiful blue teacups. I was scared sick, and the older boy who was with me did nothing to make me feel any better.
>
> "You'd better tell Mamma Newhall you smashed that cup," he said. "She's going to be awful mad and I don't want her to punish me for it."
>
> So a thoroughly frightened little Eskimo, carrying the broken pieces of the cup, went in to his doom.
>
> "See, Mamma Newhall," I quavered, "I broke your beautiful china cup."
>
> She looked at me with her lovely smile and said, "That's what I brought it here for, Simmy, to be broken."[7]

For some children the Home was literally a life-saver. One such child was Alice Devlin. She was born at Nushagak in Bristol Bay. The 1910 census listed her as the adopted daughter of Stephen and Irogenia Chukugak. In 1915 her mother took her to gather driftwood, using a sled of dogs. For some reason the dogs attacked the woman, killing her. Alice fled into the hills where she managed to survive for six weeks until making her way to a cannery in Bristol Bay. There she slept with dogs under an old building and begged food from a Chinese cook. She was discovered and turned over to the deputy marshal who took her to Unalaska. She entered the Home on Sept. 4, 1915. Emily Morgan was working as a nurse and matron at the time and helped to nurse her back to health.

Unlike the memories of good times, childhood eventually ended. Nellie Holmberg left the Home to return to Sanak in the summer of 1914. Clara Cook wrote that she was lonesome and wanted to return. "She says there is no Girls there, but all boys," wrote Cook, "and they rushed her away to the Priest to be blessed as soon as she landed."[8] Nellie had a family to return to, but for girls with no relatives or no home awaiting them, the future was uncertain. Nellie eventually married August Carlson.

The workers at Jesse Lee wrestled with the question of how to prepare students for a life outside the protective environment of the Home. They were particularly concerned with girls. "If good men were plentiful," a 1909 report stated, "all would be glad to have them marry and become homemakers. The homes made by Jesse Lee Home girls are models for those around them. But good men are scarce in Alaska, native or white, and the condition of morals is such that it is not safe for a girl to leave the Home unless married."[9]

[FROM A LETTER TO RAY HUDSON *from Edith Newhall Drugg*, Oct. 26. 1978]

… To run an institution there has to be a system and **that** they had! You knew every day what you were going to have to eat except when fresh fish had been caught. The Doctor parceled out food supplies to the kitchen once a week so that he would know what to order and keep a close eye on the stock levels.

The children were divided into groups of three ages—big, medium-size, and little. A work list was made out once a month and every child had a certain chore to do. The list included keeping dormitories swept and tidied, bed making, keeping the sewing room tidied, washing dishes, drying the dishes, sweeping rooms, hallways and stairs, filling lamps with kerosene and washing the lamp chimneys each day. These chores were done by both boys and girls. The boys also had the added chores of carrying kindling and coal and emptying the ashes from the stoves in both buildings.

Doctor and the big boys got up at 4 A.M. on Mondays to start the fires in the laundry and to get the laundry started. They washed clothes until breakfast time. This involved boiling the white clothes in large containers and using a hand-operated wooden paddle in a big tub to wash the colored clothes. It took real muscle power to do the washing in those days! The big girls were excused from school on Monday mornings to take over the washing chores after breakfast.

The boys kept their own building clean (sweeping, mopping, dusting, etc.) and also took care of the barn. The mission had two cows and two goats. The goats became quite a nuisance and finally ended up as our Thanksgiving dinner!

Beds and dishes had to be done before school. Rising gong was at 6 A.M. with the sound of an old-fashioned iron triangle which hung outside the kitchen window. Breakfast was at 6:30 A.M. in order to get the work done before school.

The children were instructed in sewing, mending, embroidering and knitting. The bigger girls knitted all the stockings for the entire "family" of 35 to 40 children. The boys learned shoe repairing from Doctor Newhall and took care of the "shoeing" of the children. The girls learned cooking and bread-making. Those who were interested or talented, took piano and violin lessons which were graciously taught by Mrs. Goss, a trader's wife. Doctor taught the children to sing "in parts." The children knew how to take care of themselves and to run their own homes when they left the mission. …

Harriet Barnett had recommended purchasing a small farm in Southeast Alaska or Washington state "where the boys and girls from Jesse Lee Home could be taken when ready to leave the Home, and have better opportunities for earning a living and for leading virtuous and Christian lives."[10] "It does not seem to me that we need a large piece of land," she wrote, "but a good commodious house, and land enough for a good vegetable garden, and a chicken house. My thought is that the children would not be there very long at a time, that places in families would be found for them, that it would be a kind of employment bureau—a place to which they might return if the family to which they were sent did not prove a suitable one to get along with them. In short, a *real home*, where they could always be kept under the eye and mind of the one in charge."[11] She knew that Captain Daniels of the revenue cutter *McCulloch* would be happy to transport the young adults free of charge. He had just witnessed the marriage of Alexandra Peterson to Peter Bourdu-kofsky and been quite impressed. He had also found the Home very willing to part with used clothing for him to take to Akutan where the people were in severe poverty.[12]

From its earliest days the Home had sent promising students to the States for further training. Most often this was to the Carlisle Indian School, but occasionally they were sent to other institutions or to private homes. When the Jesse Lee Home was first conceived and during its early years, backers of the program had solicited support by promising that Native girls would become missionaries to their own people. In 1908, *Woman's Home Missions* asked Dr. Newhall to explain why this had not happened.

> Theoretically it would be nice to have girls take positions in the Home. Practically we have never seen any who could do so. The Aleuts will follow, but cannot lead. They lack strength of character and dignity, also the power to maintain discipline. They do not mature as our American girls do, from sixteen to twenty, but they are quite childish and dependent, even when advanced in years.
>
> A teacher in a Mission Home in a mining country, or in a place where sailors or naval officers abound, is in a peculiar place of temptation. Open to invitations, attentions and flatteries, which if responded to would soon bring reproach to them and the work, the teachers must be of strong character, of strong will power. Our girls would not succeed in such positions. The natives have not reached that state of development yet. The priests, too, would have far more influence over the girls, directly and indirectly, for they would intimidate native workers.[13]

This was harsh criticism and ignored women like Matrona Salamatoff, a woman of Aleut descent who had taught in the public school at Unalaska and was still doing so at Afognak. A number of children who passed through the Home would in fact become successful teachers and missionaries. However, two years later the annual report for the

PLAYING "IN AND OUT THE WINDOW," *with Mt. Ballyhoo in the distance. Courtesy of the Unalaska City School District (Clara Cook Collection).*

Woman's Home Missionary Society quoted Dr. Newhall: "Alaska is a frontier country with all the good and evil influences found in such places. At first the rougher element predominates, but with the increase of population the influence of good people and Christianity is felt." The report continued, "We do not expect to do great things, but we are trying to work for the Master, to care for the orphan and to minister to the afflicted ones, to care for the dying, to lend a hand wherever needed—'Just to do what our hands find to do.' Our faith and trust is in God, and we know His blessing has been on the work."[14] This suggests that expectations had lowered.

When Adlooat was with the Newhalls on the East Coast he wrote to Annebuck at Carlisle. She had entered the school in November 1897, a few months after Elizabeth Mellor had brought girls from Unalaska. She was from Port Clarence and does not appear to have passed through the Jesse Lee Home but to have been placed at Carlisle by Sheldon Jackson himself. By the time she graduated in 1906, her name had been divided into "Anne Buck." She returned to Alaska with Mollie Delilak, another girl from Port Clarence. They arrived with no place to live and no money; they knew no one and could no longer speak fluent Eskimo. Her subsequent letters to Jackson are extraordinarily frank. "I don't think any body has right to civilize a native unless they present her or him a house, stove and sewing machine to live with," she wrote. "I think an Eskimo would be more comfortable and enterprising if he has a house to live in than in a one hour sermon with a dirty clothes on."[15] Anyone with common sense, she wrote, ought to consider the result of educating children far from home and in a different culture. Fortunately, she met a woman who gave her a place to stay along with encouraging her. "She told me to feel that wherever I am I have right to feel independent," she wrote Jackson, "and the universe is mine."[16] Through W.T. Lopp she secured a job as an assistant teacher at Deering. Initially, she was repelled by Native life. "Dr. Jackson, I don't like Alaska any more," she wrote, "because I can't stand the Eskimo life any more." She wanted to continue her education and requested assistance to do so. Her report in June 1907 is more upbeat. She found the children bright, quick to learn, and obedient. In discipline, the teacher had to use firmness, but one that was neither mean nor rough, as the people knew the "differences between kindness and unkindness." She visited homes and when school closed went out to where the reindeer were being herded. "I never saw such a kind gentle race of people," she wrote. "We will leave everything to God for he makes no mistakes." We do not know anything about her subsequent life, but the problems that faced her were also those that faced the children who grew up in the Home.

By 1913 Newhall was rethinking the policy of sending children to the States. That year the superintendent of the Chemawa Indian School in Salem, Oregon, attempted to recruit students from the Jesse Lee Home against the wishes of the Home. He sent applications to older children and promised them free transportation. Chemawa opened in 1880; by 1913 there were 173 Alaskans among 690 students. There were few graduates, however.[17]

TENDING THE CATTLE, *behind the girls' building. Chester Newhall is the boy with apron in the center. Courtesy of Alaska Children's Services, Anchorage.*

From Annie Swanson Hatch's album, A VISIT TO THE JESSE LEE POULTRY YARD. *The woman in the dark dress is believed to be Mary Winchell. Courtesy of the Hatch family.*

Newhall complained about this recruitment to W.T. Lopp, in charge of education for Alaska. His anger was reflected in an appalling paragraph.

> It is unwise to send the young children out to the states. They are typical Aleute, not as bright as the normal child, and after three years schooling or more, they cannot read or write—do not know their letters. They are only adapted to live in this country. They will absorb little education, will get a veneer of civilization, the boy will probably take on the vices of city life (judging by the Alaskan boys who have failed to get thru Seattle) while the girl will go into the dance and may land in the institutions or into the lives where so many have been wrecked. Here they could learn to fish and hunt and they would be contented to do it and that is all they are fit for.[18]

Newhall remembered how Henry Swanson had been lost to the Home while Dr. Spence was in charge. Newhall was now incensed because shortly after the recruitment attempt, Nick Hatch arrived from Chemawa and tried to talk his brother Peter into joining him and their brother Tracy there. Then an attorney demanded the release of the Hatch children from Jesse Lee. The "floating court" decided that the contract with the Home could not be broken. Nevertheless, Newhall reluctantly agreed to send two of the Hatch boys to Chemawa in 1915. Peter Hatch, Newhall wrote, was "a bright boy . . . polite, good and free from all bad habits." In two or three years he might have enough moral strength to resist the temptations that would come at Chemawa. For the time being he was still too impressionable to live with his half-brother Nick who "swears and when occasion requires uses vile language."

Newhall concluded his letter with a summary of the removal of children from the community.

> Jesse Lee Home has in times past sent many children to the states, some to Carlisle and others into homes, but the experiment has not been a success. Few are contented to either stay in the States or return to this land. It does not seem hardly wise to strip Alaska of the best of its children and leave only the dregs. . . . We wish the Chemawa school well and hope they will do much good. With ourselves they are trying to better the condition of the Alaskans, but we shall not interfere with their school, nor try to get children away, and trust that the same courtesy may be shown to us.

Robert Scott, the schoolteacher, agreed. "I would not advise the sending of native children to the States for special training," he wrote, "for when they return they are not trained to live a life such as they must live here with little or no employment."[19] Henry Swanson found Chemawa offered him little in the way of training. "I hated the place," he said. "When I went to Chemawa they put me in the eighth grade right away. And I stayed in

CHILDREN FROM JESSE LEE *dressed for a winter walk, with a woman identified in Annie Swanson Hatch's album as "Mary"—probably Mary Winchell. Courtesy of the Hatch family.*

THE BOYS' HOUSE, *on a rare day suitable for drying clothes outdoors. From Annie Swanson Hatch's album, courtesy of the Hatch family.*

the eighth grade for four years 'cause I ran away all the time. . . . You know, the place was full of wild Indians."[20]

Nevertheless, Peter Hatch left Unalaska in 1915 to attend Chemawa. In 1917 he married Annie Swanson, a girl from the Home. Among their children was one they named Jesse Lee Hatch.

Peter's brothers, Nick and Tracy, had successful years at Chemawa.[21] Both learned tailoring as a vocational skill. Tracy followed that vocation, but Nick enrolled in a technical high school in Portland as he was interested in engineering. Following graduation, he enlisted in the Navy near the end of World War I. After his discharge he returned to Portland, married, and raised a family. He returned to Alaska for a time and taught school. Unlike the comment from Dr. Newhall, Nick's son Kenneth recalled his father as some-one who never swore, but was a good citizen and protective of his children.[22]

Another successful graduate of schooling in the States was William Baylies (Catua). He was 11 or so when he arrived about 1904. He is said to have stowed away on a whaler to reach Unalaska. "He is ambitious and eager to advance in his studies and lifework," wrote one of his teachers. "His heart's desire is to go through music, and in that he excels, although he adapts himself to everything that is to be done here. All the boys look up to him, and the teachers depend on him. History is his delight, and his taste in literature is good."[23] He was a highly skilled, dependable member of the Home family. The society looked for someone to sponsor his further training.

He left on Oct. 9, 1911, and was enrolled in the Cushman Trades School at Tacoma, Washington. Nine others had left with him, but Clara Cook missed William more than the other nine combined. Three pieces of furniture he made at Cushman were displayed at the Panama Exposition at San Francisco.[24] In 1913 or 1914 he went to Nome to assist Dr. Baldwin, because, as the annual report of the WHMS stated, "his health needed the cold of his native country." In 1920 Dr. Newhall recalled him with affection and said he had been "a manual training teacher at Nome for a time ere he fell ill with pneumonia."[25]

Dr. Newhall liked to keep lists. In 1912 he reported that since he and his wife had first become involved with Unalaska there had been 164 children in the Home. Of these, 14 between the ages of 10 and 20 had died. Eighteen younger children had also died, for a total of 32 deaths, but "all of these children did not pass away while in the Home."[26] Of those who were alive, he wrote cryptically, "more than sixty are living with good records." What he meant by that, he tried to explain, was that bad news travels fast and he had received no reports of former children going astray. "Some of them are earnest Christians as we under-stand the term," he wrote. "Others may be Christians judged by the light they have had and the conditions and influences under which they live." Given the harshness of the moral climate that Newhall perceived in Alaska, he was satisfied if former students stayed away from alcohol and immorality.

1. Tape-recorded conversation with Simeon Oliver, Henry Swanson, Philemon Tutiakoff and Ray Hudson, May 25, 1979.

2. Cook, letter, Aug. 18, 1912. Robert Collins Collection.

3. Winchell, *Home by the Bering Sea*, 27.

4. Cook, letter, Aug. 18, 1912. Robert Collins Collection.

5. *Ku-eu-it*. May 1927. Comments from the graduating class, unpaginated.

6. Simeon Oliver to Myrtle C. Hatten, June 4, 1931. *Ku-eu-it.*

7. Oliver, *Son of the Smoky Sea*, 37.

8. Cook, letter, Aug. 31, 1914. Robert Collins Collection.

9. *WHM*, October 1909:11.

10. Woman's Home Missionary Society, Reports from Bureaus. 1908–09:140.

11. *WHM*, October 1909:11.

12. Woman's Home Missionary Society, Reports from Bureaus. 1907–09:130.

13. *WHM*, November 1908:210.

14. Woman's Home Missionary Society, Reports from Bureaus. 1911–12:183.

15. Anne Buck to Jackson, Sept. 7, 1906. PHS. RG 239. Box 7, folder 25.

16. Anne Buck to Jackson, November [no day] 1906. PHS. RG 239. Box 7, folder 25.

17. Herbert Reinken in 1913; Lubova Sifsof in 1915; John Beyers in 1916; and Marie Shaishnikoff and Agnes Swanson in 1918.

18. NARA, RG 75. Entry 804. Letters Received. Newhall to W.T. Lopp. Sept. 1, 1913.

19. Scott, Robert. *Teachers Annual Report, 1912–1913.* NARA. RG 75. Incoming Correspondence.

20. Swanson, *The Unknown Islands*, 34.

21. Godfrey, Harriet. Untitled writings about her family. Copy supplied by Kenneth M. Hatch.

22. Kenneth M. Hatch to Ray Hudson. Jan. 20, 2006.

23. *WHM*, October 1909:11.

24. Woman's Home Missionary Society, Reports from Bureaus. 1913–14:196.

25. *WHM*, June 1920:5.

26. *WHM*, October 1912:8.

A Few of the Girls, A Few of the Boys

"THANK GOD FOR THE HOME," WROTE ANNIE PETERSON WEATHERS in 1975. She had lived there from 1902 until 1915 when she married Dan Sipary, one of the Jesse Lee boys. However difficult the lives of adults became after they left the confines of the mission, many of them remembered the Home with fondness. It may have been the landscape of Unalaska Island with its mosaic of green hills, horizontal snow, enveloping fog, and always the sea pushing against the rocky beach. It may have been the staff: the Newhalls, Emma Supernaw, Clara Cook and Mary Winchell among others. It may have been the fellowship of children living in similar situations. The reasons for these fond remembrances are as varied as the people themselves. Mary Winchell once recalled Agnes Newhall watching the children. She turned to Mary and said, "Whatever else we may be able to do for these children, at least we have given them a happy childhood."[1]

Marie McLeod

Among the girls Elizabeth Mellor took from Unalaska in 1898 were Marie McLeod and Kathryn Dyakanoff. Details of Marie's story remain largely unknown. She was born on Kodiak Island and entered the Home in 1893. She was taken to the Carlisle Indian School by Elizabeth Mellor in 1898. Before leaving Unalaska, she became engaged to Charles Anderson. His full name was Hans Fredrick Carl Christian Peder Anderson. A few weeks after Marie left, Anderson took his small fishing boat to Unimak Island to hunt fox and sea otters. In his journal he complained of not feeling well on April 9, 1899. He grew increasingly sick and died around June 19. His body was discovered by men from Akutan a month later and they reported it to the Revenue Cutter Service. However, a year later Samuel Applegate learned that the body had not been buried and he saw that this was done. He found Anderson's journal and made a copy which he gave to a reporter from the *San Francisco Examiner* who promised to send it on to Marie.[2]

Marie did well at Carlisle. She eventually did missionary work in Southeast Alaska and at Kotzebue. She taught school at Deering, Alaska, for three years. In 1919 she returned to Unalaska as a member of the Jesse Lee Home staff, filling in as a teacher in the public school in 1922. In 1924 she married Daniel Ross, the deputy U.S. marshal at Unalaska.

Kathryn Dyakanoff

Kathryn was an excellent student at Carlisle and received a scholarship to the State Normal School in West Chester, Pennsylvania, even though the scholarship was for Indian students and, according to her, she technically did not qualify.[3] Near the beginning of her studies there, she wrote to Sheldon Jackson about teaching in Alaska. Specifically, she wanted to know if her way would be paid to Alaska and what the salary was for a teacher. Although she occasionally received funds from her family at Unalaska, the mail was slow and money was tight. On one occasion she requested a loan from Jackson himself. Expecting to graduate in 1909, she planned to work during the 1908 summer vacation, but officials at Carlisle objected to this. She considered having her name removed from the roll. Jackson cautioned her against this as she would then be ineligible for transportation back to Alaska.[4]

As mentioned in an earlier chapter, following graduation Kathryn applied for the job of assistant teacher at Unalaska. Instead, she was assigned to the school in Sitka. In 1910 she married Harry G. Seller in Seattle. That same year she secured the position of first government teacher at Atka, in the central Aleutians. She and her husband arrived on Aug. 1, 1910. Their first project was to erect a school building. Kathryn found that her knowledge of the Aleut language enabled her to communicate effectively with her students and accelerated their progress in English. She taught at Atka for three years, and her reports are among the most detailed that exist for the Aleutians from the period 1910 to 1920. Harry Seller organized a community store and became embroiled in economic controversies pitting the A.C. Co. and A.C. Goss against Seller and H.O. Schaleben, superintendent of the Southwestern School District. In 1914 charges and counter-charges of rape were filed against Goss and Seller.[5] Appearing on Goss's behalf at his trial at Unalaska were Peter Kashevaroff and Dr. Newhall. Undoubtedly, Clara Goss's work for the Home and the support the staff gave to A.C. Goss alienated Kathryn from her former friends. The judge determined that rape had occurred, and Goss was ordered to trial at Dillingham and then Valdez. In the meantime, Seller was arrested. In October he pleaded guilty to adultery and was sentenced to 60 days in the Valdez jail. During this ordeal, Kathryn served as assistant teacher at Unalaska.

Eventually Kathryn and her husband moved to Anchorage, and she continued to work for territorial schools. In 1922 *The Pathfinder of Alaska* asked her to write a series of articles about Aleuts. Busy teaching and raising her own four children, she undertook the project somewhat reluctantly. The three articles were published in 1923 and contained fascinating details about ancient Aleut life, contemporary practices, and the transition into the 20th century. She praised the work of Orthodox missionaries. Although never mentioning the Jesse Lee Home by name, she dedicated the articles "to the Pioneer Missionaries and Teachers of Alaska." After 29 years of teaching, she retired and moved to San Francisco where she began a second career as a public speaker. One of her topics, following World War II, was the "hardship and evacuation" experienced by Aleuts during the war and the difficulties they faced following this traumatic period. She was decades ahead of the general population in discussing this miscarriage of justice.

Pelagia Dyakanoff McCurdy

Pelagia was living in the Home the year her Aunt Kathryn taught at Unalaska. "Personally, [I] don't think the Jesse Lee Home was so great," she wrote in 1981.[6] Pelagia was taken from her grandparents' home on Hog Island at the age of six and allowed no contact with the Orthodox church or community. Inspired by her Aunt Kathryn, Pelagia herself became a teacher in Alaska and California. Today a scholarship fund for Aleut students is named for her and administered by the Ounalashka Corporation.

Polly (Pelagaia) Dirks

Polly, who with her brother had lived on the East Coast with the Newhalls, returned to the Aleutians. At Atka on July 12, 1914, she married A.B. Somerville aboard the Coast Guard cutter *Unalga*. The witnesses were William Dirks and Kathryn Seller. Somerville had been trading for furs at Attu since 1911. Before that he had served seven years as first officer aboard the *Dora*. In 1915 he unsuccessfully attempted to persuade the U.S. Commissioner of Education to open a school at Attu with his wife as teacher. He and Polly established a home at Unalaska, a small white house near the Iliuliuk River. While visiting San Francisco in 1918 she contracted influenza and died.

Sophia Swanson

When Mabel Benedict left Unalaska in 1908, she too took girls with her. The annual report for 1907–08 noted that these were girls "for whom Christian homes had been found." The girls may or may not have attended Carlisle. Among them were Sophia Swanson, Nellie (Eleanor) Tilton, and Anna Irene Gould. As noted earlier, Benedict had grown so fond of Sophia "that she could not bear to leave her." Henry Swanson remembered that two girls originally from the Pribilof Islands, Stepandia and Alexandra Oustigoff, had also left with Benedict. Lavinia Young, then secretary of the WHMS Alaska bureau, wrote to the Bureau of Education seeking transportation for these two to Connecticut.[7] They were enrolled in a school, but according to Henry Swanson died within a few years from tuberculosis. The 1910 census has both Sophia and Nellie living with Mabel Benedict in Ramapo, New York. Benedict was recorded as a teacher in the public school. Sophia was listed as her "adopted daughter."

> She took the girls with her and put them in some school back east. The two Oustigoff girls died out there. They had T.B., I guess, or something. Those were two nice looking girls. Of course, at that time I wasn't too interested in girls, you know. But they were two nice looking girls. When I was in the Navy in World War I, I stopped there in New York and visited. The Oustigoff girls were gone then, but my sister [Sophia] was there and this Eskimo girl.

Nellie Tilton's subsequent life remains unknown. Her enrollment card merely notes, "Married." Sophie grew up a strong-willed and independent woman. She married in 1917, but this ended in divorce. In 1920 she married a singer in the Metropolitan Opera. "He wasn't one of their top singers," recalled brother Henry, "but he was in the chorus or something." She wrote to Henry asking for a copy of her birth certificate. She needed a passport because she was accompanying her husband to Paris. A few years later, he died while they were still in Europe. Sophie returned to the States, bringing along a Model-T Ford. She drove the car across the country to visit her sister Louise in California.[8]

Anna Irene Gould

Anna Gould, half-sister to Eliza Gould Kashevaroff, left Unalaska at 16 in 1908 and became a domestic in Glencoe, Ohio. Although successful as a family helper, she had other ambitions. According to a 1909 report, "She writes that she has a good home, but would very much like the opportunity of going to school, and later becoming a missionary."[9] While working for a family that owned a farm, she was able to welcome her brother Gordon in 1914. He had left Unalaska with the aim of furthering his own education. Instead, he found himself essentially indentured as a farm laborer. The man who owned the farm would not allow him any further schooling. In 1917 he arranged to visit Robert Scott, who had taught at Unalaska. When the Scotts heard how he and Anna were being treated they arranged for her to be hired by a banker in Claysville, Pennsylvania. Gordon credited his sister with the financial and emotional assistance he needed to escape the farm. "Words are inadequate to express all I owe to my sister Anna," he wrote. "No sister could have helped her brother with more utter devotion and sacrifice than she, sharing with me her earnings and encouraging me when the way was hard."[10]

Anna's own missionary goals never dimmed. Eventually she met a Methodist deaconess and through her was able to enter the Pittsburgh Deaconess Home as a cook in 1918. During the four years she was there she worked summers for the Epworth League Fresh Air Home near Pittsburgh.[11] In 1925 she secured a position at the Jesse Lee Home in Seward and became the Home's dietitian. On Jan. 5, 1932, she married Ralph Williams in the Home's Newhall Chapel before a large crowd of friends and home folks. The chapel though plain, "even barren," was "transformed into a vision of loveliness."[12]

Auxinia Dushkin

Auxinia Dushkin was from Morzhovoi and had entered the Home in 1901 at the age of 8. Her story is brief and tragic. The contract that had entrusted her to the Home was scheduled to expire when she turned 18, and her relatives wanted her back in Morzhovoi. The society put out "an urgent call" for someone to take her into their home "to save her from a life worse than death." She was a "well-trained girl who would most faithfully work to repay the expense of transportation."[13] During the annual meeting in Los Angeles in 1909 there were six volunteers to take her. She eventually went to a home for Mexican girls at Tucson, Arizona, and after a few months she entered the home of Mrs. Anna Kent, one of the "Home Missionary ladies" living in East Orange, New Jersey. Auxinia soon longed to return to Alaska. She "was finally allowed to move to Los Angeles" where she lived at the De Pauw Industrial Home while taking courses in domestic science and dressmaking. Once again she became a domestic for a "Christian family" to earn money to pay her passage to Unalaska.

> So capable and pleasant a maid she proved to be that the family greatly desired to retain her services, but the seeds of tuberculosis were in her system and a sudden cold developed them rapidly. From the first no hope of recovery was given by the physicians, and after three weeks of tender care in the little hospital of De Pauw Home, she was admitted to La Vina Sanitarium for tubercular patients near Pasadena. During the remainder of her short life she received the best of care, and she was so patient and thoughtful that the superintendent expressed her gratitude that she had been in the Home, since she had proved "a benediction to all about her."[14]

Tuberculosis accounted for the majority of deaths at the Home, and for many of the deaths of children who left. The missionary society estimated, from the partial records that were available, that at least 20 percent of the children who lived at the Home had died of this disease.[15] In part this mortality was attributed to accepting children into the Home no matter how advanced their illness. However, even after the Home moved to Seward and a policy was eventually adopted by which only children with a clean bill of health could be admitted, the disease continued to claim victims.

Helen E. Swanson

In her old age Helen Swanson Malcolm reflected on the sheltered life she and other girls had lived at the Jesse Lee Home.[16] She entered the Home in 1902 or 1903 at the age of a year and a half, with her sister Annie. The concerns of Harriet Barnett and others were not unfounded. On reaching young adulthood, the girls were unprepared. "And then when you were 18," Helen said, "they looked for someone for you to marry. And you were married off at 18." (The hope, of course, was that this would ensure the girls' well-being.) Like the other older teenage girls, Helen found it strange to be courted. The girls had never mixed with men outside of the Jesse Lee Home. She laughed as she recalled men coming to church to look for prospective brides. Her own future husband came to Unalaska, purchased a house, and then began visiting the Home. She would be sent down to the main floor of the girls' building to sit with him. Finally, he proposed and she accepted. "Well," she said, "they wanted me to get out of the home, so I got married."

She knew nothing of married life. She and her husband had a son, Cecil, and two years later her husband developed tuberculosis and died. With her life plummeting into diffi-

LUCY LEAVITT AND WILLIAM ROSENBERG *at Unalaska shortly after their wedding. Courtesy of the Unalaska City School District (Clara Cook Collection).*

culties, she abandoned her house, took Cecil and moved back into the Home. When Helen was a child, financial support had been given to the Home in her name by a wealthy woman who supported the missionary work. Called a "sponsor," this woman now invited Helen to live with her. In 1923 the Newhalls left on a year's sabbatical and took Helen and Cecil with them to Harrisburg, Pennsylvania, and to her "sponsor's" home. Here again, Helen's lack of training showed itself. She accompanied the woman to church, did her cooking, and called her "my lady." She had little money of her own and less independence. Eventually she escaped to Seattle and then moved back to Alaska. In Seldovia she lived with her sister, met a man working at one of the canneries, and married. Several times in her account, Helen emphasized how unprepared she had been for adulthood. "We just grew up there," she said, "and we had to make our own ways afterward. I mean, we had to learn to make our way."

Lucy Leavitt

On Aug. 14, 1913, William Rosenberg and Lucy Leavitt were married at the Jesse Lee Home chapel. She was 18; he was four years older. William had lived at the Home from 1901 to 1904 and was now assistant lighthouse keeper at Cape Sarachev on Unimak Island. Charles Rosenberg, his father, had immigrated from Germany; he and his wife, Martha, had a home at Unalaska, but he and his sons trapped and hunted on Unimak Island. They also patrolled the beaches for any sea otters that might have washed ashore. As they grew up, all the Rosenberg children—William, Katherine, John or Jack, Daniel, and Lilly—lived at the Home for periods of time. For Lucy and William's wedding his father, stepmother, brothers and sisters came from Unimak. Also attending were men associated with the lighthouse. Clara Goss and Mrs. Applegate were present along with two convalescent patients. Fred Chipitnoi played the wedding march. Dr. Newhall, assisted by teacher Robert Scott, conducted the ceremony. The day after the wedding a dinner was given in honor of the couple by Captain Pedrick, the port engineer. Guests included the Newhalls, Emma Supernaw, and Annie Petersen and Daniel Sipary, two Home residents who would marry each other two years later.

Mrs. Applegate was living at the Home while her husband was absent, so she loaned her own home to the newlyweds until they were able to secure passage back to Unimak Island. With them went William's stepmother, his younger brother Paul, and his sisters. The ship set them ashore at Urila Bay, some 50 miles from their destination. A trapper's cabin provided shelter. Dinner consisted of dried plums, apricots and a little candy. The next day William and Paul shot a deer. Once fortified, the group set off walking. Dr. Newhall told the story:

> All the party loaded up with as much luggage as they could pack and soon were on the way. The women traveled in "bloomers" and they were laughed at

In the Eliza Jane Baker Chapel *at Jesse Lee: "In loving memory of Daniel Rosenberg, age 18."*
From Annie Swanson Hatch's album, courtesy of the Hatch family.

by the men folks traveling behind. There were valleys to cross, hills to climb, cliffs to scale, and mountain ridges to get over while the miles of soft yielding tundra moss and the many rivers to cross did not make the journey an easy one. The first day twenty-one miles were made and at night camp was made by "Big Creek." Here a fire was made, and food eaten and then under the tented canopy of heaven they all lay down and slept.[17]

A change in the administration of the lighthouse ended William's job. He trapped fox and provided subsistence for his wife. When Lucy became pregnant he sent her to Unalaska to be near the doctor, and William himself returned there occasionally to work. Their son, Karl Leavitt Rosenberg, was born Sept. 10, 1914. Lucy remained at Unalaska through the winter. Karl was baptized by Dr. Newhall in June 1915. In 1920 Mary Winchell wrote to Clara Cook (now Mrs. Lawrence) recalling April 3, 1916, as a day with "the worst storm of the year." On that day Lucy gave birth to her second child, Esther Woodward Rosenberg. When Winchell wrote *Home by the Bering Sea* in 1951 she devoted a chapter to "The Coming of Esther." It began

> On the night of April third, a driving gale from the Bering Sea threatened to blow our mission-orphanage and all the village back against the mountains. The houses rocked like ships at sea, but they remained on their foundations. They were used to gales, and so were we.[18]

Suddenly Dr. Newhall was knocking at her window, having climbed up the fire escape. *"Mirabile dictu!"* he exclaimed and announced that Lucy was about to give birth. Mary lit a fire in the downstairs corner room while the doctor went for Lucy, who was staying with her son at the Rosenberg home in the village where her sister-in-law Katherine was living. Emma Supernaw warmed some bedclothes and made up a narrow bed. Once Lucy was settled, the women picked up their knitting and waited. A quilt had been nailed across the room's window, but even so the snow sifted through and piled up on the floor. Winchell emptied six coal buckets of snow during the long night.

The delivery was extended and painful. Newhall reassured Mary that this was not unnatural and paraphrased Goethe about births that came "through the sacred arch, under which all kings and queens, and little Eskimos must pass." Esther was born at 3 o'clock in the morning.

Shortly after seven, while Winchell was rubbing Esther with olive oil, Lucy went into convulsions. Newhall ordered water and bricks to be heated. They placed the hot bricks at her feet and covered them with thick cloth wrung from a tub of hot water. Hot, wet blankets were laid over her. But every half hour or so the convulsions returned and the women would have to hold her as still as they could while her body shook. At some point Mary fetched the deputy marshal, who kept watch while Mary or Emma caught a short rest.

Periods of calm and convulsive outbreaks alternated through the day and the following night. Dr. Newhall feared that even if she lived, Lucy's mind would be damaged. About 5 the following morning, two hours after her last convulsion, Lucy opened her eyes. She smiled and, turning to the marshal, asked, "Do you know that I have—a little baby girl?" And she recalled her child's name. "We looked at each other in speechless surprise," wrote Winchell, "and immeasurable relief." She continued, "The marshal got up and went to the window. He took down the quilt. The storm had ceased. We looked out into a white morning, mountains and valley beautiful and serene."

Lucy stayed with her sister-in-law, planning to return to Unimak as soon as she was fully recovered. The summer of 1916 was a summer without a mailboat from May to October.[19] The first letter Lucy received from William told her to stay at Unalaska as he was coming to see Dr. Newhall. His younger brother, 18-year-old Daniel, suffered from tuberculosis, and this had worsened after he was chilled while hunting. William, Jack, and their father carried Daniel to the western end of Unimak where they hoped to catch the mailboat. Twice it passed without being able to land. Daniel lived for six weeks and then died on May 13. Six weeks later, on June 27, his father hanged himself. "The father, bowed down with grief," wrote Newhall, "became unbalanced in his mind and in a short time took his life."[20]

An article in *Woman's Home Missions* suggests Lucy did not return to Unimak. Her brother-in-law Jack came to Unalaska where he joined the newly formed Methodist church. Lucy was living at Unalaska in the spring of 1918 when her stepmother married a Mr. Jacobson as soon as Great Lent was over. According to Winchell, he was "a hardworking Norwegian fisherman of about her own age."[21] Following the service at the Orthodox church, Lucy served tea and cake at her home. In 1917 Jack decided to travel to Seattle and so signed on as a crewman aboard a ship. In the meantime, William himself had become ill. Jack left Unalaska on June 9 and stopped at Unimak where he saw his brother. William died on March 29, 1918. Lucy, now widowed with two young children, moved back into the Jesse Lee Home where she was able to work.

On Oct. 15, 1919, Lucy, her sister-in-law Katherine, and Sarah Morton left Unalaska aboard the Coast Guard cutter *Unalga* for Seattle. According to the ship's log they went "to better their condition as there is no means of support for them at Unalaska."[22] Leaving Karl and Esther was difficult but Lucy wanted to improve her skills as a seamstress to be able to provide more for her children. Karl soon latched onto Paul Morton, himself a former resident of the Home and now working there, and called him his Uncle Paul.[23] Captain Coffin of the U.S. Coast Guard invited Lucy to live with him and his wife in Berkeley. She had not been in California long before she became ill and was diagnosed with tuberculosis. Coffin paid her way to the Methodist tuberculosis sanitarium at Albuquerque. According to Simeon Oliver, she died of the disease.[24]

Esther and Karl continued living at the Home their mother had known so well. In 1925 they were part of the move to Seward, where in 1930 Karl was 15 and Esther, 13.[25]

Peter Gordon Gould

Among the boys who lived at the Jesse Lee Home, only Peter Golovin (Peter Gordon Gould) entered the ministry. He arrived at Unalaska around 1908 at the age of seven, a curious energetic boy. "Peter Golovin," wrote Nellie Holmberg during school in 1914, "the boy that sits in front of me moves around in his seat so much that I can't write straight." In 1914 Dr. Newhall arranged for him to work on the farm in Ohio where his sister Anna was living. Peter left in late June with Mary Winchell, who was beginning a year's furlough.

Aboard the vessel, the mail clerk loaned the 13-year-old Peter books. After finishing one, he said to Mary Winchell, "Well, this book turned out all right. They got married in the end."

Mary wrote that she then asked, "Isn't that book a little too old for you?"

"'Oh no,' answered Peter, whose aim in life was to appear as grown-up as possible. 'I've been reading this kind for years!'"[26] Winchell's account is filled with examples of how amazed and delighted Peter and two other children from Unalaska were by new discoveries on ship and shore. The perspective from which she saw things was, of course, her own. Years later, Peter recorded one of his own first impressions. Arriving in Seattle, they were met by a well-dressed cultured woman who spoke with Winchell while Peter was a short distance away.

> "My, isn't he cute?" said the lady and I strained my ears for what was to follow, and I heard, "but you can't expect anything from these Alaskans, can you?"
>
> It was only a chance remark, but it was spoken with an air of a foregone conclusion that reflected the general attitude of even some of the best people in regard to us Alaskans. While they were spoken with no intent to hurt or harm still they were like a two-edge sword piercing even to the quick leaving a bleeding wound. For the briefest moment there seemed to be genuine friendliness and appreciation, but it was soon apparent that this stemmed not from a sense of intrinsic worth but from a shrewd measuring of possible gain that might be had from exhibiting one to the public gaze as "exhibit A."[27]

Always a boy with his own mind and a strong will, Peter became even more determined to succeed. After a short stay with Mary Winchell in Denver, Peter boarded a train for Chicago and on to Ohio. To avoid confusion, he took his half-sister's last name and often called himself Peter Gordon Gould. After he and Anna escaped from the farm and its tyrannical owner, they lived in Claysville, Pennsylvania. Through the generosity of

R.R. Griffiths, a local minister, Peter found employment and furthermore decided to attend the Williamsport Dickinson Seminary, from which he graduated in 1923. He enrolled at the University of Syracuse and began his preaching career there. That winter, Dr. Newhall visited him and found him "indeed a very fine young man and doing well at school." Peter described their visit.

> It was during my first winter in Syracuse that Dr. Newhall visited me for a day. I cut classes so as to spend all the time I could with him. That night as we were shown our room in the hotel, he put his arms around me and hugged me with all the warmth of a father's love for a son whom he had not seen for many years and what he said I shall never forget.
>
> "So many of the boys and girls that have been trained in our Home have gone out into the world and slipped back into the old life from which we have tried to save them. When I find one like you fighting to make good as you are, it makes me feel that all my life in the Mission in Alaska is amply justified."[28]

After a successful career as a Methodist minister in the east, Peter Gould returned to Alaska in 1948 as superintendent of the Alaska Mission. As he was beginning his new work in Alaska, he wrote:

> I am profoundly grateful to God who in His wise providence has never left me alone, and has seen to it that at the crucial times along the way someone has been ready to stand by and help. I am very humble when I think that "unto me, who am less than the least of all (His children) has this grace been given, that I should preach the unsearchable riches of Christ."[29]

Through his efforts Alaska Methodist University (now Alaska Pacific University) was established in 1957. In January 1989, shortly after his death, the Alaska Legislature issued a memorial tribute for "his tireless humanitarian efforts."

Simeon Oliver

Unlike Gordon Gould, Simeon Oliver never found one calling to which he could subordinate all else. He was, as he told a newspaper reporter while on his way to Unalaska in 1979, "a sort of jackass of all trades."[30] But what trades: concert pianist, author, folklorist and nationwide lecturer. Initially, however, Oliver wanted to become a doctor. Dr. Newhall was prompted to write to Simeon's father to tell him about his son's decision. James Oliver wrote to Simeon and told him he and Dr. Newhall would finance his education at Northwestern College in Naperville, Illinois, provided he earned the money to get there. Oliver immediately went to work at the sulfur mine on Akun Island, about 50 miles east of Unalaska.[31] In 1920 Simeon and Chester Newhall left Unalaska for Illinois. The superintendent of the sulfur company wrote Simeon a glowing recommendation without being

This may be the RECITAL IN 1913 *for which Dr. Newhall wrote out the program: "Hilarity March," Lucy
& Jennie; "Lone Star Reverie," Alexandra Visilof; "Boys of the Nation," Peter Golovin; "Minuet," Alexandra,
Annie S. (second from left in photo), Mary; "Class Reception March," Simeon (Oliver, far left); "Two Juveniles,"
Peter S. & Fred; "Visions Sweet—Reverie," Annie; "Springtime," Edith Newhall (far right); "Daisy March,"
Nellie; "Wayside Chapel," Lucy; "Fireballs Mazurka," Edith, Peter, Simeon; "Con Amore," Daniel; "Clover
Blossoms," Mary; "Tannhauser March," Daniel & Fred; "Angels' Serenade," Fred; Medley—piano, cello,
mandolins, "National Airs," Fred, Daniel, Lucy, Mrs. A.C. Goss, P. Kashavaroff. Photo from Annie Swanson
Hatch's album, courtesy of the Hatch family.*

An Aleut Lullaby

©1940 by Simeon Oliver.

asked to do so. The next summer the two young men worked on a farm for their board. In the course of that summer Simeon decided to make music his vocation. Chester returned to Northwestern while Simeon enrolled in a music school in Chicago where he became staff pianist for the radio station WJJD.[32] Working at the station he met numerous celebrities including Harry Houdini and Amelia Earhart. In 1925 he embarked on a musical tour to nearly 30 radio stations that lasted four months. He was made the "First Honorary Eskimo Kentucky Colonel" and an "Admiral in the Navy of Nebraska"—which he called "those wonderful and dubious honors" bestowed by the states' governors. When Simeon was stopped for speeding, the Nebraska honor produced "a double-take" from the police officer, who said, "Follow me!" and gave him an escort to his next speaking engagement at Father Flanagan's Boys Town.[33] He visited Hollywood and met Douglas Fairbanks, Mary Pickford, Joan Crawford, and others. He was on the set while Rudolf Valentino made part of *The Eagle*. He heard the organ in the Tabernacle in Salt Lake City and later swam in the lake after a hot bus ride.

By 1926 Oliver's musical career was gaining speed. He wrote to Newhall in Barrow asking him to buy a set of Eskimo clothing for which he would repay the doctor. His reputation as *the* Eskimo pianist provided him access to vaudeville stages and recital halls. He found the vaudeville audiences tough, a sentiment Dr. Newhall wrote that he shared while admitting he was completely ignorant of vaudeville. Newhall was gratified with Simeon's career. Echoing his earlier praise of Simeon's boyhood friend Peter Gould, he wrote, "I felt repaid for the years spent in the Jesse Lee Home, Simeon, just to think what it has done for you."[34]

Simeon married Betty List of Carlyle, Illinois, around 1929. They had two daughters, Cora Louanne and Juanita, and Simeon supported the family by lecturing and giving piano concerts. This, of course, entailed extensive traveling. While he was away on one of his trips, Betty died in late 1933 or early 1934. Simeon began several years of despondent wandering across the United States, finding odd jobs here and there, leaving his daughters with Betty's mother. In June 1938 he returned to Unalaska for part of the summer.[35] Back in New York he met Alden Hatch, a professional writer, with whom he collaborated for two books: *Son of the Smoky Sea* (1941) and *Back to the Smoky Sea* (1946). The success of the first book helped him overcome the depression he had been experiencing. At the outbreak of World War II he enlisted. He worked for Army intelligence in Alaska and wrote a booklet on surviving in the Aleutians. In 1943 he married Ethel Ross and they settled in Anchorage. The time they spent at Atka, June 1946 to June 1947, is the subject of Ethel Ross Oliver's book *Journal of an Aleutian Year*. In 1949 Simeon's "Aleut Lullaby" was premiered by Metropolitan Opera star Marita Farell and the Anchorage Concert Chorus. During the last years of his life, Simeon lived in Spokane, Washington, near his daughter, Juanita.

In May 1979 he returned to Unalaska to deliver the high school commencement address. He arrived on a perfect day for homecoming: blue sky over Ballyhoo, a few white clouds, a slight breeze, and over the hills the bright green of early spring. While there, he remarked that the melody for his "Aleut Lullaby" had been given to him by Michael Tutiakoff, a student and later teacher at the Russian school. Simeon impressed everyone with his warmth, good humor, and knowledge of the Jesse Lee Home and Unalaska "in the early days." The evening he arrived, there was a community reception and potluck. The Ounalashka Corporation "adopted" him and gave him the name *Oong-Nghee-Kux,* "story teller."[36] "I've always wanted to be an Aleut," he said in his gracious acceptance remarks. He showed he still retained an excellent piano technique at 76 by playing selections from Romberg's *The Student Prince.* In his talk at the graduation he urged people to work to preserve the Aleut language and traditions.

George Porter (Oslooluk)

George Porter was the son of Mary Kappak from Kotzebue Sound and W.P.S. Porter, an American whaling captain. George was born at Herschel Island in December 1895. He entered the Home in 1907 and remained until 1913 when he joined the crew of Henry Swanson's stepfather, C.T. Pedersen, on the *Elvira.* Porter had an adventurous youth as a reindeer herder, sailing on a French cargo schooner, serving in the Army during World War I. After the war, he sailed out of San Francisco and Seattle on several voyages to the arctic. In 1921 he was a member of a crew aboard a four-masted schooner that took lumber to Australia.

In 1926 he joined Pedersen's Canalaska Trading Company and was associated with this company until it was sold to the Hudson's Bay Company in 1936. By this time he had so established himself in the community of Gjoa Haven on King William Island, Nunavut, that retaining him as a trader was made a condition of the sale. Porter also served as a guide and dog team driver to the Royal Canadian Mounted Police, who tried to persuade him to join them permanently.

He remained the HBC manager at Gjoa Haven for 25 years. He married Martha Nuliajuk and they raised a large family.[37] He retired in the late 1960s.

Henry Swanson

Unlike most of the boys who spent years at the Home and then left the community, Swanson remained in the Aleutians. He worked as a fox trapper, fisherman, construction worker, and pilot and guide for the U.S. Navy during World War II. He served for many years on the Unalaska City Council. In 1970 he joined two other elderly Aleuts, Anfesia Shapsnikoff and Nick Peterson, who also had spent several years living at the Home, in filing a petition that resulted in the eventual transfer of extensive land to the local Aleut

IN THE SWING, *Edith Newhall and Hilda Lee (?). Back row, left to right: Amelia Petersen (tall girl), Annie Swanson, Lucy Leavitt (with a girl barely visible between Annie and Lucy), Nellie Holmberg (dark middy collar), Helen Swanson (holding the rope), Lena Krukoff (far right). Photo c. 1911, courtesy of the Unalaska City School District (Clara Cook Collection).*

corporation under the Alaska Native Claims Settlement Act. Henry's long years and vast experience made him an unequaled expert on the Aleutians. He was consulted by historians, scientists, and anthropologists. His numerous talks and recorded interviews were compiled by students at the high school and published in 1983 as *The Unknown Islands: Life and Tales of Henry Swanson*. After his death in 1990 his house was donated to the city of Unalaska. The Unalaska Historical Commission is presently (2006) considering nominating it to the National Register of Historic Places.

1. Winchell, *Home by the Bering Sea*, 159.

2. Alaska State Library. Alaska Historical Collections. Ms 3 (Samuel Applegate Papers). Box 2, Folder 12, Items 2 and 3.

3. The reason she did not qualify remains unclear.

4. Dyakanoff to Jackson, Nov. 15, 1907; Dec. 8, 1907; May 9, 1908. PHS. 239. Box 7, folders 28 and 30.

5. NARA. Record Group 21. Case Files 416 and 417.

6. E. Pelagia McCurdy to Ray and Shelly Hudson. March 9, 1981.

7. Young to Updergroff, Nov. 21, 1907. NARA, RG 75. Letters received.

8. Swanson, *The Unknown Islands*, 4.

9. Woman's Home Missionary Society, Reports from Bureaus. 1908–09:140.

10. Gould, *The Fisherman's Son*, 30.

11. *WHM*. February 1940:13.

12. *WHM*. May 1932:5.

13. Woman's Home Missionary Society, Reports from Bureaus.1907–08:131.

14. *WHM*. October 1912:10.

15. *WHM*. October 1929:10.

16. Helen E. Malcolm in McClanahan, ed., *Our Stories, Our Lives*.

17. Hudson, ed., *Cuttlefish, Volumes One, Two, & Three*, 163.

18. Winchell, *Home by the Bering Sea*, 117–39.

19. *WHM*. January 1917:17.

20. *WHM*. November 1916:8–9.

21. Winchell, Mary. Letter, May 26, 1918.

22. Ship's Log. U.S. Coast Guard Cutter *Unalga*. Oct. 15, 1919. NARA. RG-26.

23. *WHM*. June 1920:7.

24. Simeon Oliver to Brenda Shelikoff, Dec. 28, 1978. Hudson, ed., *Cuttlefish: Volumes One, Two & Three*, 251.

25. Esther married a Swedish immigrant, Gunnar Strindberg, and they had two children, Margaret and Ruth, both born at Unalaska. Esther was badly burned during the Japanese raid on Dutch Harbor in June 1942. She died in 1975. Following their time in the Home, she and Karl lost contact with each other. (Ruth Easters to Ray Hudson, Dec. 10, 1979.)

26. Winchell, *Where the Wind Blows Free*, 147.

27. Gould, *The Fisherman's Son*, 5–6.

28. Ibid., 35.

29. Ibid., 39.

30. Hunter, Don. "Easy modesty marks 'jackass of all trades.'" *Anchorage Daily News.* May 29, 1979:D-1.

31. Oliver, Ethel. "Simeon Oliver (Nutchuk)," c. 1989. Alaska Children's Services, Jesse Lee Home Archives.

32. Chester Newhall completed undergraduate studies in 1924 and graduated from the University of Vermont College of Medicine in 1928. In 1926 he married Nella Tillotson. They settled in Burlington, Vermont, where he practiced medicine and taught anatomy. He received many honors and was noted for his "creative sense of humor" and his dedication to medicine and teaching. He died Jan. 27, 1985.

33. Simeon Oliver to Phil and Flora Tutiakoff, Jan. 7, 1980.

34. Newhall to Simeon Oliver. Feb. 6, 1926. Alaska Missionary Conference Commission on Archives and History.

35. Oliver tells of this return in *Back to the Smoky Sea*. In the 1979 interview with Don Hunter he said he went there to work with Ales Hrdlicka. However, *Back to the Smoky Sea* does not mention the anthropologist, nor does Hrdlicka mention him among his assistants for 1938. A letter from Oliver to Alan G. May, March 16, 1944, makes clear that he was not part of the expedition but that he did meet Hrdlicka at the Explorer's Club in New York City. The various anecdotes recounted in Oliver's two books and in later talks need corroboration. These would include his meetings with Franz Boaz and Sergei Rachmaninoff that resulted from talks with Father Ponteleev, then Bishop Alexei, at Unalaska in 1938.

36. The adoption statement was written by Philemon Tutiakoff and read by Emil Berikoff.

37. "George Porter." Kitikmeot Heritage Society. Angulalik-Kitikmeot Fur Trader. Virtual Museum of Canada. www.kitikmeotheritage. ca/Angulalk/ctpeders/georgepo/george.html.

27

In the Absence of the Doctor

THE NEWHALLS WERE GONE ON SABBATICAL FROM JULY 1916 TO July 1917. The year before, they achieved one of the most personally satisfying accomplishments of their many years in the Aleutians. On Jan. 14, 1915, the first Methodist Episcopal Church at Unalaska was formally established. Dr. Newhall had been designated a "local preacher" almost as soon as he arrived in 1898. A year before, an Alaskan Mission had been authorized by the parent church although formal organization was delayed until September 1903 when three churches were formed in Southeastern Alaska: at Douglas, Ketchikan and Skagway.[1] The Unalaska church began with three members and 14 probationers. The charter members were Mary Winchell, Clara Cook and Emma Supernaw. (As the local minister and his wife, Albert and Agnes Newhall were not technically members of the congregation.) The names of the probationers read like a list of former or older Home residents. All, except for the Newhalls' daughter, were at least 16 years of age: Peter Hatch, Fred Chipitnoi, Jennie Alexander, Annie Petersen, Mary Hansen, Amelia Petersen, Lucy Rosenberg, Sara Morton, Annie Swanson, Helen Swanson, Katie Rosenberg, Lillie Rosenberg, Lena Krukoff, and Edith Newhall.[2]

On Oct. 1, 1915, the doctor wrote to Mary (Hansen) Nasenius at False Pass that Mama Newhall was "so busy that I do not think that she will be able to write as Katie Dowd was operated on here for appendicitis two days ago and is very sick but I think that she will get along. She is over at the boys' house. Just think seven new children came on this boat. What a crowd to care for. Four girls."[3] That year both Agnes and Clara Cook purchased "Perpetual Life Memberships" in the missionary society. Mama Newhall's health declined during the year. A sabbatical would give her a respite and the opportunity to consult specialists. Emma Supernaw would accompany them in part to look after her friend and also because it was time for her own sabbatical. Mary Winchell was well-experienced with the Home's operation and she would assume the position of superintendent.[4] Her brother, Karl, and his wife, Mildred, would join her for the year. Clara Cook was expected back from her own year in the states.

Karl Winchell was 26 and Mildred was 20. Thirty minutes after they were married in Denver they left for Alaska. In Seattle they joined Clara Cook on the *Northwestern*, which sailed north on June 12, 1916. At Seward they boarded the *Dora* for the last leg of the voyage. Near Afognak the vessel ran aground on a reef and remained stuck until high tide. Limping to Uyak Island, it was beached, and the passengers were marooned for eight days until rescued. Back to Seattle they went.

AMELIA PETERSON. *Courtesy of the Unalaska City School District (Clara Cook Collection).*

When the Newhalls realized the *Dora* was out of commission, they made arrangements to leave Unalaska on the Coast Guard cutter *McCulloch* when it departed July 10. Clara Goss moved into the Home to assist Mary Winchell until Mary's brother and sister-in-law and Clara Cook arrived. Joseph Coleman, the public school teacher, slept in the boys' dorm at night.

In Seattle the captain of the *Great Bear*, a three-masted schooner, agreed to take the Winchells and Cook to Unalaska. This vessel belonged to Mr. John Borden of "condensed milk" fame and was heading north to bring relief supplies to the Steffanson expedition. They sailed from Seattle on July 26 and arrived at Unalaska two months after the Winchells had first departed from Denver. According to Newhall, the *Great Bear* continued north, struck a submerged pinnacle, and sank before delivering the supplies.

Life at the Home was different without the Newhalls but many things continued as normal. From August 1916 to August 1917, 233 new garments were made by Clara or the older girls following her instructions: "Shirts 27, Bloomers 31, Overalls 10, Aprons 61, Night Gowns 41, Dresses 30, Drawers 12, Union Suits 4, Rompers 5, Under Waists 12."[5]

What the staff feared in the absence of a physician, however, soon appeared. Monia (Morna) Wilson was well on Oct. 8, 1916, but the next morning she suddenly became ill and had convulsions. At one the following afternoon she died. The assistant surgeon aboard a Coast Guard cutter certified that she had died from spinal meningitis.[6] Two weeks later the Home was struck by a sudden wave of illnesses with the same symptoms except for the convulsions. Seventeen of the girls were confined to bed. Seven of them were critical at the same time. The boys seemed to be untouched by the illness. A wire was sent to the cutter *Bear* at Nome and it returned with a physician. In the meantime, Karl Winchell began reading Dr. Newhall's medical books searching for treatments for dysentery. The marshal's wife had been a nurse and came to assist. Drinking water and dishes were boiled. Louis Strauss at the A.C. Co. offered rooms to segregate healthy children from those who were sick. For two weeks Clara Goss supervised two improvised dormitory rooms and a playroom next to her own suite at the Company House.

The weather was atrocious so the youngsters had to stay indoors most of the time—and you know what that means. It kept me on the "go" most of the time. I sewed doll rags, told stories, read etc. but kept the older girls busy an hour both afternoon and morning on either knitting or fancy work. Little Charlotte Smith, aged 4, was my youngest, and Elizabeth Stankus the oldest. E. and Dolly each had a Birthday, so I gave them a party. Had 20 candles (tiny ones you sent me in rose holders) on cake, 11 for E. and 9 for D. Had cocoa for supper which is a treat to them, fixed the table as I would for a big party—with candles etc., and had a little present at each place. After supper Mr. S[trauss] invited us all into his room to "sing" then he & Mr. Goss came upstairs and played games until bed time, and even stayed to "prayers" which pleased the kiddies immensely. When I tucked them in bed, they all declared it had been a "lovely party." When they could be out of doors I had to be so vigilant, as we were really in quarantine. When the children went back home, I really missed them terribly, and so did the men—but they wouldn't acknowledge it.[7]

By the time the *Bear* arrived with a physician, all were well.

Early in 1916 Harriet Barnett left for the States. She had spent 1915 at Unalaska, filling in during Mary Winchell's leave. Back in Nome, she became ill and went south for medical treatment. All the doctors she consulted concluded her illness was terminal. She died on December 15 at Verdon, South Dakota, in the home of her sister.[8] She was 61 years old.

By 1916 the society had appropriated funds for a chapel and a hospital. Because the United States entered the World War, however, the cost of materials rose while shipping facilities declined. "We hope in the next year our buildings will be completed," the annual report for 1916–1917 enthused, "and the 'Methodist Episcopal Church farthest West,' and the only hospital of any kind for nearly a thousand miles in any direction, will send their beacon lights across the cold dark waters and the sailors will be guided by day by the sight of the clean white outlines of the buildings like a sunbeam on a winter's day, guiding the travelers to a safe harbor."[9] The following year, hope was expressed that the buildings might still be shipped "as soon as transportation can be reasonably secured." For that, however, more funds were needed.

Overall, the year 1916–17 had gone smoothly at Unalaska. The Winchells were well-liked and efficient. Their youthful energy found them roaming the hills with the children, climbing Mt. Ballyhoo near Dutch Harbor, and venturing out in the Home boat. A Miss Calkins arrived late in 1916 or early in 1917, but she stayed only a few months before returning to the States to be married.[10] The Newhalls arrived back at Unalaska in July 1917. The joy with which the staff and children greeted their ship soon turned to sorrow.

KARL WINCHELL AND BOYS, *c. 1916. Courtesy of the Unalaska City School District (Clara Cook Collection).*

An outing to Expedition Island, c. 1916. Left to right: Perhaps Mildred Winchell (in profile), Clara Goss, Mary Nielson, Jennie Alexander, Helen Swanson (lying on ground), Amelia Peterson (dark hat), Joseph Coleman or Karl Winchell, Lena Krukoff, Annie Swanson, Lucy Leavitt, Hilda Lee. Courtesy of the Unalaska City School District (Clara Cook Collection).

NOTES

1. Gould, *Methodism at Work in Alaska*, 16.

2. Bound volume of records of the Unalaska Methodist church in possession of Coe Whittern. Copy supplied by Alaska Missionary Conference Commission on Archives and History.

3. Alaska State Historical Library. MS 106. Folder 9.

4. *WHM*. June 1917:9.

5. Hudson, ed., *Cuttlefish: Volumes One, Two & Three*, 179. In the original scrapbook this was added in Clara Cook's handwriting.

6. Statement of Edward C. Ernest, M.D., Oct. 10, 1916. Jesse Lee Home Correspondence, Unalaska City School.

7. Clara Goss to Mrs. Applegate. Nov. 10, 1916. Alaska State Historical Library. MS 0003.

8. *WHM*. June 1917:8.

9. Woman's Home Missionary Society, Reports from Bureaus. 1916–17:131.

10. *WHM*. June 1917:8.

AGNES NEWHALL. *Courtesy of the Unalaska City School District (Clara Cook Collection).*

28

The Death of Mama Newhall

WHEN THE NEWHALLS RETURNED TO UNALASKA IN 1902, Agnes went with the expressed decision that she would have no official role. She would do what she had energy for around the Home, help with medical work, and visit families in the village. She became affectionately known as "Mama Newhall." Anfesia Shapsnikoff never lived in the Home, but she went there for special events or to play with other girls. She had an abiding affection for Agnes Newhall.

> She went and looked after everyone in the Jesse Lee Home as well as in the community. She shared the school, the public school, and learned us how to knit and sew our clothes. She shared her food. Many of times the Russian School boys would receive a big pot of baked beans and my brothers would come past the house—they stayed in the Russian School—and they would tell Mama how nice Mama Newhall sent a big pot of beans and they were happy to get that. Although we were not hungry, but something like that was always appreciated.[1]

Agnes Newhall's attempts to take no official position were constantly derailed by staff shortages. As late as 1915 she was referred to in *Woman's Home Missions* as the assistant superintendent at Unalaska. Both she and Albert were looking forward to a year's absence from the perpetual activity at the Home. Her health forced them to leave before Karl and Mildred Winchell arrived.[2] They departed Unalaska on the *McCulloch* on July 10, 1916, with their children, Chester and Edith, and their constant friend Emma Supernaw. They didn't get far. At a port in Bristol Bay the Unalaska deputy marshal Paul Buckley received three prisoners—two involved in a stabbing and one murderer—and seven insane men. The bay was crowded with more than 40 fishing vessels at anchor awaiting the arrival of salmon. The *McCulloch* returned to Unalaska and left again on July 22. At Valdez they transferred to the *Admiral Watson* for the trip to Seattle.

These "vacations" did provide time for rest, but there was also continual promotion work for the Home. During this particular absence, Dr. Newhall gave more than a hundred addresses in Washington, New York, Vermont, Wisconsin, Michigan, Indiana, Pennsylvania, Massachusetts, New Jersey and Rhode Island. At the annual meeting of the missionary society in Columbus, Ohio, in mid-October, Albert, Agnes and Emma sat "in their interesting corner in the balcony" and told stories about the Home and hospital and showed the needlework done by the students.

After they reached Massachusetts on September 2, Dr. Newhall convinced Agnes to see specialists in New York City. She went to the Skin and Cancer Hospital in early December and shortly afterward underwent surgery, remaining in the hospital until the middle of January 1917. While there she was encouraged by letters from women in the society. "On the day of my operation I felt great peace," she wrote, "knowing that my friends of the Woman's Home Missionary Society were praying for me."

On Christmas Day I received that rich telegram from Miss Grace Roraback, telling me that some friends had a purse of fifty dollars for me. It has since been added to, and Miss Roraback has sent me seventy-six dollars. I am so thankful I do not know how to put it in words, as I needed it so much. I wish, in this letter, to express my gratitude to each person who contributed.

Miss Roraback asked me to use it for myself, and I shall buy the outfit I shall need for the next five years I expect to spend in Alaska. I am so glad God answered your prayers and that I shall be physically able to return next June for another term of service.[3]

Dr. Newhall reported that she was recovering "in a gratifying way." He, in the meantime, visited several cities and gave talks about Alaska. In Arlington, New Jersey, an appreciative audience voluntarily made a large offering. Perhaps "voluntarily" is not quite the correct word. The church had two doors. One had a collection plate and the other did not. The presiding minister said people could leave by either.

While Agnes was recovering back in Stoneham, *Woman's Home Missions* had several articles about her.

"Dear Mama Newhall," as she is fondly spoken of, has spent days and nights in physical pain almost the entire time since the Columbus meeting. Mrs. Newhall has been in every sense a mother at Jesse Lee Home, possessing all the social and domestic graces, together with a beautiful Christian spirit. Her interest has never faltered, and bravely she urges Dr. Newhall to return north with no thought of self, of the lonely hours that must be hers. She has given unapplauded toil to the lowly. Besides her mother heart, big and strong, she has the delicate hand of discerning nurse, and has bound up physical and spiritual wounds for all these years.

Many earnest prayers go out from our societies everywhere, and from loving children in the north for her recovery and return to the service she so much loved and dignified.[4]

Peter Hatch, one of the former residents of the Home who was now attending school in the States, conveyed how so many children felt about her in a letter that began, "Dear

Mama—For so you have always been to me. . . ." He expressed his love for her patience and kindness and assured her he would try his best "to do that which I know is right."[5]

Agnes began her slow recovery, but in the spring she had a setback, suffering "a stroke of paralysis." "Yet her missionary zeal is not paralyzed," wrote her husband, "and she is anxious for her husband to return to the work where he is so much needed. Mrs. Newhall says she will follow as soon as she can manage crutches."[6]

"Brave, patient, cheerful in spite of suffering and weakness," wrote Mrs. W.P. Thirkield after visiting Agnes, "she has prayed constantly that God would restore her to former strength. Her heart is hungry for Alaska, and as I sat by her bedside and read the latest letters from our Unalaska Mission, I could see the response in her eyes to their appeal that she return, even if she must be taken as an invalid. Her children have caught her spirit, and as they came in from school, told of their love for Alaska. They must remain in New England for the advantage of its schools, but to them the cold of Unalaska seemed no more severe than a winter in Stoneham. With true heroism she is bidding her husband go back alone if necessary. Let all pray that the summer days may bring her healing, and the journey be undertaken in the fall as a united family."[7]

By June 25 Agnes was well enough to leave for Unalaska with her husband. "Never mind if I do die there," she told him, "it will be *in the harness* and I won't just be laid aside which is what would happen if I gave up the Alaskan trip."[8] Once again Emma Supernaw accompanied them. In Seattle Dr. Newhall used the donation from Arlington, New Jersey, to purchase a wheelchair which delighted his wife. During the 20 days they stayed in Seattle, a woman whose husband had been nursed to health at Unalaska came each day and wheeled Agnes about the long halls and corridors of the hotel.

They boarded the *Northwestern* on July 12. Agnes was lifted onto the deck while sitting in the wheelchair. Each day she was pushed around the deck where she enjoyed the scenery and counted the stops before reaching home. In Seward, the chair enabled her to get fresh air and to attend church. On the 17th day of the trip Dr. Newhall wrote, "Mama Newhall enjoys being on deck, but is getting nervous and anxious to keep well and reach home." When the ship reached Akutan, about 40 miles from Unalaska, she said that she wished the Lord would spare her life for five more years of work. She was content, her husband reported, with whatever might be ahead. After oil was taken aboard the vessel at the whaling station, the decks were washed with gasoline. The fumes were too much for her and she suffered another stroke.

On the 18th day they left Akutan at 3:30 in the morning, expecting to reach Unalaska about six hours later. Although weak, Agnes was alert and looking forward to seeing the familiar harbor. Every little while she would say, "Papa, just run out and see if we are at Priest Rock." After the ship rounded the point at that familiar landmark, breakfast was served.

"In a few minutes," wrote Dr. Newhall, "that awful headache came and my heart sank within me and Mama Newhall herself realized that it meant she would die." He told her to keep up her courage, but his had fled. Only moments seemed to pass before they were at the wharf. Agnes could move neither her head nor her feet. The teachers and children were at the dock eager to catch sight of their doctor and their "Mama."

"I tried to keep out of sight," Dr. Newhall wrote, "but they spied me and the cry went up, 'Doctor!' and the whole crowd stampeded to the end of the wharf. 'Where is Miss Supernaw and Mama Newhall?' they cried, but I could not speak and turned away."

He had the children escorted to the Home before "kind friends carried Mama Newhall ashore." She was placed in the wheelchair "which was tipped back like a bed, and slowly it made its way to Jesse Lee Home with its precious load."[9] She was conscious for two days, but could neither move nor speak. She lapsed into a coma and four days later she died, on Aug. 6, 1917.[10] The court record states that death occurred at 4 p.m. and was caused by apoplexy (arteriosclerosis) lasting five months and 19 days; a contributory cause was intestinal nephritis for three years. The Aug. 31, 1917, issue of *The Seward Gateway* strangely reported her death due to "ptomaine poisoning as the result of partaking of spoiled ham at a luncheon while in the East."[11]

"God has called our dear 'Mama Newhall' to rest after her twenty-two years of love and service in behalf of these dear children," stated the next annual report. "Her service and loving deeds will bind the teachers, children, friends, and Missionary Society together with chains of gold, until age will chink the face of many of those who knew and loved her."[12]

Peter Nielsen wrote to Dr. Newhall from Sanak on September 8 with his condolences on the "great loss" to the doctor and the children at the Home.[13] Adlooat wrote on November 8, expressing his sorrow at Mama Newhall's death. He recalled the last time he had seen her as he left Stoneham in 1902. He knew he would see her again "if I am on the right road she took." "But Doctor have courage," he said, "who knows, God only knows, maybe it was for the best for Mama Newhall to be with God. I know she had done well, she was a friend of our Saviour."[14]

Agnes Sowle Newhall was buried next to her daughter Isabella at the base of the mountain that had been known as Mt. Newhall since the early 1900s. Simeon Oliver recalled that the chaplain from a Coast Guard cutter conducted the service and an honor guard fired a salute.[15] In 1920 her friends and the children of the Home purchased a monument on which was engraved, "She hath done what she could."

Overwhelmed by sorrow, Albert began a letter to his children.

NOTES

1. Anfesia Shapsnikoff, interview with Ray Hudson. Hudson, ed., *Unugulux Tunusangin; Oldtime Stories*, 187.

2. Winchell, *Home by the Bering Sea*, 207.

3. *WHM*. March 1917:13.

4. *WHM*. June 1917:8.

5. *WHM*. June 1917:9.

6. Ibid.

7. *WHM*. July 1917:8.

8. Paraphrased from Newhall's article. *WHM*. February 1923:9.

9. *WHM*. February 1923:9.

10. Hastings, Horatius B., "A Long Ocean Voyage." *The Christian*. September 1917:3. Copy provided by Virginia Drugg.

11. *The Seward Gateway*. Aug. 31, 1917.

12. Woman's Home Missionary Society, Report from Bureaus. 1916–17:131.

13. Hudson, ed., *Cuttlefish, Volumes One, Two, & Three*, 241.

14. *WHM*. January 1919:6.

15. Tape-recorded interview with Simeon Oliver, Henry Swanson, Philemon Tutiakoff and Ray Hudson, May 25, 1979. Oliver also remarked, without elaboration, that he was the last child in the Home she asked to see.

29

The War Years

AFTER THE UNITED STATES ENTERED WORLD WAR I ON April 6, 1917, Unalaska residents rallied to do their part for the war effort. By June 30, 1918, the post office had sold $1,800 worth of "war savings stamps" to Aleut residents. Children saved candy money for these stamps. Girls in the Home reserved money from their needlework as did Emma Supernaw, who by the spring of 1918 had knit five sweaters for the Red Cross. The children at the Jesse Lee Home sang popular war songs like "Over There" and "K-K-K-Katie." Those with any connection to Swedish, Danish, or Norwegian ancestry bragged about it. Anything German was disparaged. Once Winchell discovered Margaret Seymour pestering Lena Krukoff to the point of tears by placing the only plate marked "Made in Germany" at the younger girl's place.[1]

A service flag hung in the chapel with five stars for the five Jesse Lee Home boys serving in the war.[2] Jack Rosenberg was on the SS *Great Northern* transporting troops to and from France out of New York. John Lee, who had entered the Home in 1899 at the age of three, was aboard another transport that sailed from Boston. (His younger sister, Hilda, was a greatly respected resident of the Home.) William McCurdy was on the battleship *Maine*. George Porter (Oslooluk) was stationed in Panama. He eventually served as a lieutenant. Henry Swanson, having joined the Navy in 1915 and seen duty in Hawaii and Panama, was off the coast of Europe aboard the cruiser *Charleston*.

Jack Rosenberg wrote to Dr. Newhall on June 13, 1918, telling him about his enlistment, his basic training, and his first trips across the Atlantic. "I have kept away from wicked women and drink," he assured the doctor.

Henry Swanson wasn't quite so fortunate when it came to women and wine. Having arrived at the French port of Saint Nazaire, the sailors were given a two-day pass.

> We got a 48-hour liberty in Saint Nazaire. Anyhow, me and another guy went to a town way up the river there. Two girls captured us and took us home to their place where they lived in a big stone house with doors that thick! Real old house, maybe hundreds of years old, and they dug wine out of the cellar. Gee, we got drunk. I don't remember leaving the place!
>
> We had a room in a hotel, French hotel, big feather beds in the bunks, big boxes with feather beds that thick in them. Gee, next morning I was sick, O gee! And thirsty. Well, I drank a lot of water and, boy, I got drunk again! Not

U.S.S. *Great Northern*
New York City, June 13, 1918

Dear friend Doctor,

We left Unalaska on the 9th of June at noon and steamed out to sea and called at the light house on Unimak island. I went ashore and saw my brother [William] for the last time. I am sorry to say I shall never see him on earth and the very last words he spoke was these, "Jack, good bye, take care of yourself." Then we sailed on calling at Sanak, where a school teacher came aboard—then at Morsovia a party of natives were landed. At Seward there was only myself of all the crew that wasn't drunk. After leaving that port we struck a storm which lasted three days. A man had been drinking and got crazy from it and jumped overboard and was lost. At last we reached Seattle and the mate took me round the city but I kept close to him for fear I would get lost. Then I was watchman on a steamer which was laid up for three weeks and then decided to go and visit my old Alaskan friend Mike Ladusher. I had never been on a train but bought my ticket, got on the train, started but did not know where I was going. I arrived safely at Astoria and the life saving crew took me out to the lighthouse, where I staid over night. Next day I went back to Astoria and joined the navy.

I staid at the recruiting station for three days, and they sent me to the Bremerton Navy Yard. They took us to the detention camp and made us take off all our clothes, take a bath and then put on a uniform of blue. They sterilized our old clothes. There we got four months training and then made the trip thru the canal to New York. Two days out I got the measles and I didn't see much of the voyage. I saw Panama and that sure is some piece of work. While passing thru the lake everybody was taking fresh water baths, but in seven days we were in New York and snow on the ground. They sent us up to the hospital in Brooklyn, 21 of us in the lot, 19 with mumps and three with measles. Staid there eight days, and then went aboard the "Great Northern."

Made my first trip to France but all along the course no ship was with us. We arrived safely and went ashore and saw the old houses and narrow dirty streets and the strange dress of the people and heard their strange language. To talk French—I could not. We have made five trips now and have not even seen a submarine.

On one trip we rescued the survivors of the "S. S. *President Lincoln*" [a transport torpedoed by a German submarine on May 31, 1918]. They sure were pretty well nerve shattered. What if we had had such a squeeze as they had. They were brave enough to face it. The sub shot a couple of holes in the vessel and then came to the surface and while the survivors were floating about in the boats, the sub was going around among them looking for the captain and they asked for him, but he got into a sailors suit and they could not tell him from the sailors.

I have kept away from wicked women and drink and I have no desire for either. With your help I will keep away from evil. When you write give me the address of your children, Chester and Edith, as I may go and see them some day.

Doctor, I hope to see you again some time. I will write again and I am always ready to receive your good advice and warnings of bad habits.

With love and best wishes to all and to my good teacher and friend,

"Jack" Rosenberg [3]

like I did the night before, but, you know. Anyhow, I never drank any wine again after that. Gee, that cured me from drinking wine. Well, I never drink a lot anyhow of anything, but I did on that liberty at Saint Nazaire.[4]

While on the East Coast, Henry and men from his ship were taken to a firing range for practice. It was outside Stoneham, Massachusetts, and Henry recalled that this was the place where the Newhalls lived when they were not at Unalaska.

Dr. Newhall and Emma Supernaw, the "faithfuls," continued their work. Clara Cook returned to Muskegon, Michigan. She married a Mr. Lawrence and lived for years in South Bend, Indiana.[5] Earl and Margaret Lewis had arrived in the autumn of 1917. She was 22 and worked as the sewing teacher while he took care of the outdoors and the upstairs. Margaret gave birth to a baby boy the third week of May 1918, but he lived only a few days. "We all felt so sorry for them," wrote Winchell, "but she is getting along all right so that is a great blessing."[6]

Margaret Smythe, the cooking teacher, married Captain Newland of the *Dora* on June 1, 1918. The women and children spent the day decorating the chapel with wildflowers, freezing ice cream and baking cakes. Shortly after the wedding the newlyweds boarded the *Dora* for a trip to Nushagak. Margaret Lewis was well enough to help with the upstairs rooms in the girls' dorm during Smythe's absence. In 1918 Lotta Ketcham arrived from Berwick, Pennsylvania. Also joining the staff was Edith Gavitt, "from war work in Columbia, S.C." Gavitt had attended the Kansas City Training School. These two women had "many hardships" reaching Unalaska. Ketcham sailed on the *Dora*'s last trip of the season.[7] Gavitt and the public schoolteachers arrived on an ammunition boat. Mary Winchell, now the matron, left for a year's furlough at her mother's in Santa Clara, California.

Clara Goss continued her support of the Home. For several years she had taught school at Sanak while Albert was at Atka. "Through her influence," wrote Miss Gavitt, "about twenty Sanak children have come to the Jesse Lee Home in the past five years." During the months Clara Goss lived at Unalaska, her suite of rooms in the A.C. Co. house became a "haven of rest" for the women from the Home. She encouraged the girls in their needlework and often finished their projects for them.

Peter Hatch returned from school in Tacoma and on Oct. 23, 1917, he and Annie Swanson were married. They promptly boarded the *Bear* and spent the year at Atka. In 1918 they returned, built a home, and began to raise a family. Peter initially worked at the Home, as did Annie's sister Helen. In 1925 Peter and Annie moved to Seldovia. Their success bolstered Dr. Newhall's spirits. He wrote about them glowingly in 1920.[8]

The mission boxes that arrived from well-intentioned congregations in the States were sometimes filled with the oddest contributions. Once a barrel of straw hats arrived—to a place where, as Winchell put it, the wind blows the hair off a dog. They received a shipment of fans and a dozen black swallow-tailed coats. Men from Biorka village eventually took the coats, leaving Winchell to reflect how coats that had once attended concerts in Boston now hunted ducks along the Biorka shore. Occasionally specific items would be requested: stout underwear, heavy stockings, white cotton sheets, two good 12-gauge shotguns for duck hunting, a new kitchen range. There was, at least once, a "not needed" list: post cards, old newspapers and magazines, thin underwear, petticoats, and swallow-tail jackets.

. .

THE REVOLUTION IN RUSSIA reached its climax in October 1917. One result of the trau-matic change in government was the end of subsidies to the Orthodox Church in Alaska. The commissioner of education in Washington, D.C., asked Arthur H. Miller, superin-tendent for the Southwestern District, what the withdrawal of support for the Orthodox Church meant for Native communities. Miller made three points. A staunch Protestant, he distrusted any religion with priests who were (as he understood it) essential for "access to the divine ear." He thought priests, now dependent on local congregations for their support, would take advantage of their communities. Even white congregations in Alaska, he wrote, were generally unable to support a minister on their own. This section of his reply sounded like a Reformation tract. Second, he felt the withdrawal of support and the absence of a resident bishop resulted in disorganization. The priest at Unalaska told him that each resident priest in the territory now had an assigned territory "in which he might conduct religious services." This, however, was exactly what had existed for decades. The only positive outcome, in his mind, was the third effect: with the withdrawal of support by the Russian government "the American government may insist that this church be Americanized." He wanted headquarters in the United States, priests educated in American seminaries, and less emphasis on "religious Russian festivals and holidays" that interrupted the work schedule.[9]

The WHMS repeated the belief that with funds cut off from its Russian center, the Orthodox Church in the Aleutians would inevitably decline: ". . . the natives are left like sheep without a Shepherd," a report stated, "and, having never been taught self help or reliance under these missions, are fast dying through neglect."[10] Mrs. J.H. Parsons found prospects encouraging.

> The withdrawal of all support from the Russian Greek Church means an opportunity for Protestantism. The younger people do not care much for the church now. The older people take kindly to our efforts, and in a few years the priests will not bother with them much. The Greek system has not been an uplift to these people at all. Little by little the gospel will reach them, and the Sunday school is the medium through which the children may be reached.[11]

This sentiment continued for years. "The Russian-Greek Church here is now a thing of the past," stated the annual report for 1920–21.

Mary Winchell has left two accounts of the formation of a local Red Cross chapter and both provide insight into the complex factions within the community. "Doctor Talks About the Red Cross," a chapter in her 1951 *Home by the Bering Sea*, enlarges what she wrote in a letter on May 26, 1918. Briefly, Dr. Newhall had decided to organize a local chapter because anything done at Unalaska was being credited to the Red Cross chapter in Seward. He called a meeting "to talk about a Red Cross organization." It was held in the large community room on the second floor of the A.C. Co.'s laundry building. Notices were posted and sent to Chief Alexei Yatchemeneff and to Father Dmitrii Hotovitsky. Winchell was under the impression that the priest knew only a little English; however, he had been in the United States since 1908. The meeting still faced major linguistic and factional obstacles, as Mary Winchell explained in her letter.

> There was a good crowd but with the natives who could understand neither English nor Russian well, and the Priest who could understand neither Aleute nor English clearly and the white folks who could understand neither Russian nor Aleute coupled with the lack of unity among the white folks on account of industrial[,] political[,] racial and religious reasons it was finally given up and also for the fact that the Priest rose up after a long spell of misunderstandings —explainings and interpretations of both in Russian and Aleute and said the Greek Brotherhood had already organized a Red Cross (unbeknownst to us all) and there couldn't be two and he was quite excited.[12]

Father Hotovitsky understood that the meeting had been called to *talk about*, not to organize, a Red Cross chapter. He announced that one had already been formed by the St. Ponteleiman Brotherhood. They had been selling pins for more than a week to raise money. That ended the meeting. The next day when Newhall took the Home's scissors to Jimmy Lavigne's for sharpening, Mary Lavigne, the great basket weaver, remarked that she had met a woman a few days earlier who was wearing one of the pins. She thought it would protect her in case of a German invasion. Jimmy Lavigne burst out laughing and said in his Virginia accent that he didn't have much interest in the Red Cross anyway. "Not very patriotic," remarked Winchell in her letter, "but he sharpened our scissors for nothing like the good neighbor that he is."

NOTES

1. Winchell, *Home by the Bering Sea*, 84–85.

2. *WHM*. February 1919:17.

3. Newhall Manuscript, 300.

4. Swanson, *The Unknown Islands*, 50–51.

5. Edith Newhall Drugg to Ray Hudson, Oct. 26, 1978.

6. Winchell, Mary. Letter, May 26, 1918.

7. *WHM*. February 1919:17.

8. *WHM*. June 1920:5.

9. Arthur H. Miller to the Commissioner of Education. Aug. 2, 1918. NARA. RG 75. General Correspondence.

10. Woman's Home Missionary Society. Report to Bureaus, 1918–19:138.

11. *WHM*. February 1919:17.

12. Winchell, Mary. Letter to "Dear Folks," May 26, 1918. Alaska State Historical Library. MS 0003. Box 2, Item 4.

30

The Pandemic of 1919

Bʏ ᴛʜᴇ ᴛɪᴍᴇ Wᴏʀʟᴅ Wᴀʀ I ᴇɴᴅᴇᴅ ᴡɪᴛʜ ᴛʜᴇ ꜱɪɢɴɪɴɢ ᴏꜰ ᴛʜᴇ ᴀʀᴍɪꜱᴛɪᴄᴇ on Nov. 11, 1918, an influenza epidemic had crossed the United States and arrived on the West Coast. In two years this pandemic would claim 50 million victims worldwide, including 675,000 Americans. Thousands of revelers in San Francisco wore protective face masks as they danced in the streets to celebrate the peace. Officials in Alaska were understandably worried. At Unalaska the dance halls and pool rooms were closed. Sailors were not allowed ashore.

The winter was stormy, but the general health of the people at Unalaska remained good. By spring, the threat seemed to have passed and life returned to normal. Dr. Newhall made a slightly ironic list of things to be thankful for: the local boys who had served in the war were unharmed; the flu had spared the village; snow was only five feet deep between the two Jesse Lee Home buildings; it was too stormy to dig clams, but plenty of clams were still waiting on the beach; the store was out of white sugar and table salt, but soft coal was only $25 a ton.

As May drew to a close, the weather cleared. The USS *Saturn* was in port to service the Navy radio station. Father Hotovitsky returned from visiting one of the outlying villages. Then on Friday, May 23, people began falling ill.[1] The speed with which the flu permeated the village was phenomenal. By Monday the influenza was epidemic, and the commanding officer of the *Saturn* wired Captain F.E. Dodge on the Coast Guard cutter *Unalga* anchored in Seredka Bay on Akun Island.[2] As Dodge took the *Unalga* toward Unalaska, a wire came from Dr. Linus H. French at the Kanakanak Hospital that the entire Bristol Bay region was being ravaged by influenza. On anchoring at Unalaska and inspecting the village, Dodge decided to remain at Unalaska. He wired Coast Guard headquarters in Washington, the governor of Alaska, and Dr. French about his decision.

On Wednesday morning, May 28, the *Unalga* tied up at the A.C. Co. dock in order to be better able to deliver assistance. Five people had died since the illness began. Dodge inspected the village, the Dutch Harbor settlement, and the naval radio station near Dutch Harbor. The magnitude of what he found was reflected in the repetition of his report:

> . . . native population all down and helpless, unable to cook or care for themselves in any way. All teachers and inmates of the Jesse Lee Home sick and helpless, all government school teachers sick and helpless, the people at the jail and A.C. Company house sick and helpless, all at U.S. Naval Radio Station sick and helpless, except the Chief Operator who is working night and day . . .[3]

"It appeared to be a case where it was necessary for the entire ship's force to co-operate," he wrote, "without a thought of their own personal health or comfort in order to combat the situation with assurance of success." He called for volunteers. The ship's surgeon, F.H. Johnson, oversaw all medical relief. He was assisted by the pharmacist's mate, E.S. Chase. The officer in charge of the commissary prepared food. Overall relief work and the distribution of food fell to the executive officer, along with the job of getting a service hospital in shape in case members of the crew fell ill. While the ship's carpenter N. Bruinilla built coffins, Boatswain S.B. Johnson and a detail of men dug graves. Three volunteers headed by Dental Surgeon E.W. Scott went to the naval radio station and to Dutch Harbor. The village itself was covered by three men under Lieutenant C.E. Anderson with headquarters at the A.C. Co. office. The Jesse Lee Home became the responsibility of Captain of Engineers T.G. Lewton and six men: ordinary seamen L. Straley and F.E. Honeywell, seamen 2nd class F.K. Briggs and M.V. Wilson, and firemen 3rd class S.O. Johnson and J.B. Sowell. Other men would be added to these lists.

Dr. Newhall was one of the first to fall ill. He was bedridden, and within a short time the entire staff followed. Only five children escaped. Simeon Oliver remembered that Benny Benson was one of these. "Why he didn't come down with it, no one seemed to know," Simeon said, "probably too ornery or something of this sort. He was a lonely boy. We'd hear him outside singing to himself. He never strayed far from our open windows. We could always hear him singing or talking to himself or tapping stones. There wasn't even a dog around with which he could play."[4]

The Home became even more crowded when Lucy Rosenberg and her children sought shelter. They were followed by Andrew, Paul and Sarah Morton. The doctor was relieved when Captain Lewton and his six men arrived. The women on the staff, on the other hand, were nervous about un-chaperoned sailors roaming the halls of the girls' dorm and chatting with those well enough to talk. Too sick to protest, however, they stayed in their rooms confined to bed. Dr. Newhall was thankful.

It was a good thing they could not get down into the kitchen. Oh, that kitchen—grease, grease, grease—the floor was a veritable skating rink. Slid quite a ways on a fried slice of bacon and that at 75 cents per lb—The greasy dishpan with its never ending pile of dirty dishes. All kinds of dishes were used and it made no difference how they went into the dish pan. Company dishes, cut glass, silverware, pots and pans all the same, around the scummy pan they swished. Washcloths that belonged to the girls with crocheted edges were used for dish rags and they wiped on any old thing, roller towels, etc., and they didn't get washed after every meal. The sink spout must have become disjointed the first day or so and all kinds of dirty water etc. was going on the floor under the sink. The sailors liked boiled beans the best but they were not always well done, and often were not salt[ed] enough. At last the convalescents got solid food. Fried eggs reeking with grease, toast soaked with butter, potatoes peeled and fried until they were dark with grease, beef steak served cold sometimes and half an inch more or less of grease on it; bacon, Oh! such thick slices. The doctor, before the flu, thot he had indigestion and couldn't eat greasy things, but guess he was cured after the grease diet. But the sailor boys were happy—they smoked and chatted and every and anon feasted on the good things sent up from the cutter. Out on the beach the seagulls and ravens held high carnival and daily banquets.

By May 29 the situation had worsened. Captain E.A. Coffin joined Lewton at the Home, "nursing, feeding and doctoring them as all are sick and helpless there," according to Captain Dodge. By the end of the day, the total dead in the village had reached nine. Men from the ship went into homes to build fires, deliver food, nurse the sick, and carry out the dead. On May 30 Anna Lukanin and her newborn child were found dead while her four other children stood shivering in the cold house. They had gone hungry for two days. The father or father-in-law died later that day. May 30 also saw the death of Alexandra Sokolnikoff. Her husband, Vasilii, had died a few days earlier at the whaling plant at Akutan where he worked. Dodge ordered a vacant house to be thoroughly cleaned and turned into a temporary home for orphans or children whose parents were too sick to care for them. Master at Arms Peter Bugaras and three other men were placed in immediate charge of 12 children. Eighty-five years later, Alexandra and Vasilii Sokolnikoff's son recalled being taken with his sister to "one of the warehouses used by the A.C. Company."[5] The boy, Vasilii, would eventually be adopted by Afenogin Ermeloff of Nikolski and become known as Bill Ermeloff. By June 4th there were 26 children crowding what was called "an improvised orphanage."

For decades people remembered teams of sailors delivering food to homes. Most frequently, pails of soup were carried from house to house with long waits between deliveries. The boys in the Home referred to the soup as belly wash. It didn't fill them up much, according to Newhall. "One most caved in before the next meal came," he wrote. "One feller said he was so hungry and so thin that his 'umbilical' button had stuck to his back bone (but he didn't say umbilical)."

> . . . a sailor was bringing up a pail of soup from the ship and he dropped his Sunday shoes in it. Two sailors were carrying two heavy pails of soup to the houses in the village when a sick man looked out and saw them set down their pails and have a smoke and a chat while in the meantime two dogs were licking away at the soup in the pails. The sailors laughed and went along on their

errand of mercy. O finicky folks—what they don't know they needn't worry about. However, that patient didn't eat any of that soup.

One of our convalescents went over to the other house and they had fried beefsteak for dinner and it was in liberal pieces but greasy and tough. The poor fellow was weak in body and in the jaw but he chewed and he chawed looking at me with a most solemn mien until I had to laugh and asked him what was the matter. "Well," he said, "I am trying to make out whether this is bull meat or belt leather."

Dr. Johnson visited Margaret Lewis at the Home on May 29. She had given birth to a son a few days earlier and complications had developed. He performed surgery and administered an anti-streptococci vaccine and a saline solution, "all of which did no good." She died on the evening of May 31. She was 24 years old. Lotta Ketcham was the member of the staff who stayed on her feet the longest. She was able to care for the infant until she finally fell ill and handed the job over to one of the seamen. He was a tall, lanky man, as Dr. Newhall described him, who came into the doctor's room and said, "Wall, I've got a new job—got to take care of that kid and feed 'im."

Newhall looked at him and asked, "Are you going to bring it up on the breast or the bottle?"

The sailor stood dazed for a moment and then burst out laughing. "Wall, by gosh, guess it will have to be the bottle—breasts are pretty dry."

On June 1 Leontii Sifsof died. He was a deacon in the church and an accomplished linguist who had assisted Waldemar Jochelson in the collection of Aleut folk tales in 1909 and 1910. Nekifor Dyakanoff also died that day. He was the head of a prominent family and several of his children and grandchildren, including Kathryn Dyakanoff Seller, had lived at the Home. His home was on Hog Island in Unalaska Bay. Although warned to stay on the island, he came into the village and contracted the illness.[6]

The next day, Peter Kashevaroff died at noon. He was survived by Eliza and five children ages four to nine. His body, like so many others, was placed in a simple coffin and taken to the cemetery on a cart. Newhall wrote about "the rattle of the wheels on the beach stones" passing the Home, "telling of one more victim—that was all." The dead were buried in rows. Eventually the Iliuliuk Club purchased a stone marker for Peter's grave on which was engraved his service as president of the organization. He was not quite 35 when he died.

Lilly Rosenberg Anderson, who had lived at the Home off and on and who had recently married, also died on June 2. She was Lucy Leavitt's sister-in-law. With the death that same day of Mary Prokopeuff Lavigne, the noted basketry teacher and a close friend of Dr. Newhall, the casualties had reached 31.

Simeon Oliver looked out his dormitory window and saw coffins sitting outside houses waiting for someone inside to die. Day after day Captain Dodge sent radiograms telling of no improvement. The entire ship's company was employed in relief work. More orphan children were placed in the improvised home. From May 28 to June 1, 350 rations had been distributed each day. On June 2 the number slightly decreased. On June 3 the *Bear* arrived in port with Captain Uberoth, commander of the Bering Sea fleet. The surgeons from the *Bear* and *Unalga* divided the work on shore, with the *Bear*'s surgeon taking the portion of town from the marshal's office eastward. Governor Riggs wired that the Navy vessel *Marblehead* was being sent with Navy doctors, public health doctors, and nurses. Dodge wired back that while he needed help nursing the ill, the *Marblehead* could not offer sufficient assistance to the Bristol Bay region. The governor felt unsupported by the federal government. On June 5, he wired Dodge, who had fallen ill himself the day before:

> Can get no satisfaction from Washington, they passed the buck to me last epidemic and evidently doing same thing again. My funds very small but allot you additional five hundred. Appreciate your splendid work and will cooperate best of my limited ability. Do not spend too much money on coffins for dead, but conserve all available funds for care of living. Keep me constantly advised so that I can punch up Washington. Am asking ten thousand for your immediate use.

Twelve men from the *Bear* came ashore to help dig graves, carry coal, and deliver food under the direction of officers from the *Unalga*. Deputy U.S. Marshal Paul Buckley had also arrived on the *Bear*. He readily agreed to the transfer of the 12 oldest children from the temporary home to the jail to relieve crowding. The two schoolteachers, Agnes Danford and Miss Gard, were also taken to the jail after they contracted the flu.

Reports of influenza reaching Akutan arrived on June 3. The village was quarantined and no ships were allowed to land. By June 6, 33 women and children in the village were ill. The men, working at the whaling station across the bay, were also stricken.

On June 4, Feodore Moriss, the adopted son of Annie and Mark Moriss, died. He was 15. Annie herself died three days later. On June 6 Dr. Newhall was well enough to relieve the sailors, who then returned to the *Unalga*. They gave the kitchen a thorough scrubbing before they left. Throughout the village, people began to convalesce. The number of rations distributed was down from 350 to 90. People were still seriously ill, however. With the deaths of Zoe Borenin on the 11th and Nicolai Kudrin on the 13th, the epidemic came to a close. According to Captain Dodge, there had been 46 deaths. Newhall said 44 had died, and this number is reflected in district court records.

The children in the "improvised orphan's home" were returned to parents who were still alive. "Those whose parents were dead," wrote Dodge, "were taken by other native families in the village, under the directions of the Rev. D.A. Hotovitsky." On the 12th the building used for the children was cleaned and locked. Dodge submitted a bill to Agnes Danford, as the representative of the Bureau of Education. There had been 3,120 rations distributed costing .98953 cents each, for a total of $3,087.3336. In addition, he gave her an itemized bill for miscellaneous expenditures for $1,088.44.

On June 17 the *Unalga* sailed for Bristol Bay. Father Hotovitsky and Chief Alexei Yatchmeneff wrote to Captain Dodge on July 1 thanking him on behalf of the community for "the heroic work" he and his men had done. "We feel had it not been for the prompt and efficient work of the Unalga, when everyone willingly and readily exposed himself to succor the sick," they wrote, "Unalaska's population might have been reduced to a very small number if not entirely wiped out." They offered prayers "for the welfare of everyone of the good ship Unalga, who so cheerfully risked their lives to save the people of Unalaska."

The staff at the Home followed the next day with a letter expressing gratitude for "the aid and kindly ministrations given to the sick at the home." The Home and the village had indeed been fortunate, wrote Dr. Newhall, "that the U.S.C.G. Unalga was near and that Captain F.E. Dodge came to our help so promptly, and so efficiently took charge of the situation." The letter was signed by A.W. Newhall, Edith Gavitt, Emma E. Supernaw, Earl R. Lewis, and Lotta Ketcham.

On September 15 Dr. Newhall and Alexei Yatchmeneff filled out 44 death records for the district court.[7] The *Unalga* returned to Unalaska at the end of the season and prepared to sail south. Eliza Kashevaroff left aboard the shiip on October 15. She took her five children: Elinore, 9; Chester, 8; Victor, 6; Ethel, 5; and Mildred, 4. According to family tradition, Peter Kashevaroff's dying request to his wife had been that his children receive an education in the States.[8] Also leaving were Lucy Rosenberg, Katie Rosenberg, and Sarah Morton.[9] Samuel Applegate and the agent of the Alaska Commercial Company had requested passage for all of them. The log of the vessel noted that they were leaving because "there is no means of support for them at Unalaska, their natural protectors having passed away during the epidemic of influenza." Eliza Kashevaroff lived to be an elderly woman. For her 90th birthday she showed her younger relatives that she could still bend at the hip and touch her hands to the floor.[10]

Throughout the epidemic the weather had been unnaturally fine: sunny days and calm nights. Years afterward, whenever good weather persisted for more than a couple of days, the older residents of the village who had been alive in 1919 began to get nervous.

NOTES

1. Newhall, undated three-page article on the influenza epidemic. Alaska State Historical Library. MS 0106.

2. F.E. Dodge, Commanding U.S.S. *Unalga,* to M.E. Reynolds, Commodore Commandant, U.S. Coast Guard. "Report of operations of this vessel during influenza epidemic." June 30, 1919. NARA. RG 75. General Correspondence, 1919–20. Box 97. Unless otherwise stated, all material in this chapter is from Newhall and Dodge.

3. F.G. Dodge to M.E. Reynolds, Commodore Commandant, U.S. Coast Guard. June 30, 1919. NARA. RG 26, Box 1846.

4. Simeon Oliver, tape-recorded conversation with Henry Swanson, Philemon Tutiakoff and Ray Hudson, May 25, 1979.

5. Bill Ermeloff conversation with Ray Hudson, Sept. 1, 2005.

6. Walter Dyakanoff conversation with Ray Hudson, April 25, 1996.

7. Third Judicial District. *Unalaska Record Book,* pp. 71–114.

8. Elizabeth Haralson conversation with Ray Hudson, Jan. 17, 2006. She is a granddaughter and namesake of Eliza Kashevaroff.

9. Ship's Log. U.S. Coast Guard cutter *Unalga.* Oct. 15, 1919. NARA. RG-26.

10. Elizabeth Haralson conversation with Ray Hudson, Jan. 17, 2006.

In her book Home by the Bering Sea, *Mary Winchell writes that this photograph is of* "Miss Smith, boys' matron, *trying to write on mail day while the boys look at 'funny papers' given them by the mail clerk on the boat."* *From Annie Swanson Hatch's album, courtesy of the Hatch family.*

Now or Never

Waves of rheumatism, meningitis, and whooping cough followed the influenza epidemic.[1] No one at the Home had strength enough to plant a garden. Emma Supernaw developed inflammatory rheumatism and became dependent on crutches. Mary Winchell cut short her vacation by two months and returned as soon as she realized the Home needed help. In July, Olive Smith arrived. Although orphans from Unalaska were adopted by friends or relatives,[2] 1919 saw the largest number of new residents in the history of the Home: 21 girls and 14 boys. The enrollment reached 70. Most of these came from communities on the Alaska Peninsula or around Bristol Bay.

> The family is large, owing to the "flu" and other conditions, and at present there is neither sufficient bedding or beds. Some teachers have from one to three children in their rooms. One boy sleeps on a sick chair and another on the soft side of a pine board. . . . Forty girls sleeping on the third floor of a large old house, which is hog-backed and leaning toward the river, is not just desirable. The winds are very high, but it is fire that we most fear.[3]

For several years Dr. Newhall had been urging a major reconstruction program. Now he laid out specific goals for expanding the facilities. In addition to a general renovation of the dormitories, a recreation room and a more suitable sewing room were needed. He continued to make repairs and improvements. A new pump house was built and sodded on all sides like a barabara. A new water line was laid and a pressure tank installed. Water was now being taken from a mountain reservoir built above the village lake, some 2,500 feet from the Home. This waterline was installed to avoid the annual fall pollution from dying salmon in Iliuliuk Creek and the village lake. A fine Otter boat was purchased with earmarked funds; once a gasoline engine for it was secured it would be used for towing the seining skiff, taking teachers to the rest camp, and giving the children outings along the shore. A Delco electric plant was installed to provide lights. This removed the constant danger from kerosene lamps.

In 1919 the treasurer of the Woman's Home Missionary Society informed the Alaska Commercial Company that the society had a yearly income of over one million dollars.[4] From June 20 to July 13, 1919, the Methodist Church sponsored a centenary celebration in Columbus, Ohio, an elaborate affair with pageants and parades. Jennie Alexander took part dressed in her Eskimo parka. She was introduced as "a converted Alaskan girl . . . a product of missionary work."[5] She was soon enrolled in a nurse's training program at the

Methodist Hospital in Rapid City, South Dakota. She married John Para and they settled in San Francisco where she stayed in touch with former Unalaskans like the Applegates. In her later life she did private nursing, and one of her patients was William Wrigley Jr. (1861–1932), the founder of the chewing gum empire.[6]

Shortly before Christmas 1919, Marie McLeod arrived on a steamer from Seattle. A grand Aleutian storm was in progress with snow blowing horizontally across the bay and village. She had left Unalaska with Elizabeth Mellor in 1898. Now after many years as a teacher and missionary she was returning to assist in the Home she had loved as a child. The "sweetest memories I have in life," she said, "are those of 'Mamma Newhall,' as she gathered all the little girls around her knees in the evening and told stories of Jesus, and taught us our prayers and then tucked us into bed."[7] Dr. Newhall and several of the boys were at the dock. She had brought a special gift: a Christmas tree. She also had boxes of apples, candy, raisins, peanuts, and popcorn, all donated by well-wishers. The doctor and the boys piled them on a large sled and pulled it through the village distributing the treats to every house. "It was a bitter cold day and a howling blizzard was on," he later wrote, "but the day spent was a pleasure, for so much of good cheer was brought to every home."[8]

For Christmas that year the Home once again held a community program. Newhall began his description of the evening with Clement Moore's famous lines, "'Twas the night before Christmas, and all through the house/ Not a creature was stirring, not even a mouse."

> But that was not in Jesse Lee Home, for out in the kitchen more than seventy boys and girls were laughing and talking and getting in line to march into the large room, where all the village had gathered. The room looked very pretty with its decorated platform and a Christmas tree on either side. The exercises went off finely. There were Christmas carols, recitations, a Christmas message, and prayer. Then a tinsel drill, a Christmas dialogue, and it was nice when "Tiny Tim" said he didn't know any verse but he would just say, "A merry Christmas to all, and God bless you every one!" . . . Even with raisins 25 cents per pound, popcorn 25 cents, and peanuts 35 cents, there was enough for all the village. Kind friends had donated cash, candy, apples, etc. Each child in the village received a package of a dozen old post cards.[9]

The program featured a very un-Christmas-like skit in which "Boy Cadets" fought Indians. They put on a fierce battle, especially when one of the cadets and one of the Indians briefly lost their tempers for real. On Christmas morning the children arrived and found a semicircle of chairs with an initialed flour sack on each.

> At 7 a.m. the boys and girls rushed in, and some friends were along to see the fun. What a racket! Horns a-tooting, whistles blowing, seventy mouth

organs all going at one time; boys and girls charging here and there to show their presents—yapping dog or climbing monkey, and goodness knows what not. All were very happy. The toys, games, etc., sent by mail during the year, made this possible. . . . The children wish that Christmas came every day, but the teachers do not.

Clara Goss visited the States in the summer of 1919, returning in mid-December. She gave a dinner party on Christmas afternoon for some of the Home staff. Those who stayed back to take care of the children went to her suite for dinner on New Year's Day. Simeon Oliver was also invited. He was becoming an excellent musician and played the piano for Clara and her guests. "Mrs. Goss had such lovely linen, silver, and new hand-painted china set," wrote Edith Gavitt. "Her table was unusually beautiful and the dinner the finest I have had up here, anyway, and I don't remember a better one."[10] The New Year 1920 was ushered in with several clear days and nights filled with moonlight.

The calm weather continued through January 12, the night the girls' dormitory caught fire.[11] This was the original building, now three stories of weather-stressed and rotting wood. Evidence suggested the fire began when a bracket lamp exploded in the sewing room. Mary Winchell had been there shortly before supper, had turned down the lamp, and noticed that the fire in the stove was almost out. After Hilda Lee, one of the older girls, finished her meal she went upstairs and saw smoke coming from under the door. There was a roaring, crackling noise within. Quickly but quietly she ran downstairs and informed the teachers. She then hurried to the boys' dormitory with the news.

Dr. Newhall and people from the village arrived almost simultaneously. Eddie Anderson, a village boy who happened to be outside, had seen the blaze through the windows and notified the marshal. Dr. Newhall described the crisis:

> Paul [Morton], Miss Supernaw and I rushed up stairs and opened the sewing room door and a volley of smoke and flame burst forth throwing Paul back against the wall and singeing him somewhat. He had a fire extinguisher but it could not be used there. The house is doomed, we said and I rushed down to the girls' dining room where all the children were assembled and told Miss Winchell the house was without a doubt doomed and then I told the children to go quickly and quietly to the other house and Miss Smith was delegated to see that they kept away from the big house.

Paul Morton, Chester Newhall, Simeon Oliver and Dan Sipary climbed up the outside fire escape, broke a window and crawled along the floor to where the water tank was stored. They opened the valve and soon a bucket brigade was flooding the floor above the fire with water. A boy was sent to keep the electric pump going. This cooled the floor, but the fire spread into the hallway and was threatening the third story itself. While the marshal and men from the village joined the older boys in attacking the fire, others rushed about in a purposeful chaos trying to rescue valuables.

Dr. Newhall and a few of the older girls piled 200 loaves of bread in tablecloths, tied them up, and dragged them outside where a posse of smaller children took them to the boys' building. Dishes were saved the same way. Canned goods were stacked in the yard. Up on the third floor, Paul Morton was directing Simeon and Chester, who threw mattresses and bedding through windows out onto the ground. One of the teachers, unnamed by Newhall, rushed into her room in a frenzy and threw everything—clothes, trinkets, and bureau drawers—through a window or down the fire escape. All her good clothes were ground into the mud.

Emma Supernaw was trapped in her room when the hallway filled with smoke. She had returned to save about $900 she had been safeguarding. Five hundred belonged to a man at the wireless station, another large sum belonged to Clara Goss, and smaller amounts belonged to her, the girls, and the Sunday School class. For 15 minutes she stayed in the room as the air thickened and breathing became more difficult. She was about to throw a mattress out the window followed by a feather bed and then herself when two men appeared below her window with a ladder. One climbed up and she handed a dresser drawer with the money to him. He promptly dropped it to the ground. Then he and another rescuer climbed into her room where they offered to carry her down. She demurred. "If I can get onto the first rung," she told them, "I can get down." As she left through the window, the two men rushed to save anything they could grab. One descended the ladder with a box of old post cards. The other came down with a pair of worn out corsets. Emma explained about the money, a flashlight was produced, and the hunt began.[12]

Lotta Ketcham rushed into the barn adjoining the house and rescued the goats. She had an affinity for animals and Dr. Newhall once described her as "skilled with the needle and good at raising chickens, ducks, and goats."[13]

> The bucket brigade and the pipe line worked well for the water was coming thru the floors everywhere like rain. . . . Great credit should be given to the men who worked to save the home for they worked like Trojans. The house was well soaked with water and was desolate enough indeed but it remained as a shelter for us until something better could be had. The fire was out but the sewing room was a blackened mess and the six sewing machines were a sight and their needles twisted all out of shape by the heat. The boys lost shirts, stockings, overalls, etc. and there was also lost a lot of new fancy work material as well as sewing supplies. A large hole was made in the roof to let out the smoke and Dan, Chester, Simeon and Paul went on guard for the night lest the fire again break out.

Fortunately, it had been a rare calm evening without rain or wind.

Twenty-one of the smallest girls slept in the jail that night and were treated to a fine breakfast the next morning. The other girls slept in the boys' house, crowded together on the floor. Forty mattresses and 200 loaves of bread. One girl cried out, "Oh, dear, we are so close together we can't grow."

"Well," said Emma Supernaw, laughing, "stop growing for one night."

Just as things quieted down, there was a knock at the door. A village boy had fallen down a bank and his leg was bleeding badly. Dr. Newhall rushed to him and found he had probably severed an artery. The doctor ordered pressure applied to the wound and the boy carried to the Home. The room used for surgery in the boys' house was packed with mattresses and stacks of bedding. The parlor was in the same condition. Finally, the 200 loaves of bread were taken from a table and piled on the old grand piano and the table was prepared. When Emma Supernaw was told ether would be used, she insisted the bread had to be moved farther away or it would be inedible. The loaves were carried into a crowded room and left on the floor. Once the patient was in place, Olive Smith administered the ether and the doctor went to work. He successfully finished surgery at 1 a.m.

An exhausted staff assembled for breakfast the next morning. "A woebegone looking crowd" is how Newhall described them. "And yet," he wrote, "there were enough funny things that had happened to make folks laugh and keep up their spirits." One girl cried because her doll had been left in the attic; another rejoiced that the cat had been saved, and a third was "indignant because her old cloak which she hated" hadn't burned. Belongings were gradually recovered and sorted. A prized Bible was found in a kindling box. One teacher's false teeth were brought in by John Carpenter, who smiled as he said he'd tried them on. The matron couldn't understand why bread had been wrapped up in her best silk skirt. And the considerable sum of money with which Emma Supernaw had been entrusted was returned to her.

That morning the marshal arrived with a crew from the *Eider*. They set to work clearing away debris, scrubbing floors and walls, and setting up beds in the parlor, library and chapel of the first floor. Paul Morton and the older boys washed the sewing room and white-washed it. They set about 72 panes of glass into repaired window panes. The girls did not return to the third floor but slept in every available corner: in the chapel, the library, the living room, and in the teachers' bedrooms. "We shall be glad when we have a new house," wrote Newhall at the conclusion of his account, "one and a half stories big of proper dimensions and with conveniences."

It should be equipped with electric lights, hot water heat and some fire hose. It was a good thing the water tank was put in last year for the water was needed and there was plenty of it. Mr. Strauss, the agent for the Alaska

JESSE LEE HOME, UNALASKA. *Left, the boys' house; center, girls' house (the original Jesse Lee Home); far right, dark with white trim, the public school. Photo by W. D. Weaver from E. Pelagia McCurdy, in the author's collection.*

Commercial Co., wired us that the company house and the Dutch Harbor hotel was at our disposal. It was very kind as the bedding was included but we did not need them.

The night after the fire, the United States marshal made a lot of ice cream and all the home folks were invited to call and they were treated to ice cream and cake and nuts. The smaller children thot the whole experience was a sort of holiday affair gotten up for their benefit. Such is child life—so care free— and they may well be so for the cares of life will be upon them soon enough.

In his next report Newhall became as emphatic as he ever was. "The time has come when Jesse Lee Home must be put on an up-to-date basis," he insisted. Construction of the needed buildings could not be postponed again. The 1920–21 annual report graphically described conditions.

The Mission plant consists of the following buildings: Jesse Lee Home; the boys' house; a building used as a barn and laundry combined; a chicken house; a power house for the electric light system; a shop and a boat house for the dory. Jesse Lee Home, the largest of the buildings, is in bad shape; as it stands it is neither safe nor suitable as a Mission building. It is hog-backed and leans toward the river. The third floor creaks and bends when one walks over it, and it is so old and so high that the strong wind racks it much. It is too high for this country. Since the fire it has not been considered safe to have the girls sleep on the third floor, and so they have been sleeping in all sorts of places— in the chapel, parlor, halls, play-rooms, in teachers' rooms, etc. For this reason a temporary sleeping barrack is being built for the girls. A new building should be built, having an up-to-date kitchen, dining room, and sewing room on the first floor, and dormitories and teachers' rooms on the second floor. As it stands now, the floors are in a wretched condition, and the dining room is so crowded that there is not elbow room. The boys' house was at first a dormitory and hospital—two wings being devoted to the latter work. But our increase in the number of boys has demanded the whole house, and then not too much room. At present Dr. Newhall has his office and sleeping room in it. Two of the teachers, with Paul Morton, also sleep here. There is only one room in which to care for the sick. New floors are absolutely necessary here.

The laundry, for a family of seventy, is worse than nothing. Certainly some modern methods of washing the clothes should be installed. When the clothes are ready to be dried, they are put into cracker boxes and carried up three flights of stairs and dried around small stoves. The teachers swelter and sweat, for there is hardly a week when the things can be dried out of doors. It means a big waste of energy, a waste of coal, and a fire risk as well.

For years he had urged the establishment of a hospital. The immediate pressure was lessened because the number of marine injuries and illnesses had diminished with fewer vessels on patrol in the aftermath of the war. In 1918 the teacher, Joseph Coleman, recommended a hospital be established under the Bureau of Indian Affairs. He called the present system of medical care "haphazard and unsatisfactory." Of necessity, Newhall could only respond to emergencies. Coleman felt that venereal diseases went untreated because of moral strictures and were, in fact, frequently diagnosed as tuberculosis. "Practically no treatment of venereal diseases is given," he wrote, "as the doctor is very much religiously inclined and gives these unfortunate people such lectures on their sin and immorality that very few of them ever attempt to obtain medical treatment."[14] Despite his statement that Newhall harangued patients suffering from venereal diseases, this is not supported by other testimony. The fact that he was a Methodist missionary within a religious community that disapproved even of dancing was probably enough to discourage visits by people with these diseases.

A 1921 report from the U.S. Coast Guard, written shortly after the fire, described conditions at the Home with 41 girls and 24 boys, praised Newhall for his humanitarian and medical work, and mentioned a possible new hospital.

> Dr. Newhall is a graduate of a medical institution and appears to be thoroughly competent to look after the ordinary cases of sickness and accident brought to his care. Being the only surgeon and doctor in connection with the Home, his work is very heavy, however, and if a Public Health Surgeon were assigned to the staff of the Commander, Bering Sea Patrol Force, this officer could be of material assistance to Dr. Newhall, especially in looking after cases brought to Unalaska by the Cutters for hospital and surgical treatment. The Home also maintains a relief station where sick and disabled seamen are cared for. Plans have been made for a new hospital building, which Dr. Newhall states will be of sufficient character to well care for any and all cases which might be brought there for treatment.[15]

Living among children supplied moments of diversion that must have helped the staff deal with crowded conditions and a series of great losses. Olive Smith was now the matron at the boys' dormitory. Dr. Newhall described her as "so jolly and full of life that the boys consider her 'one of them.'"[16] She delighted in her young charges and described the five smallest boys as "the nightgown brigade." They would assemble in her room every evening to get dressed for bed near her fire. After repeating "Now I Lay Me" they would cluster around for a story and a treat, "a few nuts or a bit of candy . . . or may chance a cookie, donated by the A.C. Co.'s cook, Sam, the Hawaiian."[17] Among this brigade was Benny Benson, who had the nickname "Brown Beans." "Such a sturdy little man he is," wrote Smith. "Whistles through his teeth when he talks, and he uses good, almost classical

English which he has learned, apparently, of Dr. Newhall and Miss Winchell. . . ." There was Benny's younger brother Charley [Carl], who had just moved from the girls' house to the boys' dormitory. Whooping cough had nearly killed him, but he was rallying. And there was Andy Peterson who, when asked his name, would reply in his piping voice, "Andrew-Peterson-high-boat-Nushagak-Kvichak-down-by-the-Wood-River." During a bout of whooping cough he had time for reflection, and he remarked to Smith, "Seems like most all the angels be ladies, don't they?" Smith was impressed by all the boys. "I have never been among a bunch of boys who use so little rough, coarse language and real swear words so seldom," she wrote, attributing this to the example set by Dr. Newhall.

Three-year-old Esther Carlson, however, could and did swear proficiently. Mary Winchell described her among several new girls who had arrived. She was "such a growler" who kept them laughing with her picturesque English.

> At first she would swear very fluently, kicking doors and swearing to be let in; but not hearing it, she has dropped it now. She is rather a nice-looking child and smiles sweetly when not growling. . . . She didn't want me to go to Huntsville and said: "I don't want you to go; I fraid I bin lose you." "Oh, no," I said, "you won't lose me." "But I bin lose my mamma at Sanak." "Well, your mamma died." "Yes, somebody bin kill her—somebody bin kill you." I tried to explain to her that no one killed her poor mother. She died last year suddenly, but I don't know that she was convinced.[18]

Six-year-old Alice Carlson loved to be around the doctor, whom she called "Dockie." He was cutting a boy's hair one day when she walked in. She said the teachers had told her to have him cut her hair, also. So he did—"greatly to my dissatisfaction," wrote Winchell. "The next day she wanted a ribbon on it, being quite vain, and I said, 'No; you had your hair cut; you can't wear a ribbon.' She looked in the glass and said, 'Dockie was kazy; I never wanted my hair so small as thats.'"

Edith Gavitt had arrived in September 1918 from the Kansas City Training School and served as matron, but in the summer of 1919 she became the cooking teacher. She enjoyed the change but missed regular contact with the smaller children. "It is no more drying day, darning day, mending day, etc., but bean day, fish day, etc." she wrote. "The problem isn't being able to cook and teach cooking so much as it is to know how to make the most of the requisitioned supplies, for there are many things we do not have, and all are so expensive up here."[19] She left in the fall of 1920.[20]

Ellen Coughlin Keeler completed a history of the first 40 years of the Woman's Home Missionary Society in 1920. She was a graduate of Wellesley College and the wife of the director of publicity for the Board of Home Missions and Church Extensions. When *The Balance Wheel* was published by the society, readers interested in the Jesse Lee Home were given a chaotic survey of events embroidered with imaginary details.[21] It is impossible to distinguish fact from fiction. The first year of the public school under John Tuck and the opening of the Tucks' own home to a few girls were summarized in the sentence, "The first Home filled up in three weeks with the child aristocrats of the place, one-half of whom were the grandchildren of the former Greek priest." According to Keeler, the Unga cottage was built at Unalaska and filled with girls "packed in like sardines in a box." Anna Beiler's visit was eulogized with florid passages from her reports merged into single sentences: "Once their homes were holes in the ground, now they are in a safe place, yet human wolves from whale ships and war vessels come and gaze in the windows or try to talk through cracks and knot-holes in the fence." Even Beiler would have known the men could have talked *over* the fence. Bits of information from Dr. Newhall's reports were spliced into paragraphs. The doctor and his wife appeared to be the only staff members from 1900 to 1920. She discussed the transition for girls from the Home to adult life, suggesting difficulties arose only after the superintendent of the Carlisle Indian School refused to take any more children because he wanted only full-blooded Indians and the Aleuts, she wrote, were of Japanese origin. The solution, according to her history, lay in teaching girls Aleut basketry. Near the conclusion of her section on the Home, she wrote that because of the war, mail was infrequent and the cost of living was high. This "presented a serious problem for Alaska." Consequently, the society faced an urgent situation and placed Alaska "in its special survey and reconstruction program."

. .

IN FEBRUARY 1921 measles swept into the village and afflicted 170 people. Hilda Lee, an older girl who had shown great promise, died on the 11th from tuberculosis with complications of bronchial pneumonia and hemorrhaging of the lungs. She and Paul Morton had grown close and were, for all purposes, engaged. Paul had been a student in the Home before joining the staff as the person "who makes things go—the motorboat, the electric dynamo, the pumping plant." Newhall wrote, "He can use tools, make and repair things. He wired the buildings for electric lights, and when the button was turned all the lights came on. Yes, Paul is the doctor's right-hand man."[22]

The year held quiet joy as well. As a preface, Emma Supernaw and Mary Winchell visited A.B. Somerville and his wife, the former Polly Dirks, after the couple returned from three years at Attu. The Somervilles were living in a small house by the Iliuliuk River. The Home women admired the down blanket tucked around two sleeping babies. Both Winchell and Supernaw had hopes of eventually securing enough eiderdown to make a quilt, but Captain Somerville merely laughed when they asked to purchase some. "I won't sell it," he said, "but I'll tell you what I will do." He looked at the two 40-ish spinsters and continued, "I will give enough down for a quilt to the one who is first married."

In September 1921 Dr. Newhall and Emma Supernaw boarded a vessel for the 800-mile trip to Kodiak. On September 26 they were married by the Baptist minister in the

DR. NEWHALL AT THE UNALASKA DOCK. *Courtesy of the Unalaska City School District (Clara Cook Collection).*

EMMA SUPERNAW NEWHALL. *From Annie Swanson Hatch's album, courtesy of the Hatch family.*

Baptist chapel on Woody Island. "There was an aisle of evergreen from the door to the altar," wrote Newhall. "The chapel was prettily decorated. While the ceremony was going on a phonograph tweedled out 'Loves Sweet Lay.'" They had been told that following the ceremony they should stroll slowly down the aisle "so the folks could see what the bride had on." A stately wedding march would accompany them. The young woman in charge of the phonograph, however, got "flustered." She put on a fox trot. "And we went out of that chapel," wrote the doctor, "with a hop, skip and a jump."[23] At a prayer service the next morning, the minister said, "Let us now sing hymn number 374, 'The Fight is On.'" Emma Newhall burst out laughing.[24]

When Captain Somerville eventually came to call at the Home and offer his congratulations, Winchell tactfully reminded him of his promise. He merely smiled. The Somervilles had a reputation for thrift. Dr. Newhall described them as "tight as bark on a tree." The captain was "precious" for his down, as Winchell said the local expression went, and was reluctant to surrender any. Eventually Winchell received a paper bag filled with delicate down. The new Mrs. Newhall, however, opened a bulging pillow slip to find it stuffed with wild goose feathers. Everyone had a good laugh, and "Mrs. Doctor," as Winchell referred to Emma, used the feathers to stuff pillows.[25]

In the spring of 1922 the newlyweds were given an entertainment in their honor at the Home. Clara Goss, "at the eleventh hour, wishing to have something brand new, and typically Alaskan," sat down with one of the schoolteachers and wrote a song for the occasion. "Dear Alaska" was set to the tune "Virginia" and was so enjoyed that Goss wrote to the commissioner of education suggesting it might be used as a state song until something better appeared.[26]

"Just one year ago today we were married," Newhall wrote to Clara Cook Lawrence that fall. "And we aint sorry that we were—think we will try living another year together and don't contemplate a divorce. It has been a very happy year indeed."[27]

The staff in 1922 consisted of Olive Smith, practical nurse and boys' matron; Mary Winchell, girls' matron; Marie McLeod, sewing teacher; Estella McMillen, cooking teacher; Clara Goss, fancywork and music; Emma Supernaw Newhall, knitting teacher and general helper; and Nels Drugg, ivory-work teacher and general repairman. The 63 children, 24 boys and 39 girls, ranged in age from 6 months to 16 years. It was a congenial staff, although McMillen, at 64, found cooking for the crowd a bit difficult. That year there was $4,000 in the fund for a new chapel.[28]

In 1923 a territorial school was approved and both Dr. Newhall and Nicholas Bolshanin were elected to the school board.[29] In February Clara Goss wrote the commissioner recommending her sister-in-law, Flora Goss Willis, as principal. A widow with 35 years experience as a teacher, Willis had worked in Vermont, New York, and Virginia. She was hired. In April, as the last term of the government school was coming to a close,

87 students were enrolled. Goss expected more than 100 when the territorial school opened in the fall. "It is understood locally," Clara wrote to the territorial commissioner of education, "that all the children of the community will attend. Dr. Newhall is planning to send all of the Mission children and it is a certainty that no children would attend the Gov. school if they could by attending the Territorial school be classed as 'Whites'. It is understood now that the Gov. school will discontinue altogether."[30]

NOTES

1. *WHM*. June 1920:6.

2. Danford, Agnes. Annual Report, 1918–19. NARA, RG 75, Incoming Correspondence. Unalaska.

3. Newhall, "Christmas at Jesse Lee Home, Unalaska," *WHM*, June 1920:5.

4. H.C. Jennings to Alaska Commercial Company. May 6, 1919. Jesse Lee Home Correspondence, Unalaska City School District. Edith Newhall Drugg wrote, "The monetary support for the Jesse Lee Home was a 'sure thing.' The missionaries got paid $50.00 per month plus their room and board. They were well supported by the 'Woman's Home Missionary Society' of the Methodist Church. . . ." (Letter to Ray Hudson, Oct. 26, 1978.)

5. *WHM*. August 1919:1.

6. Their two children were Jennie Belle and Joseph Para. (Edith Newhall Drugg letter to Ray Hudson, Oct. 26, 1978.)

7. Woman's Home Missionary Society. Reports from Bureaus. 1919–20:146.

8. *WHM*. June 1921:5.

9. *WHM*. June 1920:5.

10. *WHM*. June 1920:9.

11. Newhall's account is undated, but a letter from Edith Gavitt dates the fire to Monday, January 11, in either 1919 or 1920. January 11 fell on a Monday in 1920. An unnamed newspaper article about the fire in the Eva Alvery Richards *Scrapbook #2, 1918–1933*, is dated Feb. 21, 1920. (Archives of the Arctic and Polar Regions Collections of the Elmer E. Rasmuson Library at the University of Alaska Fairbanks.)

12. For a detailed account of the money rescue, see Winchell's *Where the Wind Blows Free*, 83–91.

13. *WHM*. June 1921:6.

14. Coleman, Joseph. Annual school report. NARA, RG 75, Alaska Division, General Correspondence. Unalaska, FY 1917–18.

15. NARA, RG 26. Box 1849.

16. *WHM*. June 1921:6.

17. *WHM*. June 1920:6.

18. Winchell, Mary. Letter to Karl Winchell and Clara Cook Lawrence. Undated. *WHM*, June 1920:7–8.

19. *WHM*. June 1920:8–9.

20. Newhall to Mrs. Lawrence (Clara Cook). Oct. 2, 1920. Alaska State Library. MS 106.

21. Keeler. *The Balance Wheel*, 117–25.

22. *WHM*. June 1921:6.

23. Newhall to Simeon Oliver, Oct. 4, 1927. Alaska Missionary Conference Commission on Archives and History.

24. Newhall to Mr. and Mrs. Lawrence. Sept. 30, 1927. Alaska State Library. MS 106.

25. Winchell, *Home by the Bering Sea*, 206–09.

26. Goss to Henderson, April 17, 1922. Alaska State Archives. RG 05, RS 01, Box AS4477. Folder: Unalaska 1921–1932; 4586-62. The song appears in Volume II of *Family After All*.

27. Newhall to Mrs. C.A. Lawrence. Sept. 26, 1922. Alaska State Library. MS 106.

28. Ibid.

29. John Carpenter received a "certificate of promotion" from the Department of Education, Territory of Alaska, for successfully completing the eighth grade at Unalaska, dated June 30, 1923. This entitled him "to enter any High School in the Territory without examination." Copy accompanying letter from John Carpenter to Ray Hudson, July 21, 1978.

30. Clara Goss to L.D. Henderson, Commissioner of Education, Juneau. April 21, 1923.

In this photograph taken from Cemetery Hill, the Jesse Lee Home buildings are nearest the camera. From the original caption: "VIEW OF TOWN OF UNALASKA, ALASKA, with U.S. flag flying from one building, Russian Orthodox Church in far center background, and pier in far right background with vessel docked there. Photo taken during National Geographic Society expedition on the way to Katmai area, 1918." Courtesy of the Consortium Library, University of Alaska Anchorage, Archives & Manuscripts Dept. (National Geographic Society, Katmai Expeditions Photographs, 1913-1919, Jasper Dean Sayre, photographer; hmc-0186-volume4-3864.)

Departures

THE WOMAN'S HOME MISSIONARY SOCIETY FINALLY RECEIVED TITLE to the Unalaska property via a deed granted by the U.S. government on Oct. 15, 1923.[1] Membership in the Methodist church had grown to almost 60, of whom 23 were older children in the Home. That year saw several changes to the staff. Mary Winchell and Marie McLeod left. Winchell had completed 12 years of service. Nellie DonCarlos took her place as matron at the girls' dormitory. McMillen, Smith, and Drugg remained, and Ida Young arrived to help in the boys' building. Mrs. Ethel Robbins became the sewing teacher and Emily Morgan took the position of nurse. Albert and Emma Newhall went on a year's sabbatical, accompanied by Chester and Edith. The captain of the Coast Guard cutter *Haida* noted, "The Doctor's departure left Unalaska without the presence of Medical aid, except such as might be offered by the Cutters when in port."[2] Edith, now 20, had become a fine pianist and organist and had taught school at Unalaska for the 1922-1923 term.[3]

The Newhalls' replacements for the year were J.C. Dorwin and his wife. On Alaska Day, 1923, J.C. Dorwin represented the "future" in a school program that included U.S. deputy commissioner Bolshanin as the "present" and Father Orloff as the "past."

On August 2, after a trip to Alaska, President Warren G. Harding died in San Francisco. Three days later the Home hosted a community-wide memorial service. The chapel was draped with bunting and there was a display of articles and flags. Men from the Bering Sea Patrol attended and the office log noted that the village population turned out "en masse." Flags in the village were at half-staff and the village was "in mourning." But not for long—on August 9 a visiting ship from San Francisco entertained the children at the Home with photographs of South Africa and music by the saxophone sextet the Brown Brothers.[4]

The Newhalls attended the annual meeting of the WHMS, Oct. 10–16, 1923, in Sioux City, Iowa. They reunited with Jennie Alexander, who was in nursing school there. Dr. Newhall was able to provide an accurate description of the Home, detailing the necessity for a new girls' dormitory. He emphasized once again the urgent need for a hospital. "All who come to the Jesse Lee Home," a report on the meeting stated, "commend its work, but not its buildings and equipment."[5]

At a meeting in January 1924, the Board of Trustees decided to build a hospital and chapel at Unalaska. The dormitory would be repaired enough to make it comfortable, but replacement would have to wait for sufficient funds.[6] In the spring "the lumber for a new hospital, church, and dormitory will be sent on the first boat that goes direct to Unalaska," declared the annual report. "The need is very great for these buildings and we are sure [they] will be greatly appreciated by all the workers, the children and the village people as well."[7]

After the meeting in Iowa, the Newhalls continued on to West Chazy, New York, to visit Emma's family. While there, Edith wrote to Nels Drugg intending to call an end to the budding romance between them. Edith had other suitors, but Nels was persistent. In the spring he caught a ship to Seattle where he met Albert and Emma, on their way back to Unalaska. Dr. Newhall did his best to remain noncommittal. Either encouraged or stubborn, Nels went north to Prince Rupert and then took the Canadian railroad east to West Chazy. "I do not think she could do to his face what she did by letter," wrote Newhall to Simeon Oliver.[8] Before the Newhalls had heard anything, Edith and Nels were married. She dropped her plans for attending a teacher's college, applied for a job at Unalaska, and the newlyweds arrived. "All's well that ends well," wrote her father. "They seem very happy together and as you say Edith likes a home and will make a good wife."

Back at Unalaska, the Newhalls were joined by Isabelle Knapp, the new matron for the girls, and Pauline Collins, the boys' matron. When the staff received a report of the society's annual meeting held in October 1924, they were astonished to learn that plans had been drawn up for a new orphanage in a new location.[9] "The reason given for finally moving the home to Seward," wrote Edith Drugg, "was that it would be cheaper to run in a less isolated place, with lower freight rates than to Unalaska." She went on to add that her father "was not in favor of the transfer. He felt the *need* was in Unalaska as it was more central to the huge area of the Aleutian Islands, north to Point Barrow and Herschell Island and as afar as Chignik to the east."[10] At the beginning of December 1924, Newhall wrote to Simeon Oliver.

> Now another surprise—"The powers that be" at the annual meeting decided that Jesse Lee Home in Unalaska should be no more and I have been officially notified to that effect. Another home will mayhap be built out some five or so miles on the railroad from Seward and some of these children transferred there. Mr. Bolshanin is quite peeved and intends to try and get the prespbterians [sic] to come in here. No orphanage will be here, but they will just have a man and wife maybe and services.[11]

Newhall felt he would not be considered for the Seward job because the town already had a physician who could be paid $300 a year to treat children at the Home. "Our work is very evidently finished here," he told his former student. "We are very minus on dough but must look elsewhere." The society hoped that he would remain at Unalaska as a local minister. "We did not wish to see the children taken from the place," he wrote, "and we be left like two old coots on the beach."[12] He applied to the Presbyterian Board of Missions and accepted a position at Barrow. Dr. Spence, the Newhalls' replacement back in 1908, called at mission headquarters in New York and highly recommended them. Spence had served the Presbyterian church in Alaska from 1916 to 1921.

The relocation of the Home would have a tremendous effect on the local school, cutting enrollment and teaching staff by half. Flora Goss Willis heard the news through a letter written by Louis Strauss of the A.C. Co. to Clara Goss. He had learned of the anticipated move while wintering in San Francisco. At first, Willis thought no move would be possible until the summer of 1926. However, on March 10, 1925, she learned that the transfer to Seward would take place the coming summer. "This is decided," she informed the commissioner. "Everyone here regrets that the Mission is to be moved," she wrote on May 20. "It will leave the school very small and un-interesting."

Dr. Newhall had been elected to the school board in October. Unfortunately, this position heightened the stress of his last months at Unalaska. He had a running battle with Flora Willis. They disagreed on almost everything, from school holidays to discipline to teacher qualifications. Clara Goss sided with her sister-in-law, crediting the doctor's behavior to his personality and to "his ignorance." She had not been impressed with Edith Newhall's teaching and wrote to the commissioner forestalling any thought he might have had of hiring the young woman permanently. "She has returned as Mrs. Drugg," wrote Goss on July 26, 1924, "and I think you ought to know that as a teacher she is absolutely useless." Dr. Newhall wanted to hire only teachers who did not dance. The commissioner attempted to bring the two warring parties together. "Ability to refrain from dancing," Henderson wrote, "may or may not be a virtue."[13] There was no happy medium to be found. In the end, all four teachers left during the summer, and an entirely new staff of two arrived.

In early 1925 Newhall wrote a valedictory letter which he sent to many who knew him. The lines of each of the six paragraphs were indented so that the text as he typed it resembled poetry. The first paragraph reads:

> Owing to official notice—moving the home and other changes
> Resignation from this work takes effect by May of the present year.
> This closes a service of 30 years by the Newhalls. A.W.N. 27 yrs.
> The next field of labor is Point Barrow.
> The most northerly point in North America.
> The land of ice and snow—land of the midnight sun.
> Six months night and six months day
> We will get there about evening.
> Good Night.

He looked on his new job as:

> "A fine chance to preach the gospel.
>   A fine chance to give out pills.
>   A fine chance to pull teeth.
>   A fine chance to scratch."

"Our courage is good," he concluded. "We are happy. Who should worry[?] 'Ask of me and I will give thee the heathen for an inheritance and the uttermost parts of the earth for thy possession.' When 20 years old that was our petition––It is granted."[14]

Gordon Gould, most moderate of men, described the decision to move the Home as a "selfish mistake" on the part of the WHMS. He described Newhall as "a saint of God if ever there was one." In 1950 he wrote, "It was a sorry day for the boys and girls of the Aleutian Islands when the Woman's Home Missionary Society refused to accept his judgments and ideals for these people. But God makes even the selfish mistakes of Mission Boards to praise Him. . . ." The doctor had written to him, quoting the "Ask of me . . ." verse and adding, "I have asked Him and my inheritance is great."[15]

After the Newhalls packed their belongings, they had to wait several weeks for a ship.[16] On March 28 Albert wrote to several friends.

> Ere this reaches you, we will have resigned from this work, packed up our baggage, and be on the *Herman*, bound for Point Barrow for the next four years. The society on receiving our resignations, or rather Alaskan Committee, offered a raise of 600 per year; repairs on the house, buy a house—put up a hospital— let us use the $1400 chapel fund—a mixed wire. Money did not influence us—our work here is done—with the moving of the home—but honest we hate to leave the boys and girls—especially the boys and hope the next man will be good to them and love them—and we hate to leave the cat. . . .[17]

When the *Chas. Brower* arrived (not the *Herman*), two of the older boys took their luggage to the dock: three trunks with clothing and bedding; an old suitcase with medical supplies; a bundle of papers wrapped up in a parka; a barrel of fine dishes; a box of books; a portable typewriter; a barrel of salted cod.

"Never mind the farewells," wrote the doctor. "The children were sad to have us go and we sure did not want to leave them."

On May 7 they boarded the three-masted vessel. The teachers and children from the Home accompanied them, inspected the ship, said their farewells, and wished them a safe trip. The next morning Edith and Nels Drugg stood for hours on the wharf until the ship finally pulled away from the dock at 11 a.m. As it passed along the front beach the

Newhalls saw folks waving goodbye—workers at the A.C. Co., the Orthodox priest, Ole Quean, Nick and Olga Bolshanin, people from the town and boys from the Home.[18] The buildings of the Jesse Lee Home had long dominated the eastern end of the village. As the *Chas. Brower* turned north, the two largest buildings, the girls' and boys' dormitories, gradually receded.[19]

For two days the ship tossed and rolled. Crawling into their bunks they discovered the beds had no springs. On the third day, May 10, they reached the ice floes and immediately the seasickness stopped. "As far as one could see an undulating expanse of snow white glistening ice in fragments from two feet to six feet thick." The *Chas. Brower* had a cast iron shoe on the bow to buck the ice. In the evenings the Newhalls heard the cook in the galley singing. One hymn recalled to Albert his earliest days in missionary work: "Come ye that love the Lord and let your joys be known," it began. Each verse ended with the triumphant refrain, "We are marching to Zion, beautiful, beautiful Zion. We are marching upward to Zion, the beautiful city of God." The second verse contained the lines, "That rides upon the stormy sky/ And calms the roaring seas."

· · ·

CLOSING THE HOME was a tremendous undertaking. For weeks the staff and children sorted the accumulation of 35 years. Clothes were given to people in the village and sent to Nikolski and Biorka villages. "We gave away and threw away from early in August until late in September," recalled Isabelle Knapp. "Some of the old clothes . . . surely must have dated back to Noah's time."[20] On September 20, the Rev. A.M. Lambert and his wife arrived and took charge of the mission. There was still hope that a chapel would be built. They would minister to the small congregation and do whatever they could to promote good works. Four days later, Ethel Steele Robbins and 25 boys boarded the *Bear* for a six-day voyage to Seward. A report from Captain Jacobs named the students: John Wanka Andre, Charles Nelson, Aleck Cann, Charles Carlson, Ephraim Kalmakoff, William Lyons, Benjamin Benson, Nick Heidel, Mike Kalmakoff, Fred Pestrikoff, Andrew Peterson, Carl Rosenberg, Mike Riley, Carl Benson, William Anderson, Harry Olsen, Steven Paulson, Nick Gardiner, Charles Peterson, Joseph Bean, John Balumatoff, Steven Kristensen, Inikenti Kalmakoff, Stanley Kristensen, and John Carlson.

John Carlson had entered the Home only two days earlier. He was the last of more than 317 children to have been enrolled since the first girls arrived in 1890.[21]

The Newhalls would have been pleased to know that the Home's favorite cat was carried aboard. However, at Seward the trained nurse would not hear of a cat living in the dormitory and so, as Dr. Newhall later learned, it made the long voyage "back to Unalaska and to jail where it lives with Mrs. Ross."[22] She was, as noted earlier, Marie McLeod who had a long association with the Home.

The 35 girls and the rest of the staff went aboard the Coast Guard cutter *Haida* two days later. At 11 a.m. on Saturday, September 26, they steamed out of Unalaska Bay and past Priest Rock. With all but five of the girls seasick, the captain did his best to make good time. Instead of a week for the trip, he brought the cutter into Seward in three or four days.

. .

WHEN MARY WINCHELL was writing *Home by the Bering Sea*, published in 1951, she used the formation of a Red Cross chapter in 1918 to contrast Seward and Unalaska. She had Dr. Newhall say that "Seward *was* a good base station for that part of the country, but that the Aleutian Islands should also be recognized. . . . Surely, this village is of some importance, since it is the last port of call for the mail boat, and, in summer, the headquarters of the Bering Sea Fleet."[23] Winchell went on to confess that she had doubts. No one knew where the Aleutian Islands were, let alone Unalaska, and once told they soon forgot. In 1967, 89 years old and essentially blind, she wrote to Dorothy Jones that she had published her two books because the Home had been moved to Seward "and I feared that our good life in the Children's home would soon be forgotten."[24] Built upon that past, new adventures were beginning for the children and for the Newhalls.

On his 54th birthday, Feb. 6, 1926, Newhall wrote to Simeon Oliver announcing that Emma had given birth to a son on December 4. Warren Blake Newhall began losing weight, but by six weeks he was again at his birth weight. Newhall had hope that his son would be healthy. He recalled how when he himself was born an old woman had declared him to be "only a few crows legs with a piece of skin tied over it." But now, he laughingly told Simeon, he was "fat enough, at least in one place." Edith Drugg had given birth to a daughter a few months earlier at Unalaska. Virginia Isabelle was named after "grandma Supernaw" and the Newhalls' son took the grandmother's maiden name. But on April 23, 1926, Newhall wrote to Clara Cook Lawrence, "Our little boy Warren Blake died very suddenly—we did so love the little one."

Plans were being made for a family vacation trip in 1929. Edith and her daughter would meet her father and stepmother in Seattle and travel east "visiting on the way as we were wont to do in times past and that will delight us."[25] Edith and Nels Drugg were living in Sitka where Nick Bolshanin had helped Nels find work at the local power house. The vacation would give the Newhalls time to do things they had been holding in abeyance. Newhall had been told by Presbyterian officials that the Presbytery of Yukon hoped he would visit Fairbanks or Anchorage where he would be ordained to the ministry.[26] He also needed extensive dental work and a thorough medical checkup. Since a severe cold a year earlier he had experienced difficulty breathing. He described his condition as having "a whole family of cats and kittens within by spells."

Asthma is in our family but this does not act like the spasm asthma. At times the wind is short and I would like to have the heart examined as well. Thot I would go to the Presbyterian hospital in Seattle while passing thru and see what they think about it. Mrs. Newhall has the asthma since childhood and we don't make much progress in a head wind except to grunt and blow.[27]

Always young at heart, the doctor sympathized with a young nephew who was trying to decide what to do in life. "When I was a boy I didn't know just which I wanted to be most," he wrote, "a doctor, a minister or a clown in the circus. The last struck me best and I made a clown suit from an old striped shawl my mother gave me. I was always getting up shows. Even now I like to get up entertainments with children and put the boys thru some stunts."[28]

He told his nephew in December 1928 that this was perhaps the last letter from Barrow as he and Emma would be leaving for West Chazy, New York, in the spring. They would stay a year and then return to Alaska, but not to Barrow—"to another place and more isolated." In July he had informed A.J. Montgomery of the mission board that he and Emma would be willing to go to St. Lawrence Island. Each year people from St. Lawrence Island stopped by on a whaler and asked when the doctor and his wife would move to their island in the Bering Sea. He still, of course, missed Unalaska. "Unalaska was a beautiful place especially in summer," he reminisced. "I never saw grass so green nor so many flowers and berries. Here there are no flowers; no nice green grass but we do have plenty of snow, ice, dogs and polar bears."[29]

On the last day of 1928 Dr. Newhall wrote, "It was glorious red at the horizon this morning so we know that in three weeks or so the sun will rise again. Just now the days are dark but fine moonlight." The sun was back when he fell critically ill in mid-March. The pioneering commercial pilot Noel Wien attempted to bring in a plane to evacuate him to Fairbanks, but weather intervened as it so often does in Alaska. Albert Warren Newhall died on March 17, 1929. He was 57. Emma arranged for his burial beside their infant son.[30]

Mary Winchell was in Seattle at the Catherine Blaine Home preparing dinner for a group of basketball-playing Japanese boys when she heard the news over the radio. She found she couldn't visualize him dying at Barrow. She could only see him at Unalaska. "All day I kept thinking of him in so many places where I had seen him at work," she wrote in a beautiful tribute, "—digging clams on cold, dark nights, with other teachers and children, at Agnes Beach when the tide was out; lanterns flickering, gunny sack of clams—tide coming in—home in the boat."[31]

I could see the Doctor with the boys, cutting and loading hay into the boat at Margaret Bay for the silo, getting it out of the boat and up the rocky beach, where we all carried it into the barn, Doctor directing the work and telling amusing incidents of the day.

I thought of him with teachers and children, going in the motor boat, with a trailer behind, to Ruff's Bay for blueberries to can and dry. We often brought back two hundred quarts. Going always with the big boys at four, Monday mornings, to the laundry, and often that was not easy, with the storms from the Bering Sea rolling over us.

Then she shifted tenses as though his death were not real.

I can see him now, cutting up fish to can; working in the garden; leading the Sunday school; drilling the choir; preaching at the afternoon service, with the rows of little ones in front, the older ones next, and the visitors at the right. I can so clearly hear him sing "I love to tell the story," and lead the children in reciting the first Psalm.

Winchell recalled his medical work, most frequently for patients too poor to pay, and how the rug had been rolled back many times to make room for the operating table. Births and burials came to her mind. She remembered the Christmas programs, the children's parties, and how "on stormy days it was his task to take care of a roomful of noisy little boys, studying Latin or French at the same time." Near the end of her tribute, she paused to say, "It is hard for us who lived and worked there, where our lives were so full of joy and sorrow, to write about Doctor Newhall. We do not know what to leave out."

Charlie Nelson had lived at the Home since he was five. Now in Seward and 19 he wrote an appreciation for the Home's newspaper. The doctor, he said, was "easy to look at for he most always had a smile." Always meticulously organized, the doctor could get any job completed by his sheer will. Nelson recalled the construction of two additions to the storehouse. "Doctor was no carpenter," he wrote, "but by will power and head work he managed to build those additions and in the end was quite proud of them." In front of a large piling or driftwood log he would figure silently and then assign each boy so many pieces of wood to split. His calculations were always correct. He was "a man among men, with a heart as big as himself." He was also someone who always seemed to have extra fish hooks on hand for boys. "But he would make this bargain," wrote Nelson. "For every hook we were to give him a fish." And so, "happiness was ours and also his."

"So far I have said very little about our beloved Doctor," wrote Simeon Oliver in his 1941 memoir, "but that is not because of any lack of admiration. He was, and still remains, the man on whom, if I had the strength of character, I would model my life. He was a lovable little fellow, filled to the brim with vitality and talents. He was a New Englander of the best type, dry, witty and with something of that intellectual grandeur that once made Concord the mental capital of the world."[32]

A handy man to have around the house was Doctor. He could put in new plumbing or whip out an old appendix with equal dexterity, meanwhile conversing in French, Latin or Russian if the occasion required. From the operating room he could go straight to the piano and soothe our savage little souls with the classical music of all the world. He was doctor, teacher, priest and father to all of us and to half the people within a radius of hundreds of miles.

Oliver recalled how Newhall "never stressed doctrine." This was a lesson he had learned at Unalaska. "All he asked," wrote Oliver, "was that you be honest and loyal and have faith." He remembered the doctor's "humorous humility" and how he used to say, "The greatest service I have performed for humanity is pulling teeth."

The man who had been, in the words of Anfesia Shapsnikoff, "a friend and a doctor and a father to children that were here from all over Alaska" was gone.

"I was with your father in his last days," wrote a government employee to Chester Newhall, "and I never have met a finer Christian gentleman. He died as he had lived, thinking not of himself but of others. Even while he was gasping for breath and with but a few hours to live he insisted that he be allowed to prescribe medicine which would save the life of a poor Eskimo baby. My boy, this man of God has left you an heritage worth more than all the riches of this world."[33]

Of all the deaths at the Jesse Lee Home, Hilda Lee's had touched Mary Winchell deepest. She thought of the young woman as she reflected on Dr. Newhall's death.

> I remember . . . when our beautiful young Hilda was dying of tuberculosis. She was restless and did so want to live. She suddenly prayed to live; then called out, "Doctor, do you think God will save me?" and the Doctor answered quietly, "We are all of us safe in God's hands, Hilda." "I know," said Hilda, and was quiet and went to sleep. . . .
>
> It is hard to think of his dying so far from his old work at Unalaska, so far from his beloved children, and old home in New England. But he loved his work, too, at Barrow, Alaska, and, as he said to Hilda, "We are all of us safe in God's hands."

NOTES

1. Patent No. 920768, signed by President Calvin Coolidge. Third Judicial District. Misc. Records, Vol. 3:322–24. On June 7, 1941, the WHMS, principal office in Cincinnati, Ohio, gave a quit claim deed to the Board of Home Missions and Church Extension of the Methodist Episcopal Church for their property at Unalaska for $10.00. (pp. 324–26) On Aug. 11, 1941, J. Dean King was granted power of attorney for land at Unalaska by the Board of Home Missions.

2. NARA, Pacific Alaska Region. RG 26. U.S. Coast Guard. Records of the Bering Sea Patrol, 1926–40 (1923) Log of the *Haida*.

3. The year she taught, the school was administered by the Bureau of Indian Affairs. (Edith Drugg letter to Ray Hudson, Oct. 9, 1977.)

4. Log, *Office Bering Sea Patrol Force*. 1923. G.C. Carmine, Commanding. NARA. RG 26. ARC 297162.

5. *WHM*. December 1923:19.

6. *WHM*. March 1924.

7. Woman's Home Missionary Society. Report from Bureaus. 1922–23:171.

8. Newhall to Simeon Oliver, Dec. 4, 1924. Alaska Missionary Conference Commission on Archives and History.

9. *WHM*. March 1925:13

10. Edith Newhall Drugg to Ray Hudson, Oct. 26, 1978.

11. Newhall to Simeon Oliver, Dec. 4, 1924. Alaska Missionary Conference Commission on Archives and History.

12. Newhall to "Dear Friends," Bering Sea, Alaska. June 3, 1925. Alaska State Historical Library. MS 106.

13. Henderson to Willis. Dec. 16, 1924. Alaska State Archives. RG 05, RS 01, Box AS4477. Folder: Unalaska 1921–32.

14. Alaska State Historical Library. MS 3, box 2, item 12.

15. Gould, *The Fisherman's Son*, 35–37.

16. Newhall. "The Trip—Unalaska to Barrow. 1925," Alaska State Historical Library. MS 106.

17. Newhall to "Dear Friend," March 28, 1925. Courtesy of Virginia Drugg.

18. Coincidentally, on this same day a news story left Unalaska that said word had arrived praising Emily Morgan, a former nurse at the Home and now a Red Cross nurse, as "the heroine of the Nome diphtheria epidemic." The story reported that this was no surprise to local people as for 18 months Morgan had worked with the only doctor within hundreds of miles braving "the blizzards of these Aleutian islands to bring gladness into the dingy homes of the natives." The article said she had also been the matron of the Home maintained "for destitute waifs." She had been there when Alice Devlin arrived after surviving her mother's horrible killing by dogs, and she had "nursed her back to health." "Nurse Makes Heroic Record in Alaska." *The Washington Post*. June 7, 1925:SO8.

19. The boys' building has survived to the present time. It is now owned by Coe and Phyllis Whittern. The girls' dorm was torn down in July 1926. The school purchased the "beaver board" that covered the walls and ceiling in one of the rooms and used it to repair the school classrooms. (Clara Lambert to Henderson, Aug. 2, 1926. Alaska State Archives. RG 05, RS 01, Box AS4477. Folder: Unalaska 1921–32.)

20. "Reminiscences." 1932–33 *Kueuit* yearbook.

21. See Appendix for initial enrollments by year.

22. Newhall to Simeon Oliver. Feb. 5, 1926. Alaska Missionary Conference Commission on Archives and History.

23. Winchell, *Home by the Bering Sea*, 98.

24. Mary Winchell to Dorothy Jones, Pasadena, Calif., Sept. 22, 1967. Copy provided by Dorothy Jones.

25. Newhall to Simeon Oliver, Oct. 4, 1927. Alaska Missionary Conference Commission on Archives and History.

26. A.J. Montgomery to Newhall, Feb. 4, 1928. PHS. RG 301.3. Box 2, Folder 48.

27. Newhall to A.J. Montgomery, Dec. 4, 1928. PHS. RG 301.3. Box 2, Folder 48.

28. Newhall. Letter to "Dear friend Frank," Dec. 12, 1928. Alaska State Library. MS 106.

29. Newhall. Letter to Frank Newhall, Feb. 6, 1928. Alaska State Library. MS 106.

NOTES

30. In the spring she returned to her family home in West Chazy, New York, near the Canadian border, where she lived until 1971.

31. *WHM*. November 1929:11.

32. Oliver, *Son of the Smoky Sea*, 35–36.

33. This was from a Mr. Vincent and was read to me by Edith Drugg during an interview on Feb. 13, 1976. She thought he was a school teacher.—R.H. It is also found in a tribute written by Elmer Newhall, a brother to the doctor. Lowder, *A Great Physician*, 195.

DR. ALBERT W. NEWHALL SHARED *his love of music with the children at the Jesse Lee Home, and "There's a Wideness in God's Mercy" is said to have been his favorite hymn. Written by a former Anglican clergyman who converted to Catholicism, the song has been in the Methodist repertoire for generations. Four of the dozen verses written by Frederick William Faber in 1854 appear in the current hymnal, with a melody composed in 1878 by a young New Englander named Lizzie Tourjée, for her high school graduation. It seems altogether a fitting coda to the first half of the Jesse Lee story. —J.P.*

There's a Wideness in God's Mercy

Children Enrolled in the Jesse Lee Home
1890-1925

THERE IS NO DEFINITIVE LIST OF CHILDREN who attended the Jesse Lee Home at Unalaska. Following is a compilation of two sets of index cards in the archives of Alaska Children's Services in Anchorage: "Register by Number" cards and individual file cards. No attempt has been made to standardize the spelling of names, which sometimes varies between entries (i.e., Gromoff for Grumoff, etc.). In this compilation, numerals and primary name spellings are from the "Register by Number" list. Alternate spellings from individual cards are in [brackets]. A date in **bold type** indicates that the year of entrance on the individual card differed from the numerical order. There is a third list of children among Dr. Newhall's undated manuscripts. Titled "Jesse Lee Home Children 1895—" it ends with children who entered in 1912. Names that appear on his list are underlined. Underlined names without numerals and marked with an asterisk are entries that appear only on his list.

From other records it is known that Taissa and Ludmilla Prokopioff of Attu were the first girls to enter the Home in 1890. However, the "Register by Number" lists them as numbers 13 and 14. Of the 17 girls who were subjects of Tuck's 1890 petition for guardianship (see chapter 2), 12 are not on any of the three lists: Anna Ignatieff, Eudokia Krukoff, Hortina [?] Krukoff, Priscilla Krukoff, Maria Lochnikoff, Maria Popoff, Antonina Serebernikoff, Glykeria Serebernikoff, Alexandra Sovoroff, Zoya Tutiakoff, Katarina Repin, and Olga Repin. No doubt the names of other children are missing. Pelagia Dyakanoff McCurdy, for example, told the author that she lived at the Home for a period, perhaps following the death of her grandfather in 1919, but she is not listed.

Birthplaces, birth dates, and names of parents are in parentheses. Date of entry into the Home is shown as: e:month/day/year. Students who were "indentured" are so indicated. Direct quotations from the cards are in quotation marks. "Carlisle" refers to the Carlisle Indian School in Pennsylvania and "Chemawa" to the Chemawa Indian School in Salem, Oregon. The cards are frequently unclear about the relationship between the date of leaving the Home and the event that was listed next. For example, students are sometimes recorded as "leaving" when they actually died. Other students are listed as "leaving" after which a note indicates that they were married, but whether or not those students left to be married is unclear.

1890

1 Reinken, Sophia. (Chernofski. Father: Adolph Reinken.) Married Henry Swanson, Capt. Hanson, Capt. C.T. Pedersen. Died 1916 in childbirth.

2 Reinken, Mary. (Unalaska. Father: Adolph Reinken.) Married George Sipary, Alaska; Thomas Barry, Ireland. Died in Juneau of tuberculosis.

3 Bakawnoff, Salome [no info on card].

4 Sharpishnikoff, Titiana. (St. Paul.)

5 Chagin, Pariscovia. (St. Paul.)

6 Reinken, John. (Unalaska. Father: Adolph Reinken. Mother: Alexandra Reinken.) Left in 1897 to attend Carlisle.

7 Wagner, John. (Unalaska. Father: Wagner, U.S.A. Mother: Shaishnikoff Wagner, Alaska.)

8 Wagner, Helen. (Unalaska. Father: Wagner, U.S.A. Mother: Shaishnikoff Wagner, Alaska.) Left 1897? Went home. Died at Unalaska in 1899 of tuberculosis.

9 Dowd, Lizzie. (Attu.)

10 Godeoff, Annie. (St. Paul.)

11 Kudren, Annie [no info on card].

12 Prokopeoff, Taesia [no info on card].

13 Prokopeoff, Ludmelia. (Attu. Parents dead.) Entered at age 18. Left 8/31/96, married.

14 Suvoroff, Sosipatria. (Unalaska. Mother: Martha Suvoroff.) Left 1897 to attend Carlisle.

15 Evanoff, Anastasia. (St. Paul.) Entered at age 16. Left 8/1/1897. "Married John Duakanoff, dead; Logan Repin, dead; Germain Golodoff."

16 Krukoff, Lucalia. (St. Paul. Father: John Krukoff, Alaska, dead. Mother: Oulita Krukoff, Alaska, dead.) e:no information. Left 5/1/00. Went to states. Married Aphanasia Chagin.

17 Tutikoff, Palageia. (Unalaska. Father: Tutikoff, Alaska, dead. Mother: Parascovia Tutikoff, Alaska.) e:1890, age 14. Left 7/8/97, to attend Carlisle.

18 Oustikoff, Euprexinia. (St. George. Father: Zaka Oustikoff, Alaska, dead. Mother: Euprexinia Oustikoff, Alaska, dead.) **e:1892, age 15**. Left 9/16/99. "Married John Kudren, dead. She died tuberculosis Unalaska."

19 Merculieff, Lubov[a]. (St. Paul. Father: Dosofea Merculieff, Alaska, dead. Mother: Auxcinia Merculieff, Alaska, dead.) **e:1892, age 16**. Left 8/1/97.

1891

1892

20 Yatchminoff, Auxcinia. (St. Paul. Father: John Yatchminoff, Alaska, dead. Mother: Alexandra Yatchminoff, Alaska, dead.) **e:1893, age 16**. Left 7/8/98, married. Married Charles Swensen, Norway, dead. Married: Alaska. She died at Sand Point in 1923 and left two children: Annie (No. 112) and Helen (No. 113).

21 Armstrong, Katie. (St. Paul, Mother: Katherine Chagin.) e:1892, age 14. Left 8/1/97. Married Inikenti Shaishnikoff. Dead. Married Alexseoff. Dead. Married John Golodoff. [Katie Chuchagin is on Newhall's list, 1892–1897. Her mother's name was Katherine Chagin.]

22 Morgan, Nadesda. (St. George. Father: Morgan, U.S.A. Mother: Oleana, Alaska, dead.) e:1892, age 15. Left 9/15/98, married a second priest [i.e., an assistant priest]. Died of tuberculosis.

23 Fratese, Helen. (St. Paul. Father: John Fratese, from Guam. Mother: Oleana Fratese, Unalaska.) e:1892, age 10. Left 9/25/98 to attend Carlisle. Died.

24 Nevzeroff, Feckla. (Sanak.) e:1892, age 18. Left 9/18/96.

25 Sedick, Eudocia. (St. Paul. Father: William
    Sedick. Mother: Martha Sedick, Alaska,
    dead.) e:1892, age 12. Left 7/8/97 to attend
    Carlisle.

26 Suvoroff, Irene. (Unalaska. Mother: Martha
    Suvoroff, dead.) **e:1890, age 12.** Left
    9/25/98 to attend Carlisle.

27 Block, Parsha. (Attu. Mother: Martha
    Kalastrakoff, dead.) **e:1890, age 10.** Left
    8/8/97 to Chicago. "Legally adopted by
    P. B. Weir."

1893

28 McCleod, Marie. (Kodiak. Father:
    McCleod, Scotland. Mother: McCleod,
    Alaska.) e:1893, age 7. Left 9/25/98 to attend
    Carlisle. Married Daniel Ross, U.S. mar-
    shal, June 1924. School teacher Deering,
    Alaska, 3 yrs.; Unalaska, Alaska, 1 yr.;
    missionary work, S.E. Alaska, 1 year;
    missionary work, Unalaska, 3 years.

*   Kosnechoff, Agafia. 1893– .

1894

29 Diakanoff, Katherine. (Unalaska. Father:
    Nekefar Diakanoff. Alaska. Mother:
    Palageia Diakanoff. Alaska.) e:1894, age 6.
    Left 9/25/98 to attend Carlisle. Married
    Harry Seller from England. Graduated
    Carlisle Indian School and the State
    Normal School at Chester, Penn.
    Schoolteacher in Southeastern Alaska [?]
    years; at Unalaska, 1 year; Akhiak, 5 years?
    Atka, 3 years; Atka [again], 3 years?;
    Anchorage, 1 year; Anchorage [again],
    1 year.

30 Diakanoff, May. (Unalaska. Father: Nekefar
    Diakanoff, Alaska. Mother: Palageia
    Diakanoff, Alaska.) e:1894, age 5. Left
    5/25/07. "Married Kelly. Dead. Married
    Doughty. In 19— in crossing a street in
    Seattle she was run over by a trolley car
    and both legs were cut off above the
    ankles. Recovered—was paid an indemnity
    by the R.R."

31 Nakootkin, Vasha. (Unalaska.) e:1894, age
    8. Left 9/25/98. "Went to Canada. Later
    went to school Carlisle Pa."

32 Reinken, Annie. (Chernofski. Father:
    Adolph Reinken. Mother: Alexandra
    Reinken, Chernofski.) e:1894, age 8. Left
    6/8/97 to attend Carlisle. Married.

33 Reinken, Doris. (Chernofski. Father:
    Adolph Reinken. Mother: Alexandra
    Reinken, Alaska.) e:1894, age 6. Left
    7/8/97 to attend Carlisle.

34 Reinken, Olga. (Chernofski. Father:
    Adolph Reinken, Germany. Mother:
    Alexandra Reinken, Alaska.) e:1894, age 7.
    Left 1898 to go home. Married N.
    Bolshanin. Attended Carlisle, 1901.
    Graduated Carlisle, and the State Normal
    School in Chester, Penn. Teacher at
    Unalaska 1 year. Two daughters: Barbara,
    Elaine.

35 Nevzeroff, Vasha. (Unalaska. Father:
    Nevzeroff, dead. Mother Eudocia
    Nevzeroff, dead.) e:1894, age 5. Died
    7/23/02 of pertussis and tuberculosis.

36 Zaharoff, Fedocia. (St. Paul. Father:
    Emmanuel Zaharoff, Alaska, dead.
    Mother: Christine Zaharoff, Alaska,
    dead.) e:1892, age 16. Left 5/9/06 to Ilo,
    Idaho. Died of blood poisoning in 1914.
    Epileptic.

1895

37 Tetoff, Irene. (St. Paul. Father: Matve
    Tetoff, Alaska, dead. Mother: Feckla
    Tetoff, Alaska, dead.) **e: 1896, age 10.**
    Died 9/28/00 of measles and tuberculosis.

38 Tetoff, Sophia. (St. Paul. Father: Matve
    Tetoff, Alaska, dead. Mother: Feckla
    Tetoff, Alaska, dead.) **e:1896, age 8.** Left
    7/1/01 to attend Carlisle. Died at Carlisle
    of tuberculosis.

39 Melovedoff, Marcia. (St. Paul. Father:
    Anthony Melovedoff, Alaska, dead.
    Mother: Agrafina Melovedoff, Alaska,

dead.) e:1895, age 7. Left 1902 to attend Carlisle. Died in San Francisco of tuberculosis.

40 Gary, Mary. (Marshovia.) **e:1896, age 6.** Left 6/1898, home. "Died at Marshovia." [Garey in Newhall.]

41 Brown, Olga. (Marshovia. Father: Wm. Brown, English, murdered. Mother: Auxcinia Brown, Alaska.) **e:1896, age 10.** Left 9/25/98 to go home. "Died Unalaska tuberculosis."

42 King, Annie. (Unga. Father: Robert King, England, dead. Mother: Annie King, Alaska, dead.) e:1895, age 9. Indentured. Left 7/9/01. Went to Hagaman, NY. Married.

43 McGlashan, Martha. (Akatan. Father: Hugh McGlashan. Mother: Martha McGlashan, Alaska, dead.) e:1895, age 6. Left June 1898 to go home. Married Martin Monson.

44 Repin, Alexandra. (Unalaska. Father: John Repin, Alaska. Mother: Repin, Alaska.) e:1895, age 9. Died 4/6/01 of tuberculosis. Epileptic.

45 Benson, John. (Marshovia. Father Brown Bensen, Norway. Mother: Agrafina Bensen, Alaska, dead.) **e:1894, age 9.** Left 1897 to attend Carlisle.

46 McGlashan, Hugh. (Akutan. Father: Hugh McGlashan. Mother: Martha McGlashan, Alaska, dead.) **e:1894, age 7.** Left April 1897 to go home. Married Matrona Anderson.

47 Peterson, Willie. (Sanak. Father: William Peterson, Germany, dead. Mother: Mary Peterson, Alaska, dead.) e:1895, age 12. Left 5/1/97 to go home. Died at Unalaska of tuberculosis.

48 Penkoff, John Ivan. (Unalaska.) e:1895, age 7. Left 8/1/98. "Went to York, Nebraska. Died at York, Neb. Tuberculosis."

49 Ainsworthy, Olga. (Belkovsky. Father: John Ainsworthy, England, dead. Mother:

Melania Ainsworthy.) e:1895, age 14. Left: 3/6/00. "Went Home. Married Chas. Woberg Norway."

* Ainsworthy, Mary. Newhall provides no dates.

1896

50 Vereskin, Feckla. (Belkofsky. Parents dead.) e:9/1896, age 12. Left 6/1/99 to go home. Foster father Mr. Jackson.

51 Vatanabai, Molly – Myres. (Belkofsky. Father: Peter Myres. Mother: Maggie Kleboff, Alaska, dead.) e:1896, age 6. Left 6/1/97 to go home. Married John Gardiner. Children: Marguerite, Unga, Jan. 6, 1909; Anna, Unga, April 11, 1912; Dora, Unga, Dec. 12, 1913; John Peter Jr., Seattle, Wash., Dec. 22, 1914.

1897

52 Peterson, Mary. (Sanak. Father: William Peterson, Germany. Mother: Mary Peterson, Alaska, dead.) e:5/1/98, age 6. Died 1897 of tuberculosis.

53 Leonard, Rose. (Unga.) e:6/1/97, age 5. Left 8/1897. Died of tuberculosis.

54 Leonard, Dolly. (Unga.) e:6/1/97, age 7. Left 9/1/97, went home, died.

55 Peterson, John. (Sanak. Father: William Peterson, Germany, dead. Mother: Mary Peterson, Alaska, dead.) e:7/1/97, age 10. Left 5/1/98, went home.

56 Peterson, Aleck. (Sanak. Father: William Peterson, German. Mother: Mary, Alaska.) e:8/1/97, age 12. "Left 1898 May. Drowned in a bidarky."

57 Ballou, Herman. (Kodiak.) e:5/1/97, age 3. Left 9/24/98, went home.

1898

58 Mandrigen, Maggie [Magaret]. (St. Paul. Father: Leon Mandrigen, Alaska. Mother: Marfa Mandrigen, Alaska.) e: 9/1/98, age 12. Left 7/9/01, to attend Carlisle.

59 Berin, Molly [Borenin]. (Unalaska.)
    e: **1895, age 12**. Died 5/1896.

60 Popoff, Mary. (Unalaska. Mother: dead.)
    e: **1895, age 8**. "Left 1896 May Died."

61 Siftsoff, Melania. (Attu.) **e:Sept. 1895,
    age 5**. Died May 1896.

62 Nikiton, Alexandra (nee Lee). (Marshovia.
    Father: Alastaku Nikiton, dead. Mother:
    Matrona Nikiton, dead.) e:12/5/98, age 24.
    Died April 1902.

63 Benson, Annie. (Marshovia. Father: Brown
    Benson, Norway. Mother: Agrafina
    Benson, Alaska, dead.) **e:5/21/99, age 5**.
    "Left 1901 May 15. Died: Iliocolitis."

64 Reinken, Leo. (Unalaska. Father: Adolph
    Reinken, Germany. Mother: Alexandra
    Reinken, Alaska.) e:10/5/98, age 8.
    Left 10/10/99, went home.

65 Reinken, Tillie [Matilda]. (Unalaska.
    Father: Adolph Reinken, German. Mother:
    Alexandra Reinken, Alaska.) e:10/13/98,
    age 6. Left 3/23/00, to go home. Attended
    Chemawa. Married.

66 Galacktianoff, Gabriel. (Makushin. Father:
    Tekan Galacktianoff, dead.) e:8/6/98, age 6.
    "Left 1906 Nov. 27. Insane. Remarks:
    Admitted to Mt. Ivy Insane asylum.
    Portland Ore. died there. This child was
    brot to the home by the U.S. marshall. He
    had been living in an old dory abandoned
    on the beach and which had a small cabin
    hole in one end."

67 Nutbeem, Theodore. (Unalaska. Father:
    Albert Nutbeem, England. Mother:
    Nadezda Nutbeem, Alaska.) e:6/1/98, age 4.
    Indentured. "Left 1914, to work.
    Married Alice Larsen, Unga."

68 Nederazoff, Alexsea. (St. Paul. Mother:
    Agrafina, Alaska, dead.) **e:8/24/99, age 8**.
    Died 3/7/01 of tuberculosis—measles.

69 Adlooat. (Wales. Stepfather: Oong-noo-
    nek. Mother: Wey-ak-ak-meu.) e:10/29/98.

Left 9/9/01. "Married Ong-nak-luk Stella.
Died 1918 Wales Flu."

70 Fratese, John. (St. Paul. Father: John
    Fratese, Island of Guam. Mother: Akoolina
    Fratese, Alaska.) e:1898, age 10. Left 8/1/01.
    "Went home. Remark: married."

1899

1900

71 Gould, Eliza. (Bird Island. Robert Gould,
    U.S.A. Mother: Elena Gould, Alaska.)
    e:8/21/00, age 11. Indentured. "Left 1906
    July. Burlington Vt. Married Peter
    Kashavaroff 1908. He died of Flu 1919.
    Children: Flora – died blue baby, Chester,
    Eleanor, Victor, Ethel, Mildred."

72 Gould, Annie. (Unga. Father: Robert
    Gould, U.S.A. Mother: Elena Gould,
    Alaska.) e:8/21/00, age 9. Indentured. "Left
    1908 Sept. 1. Glencoe Ohio. June 24 1914.
    School Glencoe Ohio. 1917 Chester W.V.,
    1918 Pittsburgh, Penn. M.E. Deaconess
    Home, 1926 Worker Jesse Lee H."

73 Swanson, Sophia. (Unalaska.
    Father: Henry Swanson, Norway.
    Mother: Sophia Swanson, Alaska. No. 1.)
    e:10/29/01, age 3. Indentured. Left 9/10/08,
    Mt. Ivy, NY. Married.

74 Sorokovikoff, Annie. (Unga. Father:
    Ivan Sorokovikoff, Alaska, dead. Mother:
    Irene Sorokovikoff, Alaska, dead.) e:8/17/00,
    age 13. Indentured. Left 8/5/04, went home.

75 Golovin, Katie. (Koronski Is. Father:
    Theodore Golovin, Alaska, dead. Mother:
    Parascovia Golovin. Alaska, dead.)
    e:8/17/00, age 13, indentured. Died 9/13/03,
    tuberculosis.

76 Lee, Helen Mrs. (Marshovia. Father:
    Alastacku Nikiton, Alaska, dead. Mother:
    Matrona Nikiton, Alaska, dead.) **e:7/1899**.
    Left 9/1/99. "Went Home. Maiden name
    Nikiton. Married Capt. Edward Lee. She

died of tuberculosis. Children: Hilda Lee, Aleck Lee, John Lee, Charles Lee."

77 Lee, Aleck. (Marshovia. Father: Edward Lee, Norway. Mother: Helena Lee, Alaska —No. 76.) **e:7/1899, age 5**. Indentured. "Left 1899 Sept. 1. Went home. Died tuberculosis. U.S. Hospital. Fought in world war."

78 Lee, John. (Unalaska. Father Edw. Lee, Norway. Mother: Helena Lee, Alaska, No. 76.) **e:7/1/99, age 3**. Left 9/1899, "School Chemawa. Died tuberculosis. In world war navy. Married."

79 Dirks, Paul. (Atka. Father: Henry Dirks, Germany. Mother: Natalia Dirks, Alaska.) e:8/23/00, age 9. Left: 8/1/01 to attend Carlisle.

80 Balumatoff, Andrew. (Unga. Father: Lawrence Balumatoff. Mother: Natalia Balumatoff.) e:9/19/00, age 13. Indentured. Left 8/1/06. "Went Home. Died in Unga tuberculosis."

81 Golovin, Feofan. (Unga. Father: Theodore Golovin, Alaska, dead. Mother: Pariscovia Golovin, Alaska, dead.) e:9/19/00, age 7. Indentured. Left 8/5/07. "Married Nellie Peterson (No. 106). He died at Cold Bay 1909? tuberculosis. Child: Stanley Golovin. Died. See No. 157."

82 Shaposhnikoff, William. (Unga. Parents dead.) e:9/19/00, age 13. Died 4/22/02, tuberculosis.

83 Cushing, William. (Unga. Father: George W. Cushing, U.S.A. Mother: Christine Cushing, Alaska, dead.) e:9/19/00, age 9. Left 8/22/03. Went home.

84 Cushing, Albert. (Unga. Father: George W. Cushing, U.S.A. Mother: Christine Cushing, Alaska, dead.) e:9/19/00, age 7. Left 8/22/03. "Went Home. Married Unga."

85 Swanson, Agnes. (Unalaska. Father: Henry Swanson, Norway. Mother: Sophia Swanson, Alaska—No. 1.) e:9/1/00, age 1. Indentured. Left 1910. "Went to states with Mrs. Brown. Married."

86 Swanson, Henry. (Unalaska. Father: Henry Swanson, Norway. Mother: Sophia Swanson, No. 1.) e:9/17/00, age 5. Left 4/21/10. "Abducted. At school Chemawa, Oregon."

87 Orchiden, Titiana. (Marshovia.) e:9/14/00, age 10. Died 1/5/07, TB. "Was made blind by her father, when drunk, throwing red pepper in her eyes. Rep.[?] She learned to read by Moon raised type talk-books from Phila. public library."

115 Swanson, Ruth. (Unalaska, 9/1/00. Henry Swanson, Norway, dead, drowned 1899. Mother: Sophia Swanson, died 1916.) e:9/1/00, age 0. "Left 1900 Sept. 8 Died Inanition— measles."

1901

88 Shemakensky, Alexandra. (Unalaska. Father: Zachar Shemakensky, dead. Mother: Euprexinia Shemakensky, dead.) e:1/12/01, age 1. Died 3/14/01, tuberculosis of the hip.

89 Dusken, Sophia. (Marshovia.) e:1901, age 16. Left 1901, married, Umnak.

90 Vereskin, Annie. (Belkofsky. Father: Ivan Vereskin, dead. Mother: dead.) e:5/16/01. Left 7/9/01, to attend Carlisle. Died at Carlisle, diphtheria.

91 Duskin, Auxcinia. (Marshovia.) e:6/15/01, age 8. Left 10/20/09 to East Orange, N.J. "In a Spanish W.H.M.S. home. Cal. Died at Long Beach Cal. Tuberculosis."

92 Dupeet, Samuel. (Sanak, 4/30/93, Father: Dupeet, dead. Stepfather Andrew Grosvold—Sand Point.) e: 8/6/01. Left 1902. Went home. "Married 1914 April Grace Larsen. He died at Unga.

1919 July 3 Accident. Children Sam Dupeet, Isaac Dupeet."

93 Dirks, Palageia. (Atka. Father: Henry Dirks. Germany. Mother: Natalia Dirks, Alaska.) e:8/21/01, age 13. Left 8/5/07, Burlington, Vt. "Died in San Francisco, Cal. 1918, Flu. Lived in Stoneham Mass. 1908 to 1914. Married Alfred Somerville, St. John, New Brunswick, 1914. Children: Alfred Henry, Walter William, Julia Faith."

94 Balakshin, Annie (Popoff). (St. Paul. Father: Edward Balakshin, dead. Mother: Eudocia Popoff, dead.) e:8/21/01, age 18. Left 10/1/01. "Went home. Married Harry Kafoury, Assyrian. Married Kohler, German."

95 Popoff, Alexandra. (St. Paul. Father: Edw. Balakshin, dead. Mother: Eudocia Popoff, dead.) e:6/21/01, age 6. Left 10/20/02; reentered 6/29/03. Left 10/29/03. Went to the states. Married.

96 Duskin, Austinia. (Marshovia.) e:6/21/01, age 6. Died 6/16/09, tuberculosis.

97 Rosenberg, Catherine [Katherine]. (Unimak, 12/20/92. Father: Chas. Rosenberg, Germany. Mother: Daria Rosenberg, Alaska, dead.) e:9/1/01, age 9. Left 7/9/04, went home.

98 William Rosenberg [Unimak—no file card for him].

99 Rosenberg, Lillie. (Unimak, 11/4/99. Father: Chas. Rosenberg, Germany. Mother: Daria Rosenberg, Alaska, dead.) e:3/3/01, age 3. Left 7/9/04, went home. Married Leonti Andersen, Alaska. She died at Unalaska in 1919 of flu.

* Wagner, Vera. She left with the Newhalls in July 1901 for Carlisle. However, she may have been a public school student and not a resident of the Home.

1902

100 Rosenberg, John. (Unimak, 4/4/96. Father: Charles Rosenberg, Germany. Mother: Daria Rosenberg, Alaska, dead.) e:3/3/02,

age 8. Left 7/9/04 to go home. Served overseas in the Navy in World War I.

101 Rosenberg, Daniel. (Unimak, 12/19/97. Father: Charles Rosenberg, Germany. Mother: Daria Rosenberg, Alaska, dead.) e:3/3/02, age 5. Left 7/9/04. Went home and died on Unimak Island, May 13, 1916, of pneumonia and tuberculosis.

102 Reinken, Herbert. (Unalaska. Father: Adolph Reinken, Germany. Mother: Alexandra Reinken, Alaska.) **e:11/27/01, age 7.** Left 5/1/02, went home.

103 Sipary, Daniel. (Kuskokwim River, 1896. Father: George Sipary, dead. Mother: Mary Sipary, No. 2.) **e:11/29/01, age 5.** Left 8/12/15. Married Annie Peterson, No. 107. "Child: Winifred. Divorced from wife."

104 Torgramsen, Andrew. (Andronack Island. Father: Sigert Torgramsen, Denmark, dead. Mother: Annie Torgramsen, Alaska, dead.) **e:11/22/01, age 10.** Left 6/5/04, went home. Married Helen Torgramsen, No. 113. He died in U.S. Hospital, Wash. state, of tuberculosis. Children: Cecil, Harvey.

105 Peterson, Alexandra. (Marshovia, 4/23/91. Father: Charles Peterson, Denmark. Mother: Martha Peterson, Alaska, dead.) e:5/8/02, age 11. Indentured. Left 8/26/08, married P. Bouderkoufsky, Alaska. Children: Martha, George, Victor.

106 Peterson, Helen. (Marshovia, 5/21/94. Father: Charles Peterson, Denmark. Mother: Martha Peterson, Alaska, dead.) e:5/8/02, age 8. Indentured. Left 8/5/07. Married Aug. 4, Feofan Golovin (No. 81). Married Cushing. Children: Stanley Golovin, John Cushing.

107 Peterson, Annie. (Marshovia, 12/23/96. Father: Charles Peterson, Denmark. Mother: Martha Peterson, Alaska, dead.) e:5/8/02, age 6. Indentured. Left 8/12/15, married Daniel Sipary (No. 103). Married

F. Torstensen, U.S.A. Married Weathers. Died June 5, 1978.

108 <u>Peterson, Nicoli.</u> (Marshovia, 11/6/98. Father: Charles Peterson, Denmark. Mother: Martha Peterson, Alaska, dead.) e:5/8/02, age 4. Left 7/1/17, went to work.

109 <u>Peterson, Amelia.</u> (Marshovia, 1/22/00. Father: Charles Peterson, Denmark. Mother: Martha Peterson, Alaska, dead.) e:5/8/02, age 2. Indentured. Left 1/16/18, married John Bereskin, Alaska. Children: Chester, Wilbur.

110 <u>McCurdy, William.</u> (Unalaska, 1900. Father: William McCurdy, U.S.A. Mother: Emma McCurdy, Alaska, dead. Stepmother: Ella Darling McCurdy.) e:9/13/02, age 4. Left 6/5/04. Port Townsend, Wash. "Went to Dolgeville, NY. Served in world war. Navy."

111 <u>McCurdy, James.</u> (Unalaska, 1901. Father: Wm. McCurdy, U.S.A. Mother: Emma McCurdy, Alaska, dead. Stepmother: Ella Darling McCurdy.) e:9/13/02, age 3. Left 6/5/04, Port Townsend, Wash. Went to Dolgeville, NY.

112 <u>Swansen, Annie.</u> (Unalaska, 5/15/99. Father: Charles Swanson, Swede, died 1911. Mother: Auxcinia Swanson, "Maiden Auxcinia Yatchmanoff," Alaska, died 1924.) e:9/4/02, age 3. Indentured. Left 10/23/17, married Peter Hatch, No. 164. Children: Florence Louise, Helen Elizabeth, Annie Eugenia—died Jan. 5, 1921, Ralph Warren, Jesse Lee—June 13, 1926.

113 <u>Swansen, Helen.</u> (Unalaska, 3/3/01. Father: Charles Swanson, Sweden, died 1911. Mother: Auxcinia Swanson, died 5/5/24.) e:9/4/02, age 1. Indentured. Married Andrew Torgramsen, 1919, No. 104. "Lived in Harrisburg, Penn. Teacher in Jesse Lee Home. U.S. teacher at Umnak Island, Alaska. Children: Cecil Eric, Harvey Edward."

114 <u>Hansen, Seraphima.</u> (Unalaska.) e:1/22/02, age 3. Left 3/18/03, tuberculosis.

115 <u>Swanson, Ruth.</u> (Unalaska, 9/1/00.) Died 9/8/00, inanition—measles.

116 Koznekoff, Agafia [no other information on file card, not even year].

117 <u>Oscar Ung-er-uk</u> (Eskimo). (Golovin Bay.) e:11/18/02, age 16. Left 11/5/03, Carlisle. Mission work, Golovin Bay.

118 <u>Edward Ow-kan</u> (Eskimo). (Golovin Bay, Father: Ang-oo-luk.) e:11/18/02, age 16. Left 11/5/03, to attend Carlisle.

119 <u>Samuel Sim-oo-luk</u> (Eskimo). (Golovin Bay. Father: A-na-ruk.) e:11/18/02, age 16. Left 6/12/03, to attend Carlisle.

120 <u>Garfield Mit-a-ka-nok</u> (Eskimo). (Golovin Bay. Father: Sit-a-rang.) e:11/18/02, age 15. Left 11/4/03, to attend Carlisle. "Missionary work, Golovin Bay."

121 <u>George Se-ga-uk</u> (Eskimo). (Unalaklit. Father: Portuguese. Mother: A-wun-ga. Foster mother: Mary Antisarluk.) e:11/18/02, age 10. Left 6/6/06, to go home.

122 <u>Molly Shi-ta-ka-nuk.</u> (Golovin Bay. Father: Da-lee-luk.) e:11/18/02, age 15. Left 10/4 to attend Carlisle.

123 <u>Annie Charlie A-nee-uk</u> (Eskimo). (Unalaklit. Father: Charley, dead. Foster mother: Igloo Mary (Mary Antisarluk).) e:11/18/02. "Left 1902 Dec. 30 Died tuberculosis."

1903

124 <u>Chipitnoi, Fred.</u> (Unga.) e:8/10/03, age 5. Left 2/1/18. "Worked on S.S."

125 <u>Vereskin, Faveronia.</u> (Marshovia.) e:8/10/03, age 3. 8/10/04, adopted by Mrs. Chase.

126 <u>George, Jessie.</u> (Metrofan Island. Father: Morris George. Mother: Elena George.) e:10/1/03, age 5. Left 1906, home, died.

127 <u>Bayliss, William Ca-tu-a.</u> (Herschel Island, British America.) e:10/31/03, age 11? "Left 1911 Oct. 1. School Tacoma Wash. Missionary at Nome. Named for ship Wm.

Bayliss on which he came. Died, Nome, pneumonia."

128   Morton, Paul. (St. Paul, 5/22/99. Father: Edward Morton, U.S.A.—Boston, dead. Mother: Martha Morton, Alaska.) e:12/18/03, age 4. Indentured. Left 10/26/14 to go home. "Teacher in Jesse Lee Home—Out work."

1904

129   Oliver, Simeon. (Chignik, 7/23/02. Father: James Oliver, Norway, died 1923. Mother: Anna Oliver, Alaska.) e:9/5/04, age 2, indentured. "Left 1920 Aug. 1, school North Western College. College of music Chicago, Ill. A very fine pianist."

130   Tilton, Nellie A-la-goo-na. (Herschel Island, 7/22/95. Father: Capt. Tilton, U.S.A. Mother: Alaska, dead.) e:10/21/04, age 9. Left 9/10/08, Mt. Ivy, NY. Married.

131   Norwood, Leila I-ri-luk. (Herschel Island, British America, 12/26/93. Father: Capt. Norwood, U.S.A., dead.) e:10/21/04, age 11. Left 2/22/06. "Went to San Francisco. Berkeley High School, Cal. Commercial course. Business. Instruction Convent. Married 1923."

132   Hopson, Mary Ann Un-uk-ser-uk. (Cape Smith, 4/23/95.) e:10/21/04, age 9. Left 10/26/06, Oakland, Calif.

133   Leavitt, Lucy Pup-kee-na [no file card for her].

134   Hansen, Dick Au-choo-uk. (Pt. Hope.) e:10/25/04, age 18. Left 5/1/05. Went home. "Named for ship he came in."

1905

135   Nedarazoff, Marie. (St. Paul. Father: Demetrius Philemenoff, Alaska, dead.) e:6/3/05, age 12. Left 7/5/10, married. "Died in childbirth."

136   Peterson, George. (Atka, 8/13/02. Father: William Peterson, Germany, dead. Mother: Martha Peterson, dead.) e:7/22/05, age 3.

Indentured. Left 4/1/19, to work for a living.

137   Peterson, Henry [Innokenty in Newhall]. (Atka, 8/14/01. Father: Wm. Peterson, Germany, dead. Mother: Martha Peterson, dead.) e:7/22/05, age 4. Indentured. Left 3/1/19, to work for living.

138   Dirks, Charles. (Atka. Father: Henry Dirks, Germany, died 1923. Mother: Natalia Dirks, died.) e:8/24/05, age 9. "Left 1907 Aug. 5 Burlington Vt. School, Stoneham Mass. School. Died 1911 suicide pistol shot. At Newton Mass."

139   Oustikoff, Alexandra. (St. George, 5/26/93. Father: U.S.A., dead. Mother: Oustikoff, Alaska, dead.) e:8/23/05, age 12. Left 9/10/08, Mt. Ivy, N.Y. Died, tuberculosis.

140   Oustikoff, Stepanita. (St. George, 11/24/94. Father: U.S.A., dead. Mother: Oustikoff, Alaska, dead.) e:8/23/05, age 11. Left 9/10/08, Saugus, Mass. (Cliftondale). Died 1909, tuberculosis.

1906

141   Mobeck, John. (Sanak, 5/8/97. Father: Emil Mobeck, Norway. Mother: Feckla Mobeck, Alaska, dead.) e:4/10/06, age 9. Left 5/1/11 to go home. "Died in wreck."

142   Pedersen, Theodore. (Samalga Island, 2/24/05. Father: Christian Theodore Pedersen, Norway. Mother: Musa Diakanoff Pedersen, Alaska, dead.) e:5/5/06, age 2. Left 5/15/06. Re-entered 19–. Left 1918. School, Northfield, Mass.

143   Palutoff, James. (Sand Point. Father: Nekefa Palutoff, Alaska. Mother: Alaska, dead.) e:5/9/06, age 4. Left 5/6/19, went home.

144   Vereskin, Louise [Sohia in Newhall]. (Marshovia. Father: England. Irish, dead. Mother: Vereskin, dead.) e:5/25/06, age 11. Left 1/29/10, to attend school at Chemawa.

145 Dirks, Palageia. (Atka, 9/21/02. Father: George Dirks, Alaska, dead. Mother: Agafia Dirks, Alaska, dead.) e:8/15/06. "Left 1910 March 14. Died tuberculosis."

146 Snigeroff, Austinia. (Atka, 9/21/00. Father: Isadore Snigeroff, Alaska, dead. Mother: Isenovia Snigeroff, Alaska, dead.) e:8/15/06, age 6. Died 11/7/08, tuberculosis.

147 Ward, San Francisco. (Herschel Island, British America. Father: Capt. Newth, U.S.A. Mother: Alaska, dead.) e:9/25/06, age 12. Left 10/1/07, to San Francisco.

148 Alexander, Jennie A-buk [no file card for her].

  * Snigeroff, Palageia—1906.

  * Snigeroff, Sam—1906.

1907

149 Pedersen, Margeret. (Unalaska. Father: Christian Theodore Pedersen, Norway. Mother: Musa (Diakanoff) Pedersen, Alaska, dead.) e:3/28/07, age 5. Left 6/8/08, went home. Married.

150 Dirks, Catherine. (Atka 12/9/02. Father: George Dirks, Alaska, dead. Mother: Snigeroff, Alaska, dead.) e:4/13/07. Left 12/12/09. Died tuberculosis.

151 Mobeck, Katie. (Sanak, 1/6/95. Father: Emil Mobeck, Norway. Mother: Feckla Mobeck, Alaska, dead.) e:5/11/07, age 12. Left 5/1/11 to go home. "Married Christian Gudnerson."

152 Hansen, Mary. (Sand Point, 6/30/96. Father: Andrew Hansen, Norway. Mother: Sophia Hansen, Alaska.) e:6/28/07. Indentured. Left 7/25/14, went home. "Married Joseph Nasenius, Norway."

153 Hansen, Nicoli. (Sand Point, 12/17/02. Father: Andrew Hansen, Norway. Mother: Sophia Hansen, Alaska.) e:6/28/07, age 5. Indentured. Left 5/6/18, went home.

154 Hansen, Andrew. (Sand Point, 7/19/03. Father: Andrew Hansen, Norway. Mother: Sophia Hansen, Alaska.) e:6/28/07. Died 8/28/08, tuberculosis.

155 Gordon, Thomas. (Pt. Barrow.) e:10/15/07, age 14. Left 3/1/11, to go home.

156 Porter, George Oo-la-luk. (Herschel Island, British America, 12/26/95. Father: Capt. Porter, U.S.A.) e:10/22/07, age 12. "Left 1913. To work for a living. World War. Over the sea. Lieut."

  * Snigeroff, Katherine—1907.

1908

157 Golovin, Stanley. (Unalaska, 2/26/08. Father: Feofan Golovin, No. 81, Alaska, died 1909. Mother: Nellie Golovin, No. 106, Alaska.) e:2/26/08. Died 6/1911, meningitis.

158 Vickiloff, Alexandra. (St. Paul, 6/3/95. Father: Alaska. Mother: Claudia Koochooten, Alaska.) **e:9/11/06, age 11**. Left 1913. Married A. Melovedoff.

159 Golovin, Peter—Gould. (Unga, 7/8/01. Father: Golovin, Alaska, dead. Mother: Elena Gould, Alaska, dead.) e:6/28/08. Indentured. "Left 1914 June 24 School Glencoe, Ohio. Graduated Dickinson Seminary—1923. Williams Port Penn. Syracuse University N.Y. Local preacher M.E. Church."

160 Mobeck, Benjamin. (Sanak, 8/8/99. Father: Emil Mobeck, Norway. Mother: Feckla Mobeck, Alaska, dead.) e:8/28/08, age 9. Left 5/1/11 to go home.

161 Lee, Charles. (Marshovia, 10/16/03. Father: Edward Lee, Norway, died. Mother: Elena Lee, Alaska, died, No. 76.) e:9/5/08, age 4. Left 4/1/21, went to work. "Died Unalaska 1923 tuberculosis. Willed Jesse Lee Home nearly $1000."

162 Lee, Hilda. (Unalaska, 10/17/04. Father: Edward Lee, Norway, died. Mother: Elena Lee, Alaska, died, No. 76.) e:9/5/08, age 4. Died 2/11/21, tuberculosis, measles.

1909

163 Peterson, Anicia. (Atka, 12/1/99. Father: William Peterson, Alaska—No. 47, dead. Mother: Irene Peterson, Alaska, dead.) e:2/16/09, age 9. "Left 1911 March 20. Died tuberculosis."

164 Hatch, Peter K. [Peter Shaposnikoff in Newhall]. (Unga, 6/28/99? Father: William Shaposhnikoff Hatch.) e:2/19/09, age 10. Indentured. Left 1915 Salem Oregon, to attend Chemawa. Married Annie Swanson, 1917 (No. 112).

165 Shaposhnikoff, Agnes (Hatch). (Unga, 5/23/07.) e:6/19/09, age 3. Indentured. Left 1924, to states with Mrs. Taft.

166 Shaposhnikoff, John. (Unga, 9/5/06, parents dead.) e:6/25/09, age 3. Indentured. "Left 1915 Nov. 25. Died asphyxiation ether."

167 Mershanin, Salamida. (Unalaska.) e:6/25/09, age 13. Left 8/9/09, attended Chemawa.

168 Grumoff, Julia. (Unalaska. Mother: Feckla Gromoff, dead.) e:8/21/09, age 8. Left 4/18/10, attended Chemawa.

169 Holmberg, Nellie. (Sanak, 5/21/00. Father: Gus Holmberg. Mother: Olga Holmberg.) e:8/30/09, age 9. Left 7/28/14. "Went home. Married August Carlson. Swede."

170 Golovin, Aleck. (Unga, 5/10/05.) e:9/19/09. Indentured. Left 1910 June 14. Died, tuberculosis.

   * Saposnikoff, Peter —1909.

1910

171 Waln, Cecil. (Unalaska, 9/10/05. Father: Lincoln Waln, U.S.A. Mother: Sophia Hansen, died 1916, No. 1.) e:8/15/10, age 4. Left 5/28/22, went to father's home at Cordova.

172 Waln, Lydia. (Unalaska, 8/13/07. Father: Lincoln Waln, U.S.A. Mother: Sophia Hansen, died 1916, No. 1.) e:8/15/10, age 3. Left 5/28/22, to father's home at Cordova.

173 Seymour, Ak-a-wa-na Mrs. (Eskimo). (Herschel Island, British America.) e:10/22/10, age 30? Left 1911, went home to husband. Wife of William Seymour. Child Margeret Seymour, No. 174.

174 Seymour, Margeret. (Herschel Island, British America, 2/11/06. Father: William Seymour, U.S.A. Mother: Annie A-ka-wa-na, Alaska, No. 173.)

175 Krukoff, Lena. (St. Paul [no year given].) Married Paul Merchlieff, Alaska, dead. Married Chris. Halverson, Norway.

1911

1912

176 Pedersen, Nick. (Unalaska. Father: Christian Theodore Pedersen, Norway. Mother: Sophia Pedersen, Alaska, died 1916.) e:5/15/12, age 2. Left 10/21/12. Went home.

177 Carpenter, John Nanoona [no file card for him].

178 Carpenter, Mary Turagana [no file card for her].

1913

179 Balumatoff, Dora. (Unga, 9/20/07. Father: Oscar Balumatoff. Mother: Mattie Balumatoff.) e:8/25/13. Indentured. "Left June 1925, Sand Point."

180 Stankus, Elizabeth. (Anacortes, Wash., 11/15/05. Father: Stankus. Mother: Olga Stankus, Alaska, dead.) e:10/1/13, age 8. Left 11/1/19, to San Francisco.

181 Marchussen, Nick. (Unga, 5/4/07. Father: Harry Marchussen, Denmark, dead. "Father burned to death. House burned.") e:11/27/13, age 7. Indentured. Left 3/13/25. "Died on lonely island where he lived with old man."

1914

182 Moriss, Fedora. (Atka, 11/1/07. Mother: Martha Goley. Adopted by Mark Moriss,

Croatian.) e:7/7/14, age 10. Indentured. Died 6/6/19 of flu.

183 Peters, Louis. (Unalaska, 11/1/07. Father: John Peters, German. Mother: Martha Peters, Alaska.) e:7/9/14, age 6. "Left 1924 March 18 Drowned."

184 Seller, Reine Lois. (Atka, 3/23/11. Father: Harry Seller, England. Mother: Catherine Seller, No. 29.) e:10/1/14, age 3. Left 2/1/15, went home.

185 Seller, Alfred Ellis. (Atka, 12/2/13. Father: Harry Seller, England. Mother: Catherine Seller, No. 29.) e:10/1/14, age 10. Left 2/1/15. Drowned Akhiak, Kodiak Island.

1915

186 Kelly, Edna. (Unalaska. Mother: May Kelly, Alaska, No. 30.) e:1/1/15, age 6. Left 6/30/16, went home.

187 Peshnikoff, Annanee. (Atka, 10/1/09. Father: George Peshnikoff, Alaska, dead. Mother: Agafia Peshnikoff, Alaska, dead.) e:4/16/15, age 6. Indentured. Left 12/23/15. Died from tuberculosis.

188 Peshnikoff, Kalissa. (Atka, 5/3/12. Father: George Peshnikoff, Alaska, dead. Mother: Agafia Peshnikoff, Alaska, dead.) e:4/16/15, age 3. Indentured. "Worked at S[eward] Hospital June 1931. Married Wm. Bryan, 1931."

189 Smith, Henry Osborne. (Sand Point, 11/20/06. Father: Sidney F. Smith, Nova Scotia. Mother: Pariscovia Smith, Alaska.) e:4/27/15, age 8. Left 6/1/24, went out to work.

190 Smith, Dolly. (Sand Point, 11/11/07. Father: Sidney F. Smith, Nova Scotia. Mother: Pariscovia Smith, Alaska.) e:4/27/15, age 7. Indentured. Left 6/12/24, to California.

191 Smith, Charlotte. (Sand Point, 6/11/12. Father: Sidney F. Smith, Nova Scotia. Mother: Pariscovia Smith, Alaska.) e:4/27/15, age 3. Indentured. "Left Sept. 26, 1925 'Commander Van Boskeric' Seeking further education and home."

192 Seller, Marjory. (Unalaska, 12/31/14. Father: Harry Seller, England. Mother: Catherine Seller, No. 29.) **e:12/31/14, age 0**. Left 2/1/15, went home.

193 Olsen, Mary. (Naknek, 4/28/04. Father: Ole Oleson, Norway. Mother: Katrina Oleson, dead.) e:6/1/15, age 11. Left 8/1/19, "Went home. Married Peterson, Norway. 1954 deceased."

194 Olsen, Annie. (Naknek, 1/13/09. Father: Ole Oleson, Norway. Mother: Katrina Oleson, Alaska.) e:6/1/15, age 6. Left 8/1/19. "Went home. Mrs. Sam L. Murry. Mr. Murry—Irish-Norwegian. 1954 at Naknek."

195 Monsen, Andrew. (Naknek, 5/4/08. Father: Martin Monsen, Norway. Mother: Helena Monsen, Alaska, dead.) e:6/22/05, age 7. Left 8/1/21 to go home.

196 Andre, Ida. (Aleute). (Chignik, 5/3/06. Parents dead.) e:8/22/15. "Left 1920 Dec. Died tuberculosis."

197 Neilsen, Mary. (Sanak, 4/18/02. Father: Peter E. Neilsen, Denmark. Mother: Anna Neilsen, Sanak, Alaska.) e:10/1/15, age 13. Left 6/1/20 to go home. "To Tacoma Wash. Graduated business course."

198 Neilsen, George. (Sanak, 11/29/06. Father: Peter E. Neilsen, Denmark. Mother: Anna Neilsen, Sanak, Alaska.) e:10/1/15, age 8. Left 6/1/20 to go home.

199 Neilsen, Thomas. (Sanak, 4/17/09. Father: Peter E. Neilsen, Denmark. Mother: Anna Neilsen, Sanak, Alaska.) e:10/1/15, age 6. Left 1922 to go home.

200 Neilsen, Carolyn. (Sanak, 3/4/11. Father: Peter E. Neilsen, Denmark. Mother: Anna Neilsen, Sanak, Alaska.) e:10/1/15, age 4. Left 7/30/28 "to live with her sister Mary, Mrs. Timberlake."

201 Pomian, Annie. (Unga, 12/4/10. Father: Fred Pomian, Germany. Mother: Pomian,

Alaska, dead.) e:10/1/15, age 5. Left 3/1/24, went home.

202   Pomian, Lena. (Unga, 6/4/01. Father: Fred Pomian, Germany. Mother: Pomian, Alaska, dead.) e:10/1/15, age 6. Left 3/1/24, went home.

203   Wilson, Richmond. (Unga, 1909. Father: Edward Wilson, Norway. Mother: Alaska.) e:10/31/15, age 6. Left 1917, to go home.

204   Mikleson, Mike. (Unalaska, 11/16/09. Father: Pete Mikleson, Greek. Mother: Fedora Mikleson, Alaska.) e:10/31/15, age 6. Left 1918 to go home.

1916

205   Pestrikoff, William. (Unga, 5/27/06. Father: Fred Pestrikoff, Alaska, dead. Mother: Nellie Gould, Unga, Alaska.) e:10/1/15, age 8. Indentured. Left 1922, went home.

206   Pestrikoff, May. (Unga, 12/3/11. Father: Fred Pestrikoff, Alaska, dead. Mother: Nellie Gould, Unga, Alaska.) e:5/30/16, age 5. Indentured. Left June. "Went home to mother, Unga."

207   Nelson, Charles. (Nushagak, 12/14/09. Father: Harry Nelson, Norway. Mother: Alaska.) e:6/6/15, age 6. "Graduated Seward High School 1930. Went to work at Ahls Dairy, Anchorage, Alaska."

208   Gartlemann, Katie. (Naknek, 5/4/10. Father: Germany. Mother: Alaska.) e:6/6/16. Left 8/1/21 to San Francisco.

209   Kyander, Marie. (Naknek. Father: Oscar Kyander, Norway. Mother: Kyander, Alaska, dead.) e:6/7/16, age 6. Left 7/8/19, to go home.

210   Monsen, Martin. (Naknek, 1909. Father: Martin Monsen, Norway. Mother: Monsen, Alaska, dead.) e:8/27/16, age 7. Left 8/1921 to go home.

211   Balumatoff, Emma [Balamatoff]. (Unga, 8/4/10. Father: Oscar Balamatoff.) e:1916.

"Went to work for and live with Francis Groth 1928—continuing in High School JLH."

212   Young, Evelyn Annie. (Father: A.Y. Young, U.S.A. Mother: Alaska, dead.) e:9/4/16, age 6. Left 10/13/18 to go to the states.

213   Devlin, Alice (Eskimo). (Naknek, Alaska?) **e: 9/4/15, age 7**. Indentured. Left 4/23/25, died tuberculosis. "Mother was eaten by malamute dogs. The mother and little girl went to gather driftwood with the sled of dogs. Evidently the mother fell for the dogs ate her up while the little girl took to the hills—lived on roots and berries for six weeks. Made her way to a cannery on Bering sea side—slept with some dogs under an old shack. Begged her food from a Chinese cook—was found by the marshal dirty, lousy and half starved. Said marshall brot the child to the home and indentured her."

214   Dow [only this on register by number].

215   [Blank on register by number.]

216   Benson, Elsa. (Chignik, 9/25/12. Father: John Benj. Benson, Sweden. Mother: Tatiana Schebobin, Alaska, dead.) e:9/25/16. Left 8/22/17. "To school Chemawa Oregon."

217   Benson, Benjamin. (Chignik, 10/12/12. Father: John Benj. Benson. Sweden. Mother: Tatiana Schebobin, Alaska, dead.) e:9/29/16. Left 1932. "Designed Alaska flag 1927. Living in Kodiak 1953 with two daughters, Anna Mae & Charlotte. Works with Bob Hall airlines."

218   Benson, Carl. (Chignik, 8/13/14. Father: John Benj. Benson. Sweden. Mother: Tatiana Schebobin, Alaska, dead.) e:9/29/16.

219   Opheim, Margeret. (Sand Point.) e:9/29/16. Left 8/22/17, sent home.

220   Opheim, Olaf. (Sand Point.) e:9/29/16. Left 8/22/17, sent home.

221 Greichen, Annie. (Naknek, 9/30/14. Father: Gus Greichen, German. Mother: Alaska.) **e: 9/9/17.** "Father took home." [From an invoice, it appears she lived at the Home through June 1925.]

222 Olsen, Fanny. (Naknek, 7/3/11. Father: Ole Oleson—Christiansand, Norway. Mother: Alaska, dead.) **e:9/21/17.** Left: "Went to sisters Bristol Bay."

223 Petersen, Andrew. (Kvichak by Wood River, 2/27/14. Parents dead.) e:9/21/16, age 3. Indentured. "Father a mail carrier. He died in a hospital at Dillingham. College, Alaska, school. Sept. 1933. 1954 deceased."

224 Wilson, Morna (Monia). (Unga. Father: Edw. Wilson. Mother: Alaska.) e:9/1916. Died 1916, spinal meningitis.

1917

1918

225 Harris, James Ephraim. (Sanak, 5/3/07. Father: Harris, dead. Mother: Alexandra Harris, Alaska.) e:7/4/18, age 11. Indentured. Left May 1925.

226 [This is blank on the register by number. However, on the individual cards, James Harris is listed as No. 226.]

227 Harris, Mary. (Sanak, 9/4/11.) e:7/4/18, age 7. Indentured. "Graduated Seward High 1931. Working Mumfords Anchorage 1931."

228 Larsen, Melania (Molly). (Sanak, 3/16/07. Father: John Larsen, Norway, dead. Mother: Katie Larsen.) e: 8/4/18, age 11. Indentured. Left 19 [age? year?] Went to Mississippi.

229 Caun, Aleck. (Koggiung, 11/22/11.) e:8/13/18, age 8. "Working shoe shop Seward since 1931. Cordova Fall 1931."

230 Mumalee, Mamie (Eskimo). e:6/20/18, age 6? "Left 1923. Died tuberculosis."

231 Heidel, Nick. (Nushagak, 11/16/13?) e:6/20/18, age 6. "Name given at Jesse Lee Home."

232 Aguvaluk, Anecia [Onicia]. (Togiak, 9/12/06.) e:9/13/18. Indentured. "Went home. Married."

233 Prokopeoff, Semenid. (Attu.) e:10/5/18. Left 8/1922. Tuberculosis.

234 Morton, Sara. (Unalaska. Father: Edw. Morton. U.S.A.—Boston, dead.) **e:1916, age 15.** Left 1917, went home. "Married in W. Caravan N.F. Teacher in Jesse Lee Home."

1919

235 Carlson, Olga [no card for her].

236 Carlson, Nellie. (Sanak, 10/23/09. Father: August Carlson, Finland—Swede. Mother: Mary Carlson. Sanak, Alaska, dead.) e:5/1/19. Indentured.

237 Holstrom, Vama. (Koggiung, 8/14/08? Foster father: John Holstrom.) e:7/19/19, age 10. Died 9/6/25 from tuberculosis.

238 Holstrom, Marie. (Koggiung, 12/2/13? Foster father: John Holstrom.) e:7/19/19, age 6.

239 Larsen, Mary. (Sanak, 3/29/10. Father: John Larsen, dead. Mother: Katie Larsen.) e:8/15/19, age 9. Indentured. "Seward Hospital summer 1931. Married Geo. Race 1931."

240 Carlson, August [no card for him].

241 Carlson, Alice. (Sanak, 9/19/13. Father: August Carlson, Finland—Swede. Mother: Mary Carlson, Sanak, Alaska, dead.) e: 8/1/19. "Home with parents Sanak, Alaska."

242 Carlson, Katie. (Sanak, 12/2/10. Father: August Carlson, Finland—Swede. Mother: Mary Carlson, Sanak, Alaska, dead.) e:8/1/19. "Went to visit parents Sanak, Alaska May 1929."

243 Andersen, Minnie. (Chignik, 10/8/09. Father: George A. Andersen, Oregon. Mother: Mary Anderson, Chignik, Alaska, dead.) e:9/10/19. Indentured. "Left in

August 28 to go to Anchorage to work for Munfords."

244   Andersen, Rose. (Chignik, 2/13/13.) e:9/10/19. Indent. For parents see 243.

245   Kivik, Stephen [no card for him].

246   Kivik, Lucy Ah-noa-soo-uk. (Nome, 7/5/11.) e:11/16/19. Indentured.

247   Kivik, Larsen E-la-uk (Eskimo). (Nome, 1914.) e:11/16/19, age 5. Indentured. Died 12/1920 from tuberculosis.

248   Rosenberg, Karl. (Unalaska – Jesse Lee Home, 9/10/14. Father: William Rosenberg, No. 98, dead. Mother: Lucy Leavitt Rosenberg, Wales, No. 132, dead.) e:10/1/19, age 4. Homer homestead.

249   Rosenberg, Esther. (Unalaska—Jesse Lee Home, 4/3/16. Father: William Rosenberg, No. 98. Mother: Lucy Leavitt Rosenberg, Wales, No. 132.) e:10/1/19, age 3.

1920

250   Torgramsen, Matilda. (Unga, 10/29/09. Father: Sigvert Torgramsen, Denmark, dead. Mother: Anna Torgramsen, Alaska, dead.) e:8/1/20, age 12. Indentured. Left 12/26/21, went home. Died Unga from tuberculosis.

251   Torgramsen, Laura. (Unga, 7/9/13. Father: Sigert Torgramsen, Denmark, dead. Mother: Annie Torgramsen, Unga.) e:8/1/20, age 8. Indentured. "Went to parent, Unga, Alaska June 1921. Married Louis Bernsten—6 children at J.L.H. 1946–1954 in Unga with 3 more Wilson children."

252   Paulson, Stephen. (Naknek, 11/4/16. Father: Fred Paulson, Norway, dead. Mother: dead.) e:9/1/20, age 4.

253   Anderson, William. (Chignik, 3/30/15.) e:10/1/20. Indentured. For parents see 243.

254   Carlson, Charles. (Sanak 6/9/12. Father: August Carlson, Finland—Swede. Mother: Mary Carlson. Sanak, Alaska, dead.) e:10/1/20. "Working Seward Mach. Shop Sept. 1931."

255   Carlson, Marie. (Sanak, 11/6/14. Father: August Carlson, Finland—Swede. Mother: Mary Carlson, Sanak, Alaska, dead.) e:10/20/20.

1921

256   Bean, Clara. (Unalaska, 9/28/12? Father: Simeon Bean, St. Michaels, Alaska. Mother: Kuskokwim, Alaska, dead.) e:1/1/21, age 8. Indentured.

257   Goley, Mary. (Atka, 10/14/11. Father: Alexsea Goley, Atka, dead. Mother: Annie Goley, Atka, dead.) e:1/1/21. Indentured. "Went to sister Mary Winkle, Bremerton, Wash. June 1928." Note: A second card gives her birthdate as April 14, 1909, and says she left on June 30, 1928.

258   Goley, Annie. (Atka, 2/6/12. Father: Alexsea Goley, Atka, dead. Mother: Annie Goley, Atka, dead.) e:1/1/21. Indentured.

259   Torgramsen, Matea. (Unga, 5/17/11. Father: Sigert Torgramsen, Denmark, dead. Mother: Annie Torgramsen, Alaska, dead.) e:1/1/21, age 10. "Left Home to work for R.B. Merrill, Anchorage, Alaska May 1929."

260   Wilson, Margeret. (Kings Cove. Father: Wilson, U.S.A. Mother: Mary Wilson, Alaska, dead.) **e:1/1/20, age 4**. Left 7/23/22, to go home.

261   Wilson, Mabel. (Kings Cove. Father: Wilson, U.S.A. Mother: Mary Wilson, Alaska, dead.) **e:1/1/20, age 3**. Left 7/23/22, to go home.

262   Andre, John Wanka (Albert). (Chignik, 9/19/08.) e:8/20/21. "Left Home to work on Starr June 1929."

263   Oleson, Harry. (10/20/16.) e:10/1/21, age 5. "Jail, Valdez, from there to Atka with stepfather."

264   Gardiner, Mattie. (10/31/16. Father: William Gardiner. Mother: Irene, dead.) e:10/1/21. Indentured. "Went to her Aunt Molly Gardner False Pass 1924."

265 Moriss, John. (Umnak, 11/10/08. Father: Lawrence Galacktianoff, dead. Adopted by Mark Moriss, Croatia, dead.) **e:7/17/22.** Left "June. 'Shumgin' Bill Gardner's Fox Island."

266 Pestrikoff, Fred Alfred. (Unga, 7/29/13. Father: Fred Pestrikoff, Alaska, dead. Mother: Nellie Gould Pestrikoff, Alaska.) **e:7/17/22,** age 9. Indentured. "Left 1930—June. Went to Seattle to join Navy. Rejected—ear. Stayed with sister and when last heard of in Dillingham. Married Lucy Smith, King Cove. Several children—6?—Nellie, Christine."

267 Lyons, William. (Unga, 2/19/12. Father: Joseph Lyons. Mother: Mary Lyons, Unga, Alaska, dead.) e:7/17/22, age 10. Indentured. [1922 on card, but perhaps 1921 given the entry number.] "Working Ohls Dairy, Anchorage 1931."

268 Lyons, Lillie. (Unga, 2/26/19. Father: Joseph Lyons.) e:7/17/21, age 3. Indentured. "To father in Unga 1933."

269 Lyons, Molly. (Unga, 5/17/13. Father: Joseph Lyons.) e: 7/17/22, age 11. Indentured. [1922 on card, but perhaps 1921, given the entry number.] "Went to Father in Unga 1932 Joe Lyons, Unga."

1922

270 Nevzeroff, Melania. (Chignik, 11/6/16. Father: Maginty? Nevzeroff, dead. Mother: dead.) e:9/19/22, age 6. Left 1935 Squaw Harbor.

1923

271 Kristensen, Helen [no card for her].

272 Kristensen, Stephen. (False Pass, 7/16/18. Father: Nick Kristensen, Denmark. Mother: Jennie Kristensen, Alaska, dead, flu.) e:6/29/23, age 5. Indentured. Left April 1930 to False Pass.

273 Kristensen, Stanley. (False Pass, 1/10/21. Father: Nick Kristensen, Denmark.

Mother: Jennie Kristensen, Alaska, dead, flu.) e:6/29/23, age 2. Indentured. Left April 11, 1930, False Pass.

274 Kristensen, Florence. (Ikitan, 3/9/23. Father: Nick Kristensen, Denmark. Mother: Jennie Kristensen, Alaska, dead, flu.) e:6/29/23, age 3 months. Died 3/3/24, pertussis, whooping cough.

275 Balumatoff, John. (Kings Cove, 11/12/18. Father: Gabriel Balumatoff, Kings Cove.) e:9/4/23.

276 Larsen, Annie. (Belkofsky, 4/25/11. Father: E.H. Larsen, Norway. Mother: Mary Larsen, Belkofsky, Alaska.) e:10/1/23, age 12. Left 6/1/24, home.

277 Larsen, George. (King Cove, 2/22/12. Father: E.H. Larsen, Norway. Mother: Mary Larsen, Belkofsky, Alaska.) e:10/1/23, age 11. Left 6/1/24, went home.

278 Larsen, Henry. (Unga, 6/13/16. Father: E.H. Larsen, Norway. Mother: Mary Larsen, Belkofsky, Alaska.) e:10/1/23, age 7. Left 6/1/24, went home.

279 Larsen, Victor. (Unga, 3/21/18. Father: E.H. Larsen, Norway. Mother: Mary Larsen, Belkofsky, Alaska.) e:10/1/23, age 5.

280 Larsen, Edwin. (Umnak Is., 10/7/22. Father: E.H. Larsen, Norway. Mother: Mary Larsen, Belkofsky, Alaska.) e:10/1/23, age 1.

281 Larsen, Lydia. (Unalaska, 1/21/21. Father: E.H. Larsen, Norway. Mother: Mary Larsen, Belkofsky, Alaska.) e:10/1/23, age 2. Left 6/1/24, home.

282 Anderson, Patricia. e:3/4/24. Left:12/20/24. "Went home. Went to Unalaska with Mrs. Helge—Jan. 16, 1924."

283 McKeon, Louise. (Seldovia, 1/3/11. Father: William James McKeon, Scotland, dead. Mother: Annie McKeon, dead.) e:11/1/23, age 13. Left 3/5/25. "Care of court came of own accord."

284 McKeon, Helen. (Seldovia, 11/12/21. Father: William James McKeon, Scotland,

dead. Mother: Annie McKeon, dead.)
e:11/1/23, age 2.

1924

[285 Blank on "Register by Number."]

286 Smith, Annie. (Marshovia, 10/23/14. Father:
George Kuyakin Smith. Mother: Alexandra
Kenezeroff, dead.) e:7/25/24, age 10.

287 Dirks, Palageia (Polly). (Atka. Father: Paul
Dirks, Atka, Alaska.) e:5/10/24.
Left 2/14/25. "Went home."

288 Riley, Mike Bowk-look. (Nushagak, 7/23/15.
Father: A-roo-ruk, Little Diomede, Alaska.
Mother: Sen-me-un-na, Alaska, died 1924,
tuberculosis.) e:8/17/24, age 9. Died 4/22/27,
from tuberculosis.

289 Riley, Martha Ka-na-na. (Herendeen Bay,
5/5/18. Father: A-roo-ruk, Little Diomede,
Alaska. Mother: Sen-me-un-na, Alaska,
dead.) e:8/17/24, age 6. Left 1942. Home
closed. 1935—Dering, Alaska.

290 Kalmakoff, Mike. (Chignik, 7/20/13.)
e:8/17/24. Died 10/5/28 from tuberculosis.

291 Kalmakoff, Inikenti. (Chignik, 6/4/18.)
e:8/17/24.

292 McTay, Annie [MtFay, Annie]. (9/10/14.)
e:8/17/24, age 10.

293 McTay, Anecia [MtFay, Anecia]. (1/14/18.)
e:8/17/24, age 6. "Died TB."

294 Kalmakoff, Ephraim. (Chignik, 1/12/12.
Parents dead.) e:9/25/24. Died 1935 (?)
from tuberculosis.

1925

295 Gardiner, Nick. (11/5/17.) e:5/20/25.

296 Peterson, Susie. (King Cove, 1/12/13. Father:
Charles Peterson, Norway. Mother: dead.)
e:7/14/25, age 12. Indentured. Went to sister
Unalaska June 1931.

297 Peterson, Charles Jr. (King Cove, 12/15?/16.
Father: Charles Peterson, Norway. Mother:
dead.) e:7/14/25, age 8. Indentured.
"Lives in Seward—1955—in Flynns house
below Seward Hotel."

298 Peterson, Mary. (King Cove, 7/7?/20.
Father: Charles Peterson, Norway. Mother:
dead.) e:7/14/25, age 5. Indentured.

299 Peterson, Nina. (King Cove, 4/6?/23.
Father: Charles Peterson, Norway. Mother:
dead) e:7/14/25, age 2. Indentured.

300 Carlson, John. (Sanak, 6/26/17. Father:
August Carlson, Finland—Swede. Mother:
Mary Carlson, Sanak, Alaska, dead.)
e:9/22/25. "1931—Home—Sanak."

301 Bean, Joseph. (Unalaska, 8/17/17. Father:
Simeon Bean, St. Michaels, Alaska.
Mother: Kuskokwim, Alaska, dead.)
e:9/4/25. Indentured.

FROM LEFT TO RIGHT, *front row (all seated boys): Third from left, Louis Peters; 7 (light colored coat), Henry Smith; 8, Rufe – ; 9, Johnny Yatchmenoff?; 11, Eddie Anderson.*

Second row (all seated girls but one): 1, John Carpenter; 2 (with white hat), Emma King; 6 (blond hair), Dora Balamatoff; 11 (second girl in white with white ribbons), Margaret Seymour.

Third row (seated boys and then seated girls): 4, Sammy Supsuk; 7 (with lighter jacket), Willie Siftsoff; 8 (first boy with toy pistol), Simeon Oliver; 9 (second boy with toy pistol), George Peterson; 10, Cecil Waln; 15 (third seated girl), Elizabeth Stankus; 16, Anfesia Lazarev [Shapsnikoff, eventually].

Back row (all standing): 2, James Palutoff; 3, Lillie Rosenberg; 4, Peter Hatch; 5, Annie Swanson [Hatch]; 6, Amelia Petersen; 7, Sara Morton; 8, Helen Swanson; 9, Agnes Anderson; 10, Lucy Berikoff; 12, Agnes Yatchmenoff; 13, Edith Newhall; 15, Charles Lee; 16, Hilda Lee; 17, Peter Shapsnikoff.

Names supplied by Simeon Oliver in 1979. Photo from Annie Swanson Hatch's album, courtesy of the Hatch family.

Bibliography

Archival sources consulted

Alaska State Historical Library, Juneau, Alaska:

MS 0106. Papers of a medical missionary in Alaska, 1911-1929.

MS 0156. Candace ("Candy") Waugaman Collection, 1903–present.

MS 0003. Papers of Samuel Applegate, 1875–1925.

Archives of the Arctic and Polar Regions Collections of the Elmer E. Rasmuson Library, University of Alaska Fairbanks:

Alaska History Documents, Miscellaneous papers.

Eva Alvery Richards *Scrapbook #2, 1918–1933.*

North American Commercial Company Logbooks, 1903–06 (in Alaska Commercial Company Records 1868–1911).

Museum of the Aleutians, Unalaska, Alaska:

Correspondence Copy Book, 1903–1910.
Pat Locke Archival Collection.

National Archives and Record Administration, Washington, D.C.:

RG 21. Records of District Courts of the United States. U.S. District Court, Alaska. Criminal Files 1902–1945.

RG 22. Records of the U.S. Fish and Wildlife Service. *Pribilof Islands Logbooks.* MF A3303.

RG 26. Records of the U.S. Coast Guard.

RG 75. Records of the Bureau of Indian Affairs. Alaska Division.

Newhall, Agnes Sowle and Albert Warren

No original works by Agnes Sowle Newhall have been found. A.W. Newhall arranged excerpts from his wife's letters into what he called a "Journal of Agnes L. Sowle." These 84 handwritten pages form Part II of his unpublished and undated memoir (here referred to as Newhall Manuscript). Part I details his own early life and work in Alaska up to approximately 1912. The original was owned by the Newhalls' son, Dr. Chester Newhall of Burlington, Vermont. A copy was provided the author by Chester Newhall's son, Dr. David S. Newhall.

A.W. Newhall sent carbon copies of letters and reports to numerous individuals. His nephew Frank Newhall prepared a collection, primarily dating from 1921–1928, and deposited a copy with the Alaska State Historical Library. (A copy was given to the author in 1983.) Clara Cook pasted her carbon copies in a scrapbook which, following its donation by Steven and Kathie Assenmacher, was published in 1979 by the Unalaska City School District as *Cuttlefish Three: Home on the Bering, The Jesse Lee Home at Unalaska, 1911–1915.* More Cook/Newhall material is in the Robert Collins collection at the Unalaska City Public Library (Unalaska Historical Commission file). MS0003, the Samuel Applegate Papers, Alaska State Historical Library, contains a small amount of Newhall material.

Substantial excerpts from the David S. Newhall collection appeared as photocopies in two spiral-bound volumes prepared by Norma Lowder in 1998 (see Lowder, page 373).

Presbyterian Historical Society [PHS], Philadelphia:

RG 239. Sheldon Jackson Papers (including Sheldon Jackson Scrapbooks).

RG 301.3. Alaska Mission Records.

Stanford University, Libraries. Department of Special Collections and University Archives:

JL006. Alaska Commercial Company Records, 1868–1940.

Unalaska City School District Library:
   Jesse Lee Home Correspondence,
Unalaska City School (copy received from
Steve McGlashan). Most of this was pub-
lished in *Cuttlefish Three: Home on the Bering*.
Davenport, Noah Cleveland and Clara Ellen.
*Unalaska Days: A Diary (August 7, 1910–August
7, 1912)*. Photocopied typescript with supple-
mentary material prepared by Margaret Boaz.
A copy is available at the Library of Congress
(call number MMC-3676).

Unalaska Historical Preservation Commission,
   Unalaska, Alaska:
      Robert Collins Collection (Clara Cook
      letters).

United Methodist Church. Alaska Missionary
   Conference Commission on Archives and
   History, Anchorage:
      Jesse Lee Home file (correspondence, year-
      books: *Ku-eu-it*, Unalaska Methodist
      church records).

United Methodist Church. General
   Commission on Archives and History, Drew
   University, Madison, New Jersey:
      Woman's Home Missionary Society,
      published reports from bureaus; *Woman's
      Home Missions* [WHM].

United States Coast Guard Historian's Office,
   Washington, D.C.:
      Friench Simpson Private Log. May 21–October
      1909.

United States Library of Congress, Manuscript
   Division:
      D 49. The Alaskan Russian Church Archives.

BIBLIOGRAPHY

Applegate, Samuel
1895 "The Third of Unalaska District" in *Report
   on population and resources of Alaska at the eleventh
   census: 1890*. Misc. Documents of the House of
   Representatives for the first session of the
   fifty-second Congress, 1891–92. v.50, pt. 9.
   Serial set 3020.

Black, Lydia T., with Sarah McGowan, Jerry Jacka, Natalia Taksami, and Miranda Wright
1999 *The History and Ethnohistory of the Aleutians
   East Borough*. Kingston, Ontario:
   Fairbanks, Alaska: The Limestone Press.

Bockstoce, John
1991 *Arctic Passages: A Unique Small-Boat Journey
   Through the Great Northern Waterway*. New
   York: Quill, William Morrow.

1995 *Whales, Ice, & Men: The History of Whaling
   in the Western Arctic*. Seattle and London:
   University of Washington Press.

Brummitt, Stella Wyatt
1930 *Looking Backward Thinking Forward:
   the jubilee history of the Woman's Home Missionary
   Society of the Methodist Episcopal Church*.
   Cincinnati: The Woman's Home Missionary
   Society.

Case, David S.
1984 *Alaska Natives and American Laws*.
   Fairbanks: University of Alaska Press.

Fienup-Riordan, Ann
1991 *The Real People and the Children of Thunder:
   The Yup'ik Eskimo Encounter with Moravian
   Missionaries John and Edith Kilbuck*. Norman
   and London: University of Oklahoma Press.

Fortuine, Robert
1992 *Chills and Fever: Health and Disease
   in the Early History of Alaska*. Fairbanks:
   University of Alaska Press.

Gould, Peter Gordon
1949 *Methodism at Work in Alaska*.
   Privately printed in Philadelphia.

1950 *The Fisherman's Son*.
   Privately printed in Philadelphia.

Robert F. Griggs
1922 *The Valley of Ten Thousand Smokes*.
   Washington, D.C.: The National Geographic
   Society.

Hakkinen, Elizabeth
1974 "Col. Sol Ripinsky," Musings from the
Sheldon Museum, *Chilkat Valley News*, Dec. 12,
1974, reprinted by the museum.

Hamilton, William.
1898 "The Itinerary for 1895," *Seal and Salmon
Fisheries and General Resources of Alaska*. Vol. III,
Appendix A, Serial 3578. Washington, D.C.:
Government Printing Office.

Harris, W.T.
1898 "Explanation of the Policy Pursued in
Regard to Industrial Education in Alaska."
Education in Alaska. 55th Congress, 2d Session,
Senate, Doc. No. 137. Serial 3599.

Haycox, Stephen W.
1984 "Sheldon Jackson in Historical Perspective:
Alaska Native Schools and Mission Contracts,
1885–1894." *The Pacific Historian*, Vol. XXVIII,
No. 1, pages 18–28.

Henderson, Alice Palmer
1898 *The Rainbow's End: Alaska*. Chicago and
New York: Herbert S. Stone & Co.

Hudson, Ray, ed.
1992 *Unugulux Tunusangin; Oldtime Stories.*
Unalaska: Unalaska City School District.

2005 *Cuttlefish: Volumes One, Two & Three,
Stories of Aleutian Culture & History*. Unalaska:
Museum of the Aleutians. 2005. This volume
reprints *Cuttlefish One* (1977), *Four Villages:
Cuttlefish Two* (1978), and *Home on the Bering:
The Jesse Lee Home at Unalaska, 1911–1915*,
(1978–1979).

Jackson, Sheldon
1886 *Report on Education in Alaska with Maps and
Illustrations*. Washington: Government
Printing office.

1897 *Education in Alaska 1895–96*. Washington:
Government Printing Office.

Jochelson, Waldemar
1928 "People of the Foggy Seas." *Natural History.*
Volume 28, July 1928.

Jacobs, Jane, ed.
1997 *A Schoolteacher in Old Alaska: The Story of
Hannah Breece*. New York: Random House.

Keeler, Ellen Coughlin
1920 *The Balance Wheel: a condensed history of
the Woman's Home Missionary Society of the
Methodist Episcopal Church 1880–1920.*
New York City: Woman's Home Missionary
Society, Methodist Episcopal Church.

Kitchener, L.D.
1954 *Flag Over the North, the story of the Northern
Commercial Company*. Seattle: Superior
Publishing Company.

Lopp, Ellen Louise Kittredge
2001 *Ice Window: Letters from a Bering Strait
Village 1892–1902*. Edited and annotated by
Kathleen Lopp Smith and Verbeck Smith.
University of Alaska Press. Fairbanks, Alaska.

Lowder, Norma
1998 *The Great Physician* and *We Gratefully
Come, Remembering, Rejoicing*. Two spiral-
bound photoduplicated volumes.
Privately printed.

McClanahan, Alexandra J.M.
1986 *Our Stories, Our Lives: A Collection of
Twenty-Three Transcribed Interviews with Elders
of the Cook Inlet Region*. Anchorage, AK:
The CIRI Foundation.

McKinlay, William Laird
1976 *Karluk: The Great Untold Story of Arctic
Exploration*. New York: St. Martin's Press.

Muir, John
1917 *The Cruise of the Corwin: Journal of the Arctic
Expedition of 1881 in Search of DeLong and the
Jeannette*. Boston and New York: Houghton
Mifflin Company.

Oleksa, Michael, ed.
1987 *Alaskan Missionary Spirituality*. New York:
Paulist Press.

Oliver, Simeon (Nutchuk) (with Alden Hatch)
1941 *Son of the Smoky Sea*. New York:
Julian Messner, Inc.

1946 *Back to the Smoky Sea.* New York: Julian Messner, Inc.

Niedieck, Paul

1909 *Cruises in the Bering Sea.* London: Rowland Ward, Limited.

Ray, Dorothy Jean

1975 *The Eskimos of Bering Strait, 1650–1898.* Seattle and London: University of Washington Press.

Shepard, Bea and Claudia Kelsey

1986 *Have Gospel Tent Will Travel: The Methodist Church in Alaska since 1886.* Anchorage: Conference Council on Ministries, Alaska Missionary Conference of the United Methodist Church.

Strobridge, Truman R. and Dennis L. Noble

1999 *Alaska and the U. S. Revenue Cutter Service, 1867–1915.* Annapolis, Maryland: Naval Institute Press.

Swanson, Henry

1982 *The Unknown Islands, Life and Tales of Henry Swanson.* Cuttlefish VI. Unalaska City School District.

Winchell, Mary E.

1951 *Home by the Bering Sea.* Caldwell, Idaho: The Caxton Printers, Ltd.

1954 *Where the Wind Blows Free.* Caldwell, Idaho: The Caxton Printers, Ltd.

GOVERNMENT PUBLICATIONS

Proceedings of the Department of Superintendence of the National Educational Association. Bureau of Education at its Meeting at Washington, March 15–17, 1887. Circular of Information No. 3, 1887. Washington: GPO. 1887.

Fur-Seal Fisheries of Alaska. 50th Congress, 2nd Session. House of Representatives Report No. 3883. Serial 2674. Washington: GPO. 1889.

Report on population and resources of Alaska at the eleventh census: 1890. Misc. Documents of the House of Representatives for the first session of the fifty-second Congress, 1891–92. v.50, pt. 9. Serial 3020. Washington: GPO. 1895.

Education Report, 1896–97. Government Printing Office. Washington. 1898.

Annual Report of the Supervising Surgeon-General of the Marine-Hospital Service of the U.S. FY 1900. Washington: GPO. 1901.

House of Representatives. Hearings before the Committee on the Territories. Volume II. Washington. Government Printing Office. 1904.

Report of the Commissioner of Education for the Year 1903. Volume 2. Washington. Government Printing Office. 1905.

NEWSPAPERS

The Alaskan

The Alaskan and Herald Combined

Anchorage Daily News

Chicago Daily Tribune

Daily Alta California

The Indian Helper

New York Christian Advocate

The New York Times

The North Star

Seattle Post Intelligencer

St. Louis Republic

Index

About the name "Unalaska": Beginning in 1890, the U.S. Board on Geographic Names tackled Alaskan place names derived from a multitude of languages. The board's first report, in 1892, assigned the name Unalaska to the local post office. With the publication of a second report in 1900, Unalaska had officially won out over all contenders, including Unalashka, Oonalashka, and Ounalachka. The unusual name has nothing to do with "un" as a negative prefix. The "un" was a gradual corruption of an Aleut demonstrative meaning "there," *awan* or *naakun*. The island's original name had been *Nawan-Alaxsxa* or *Nagun-Alaxsxa*, a reference to the island's proximity to the mainland.

Lacking a Board on Personal Names, and where the official form cannot be known with certainty, we have generally kept the varied spellings for people's names as they appear in sources of the time. Russian surnames, for example, began as transliterations and are sometimes spelled differently even within a family: Siftsoff/Sifsof/Siftsov. Scandinavian names offer their own possibilities: Swanson/Swansen/Swensen, Peterson/Petersen/Pedersen. Even given names vary: Miss Barnett is either Harriet or Harriett or Harriette, depending upon the contemporary writer. What seems to be the principal spelling appears in the index.

The Appendix, including the group photo caption on page 369, is not part of the index.

Photo: M. Eric Drake

RAYMOND HUDSON LIVED AT UNALASKA from 1964 to 1991, during which time he taught in the public school and was the editor of eight collections of local and regional history. Today he serves as historian for the Unalaska Preservation Commission. He is the author of *Moments Rightly Placed, an Aleutian Memoir* (1998, Epicenter Press) and numerous articles on Unangan basketry and Aleutian history. *Moments Rightly Placed* was chosen one of "Alaska's best history books" for *The Alaska 67*, published by Hardscratch Press in 2006 for the Alaska Historical Society.

A woodcut artist, Hudson had a retrospective of his work at the Museum of the Aleutians in 2004. He recently edited *An Aleutian Ethnography* by Lucien M. Turner, forthcoming from the University of Alaska Press. He lives with his wife, Shelly, in Middlebury, Vermont.

Family After All: Alaska's Jesse Lee Home, Volume I

Project coordinator and editor: Jackie Pels
Book design and production: David R. Johnson
Typography and composition: Dickie Magidoff, Burney, California

Index by Andrea Avni, Vashon Island WordWrights, Vashon Island, Washington
Proofreaders: Victoria C. Elliott (text) and Peter Kupfer (index)
Music transcribed by Janet C. Smith, Bella Roma Music, Berkeley, California
CIP data by Rose Schreier Welton, M.L.S.

Printed and bound at McNaughton & Gunn, Saline, Michigan
Alkaline pH paper (Natural Offset)

Hardscratch Press
2358 Banbury Place
Walnut Creek, CA 94598-2347

phone/fax 925/935-3422
www.hardscratchpress.com